NIETZSCHE:
THE ETHICS OF AN
IMMORALIST

NIETZSCHE:
THE ETHICS OF AN
IMMORALIST

Peter Berkowitz

Harvard University Press
Cambridge, Massachusetts
London, England
1995

Library of Congress Cataloging-in-Publication Data
Berkowitz, Peter, 1959–
Nietzsche : the ethics of an immoralist / Peter Berkowitz.
p.   cm.
Includes bibliographical references (p.   ) and index.
ISBN 0–674–62442–4 (alk. paper)
1. Nietzsche, Friedrich Wilhelm, 1844–1900.   2. Ethics,
Modern—19th century.   I. Title.
B3318.E9B46 1995
193—dc20
94–34119
CIP

For my family

Contents

Preface

One reflection of the contest of extremes in Nietzsche's thought is the extreme and rival opinions that have prevailed about Nietzsche's achievement. Once considered a conservative critic of culture, later enlisted as an authority by the court theoreticians of Nazism, reviled as a teacher of evil, and rehabilitated by Walter Kaufmann as a kind of overexuberant, up-to-date Socratic champion of fearless thought, Nietzsche has since been embraced by the Left and is now revered as a founding father of postmodernism, a ground-breaking critic of the underlying moral and metaphysical assumptions of the Western tradition, a seminal figure in the elaboration of the politics of identity, difference, and self-making. Today, both those who defend and those who oppose the Canon believe Nietzsche ought to be read. And while Nietzsche considered himself an untimely thinker whose ability to understand and overcome his own age was based on his understanding of the achievements of antiquity, at the moment there is hardly a thinker in the history of philosophy who is more celebrated precisely because, it is claimed, he points the way to a fundamental break with the past.

While disagreement persists over the meaning of his philosophy, Nietzsche's influence on the dominant thinkers and major writers of the twentieth century (and through them a host of lesser lights) is well documented and undisputed. Influence, though, as Nietzsche knew, has its cost—all the more to a body of thought that rages against orthodoxy.

The authority, prestige, and popularity of Nietzsche's thought have inevitably exposed it to routinization and domestication. The question arises whether making his thought common drains his passionate opposition to orthodoxy of its passion and makes it orthodox.

Much study of Nietzsche is, I believe, "aspect-blind" in Wittgenstein's sense of the term: narrow focus on one element or observation from a single angle has occluded vision of other elements and of the whole. To take one example, many recent scholars exhibit exquisite deference to a select group of Nietzsche's opinions, especially his imperious and sweeping denunciations of morality, religion, and reason; his extreme speculations about perspectivism, nihilism, and the human origins of justice and holiness; and his bold pronouncements on the primacy and the glory of the will, creativity, and power. But these same readers often overlook, or devise excuses for dismissing, his pervasive use of traditional notions of truth, moral virtue, and reason.

Nietzsche depends upon these traditional notions to execute his vivisection of traditional philosophy, to issue his wrathful indictment of Judaism and Christianity, to clarify the character of the superman, to prepare the way for a philosophy of the future, to carry out a genealogy of morals, and to accomplish a revaluation of all values. The prejudices of scholars have hampered appreciation of how his ruthless criticism of convention and tradition is interwoven with and inseparable from time-honored opinions about the fundamental character of the cosmos, an enduring human nature, and intelligible moral standards binding across time and cultures.

Although beleaguered by sycophantic disciples who aped his words and paid obsequious homage to his weaknesses, Nietzsche's Zarathustra taught that "one repays a teacher badly if one always remains only a pupil." It is with this admonition in mind that I shall have occasion to question Nietzsche's claims, to doubt his interpretations, and to challenge his conclusions. What is worthy in these questions, doubts, and challenges reflects the student's debt to the skeptical spirit that Nietzsche incomparably exemplified. But first it is necessary to identify Nietzsche's claims, to understand his interpretations, and to think through his conclusions. One may repay a teacher badly if one remains a student only, but one cannot repay a teacher at all unless one becomes a student first.

Many believe, often on the basis of remarks made by Nietzsche, that texts have a multiplicity of meanings that defy or defeat an author's intention and exceed or elude his grasp. Inasmuch as this belief reflects a skeptical doubt—the recognition that all interpretations are contestable and all authors human—it provides a salutary caution, chastening the pious who make too much and the arrogant who make too little of a work. But both reason and experience attest that not all interpretations are equally contestable and not all authors are equally skilled. I would emphasize that in the contest between authorial intention and indeterminacy sometimes the one prevails, sometimes the other; the proof is in the reading. And I would add that attention should be paid not only to Nietzsche's sensational speculations but also to his routine practice. For example, he purports to uncover, among other things, the intentions governing the dialogues of Plato, the tragic drama of ancient Greece, the religious faith of Jesus, the philosophy of Spinoza, the music of Wagner, the literature of Dostoevsky. To determine what weight Nietzsche gives to his more radical theoretical speculations about interpretation and what weight to his more traditional interpretive practice, it is first necessary to notice that his theory and his practice frequently pull in opposite directions.

Others adopt a more extreme view, transforming a sound skeptical doubt into a dubious theoretical certainty by flatly denying that texts have or can have any meaning other than that bestowed or imposed upon them by the reader. But the explanations and assurances, often put forward in obscure technical language, for avoiding the hard work of looking for Nietzsche's meaning are idols of the age that ring hollow when struck. In the spirit of the skepticism Nietzsche championed, let the first dogma put in question be the scholars' self-aggrandizing claim that the only meaning of Nietzsche's books is the one the reader makes.

Nietzsche lets it be known again and again that, more than the person who has the courage of his convictions, he admires and addresses those who have the courage for, and understand the imperative that demands, an attack on their convictions. He is acutely aware that the determination to expose one's convictions to attack is itself rooted in a conviction. In a section of *The Gay Science* entitled "*How we, too, are still pious*" he declares that an ancient "metaphysical faith" animates his philosophical explorations: "even we knowers today, we godless antimetaphysicians still take our fire, too, from the flame lit by a faith that is thousands of years old, that Christian faith which was also the faith of Plato, that God is the truth, that truth is divine" (GS 344). Nietzsche's conviction that devotion to the truth is the hardest and highest service is proclaimed throughout his writings and, I shall argue, pervasively embodied in his ideas and arguments. So severe is his devotion to the truth that he is compelled to question the value of truth. But make no mistake: understanding the truth about untruth in the economy of life is for Nietzsche an obligation arising from the service of truth.

Despite his peculiar piety, proudly proclaimed and beautifully exhibited in his ruthless questioning of cherished convictions, Nietzsche's thought has by now been transformed into a collection of cherished convictions, a vast standing reserve of slogans and ideas for those who wish to champion favored causes and to justify partisan political projects. People of course are free to find inspiration wherever they like: in a torn letter, an unfinished note, a discarded draft, a phrase violently wrenched from context. And Nietzsche's books may be put to a multitude of uses—from paperweights and doorstops to propaganda for democracy—that he probably never imagined and certainly would have loathed. Happily, there is no law against using or abusing Nietzsche's writings. But it must be added that Nietzsche himself wished to be understood rather than turned into a rhetorical weapon, reconstructed for political advantage, or hailed as a new prophet.

Those who have the courage of their convictions should prove it by standing on their own two feet; those who want to learn whether they have the courage for an attack on their convictions should study Nietzsche.

Abbreviations

Works in English translation are cited by abbreviation and section number. In a few instances I have made minor adjustments in the translations. Where it is necessary to refer to the German original, I cite by volume and page number to Friedrich Nietzsche, *Sämtliche Werke: Kritische Studienausgabe in 15 Bänden,* ed. Giorgio Colli and Mazzino Montinari (Berlin: de Gruyter, 1980); and *Sämtliche Briefe: Kritische Studienausgabe in 8 Bänden,* ed. Giorgio Colli and Mazzino Montinari (Berlin: de Gruyter, 1986).

A   *The Antichrist,* trans. Walter Kaufmann, in PN

AOM *Assorted Opinions and Maxims,* trans. R. J. Hollingdale, in HH, vol. 2

ASC   *Attempt at a Self-Criticism,* in BT

BGE   *Beyond Good and Evil,* trans. Walter Kaufmann (New York: Vintage, 1966)

BKSA *Sämtliche Briefe: Kritische Studienausgabe,* ed. Giorgio Colli and Mazzino Montinari

BT   *The Birth of Tragedy,* trans. Walter Kaufmann (New York: Vintage, 1966)

CW   *The Case of Wagner,* trans. Walter Kaufmann (New York: Vintage, 1966)

DS   *David Strauss, the Confessor and the Writer,* trans. R. J. Hollingdale, in UM

D   *Daybreak,* trans. R. J. Hollingdale (Cambridge: Cambridge University Press, 1982)

EH   *Ecce Homo,* trans. Walter Kaufmann (New York: Vintage, 1968)

GM   *On the Genealogy of Morals,* trans. Walter Kaufmann and R. J. Hollingdale (New York: Vintage, 1968)

GS   *The Gay Science,* trans. Walter Kaufmann (New York: Vintage, 1974)

HC   *Homer's Contest,* trans. Walter Kaufmann, in PN

HH   *Human, All Too Human,* trans. R. J. Hollingdale (Cambridge: Cambridge University Press, 1986)

KSA   *Sämtliche Werke: Kritische Studienausgabe,* ed. Giorgio Colli and Mazzino Montinari

L   *Selected Letters of Friedrich Nietzsche,* trans. Christopher Middleton (Chicago: University of Chicago Press, 1969)

NCW *Nietzsche Contra Wagner,* trans. Walter Kaufmann, in PN

P   *The Philosopher: Reflections on the Struggle between Art and Knowledge,* trans. Daniel Breazeale, in PT

PCP   *The Philosopher as Cultural Physician,* trans. Daniel Breazeale, in PT

PHT   *Philosophy in Hard Times,* trans. Daniel Breazeale, in PT

PN   *The Portable Nietzsche,* ed. and trans. Walter Kaufmann (New York: Viking, 1954)

PT   *Philosophy and Truth: Selections from Nietzsche's Notebooks of the Early 1870s,* ed. and trans. Daniel Breazeale (Atlantic Highlands, N.J.: Humanities Press, 1979)

OPT   *On the Pathos of Truth,* trans. Daniel Breazeale, in PT

PTG   *Philosophy in the Tragic Age of the Greeks,* trans. Marianne Cowan (Chicago: Henry Regnery, 1962)

SE   *Schopenhauer as Educator,* trans. R. J. Hollingdale, in UM

SSW   *The Struggle between Science and Wisdom,* trans. Daniel Breazeale, in PT

TI   *Twilight of the Idols,* trans. Walter Kaufmann, in PN

TL   *On Truth and Lies in a Nonmoral Sense,* trans. Daniel Breazeale, in PT

UD   *On the Uses and Disadvantages of History for Life,* trans. R. J. Hollingdale, in UM

UM   *Untimely Meditations,* trans. R. J. Hollingdale (Cambridge: Cambridge University Press, 1983)

WP   *The Will to Power,* trans. Walter Kaufmann and R. J. Hollingdale (New York: Vintage, 1968)

WS   *The Wanderer and His Shadow,* trans. R. J. Hollingdale, in HH, vol. 2

Z   *Thus Spoke Zarathustra,* trans. Walter Kaufmann, in PN

Nietzsche:
The Ethics of an
Immoralist

Introduction

She told me herself that she had no morality—and I thought she
had, like myself, a more severe morality than anybody.

—*Nietzsche*

The dazzling beauty of Nietzsche's writings may blind the reader to the
explosive character of his opinions.[1] Nietzsche expounded a radical and
aristocratic egoism; poured scorn on Platonism, Christianity, modernity, enlightenment, democracy, socialism, and the emancipation of
women; denounced the belief in human equality as a calamitous conceit; and ardently championed a rank order of desires, types of human
beings, and forms of life.

Nietzsche's standpoint, which he describes as above politics (BT Preface; A Preface), has implications for politics. But what he deplores in
politics and would like to see abolished is more in evidence than what
he approves of in politics and wishes to see accomplished. In fact,
Nietzsche has little that is constructive to say about many of the leading
themes in the history of political philosophy: the types of regimes and
the characteristic citizen corresponding to each; the best regime; the
laws or the rule of law; political obligation and the limits of legitimate
authority; the fair distribution of property and the right arrangement
of economic and social institutions. It is tempting, therefore, to conclude that Nietzsche does not practice or contribute to political philosophy, for a primary theme of political philosophy is the city or citizenship
and the human being, that is, the relation between the common good
and the good of the individual.

Yet Nietzsche's evident opinion that how human beings govern themselves is an illegitimate or marginal topic of philosophy is based upon a certain understanding of the desires and longings of the human soul and the kind of life or specific virtues most conducive to satisfying those desires. By starting from an analysis of what human beings desire and what is desirable for a human being, Nietzsche moves within the domain of moral and political philosophy. He poses a radical challenge to political philosophy by accepting the starting point of political philosophy—the inescapableness or fundamental importance of questions about what is good—while denying that the good is intrinsically connected to any political regime, system of economic and social institutions, or personal attachments. The radical devaluation of political life, and the comprehensive reflection in which that devaluation is ensconced, is a proper and indispensable subject of political philosophy.

A striking feature of Nietzsche's philosophical explorations, concealed by his reputation as the last of the modern philosophers and the first of the postmoderns, is the coexistence of, and indeed contest within his thought between, characteristically ancient and characteristically modern concerns. As in ancient political philosophy, the question of human perfection lies at the heart of Nietzsche's inquiries. At the same time, modern ideas about knowledge, freedom, and mastery pervade and continuously shape his investigations. In his most ambitious works Nietzsche elevates to new heights the characteristically modern aspirations to conquer fortune, to master nature, and to actualize freedom. Yet the dizzying perspective afforded by these new heights is by his own admission decisively determined by ancient notions of metaphysics and human excellence (UD 1, GS 344, BGE 204). In effect, Nietzsche radicalizes modern principles but on the basis of, and constrained by, traditional moral and intellectual virtues. As he expounds a new ethics composed of ancient and modern elements, his thought becomes a battleground for extreme and rival opinions about history, art, morality, religion, virtue, nature, politics, and philosophy. Indeed, this contest of extremes forms his thought.

The death of God is the great speculation that drives Nietzsche's contest of extremes. Contrary to the reductivist approach exemplified by Alexander Nehamas's influential book *Nietzsche: Life as Literature,* in which the death of God functions as a premise in an argument that "allows Nietzsche to deny that the world is subject to a single overarching interpretation, corresponding to God's role or intention,"[2] the death of God describes the feeble worship of a God who is no longer vital or believable and, more important, represents the discovery that morality lacks a foundation in nature, divinity, or reason. This, at least, is the view of Nietzsche's madman, who proclaims God's death and characterizes his murder as the greatest deed yet in history (GS 125). For Nietzsche's madman, the death of God does not in the first place generate questions about knowledge and interpretation, but rather more urgently symbolizes a crushing loss of moral standards that gives rise to the intoxicating possibility and unnerving necessity of those few human beings who are fit to "become gods" (GS 125).

Nehamas's favored doctrine, perspectivism, the view that every view, including the view called perspectivism, is only one among many interpretations[3] is not even an implication or consequence of the death of God as Nietzsche understands it. For Nietzsche, the death of God—that is, the denial that nature, reason, or revelation provides moral standards for the governance of life, or the belief that, as Nietzsche puts it a few sections earlier in *The Gay Science,* "The total character of the world . . . is in all eternity chaos" (GS 109)—is the one true account of the circumstances in which human beings really dwell.[4] Paradoxically, the human condition so understood, at least in Nietzsche's view, generates specific and severe moral or practical imperatives.[5] And he views the clarification of these practical imperatives as his central task.

The common tendency today to view questions about language and interpretation as the central issues in Nietzsche's thought drastically shifts the actual center of gravity of his books. Nietzsche's fundamental concern with ethical and political questions is obscured when scholars make him over into a theorist primarily concerned with questions of how we know rather than of how we should live.[6] Actually, Nietzsche tended to avoid complicated theoretical analysis, giving pride of place instead to questions about the best life. When he does turn to epistemology and metaphysics it is usually with moral intent. For Nietzsche, as I shall argue, the chief question is not how we know but rather what we ought to do in response to the shattering knowledge within our grasp. And Nietzsche knows much—or at least his madman and his Zarathustra know much; from the true but deadly doctrine that morality lacks support in nature, reason, or God, they derive the moral imperative to invent festivals of atonement and sacred games which enable the very best human beings to make themselves gods by commanding the greatest things.[7] But what are the greatest things? What would a life in which the greatest things are commanded look like? And what makes self-deification necessary or desirable?

This book clarifies the foundations and spells out the practical implications of Nietzsche's account of the best life. At the foundations of Nietzsche's thought there is a pervasive tension between his fundamental assumption that morality is an artifact of the human will and his unyielding conviction that there is a binding rank order of desires, types of human beings, and forms of life. On the basis of this contest of extreme and conflicting views Nietzsche expounds an ethics of creativity that culminates in a radical exaltation of the human power to both understand and control the world. Speaking very generally, human excellence for Nietzsche consists in facing squarely, comprehending accurately, and overcoming the ugly necessity that governs the human condition, by bringing that necessity under the will's dominion.

Human excellence so understood requires a coherent account of the disharmony between human desire and the cosmos in which human beings dwell, an account that explains why human beings are obliged to make themselves gods. But Nietzsche's robust conviction that there is an order of rank among souls and a health proper to the soul contravenes his assumption or conviction that the world lacks a moral order. His view of human excellence and his conception of the fundamental character of the world are like two intimately related antagonists in a play who can never meet on stage because they are portrayed by the same actor. Nietzsche rejects the very idea of natural or rationally intelligible ends, yet he also affirms them and cannot do without them; this pervasive tension both binds his thought together and tears it apart.[8] His remarkable attempt to do justice to and overcome the contest of extremes that forms his thought culminates in *Thus Spoke Zarathustra* and *Beyond Good and Evil*, both of which envisage virtue without a natural end and promise redemption without God. Unable in good conscience to reject either cluster of opinions, Nietzsche thinks their conflict through to the breaking point and thereby powerfully suggests that the distinctions between just and unjust, noble and shameful, and good and bad are the hallmarks of our humanity and cannot be sus-

splenius capitis

Origin: lower half of ligamentum nuchae, spinous processes

of C VII to T IV

insertion: mastoid process, skull below lateral one-third of
superior nuchal line

n. supply: posterior rami middle cervical nerves

a. supply:

function: together - draw head backward, extending neck;
individually - draw and rotate head to one side
(turn face to same side)

deep, intrinsic

tained if their foundation in nature, reason, or revelation is altogether abolished.

The Quarrel between Ancient and Modern

Contemporary scholarship, both inspired by and devoted to Nietzsche, has obscured his bold examination of the character and the requirements of the best life. One particular prejudice that is cultivated by the new orthodoxy must be confronted at once. In this book I shall often use time-honored and old-fashioned words such as truth *(Wahrheit)*, wisdom *(Weisheit)*, soul *(Seele)*, will *(Wille)*, right *(Recht)*, virtue *(Tugend)*, justice *(Gerechtigkeit)*, nature *(Natur)*, rank order *(Rangordnung)*, nobility *(Vornehmheit)*, and philosophy *(Philosophie)*. The reason is simple: Nietzsche uses these words, and not just here and there, but pervasively, vigorously, and unabashedly both in criticism of others and in the service of his most characteristic convictions and doctrines.[9] Nonetheless, this language will jar and perhaps dismay those who approach Nietzsche on the basis of recent scholarship, and may at first glance appear as a tendentious attempt to bring foreign concepts and partisan moral categories to bear on Nietzsche's thought, a crude effort to impose terms and notions on Nietzsche that he himself sought to overthrow.

Such reactions would be an unfortunate but understandable outgrowth of the new view that credits Nietzsche with overcoming morality, breaking free of traditional modes of thought, and founding new forms of life. This pious acceptance of Nietzsche's boldest claims at once selectively takes him at his word and surreptitiously puts words in his mouth. The new orthodoxy confuses Nietzsche's intention to overcome morality with its actual overcoming, mistakes the desire to discover or invent new modes and orders of thought for their discovery or invention, and mixes up the ambition to found new forms of life with their successful establishment. Propelled by a combination of credulity and enthusiasm, the new orthodoxy equates Nietzsche's wishes and promises with their fulfillment. If, however, one probes beyond the dominant opinion, one sees that Nietzsche's radical intentions are critically shaped and continuously nurtured by traditional ideas and hopes. Although it extends to the foundations, one does not have to probe deeply to discover manifestations of the traditional dimension of Nietzsche's thought: one need merely turn from popular opinions about Nietzsche to the richly textured surface of his writings.

This is not to say that Nietzsche's persistent use of traditional moral and philosophical language is without paradox. Although he tenaciously questions the value of truth and insists on "*perspective,* the basic condition of all life" (BGE Preface), he denounces those who turn truth upside down and repeatedly equates serving or pursuing the truth with the supreme human type.[10] Although he delights in exposing pretensions to knowledge as desire for power, Nietzsche and his Zarathustra affirm that wisdom—knowledge of human nature and of the fundamental character of existence—is the ground and goal of human excellence.[11] Although he condemns the soul as a pernicious invention of Christian priests and theologians, Nietzsche and his Zarathustra frequently use the term *soul* without irony or embarrassment to designate what is finest, deepest, and highest in human beings.[12] Although he criticizes the doctrine of the will as one of the four great errors and mocks the idea of both the free and the unfree will (TI "The Four Great Errors" 7; BGE 21), Nietzsche has his Zarathustra champion a self-determining will that wills itself and becomes its own law, and Nietzsche considered himself a free spirit and regarded freedom and independence, rightly understood, as prerogatives of higher human beings.[13] Although he seeks to undermine the metaphysical basis for belief in the notion of right or rights, Nietzsche does not refrain from couching his vision of human excellence in terms of right and rights.[14] Although his Zarathustra mocks virtue as the opiate of the multitude, Nietzsche speaks of "our virtues," that is, the virtues of free-spirited philosophers like himself, and he identifies the specific qualities of character on which human excellence depends.[15] Although he argues that morality is an outgrowth or projection of desire and will, he also invokes justice as the rarest of virtues, that which governs the service of truth, giving and receiving, and valid legislation.[16] Although he affirms in unequivocal terms that nature is non-moral, chaotic, and senseless, he appeals to nature as a moral or ethical standard.[17] Although he asserts that good and evil are created by human beings, he routinely proclaims that there is an order of rank of desires, human types, and forms of life, and that the noble soul belongs to the upper echelons of the rank order.[18] And although he unleashes a devastating attack on the prejudices that have ruined philosophy in the past and bedevil it in the present, he proudly proclaims himself a knower and philosopher and enthusiastically looks forward to a philosophy of the future.[19]

Neither one side nor the other in these pairs of extremes is correctly designated by itself as "Nietzschean" or as the core of Nietzsche's thought. This is not to say that in the contest of extremes that forms Nietzsche's thought one side does not gain the upper hand. It is, however, to insist upon the centrality of the contest that holds these rival and extreme opinions together and the fundamental assumptions about human beings and the cosmos that generate it.[20]

Some will argue that Nietzsche's reliance upon traditional language stems from a misplaced nostalgia from which he never quite broke free. Others will contend that he invokes traditional language ironically, subverting or transfiguring traditional terms and categories in the very process of using them. Still others will insist that although Nietzsche rejects traditional language in favor of something brand new, he is constrained to use it because traditional language has dominated the scene for ages and remains the only game in town. One must of course be alive to Nietzsche's famous irony and explore what Nietzsche aims to reveal and conceal through its use. Like Socrates, Nietzsche uses irony to call into question traditional understandings, but precisely in using irony, the very notion of which presupposes a gap between what one says and what one believes, and hence an intelligible and principled difference between appearance and reality, Nietzsche reveals his dependence on a traditional philosophical distinction.

To excuse or to rationalize away the traditional dimension of Nietzsche's thought risks transfiguring him into a miracle worker, exempting him from ordinary rules and standards and attributing to him extravagant feats, the philosophical equivalent of spinning straw into gold. I must emphasize that it is out of respect for his achievement as a writer and thinker that I do not approach Nietzsche as if he were able to walk on water or magically transform intractable tensions into redeeming visions. For now I want only to insist that his use of traditional language is a pervasive feature of his thought the significance of which must be determined if his philosophical explorations are to be understood. Nietzsche sometimes expresses his revolutionary aim as the revaluation of all values. Just as "revaluation" *(Umwertung)* embraces "value"

(Wert), so too Nietzsche's attempts to conceive a new human type by revaluing all values, both by intention and of necessity, preserve crucial elements of the tradition he sets out to overcome.

Heidegger's Challenge

Martin Heidegger provides almost unrivaled insight into Nietzsche's fundamental conceptions—the death of God, the will to power, the eternal return, and nihilism. In his pioneering confrontation with Nietzsche's thought Heidegger argues that Nietzsche's philosophy culminates in a vain desire, rooted in the very spiritual corruption that Nietzsche sought to overcome, for a supreme form of mastery. Heidegger, who regarded Nietzsche as primarily a "metaphysical thinker," indeed "the *last metaphysician* of the West,"[21] shows that the supreme questions raised by Nietzsche's philosophy revolve around fundamental metaphysical problems. Yet Heidegger, I think, mischaracterizes the significance of the moral intentions that motivate Nietzsche's philosophical explorations and misinterprets the results of his treacherous investigations.

On Heidegger's view, "Nietzsche's philosophy is inverted Platonism."[22] Heidegger understands this inversion as the outcome of the countermovement to Western metaphysics that Nietzsche launches—where metaphysics is understood as the domain of "philosophy proper," that is, the investigation of the first principles or basic character of the cosmos.[23] Nietzsche's countermovement, Heidegger argues, necessarily remains, as a countermovement, entangled in metaphysics or "held fast in the essence of that over against which it moves."[24] But whereas Heidegger draws the conclusion that Nietzsche's attempt to overthrow the Platonism that constitutes the Western tradition in philosophy is a task that still awaits completion, I shall suggest that Nietzsche's failure to move beyond metaphysics attests to its inescapableness. Whereas Heidegger dreams of breaking free of "that over against which" Nietzsche's philosophy moves—that is, the philosophical tradition inaugurated by Plato and supposedly completed by Nietzsche—I shall suggest that Nietzsche's inability to realize the highest ambitions of his philosophy requires reconsideration of the validity of "that over against which" his philosophy moves.[25]

Heidegger's encounter with Nietzsche represents a high point in

Nietzsche interpretation because Heidegger discerned that the high point of Nietzsche's speculations, the peak where his fundamental conceptions collide, is in the effort to reconcile activities and concepts that, according to Heidegger's interpretation of the tradition, have traditionally been held apart: truth and art, knowing and making, necessity and freedom, Being and Becoming. According to Heidegger, Nietzsche attempts to achieve these reconciliations by making human power over the world absolute—but he fails. Nietzsche's failure, Heidegger insists, is tremendously important: it marks a turning point in the history of philosophy in the sense that it brings metaphysics to a close by thinking through its last possibility and revealing that its opposites could not be effectively reconciled. Following Heidegger, I see Nietzsche as a turning point. Yet, contrary to Heidegger's opinion that Nietzsche's thought represents the consummation and exhaustion of Western metaphysics, I suggest that Nietzsche's failure to overcome the tradition justifies a renewed encounter—one that is skeptical and curious rather than destructive or deconstructive—with the whole history of philosophy from which he sought to break free.

One reason, I think, that Heidegger goes astray is that he pays too little attention to the movement of Nietzsche's thought. Although he was a great reader, Heidegger was also a great misreader.[26] By insisting that Nietzsche's fundamental question is the metaphysical question "What is being?" and that Nietzsche's philosophy is grounded in the doctrine of the eternal return,[27] Heidegger projected a restrictive framework of his own making onto Nietzsche's thought, which although it revealed much also obscured much. With staggering irony, Heidegger's manipulation, exploitation, and selective use of Nietzsche's writings exemplifies the technological frame of mind that Heidegger himself deplored, purported to wish to overcome, and claimed to find in its most advanced form in Nietzsche's thought.[28]

If one places Nietzsche's unpublished notes, out of which Heidegger made so much, in perspective, and respects the context in which Nietzsche expounds his thoughts by turning to a consideration of his books, one will see the opportunity that Heidegger lost sight of and that his writings on Nietzsche buried. The opportunity consists in a nontraditional and skeptical encounter with the tradition. For the traditional notions and virtues that enliven Nietzsche's thought not only make possible the exhibition of the defects of his fundamental doctrines and highest aspirations; the crucial role of these traditional notions and virtues in his philosophical explorations also gives rise to the demand that they be given another hearing. This startling if tentative vindication of the tradition by one who set out to overcome it is perhaps a fitting tribute to a thinker who prefers to the courage of conviction the courage for an attack on one's convictions.

The Importance of Nietzsche's Books

Heidegger has contributed decisively to making legitimate an odd and indefensible practice that dominates efforts to reconstruct and expound Nietzsche's thought.[29] The common practice, cutting across a wealth of opinions about Nietzsche, is to lift Nietzsche's ideas, arguments, and philosophical explorations out of the context from which they derive the sense and significance Nietzsche gave them. In particular, Nietzsche's well-known statements about perspectivism, creativity, will, and reason have suffered at the hands of scholars and advocates a fate similar to that of a lion wrested from its natural habitat, hauled thousands of miles, and displayed for show in a cramped zoo cage where forced confinement silences its roar, dims its eyes, and breaks its spirit. While there may be good reasons for wrenching some of Nietzsche's ideas from their context and forcing them into new homes, what could justify passing off as the original these caged and broken speculations?

The standard practice involves making arguments about what Nietzsche intended or thought based on picking and choosing, mixing and matching, and cutting and pasting words, phrases, and ideas drawn from wherever they can be found in Nietzsche's *Collected Works*.[30] Wildly diverse materials, often with little or no mention of the argumentative or dramatic context from which they are taken, are marshalled to construct or reconstruct doctrines that are then attributed to Nietzsche. One sees the height of this perverse practice in the crude treatment to which *Thus Spoke Zarathustra* is routinely subjected. Even some of those who emphasize the literary character of Nietzsche's works do not hesitate to ascribe to Nietzsche isolated remarks or deeds of his literary creation Zarathustra.[31]

What accounts for the strange manner in which many scholars rummage through Nietzsche's writings for useful material is, I think, a peculiar idea about how to read books in general and Nietzsche's books in particular. The common method is based on the assumption that Nietzsche's books are not unified works, that they do not present sustained philosophical views, that their parts do not derive their fundamental significance from their place in the whole. Judging by general practice, the consensus is that Nietzsche's books are potpourris of stimulating insights mixed in with clunkers, embarrassments, unfortunate fulminations, and irrelevant notions. The dominant view holds that the decisive unit of meaning in Nietzsche's writings is at one extreme a posthumously published, multivolume entity called *The Collected Works* and at the other the brilliant, self-contained aphorism. In practice, these two extreme opinions amount to the same thing: they equally license scholars to become advocates, picking and choosing from Nietzsche's writings as they please, using what they find congenial, stimulating, or expedient, passing by in silence what they find mistaken or disadvantageous, and passing off the result as if it were faithful to Nietzsche's thought.

In fairness it must be said that Nietzsche himself advances extreme opinions that seem to sanction the crude interpretive approach to which his writings have been subject. After all, Nietzsche is the teacher of the will to power. Will to power implies that will is more fundamental than reason. Knowledge is not discovered by the mind but imposed or projected by the will on the world. As there is no enduring, stable order, interpretation is always only an expression of power. As there is no original, only text, there is no knowledge, only interpretation. We construct the text to suit our desire because we can not do otherwise. As for books, there is no point in searching for the author's intention since interpretation always bears the indelible imprint of the interpreter's hierarchy of values. Since all reading is writing, and since all interpretation is ineradicably value-laden, the reader is fully justified in treating a text as grist for his or her own mill. Thus, it seems that Nietzsche's own writing justifies the subjugation of his books to his readers' wills. Or does it? For to the extent that we establish, say, that Nietzsche thought that all reading is writing we prove that some opinions, for example, Nietzsche's opinion that all reading is writing, may be read rather than rewritten.[32]

Although sophisticated authors may pay lip service to the idea that their interpretation is one among many, in practice those who champion the perspectival, willful, and aesthetic side of Nietzsche nonetheless purport to accomplish in the interpretation of Nietzsche what their interpretation of Nietzsche implies can never be accomplished, namely to grasp the basic or defining characteristics of Nietzsche's thought.[33] I am in sympathy with the quest to comprehend the fundamental features of Nietzsche's thought, in part, as I noted in the Preface, because this comprehension is what Nietzsche explicitly wished for from his readers. My point is that scholars who attribute to Nietzsche, and themselves endorse, perspectival, constructivist, or aesthetic notions of understanding often claim, in quite traditional fashion, to understand what is basic or fundamental in Nietzsche's thought and give every appearance of wishing for their own writings to be read rather than rewritten. Thus their practice betrays their principle, undercutting the key presupposition—the idea that all interpretation is willful remaking of the world—that justifies disregarding the integrity of Nietzsche's books.

And something similar can be said about Nietzsche: his extreme theoretical speculations about the willfulness of interpretation notwithstanding, Nietzsche explicitly wrote, as the prefaces to his books abundantly attest, in the hope that some few readers would understand his meaning. To be sure, the speculation and the hope conflict. But which must yield? Is Nietzsche's hope that his writings would be understood undercut by his extreme speculations about language, interpretation, and knowledge? Or rather, must we understand Nietzsche's extreme speculations in light of his firm conviction that his writings as well as those of others were intelligible?

My view is that the extraordinary unity of conviction, purpose, and execution that marks Nietzsche's thought comes to light only if we recognize the integrity of Nietzsche's books.[34] There is considerable prima facie evidence that this is how Nietzsche wished to be understood. First, the fact that he chose to write and publish books at all, and then books with titles, chapter headings, distinctive emphases, styles, and subjects gives rise to the presumption that the form of his presentation—the book—is meaningful. Second, almost all of Nietzsche's books contain prefaces or prologues in which he discusses the specific intention informing the work at hand. Third, in *Ecce Homo* Nietzsche surveys his life's work, and in so doing treats his books as distinct and ordered wholes. And more provisionally, attention to the structure, argument, and intention in Nietzsche's books yields rich rewards.[35] In the end, of course, the proof of the opinion that the key to Nietzsche's thought lies in his books is in the reading.[36]

A Path in Nietzsche's Thought

There are many paths in Nietzsche's thought. The path I trace proceeds by way of detailed explorations of a range of Nietzsche's major books, it goes to the foundations and the peak of his reflections on the best life, and it reveals the ethics of an immoralist.[37]

Part I, "Nietzsche's Histories," deals with Nietzsche's three major attempts, spanning his career, to clarify the significance of art, morality, and religion through the exploration of ancient history. The key to understanding how Nietzsche himself practices history is found in *On the Uses and Disadvantages of History for Life,* where he sets forth prescriptions for the right use of history. His prescriptions for the right use of history openly rest upon a bold claim to metaphysical knowledge and a definite view, at once descriptive and normative, of human nature. And these prescriptions govern the manner in which he himself writes history.

In harmony with the task that he assigns the "genuine historian" in *Uses and Disadvantages,* Nietzsche, in his own histories, subordinates the acquisition of exact historical knowledge to the poetic or mythic presentation of historical figures and events so as to display the enduring truth about human excellence and human degradation. In *The Birth of Tragedy* he analyses the origins of ancient Greek tragedy to vindicate an ethics of art; in *On the Genealogy of Morals* he examines the origins of moral prejudices to elaborate an ethics of morality; and in *The Antichrist* he exposes the origins of organized Christianity and praises the moral intentions governing Buddhism, Jesus, and the law of Manu to distinguish good and bad religions and to throw light on the ethics of religion. A major part of Nietzsche's enduring legacy is embodied in his histories where, in accordance with the task of the "genuine historian," he transforms history into poetry to defend wisdom, to distinguish nobility from baseness, and to establish the "service of truth" as a resplendent vice and noble faith.

Nietzsche's histories resolutely point to but do not fully articulate the character of human excellence, "the highest type [*die höchste Art*] of all beings" (EH III, on Z, 6). In his books there are two major attempts to articulate the character of the highest type. *Thus Spoke Zarathustra* presents the superman as the highest type. *Beyond Good and Evil* puts forward the "philosopher of the future" as the peak of human excellence. The obvious question, ignored right and left, is whether the superman and the philosopher of the future are distinct and rival types or whether they amount to one and the same type. Are the superman and the philosopher of the future, when all is said and done, two or one?

Part II, "The Highest Type," examines the character of the superman and the philosopher of the future. I argue that the philosopher of the future shares the superman's goal. In both *Thus Spoke Zarathustra* and *Beyond Good and Evil* Nietzsche teaches that human excellence requires absolute freedom that is based on absolute knowledge and realized in absolute mastery. And just as in *Thus Spoke Zarathustra*, where Zarathustra eventually abandons the highest aims of the superman, Nietzsche retreats in the final parts of *Beyond Good and Evil* from the grandest aspirations of the philosopher of the future. Nevertheless, the perspectives of the two works differ. For example, whereas *Thus Spoke Zarathustra* throws light on the reasons why the superman must be rejected as the supreme type, *Beyond Good and Evil* leaves the reasons for tempering the ambitions of the philosopher of the future shrouded in shadows and silence. And whereas *Zarathustra* promises a new sobriety only at the very end, *Beyond Good and Evil* richly exemplifies throughout the free-spirited skepticism that is the identifying mark of this new sobriety. Nietzsche's two accounts of the supreme type provide complementary perspectives on the best life. Along with his histories, they constitute essential parts of his enduring legacy.

A Point of Departure

Nietzsche's reputation as the philosopher of creativity, willing, and power is not undeserved, yet it has worked to obscure the fundamental structure of his thought. For Nietzsche emphatically distinguishes good from bad exercises of creativity, willing, and power, and envisages a supreme type who practices both art and philosophy. Good art or right making in Nietzsche's thought depends upon good philosophy or right knowing.[38] Indeed, the account of the highest human activity that Nietzsche offers in *Zarathustra* and *Beyond Good and Evil* can be understood in terms of a formula: right making based upon right knowing.[39]

Generally speaking, Nietzsche is, as postmodern interpretations

suggest, a teacher of self-making or self-creation. Yet postmodern interpreters and "neo-Nietzschean" theorists overlook the foundations of
Nietzsche's imperative to self-making and underestimate the severity
of his ethics of the creative self.[40] For Nietzsche, there is a rank order of
creative activities according to which the ultimate form of making is
self-making and the ultimate form of self-making is making oneself a
god. What postmodern interpreters disregard is that Nietzsche is compelled to figure out the form of life suitable to a self-made god, one who
engages in right making based on right knowing, by what he calls the
"intellectual conscience." In other words, it is what he has been driven
to discover about the human condition by his love of truth, or what he
sometimes calls his gay science, that impels Nietzsche to reach the fantastic conclusion that the good for human beings consists in the act of
self-deification.

A brief glance at Nietzsche's *Gay Science* can provide a useful introduction to the elements of the ethics of self-deification.[41] In section 2,
"The Intellectual Conscience," Nietzsche laments that "the great majority of people"—including "the most gifted men and the noblest
women"—do not seek to rest their faith and judgments on reason
(GS 2). Virtues, Nietzsche implies, are worthless if they are not supported by knowledge. "Higher human beings" are distinguished by the
intensity of their desire for certainty. Hatred of reason is better than
unquestioning faith inasmuch as it reflects a skepticism or reasoned
doubt about the competence of human reason; that is, hatred of reason
is vindicated as an exercise and achievement of reason. Reminiscent of
Socrates' assertion that philosophy begins in wonder (*Theatetus* 155d),
questioning, on Nietzsche's account the key manifestation of the intellectual conscience, is grounded in the perception or experience of the
"marvelous uncertainty and rich ambiguity of existence."[42] Nietzsche
finds those who lack the inclination to question contemptible. He
admits that there is folly in this opinion, but explains that the folly lies
not in his exalted estimation of the intellectual conscience but rather in
the conviction that all human beings feel its sting. For a lively intellectual conscience is rare and the identifying mark of a higher human
being.[43]

What would a higher human being amply endowed with an intellectual conscience know? How would such a person live? Section 125 of

The Gay Science, "The Madman," presents Nietzsche's famous parable of the death of God. The madman, a seeker after God, is distinguished not only by what he seeks but also by what he knows. As a result of his searches, the madman knows that God is dead, that human beings have killed him, that God's murder is a catastrophe for the human spirit, and that the destruction of what was holiest and mightiest calls forth severe new obligations and fantastic opportunities. In language rich with Christian and theological overtones, Nietzsche's madman speculates that human beings who know that God is dead require comfort for their crime, need water to cleanse their blood-spattered spirits, and must invent "festivals of atonement" and "sacred games" to redeem their lives. For Nietzsche's madman, the proper and only worthy response to the death of God involves neither the negation of religious yearning nor the extirpation of the impulse to transcendence. On the contrary. Relieved of older obligations to worship or to imitate God, Nietzsche's madman discovers a new obligation for human beings: to appear worthy of having murdered God, the madman thinks, human beings must themselves "become gods."[44]

By ascribing to human beings the power to kill God and the capacity to become a god, the madman effects a profound break with traditional Christianity. At the same time, the new obligation the madman assigns to human beings preserves an important element of the Christian tradition, because of the madman's heavy dependence upon Christian language and categories to articulate humanity's new goal, and indeed because of the very need for what is sacred and holy that underlies the quest to become a god. It is as if the obligation to become a god were for Nietzsche's madman the supreme act of piety. Yet even if his madmen, yearning for "all that was holiest and mightiest," knowing that God was dead, and drawing the ethical consequences of this "tremendous event," were the supreme embodiment of piety, the question would remain as to Nietzsche's own evaluation of piety. What could piety mean for Nietzsche in view of his ruthless questioning of cherished pieties?

As it happens, Nietzsche tells us. Speaking in the first-person plural in section 344, entitled "How we, too, are still Pious," Nietzsche proclaims the faith and the moral intention that govern his philosophical investigations, his gay science: "it is still a *metaphysical faith* upon which our faith in science rests—that even we knowers [*Wir Erkennenden*] today, we godless anti-metaphysicians still take our fire, too, from the flame lit by a faith that is thousands of years old, that Christian faith which was also the faith of Plato, that God is the truth, that truth is divine" (GS 344). Nietzsche rejects the favorite words and special doctrines of Christianity and Plato because of the fundamental faith that binds him to Christianity and Plato.[45] Although Nietzsche does proceed to raise the possibility of losing what he shares with Christianity and Plato—this faith in the divinity of truth—this loss remains, at least in *The Gay Science,* no more than a possibility. And a possibility, moreover, that Nietzsche is compelled to entertain by the internal demands imposed by faith in, or service to, the truth.

Nietzsche's gay science is rooted in an ethics of knowing and a faith in the sanctity of truth. What then of willing, making, and creating? In section 335, entitled "Long live physics!" Nietzsche presents the intellectual conscience as the judge of the moral conscience or the form of conscience that is recognized by conventional morality. In its restlessness and severity the intellectual conscience reveals that conventional morality rests upon hypocrisy and self-deception. Prizing knowledge above authority or tradition, the intellectual conscience undercuts the authority of conventional moral judgments by revealing that conventional morality, far from possessing a transcendent ground in nature, reason, or divine revelation, originates in the accidents of instincts, appetites, and circumstances. What follows the painful self-discovery that conventional morality lacks authoritative or lofty foundations, according to Nietzsche, is the task of understanding the imperative or necessity to undertake self-creation. The opinion that conventional morality is groundless is one of the grounds of Nietzsche's ethics of creativity.

To truly engage in self-creation requires knowledge so as to avoid mistaking the effect of some cause, a conditioned or reflexive response, for a freely chosen deed. Indeed, for Nietzsche, *"the creation of our own new tables of what is good"* rests upon the most ruthless forms of self-knowledge and knowledge of the world. Equating self-creation with making new laws for oneself, Nietzsche views this new lawgiving as dependent upon knowledge of the old laws that still bind human beings, especially the laws of physics, for conventional morality is not the only form of necessity that deprives human beings of freedom. Thus, to become self-creators, we must become the best learners and discoverers of everything that is lawful and necessary in the world: we must become *physicists* in order to be able to be *creators* in this sense—while hitherto all valuations and ideals have been based on *ignorance* of physics or were constructed so as to *contradict* it. Therefore: long live physics! And even more so that which *compels* us to turn to physics—our honesty! (GS 335)

Since creativity depends upon what is "lawful and necessary in the world," making depends upon knowing and right making depends upon right knowing.

What exactly would those who, like Nietzsche, are governed by honesty see when they turn to physics to discover what is "lawful and necessary in the world"? One possibility is introduced by Nietzsche in the penultimate section of the first edition of *The Gay Science,* section 341, "The Greatest Weight," which Nietzsche himself regarded as containing "the basic idea of *Zarathustra*" (EH III, on Z, 1). Nietzsche asks the reader to imagine a demon who reveals that every life is condemned to infinite and exact repetition of all of its moments. Nor is this merely a thought about human life: "The eternal hourglass of existence is turned upside down again and again, and you with it, speck of dust!" This account of existence, which on first hearing, Nietzsche states, appears to be a crushing curse, is on closer inspection, he suggests, a divine thought. For the thought of eternal necessity somehow gives rise to a kind of test:

> If this thought gained possession of you, it would change you as you are or perhaps crush you. The question in each and every thing, "Do you desire this once more and innumerable times more?" would lie upon your actions as the greatest weight. Or how well disposed would you have to become to yourself and to life *to crave nothing more fervently* than this ultimate eternal confirmation and seal? (GS 341)

Nietzsche's question leaves mysterious how the fervent craving for eternal necessity confers eternal significance upon self, life, or existence.

Indeed, it would seem that satisfaction of the desire for eternal, unchanging necessity would have the opposite effect. Unless, somehow, the thought of eternal necessity were itself a freely chosen work of the will projected or stamped upon existence,[46] a work of the will that renders existence desirable or beautiful (GS 276). This then—the form of making that beautifies the world by eternalizing necessity—might even be the highest example of right making based on right knowing. But what human being could hope to exercise so godlike a power? What would the exercise of such a power look like in practice? Questions and considerations like these give a clue as to why the ultimate section of the first edition of *The Gay Science,* which contains almost verbatim the opening of *Thus Spoke Zarathustra,* is entitled "*Incipit tragoedia,*" the tragedy begins.

At this point the welcome objection may be raised that I have betrayed my own strictures by forming an interpretation of Nietzsche's thought from a few passages culled from one of his books supported by an opportunistic appeal to his notebooks. Indeed! To be sure, I have not shown that right making based on right knowing is the highest aspiration of *The Gay Science,* much less that it is the dominant ambition of Nietzsche's highest type. At best I have assembled some suggestive evidence that favors such an opinion and justifies further examination. The task of vindicating that opinion belongs to the detailed discussions of Nietzsche's books in the chapters that follow.

Let me then end this introduction by anticipating my conclusion: a contest between a peculiar combination of convictions impels Nietzsche to identify self-deification as a human being's supreme perfection. A close study of a range of Nietzsche's books, however, indicates that for human beings such perfection is not attainable.

The imperative to make oneself a god is rooted in Nietzsche's teaching that in fact, and by right, will is the ruling element in the soul. Yet if the will rules over reason there are neither facts nor rights, only projections and creations of the strongest or most efficacious wills. As I shall argue, this conundrum ultimately proves fatal to Nietzsche's highest ambition; consequently, he does not succeed in establishing the will's sovereignty. Yet what is a defeat in one sense is a triumph in another. For Nietzsche's failed effort reveals that the attempt to transcend the human by making one's will a supreme law requires the principled denial of the distinction between political liberty and legal slavery, the ruthless denigration of political life, and in the end the merciless reduction of history, nature, and human beings to artifacts of strong wills. Nietzsche's writings dis-

play how and to what a terrifying extent the coronation of the will withers the humane sensibilities, instills an indiscriminate contempt for
authority, limitation, and form, and generates impossibly high and inevitably destructive standards for ethics and politics. The pathos of
Nietzsche's exaltation of the will is that it subverts the rank order among
desires, souls, and forms of life that he cherishes, and causes him to
betray the intellectual conscience to which he professes allegiance and
which in the first place dictated the will's exaltation. Yet in displaying
the truth about this betrayal, above all in Zarathustra's self-betrayal,
Nietzsche vindicates the intellectual conscience.

The explosive consequences of Nietzsche's thought will compel humane thinkers to question his assumptions, doubt his claims, and challenge his conclusions. A different kind of thinker, impelled by the very
skepticism that Nietzsche often incomparably exemplified, a free-
spirited skepticism that treats nothing (not even Nietzsche's opinions)
as too sacred to be questioned, doubted, or challenged, will strive to test
and contest Nietzsche's thought. Finally, it is not the morality of the
humane thinker but the reason of the skeptic that is decisive in requiring
a reconsideration of Nietzsche's achievement. For reason is the not-so-
secret power behind the throne on which Nietzsche sets the will.
Nietzsche's efforts to exalt the will in the end bolster the claims of reason, because for him it is reason, not will, that crowns the will; reason,
not will, that clarifies the "superroyal tasks" of the highest type; and
reason, not will, that displays the confusion, the poverty, and the degradation stemming from the will's reign.

I do not take this conclusion to be at odds with the spirit of
Nietzsche's thought. For I have been persuaded by Nietzsche's caution-
ary words directed to "philosophers and friends of knowledge," of
whom he considers himself one, "that no philosopher so far has been
proved right, and that there might be a more laudable truthfulness in
every little question mark that you place after your special words and
favorite doctrines (and occasionally after yourselves) than in all the solemn gestures and trumps before accusers and law courts" (BGE 25).
Would it not be a fitting tribute to thought such as Nietzsche's to place
a question mark or two after his special words and favorite doctrines?
Of course, such a tribute requires that one first accurately identify
Nietzsche's special words and favorite doctrines.

Many roads converge in Nietzsche's thought; divergent paths lead out. Whatever the origin, whatever the stops along the way, whatever the destination, one will have squandered a golden opportunity if one passes by Nietzsche's thought without observing the love of truth, the courage, and the yearning for the good that animate his magisterial effort to live an examined life by giving an account of the best life.

I

Nietzsche's Histories

... it is only to the extent that I am a pupil of earlier times, especially the Hellenic, that though a child of the present time I was able to acquire such untimely experiences. That much, however, I must concede to myself on account of my profession as a classicist: for I do not know what meaning classical studies could have for our time if they were not untimely—that is to say, acting counter to our time and thereby acting on our time and, let us hope, for the benefit of a time to come.

On the Uses and Disadvantages of History for Life

Anything that constrains a man to love less than unconditionally has severed the roots of his strength: he will wither away, that is to say become dishonest. In producing this effect, history is the antithesis of art: and only if history can endure to be transformed into a work of art will it perhaps be able to preserve instincts or even evoke them. Such a historiography would, however, be altogether contrary to the analytical and inartistic tendencies of our time, which would indeed declare it false.

On the Uses and Disadvantages of History for Life

What does a philosopher demand of himself first and last? To overcome his time in himself, to become "timeless." With what must he therefore engage in the hardest combat? With whatever marks him as the child of his time. Well, then! I am, no less than Wagner, a child of this time, that is, a decadent: but I comprehended this, I resisted it. The philosopher in me resisted.

The Case of Wagner

1

The Ethics of History:
On the Uses and Disadvantages of History for Life

It is generally agreed that Nietzsche gave dramatic and ground-breaking expression to notions of historicism, relativism, perspectivism, and nihilism, notions which, among other things, imply the artificiality and transitoriness of moral and political standards. What is striking about this general agreement is that it prevails whether historicism, relativism, perspectivism, and nihilism are hailed as tokens of liberation and empowerment or denounced as scourges of the human spirit.[1] Leading scholars, both advocates and critics, converge on at least one major point: that a key feature of Nietzsche's achievement was his frank and decisive renunciation of suprahistorical moral and political standards. This scholarly consensus, however, misrepresents what Nietzsche plainly says about his undertakings and ambitions, distorts the logic of his arguments, and obscures the moral and political significance of his thought.

To be sure, the proposition that "There are no moral phenomena at all, but only a moral interpretation of phenomena" (BGE 108) constitutes a pillar of Nietzsche's thought. That phenomena lack intrinsic moral significance can be seen, for example, in his teaching in *The Birth of Tragedy* that tragic drama renders visible the chaos at the heart of the cosmos (BT 7); in the assumption crucial to *On the Genealogy of Morals* that morality and religious belief are the offspring of human desire and artifice (GM Preface); and in his vehement attack in *The Antichrist* on the "theologians' instinct" for striving to view the world from a supposedly superior yet in fact malevolently falsifying vantage point, the vantage point of pure spirit (A 8, 9). It is easy to see, and the authorities have all seen, that Nietzsche insists that morality is a human invention lacking rational, natural, or divine foundations.

One cannot, however, explain the massive attention commanded by Nietzsche's attack on foundationalism by the fact that it lies on the surface of Nietzsche's writings, for Nietzsche's appeal to foundations or reliance upon enduring and intelligible moral standards has often been passed by or underrated, though it is no less passionately expressed, prominently displayed, and pivotally placed in his philosophical explorations. For example, *The Birth* portrays tragedy as the supreme achievement of Greek genius and the model for the cultural renewal of Germany in the nineteenth century because tragedy elevates the spirit, reveals "the essence of things," and makes men wise (BT 7). The *Genealogy* places a premium on the acquisition of knowledge by the genealogist (GM Preface and I 1), proclaims truthfulness the hallmark of the noble man (GM I 5), and calls the dignity of creativity into question by making it an identifying mark of the slavish man (GM I 10). In *The Antichrist*, organized Christianity, Buddhism, and Jesus are evaluated in accordance with their capacity to recognize and respect the truth (e.g. A 9, 15, 20, 23, 27, 50, 62), while the law of Manu is offered as an illustration of a political order that conforms to the dictates of nature (A 57).

In sum, alongside and in constant tension with Nietzsche's weighty cluster of opinions affirming that the world lacks a natural, rational, or divine order, that morality is artifice and pathology, and that the will is sovereign, exists a rival and equally weighty cluster of his opinions asserting that the cosmos has an intelligible character, that there is a suprahistorical ethical order, and that knowledge of these matters brings health, liberates, and ennobles. It is the unresolved antagonism between these sets of fundamental convictions that animates and orders Nietzsche's thought.

The contest of extremes in Nietzsche's thought has been underappreciated, owing, in part, to the uncritical acceptance of commonplaces about his style, in particular that he writes in aphorisms and fragments. Both Alexander Nehamas and Eric Blondel have helpfully called attention to the fact that Nietzsche employed a variety of styles including the essay, scholarly treatise, polemical pamphlet, maxim, psalm, parable, and complex narrative.[2] Yet both scholars overlook one particular genre that Nietzsche returns to throughout his career, namely the genre or form of the history.[3]

Nietzsche produced three comparatively sustained historical studies: *The Birth of Tragedy* (1872), his first book; *On the Genealogy of Morals* (1887), a book from his prime; and *The Antichrist* (1888), one of his last works. These three major attempts, spanning his career, to derive lessons about art, morality, religion, politics, and philosophy from the study of ancient history reflect the remarkable unity of Nietzsche's thought. This unity is that of a contest with its characteristic rivals, rules, and standards. Understanding of Nietzsche's histories, in particular the moral intention and theoretical guidelines that inform them, can help restore measure and precision to the understanding of the contest of extremes that lies at the foundations of his thought.

Nietzsche's histories are, to be sure, of a very peculiar kind. They represent a form of history that sacrifices exact historical or scientific knowledge to the accurate determination of the value of rival forms of life. Contrary to popular beliefs about his thought, Nietzsche's histories are incompatible with historicism either of the moderate variety which holds that beliefs and practices must always be understood only in terms of the distinct epoch to which they belong, or with the more radical historicism which asserts that beliefs and practices, especially those rooted in morality, must be opaque to the outsider looking in and must define the horizon of the insider looking out.

Nietzsche's primary quarrel is not with claims about the possibility of objective historical knowledge or the reality of suprahistorical moral goods. His own theoretical speculations and sensational proclamations notwithstanding, he routinely takes the possibility of objective historical knowledge for granted. For Nietzsche, the key question is the value or moral significance of objective historical knowledge, especially that produced by professional scholars. His conclusion is that such knowledge is disastrously harmful. University professors misuse history, not because they wrongly presume that they can acquire objective historical knowledge, but because they succeed all too well in spreading the poisonous information about the actual foundations of religion and morality, information that in Nietzsche's view undermines the basis for bold, free, and heroic deeds (UD 7, p. 95).

Paradoxically, the general aim of Nietzsche's histories is to discover and display nonhistorical or enduring knowledge about human nature and the rank order of desires, human types, and forms of life. In the following chapters I shall sketch the ethics of art found in *The Birth,* the ethics of morality developed in the *Genealogy,* and the ethics of religion expounded in *The Antichrist.* In each case Nietzsche adapts and employs historical study as a means to reveal the character of human excellence. Indeed, in each of his histories Nietzsche transforms history into poetry to show how wisdom ought to guide life.

Nietzsche reveals the moral and theoretical basis for the poeticizing of history on behalf of philosophy in his 1873 essay, the second of the *Untimely Meditations, On the Uses and Disadvantages of History for Life.* This polemical critique of modernity's oversaturation with history advances definite prescriptions for placing history in the service of the highest forms of human life. Under the assumption that the past is intelligible, Nietzsche first emphasizes that history can serve life by providing a vantage point for identifying the characteristic weaknesses of one's own age and models for overcoming one's own time. He then distinguishes two basic ways of living: the unhistorical and the historical. This distinction roughly corresponds to that between sentience and self-consciousness. Nietzsche argues that a healthy human life requires a judicious mix of the unhistorical and the historical. The mix is achieved through a shrewd practice of the three kinds of history: monumental, antiquarian, and critical.

Contemporary culture, however, cultivates the historical sense without restraint, weakening the personality of modern man, perverting science and scholarship, and dishonoring philosophy by politicizing it and making it a subject of universal education. Philosophy or service of the truth turns out to be the *sine qua non* for good history since good history rests upon knowledge of "true but deadly" doctrines and the "true needs" of man. Good history also depends upon creativity, or the free reshaping of the past to suit the needs of the present. Nietzsche's master or "genuine historian" is both philosopher and artist: he writes edifying historical poetry based on knowledge of metaphysics and human nature for the education of higher human beings.

In sum: the art of the genuine historian springs from and reflects his understanding; his ethics hinges upon his metaphysics; his making is based on knowing. Concurring with Aristotle that poetry is more philosophical than history, Nietzsche poeticizes history to serve philosophy.

The Historical, the Unhistorical, and the Suprahistorical

Nietzsche introduces *On the Uses and Disadvantages of History for Life*, a meditation on the "value of history," with a remark from the poet Goethe which he endorses as his own: "In any case, I hate everything that merely instructs me without augmenting or directly invigorating my activity" (UD Foreword, p. 59). At the very outset Nietzsche indicates that knowledge must be understood in terms of morality or how one should live, and that morality has a knowable shape. Though his initial categories may appear biological, the structure of his argument is moral in the sense that he holds augmentation and invigoration to be good, while viewing what impedes them as bad.

Of course augmentation and invigoration lack self-evident meaning. They point to without specifying what is higher. Yet Nietzsche leaves little room for doubt that his repeated stricture that history must serve life does not refer to mere life, or self-preservation, or prolonging "the self-seeking life and the base and cowardly action" (UD Foreword, p. 59). History ought not to serve life however understood, but rather should promote a certain form of life, the "higher life" (UD 3, p. 75) and the "higher unity" (UD 4, pp. 80, 82). As Nietzsche's examination of the value of history unfolds, he increasingly specifies the form and content of the higher life, revealing it to be indissolubly bound up with philosophy understood as service of the truth and art placed in the service of human excellence.

History, Nietzsche goes on to explain, though needed to augment life and invigorate action, has in his day come to stunt life and paralyze action. Acknowledging that this critical observation may provoke public censure, he nonetheless allows that his criticism of his contemporaries could redound to the glory of his age. Risking unpopularity, Nietzsche believes, is warranted on the Socratic ground that it is likely to yield a gain in knowledge: at worst, he hopes that provoking defenses of the age and its movements will result in his being "publicly instructed and put right about the character of our own time" (UD Foreword, p. 60).

In Nietzsche's view, his age betrays distressing symptoms of a general malady: too much of the wrong kind of history. He declares his meditation untimely because while his contemporaries take pride in their "cultivation of history" he views their preoccupation with the past as a crushing burden and a consuming disease.[4] Assuming the role of physician of culture, Nietzsche ascribes paramount importance to learning the truth about the character of his time in order to cure the plague by which it is ravaged. He stresses that his untimely understanding of the menace of history and his uncommon capacity to experience history as noxious are acquired through historical studies:

> ... it is only to the extent that I am a pupil of earlier times, especially the Hellenic, that though a child of the present time I was able to acquire such untimely experiences. That much, however, I must concede to myself on account of my profession as a classicist: for I do not know what meaning classical studies could have for our time if they were not untimely—that is to say, acting counter to our time and thereby acting on our time and, let us hope, for the benefit of a time to come. (UD Foreword, p. 60)[5]

For an age saturated in history, professional, scholarly studies of the ancient world are justified on practical grounds: the objective historical knowledge they provide can liberate from contemporary prejudice and show the way to a healthy existence.

In its primary sense, history, for Nietzsche, refers to an essential feature of the human condition. Whereas animals live unhistorically, wholly absorbed in the moment, human beings live historically, in the painful and dizzying awareness not only that the past is always receding and fading from sight but that happiness is fleeting and the future uncertain (UD 1, pp. 60–61). Though men and women may envy the untroubled stupor of the animals who lack awareness of time, and may also long for the "blissful blindness" of the child who as yet lacks a past, the fact remains that the historical sense is what lifts human beings above brute existence. Since, however, an overdeveloped historical sense inhibits action by multiplying possibilities and diminishing the feeling of personal responsibility, the sense itself must be inhibited or circumscribed. Man's historical sense must be harnessed by a capacity to think unhistorically; this requires a conscious and deliberate effort to limit consciousness and act without deliberation.

To describe unhistorical thinking Nietzsche first speaks of forgetting and then more gracefully alludes to forming horizons; in both cases he stresses that structure and boundaries must be imposed by human beings on experience to subdue the ceaseless and senseless onrush of events. In language that anticipates the constellation of problems inhering in the doctrine of the eternal return, he indicates that the task for a human being is to learn to forget, to understand how the "it was" weighs down upon and confounds human existence, to recognize "what his existence fundamentally is—an imperfect tense that can never become a perfect one," and to overcome knowledge of the flux or universal becoming (UD 1, pp. 61–62). One forgets by deploying the "plastic power," that is, the power to subdue, digest, and exploit the past for the sake of life and action in the present (UD 1, p. 62). By means of such unhistorical thinking, what cannot be used is rudely excluded by impenetrable boundaries and what has outlived its usefulness is unceremoniously discarded and forgotten.

Since Nietzsche holds that the health of an individual, people, or culture depends upon the proper mix of the historical and the unhistorical, and since unhistorical thinking means forcibly closing one's mind, a healthy life inevitably rests upon injustice and errors (UD 1, pp. 64–65). Accordingly, great deeds—all beautiful works of art, glorious battlefield victories, and passionate loves—require a studied ignorance, a self-imposed blindness and deafness to obligations and dangers (UD 1, p. 64). But a few rare individuals, Nietzsche anticipates, will rise to a "suprahistorical vantage point," a vantage point from which they will discern "the essential condition of all happenings—this blindness and injustice in the soul of him who acts" (UD 1, p. 65). The "suprahistorical man" suffers nausea as a result of his correct perception that history is nothing but a meaningless series of equally valueless moments. Contrary to the historical man, who is deluded about the "meaning of existence," the suprahistorical man knows that existence rules out salvation, and that despite the great variety in the history of nations and individuals, existence is always the same, a perennial flux devoid of intrinsic significance.

In section 1 of *Uses and Disadvantages* Nietzsche comes close to saying that what is greater than great deeds is understanding the injustice and delusion that make great deeds possible. He retreats temporarily from this preference for nausea-inducing wisdom;[6] acknowledging that his choice may reflect a prejudice, he opts for unwisdom, life, health, and action. But having half-heartedly renounced wisdom in favor of life, he reaffirms that life or a good life cannot do without wisdom or philosophical questioning.[7] Enduring nauseating wisdom enables a few rare souls, guided by a "higher force" (UD 1, p. 67), to harness the historical sense so that some may live a life of bold, free deeds.

The Kinds of History

There are three pure species of history: monumental, antiquarian, and critical. Each ministers to distinct human needs and longings; each is susceptible to characteristic abuses. Reversing conventional estimations that history is the preserve of students and scholars, Nietzsche declares that history belongs to the powerful man of great deeds who, lacking models, teachers, and comforters among his contemporaries, turns to history for examples of human excellence.

Monumental history provides these men with images of past greatness. It is governed by the moral impulse or command to beat back all that is base and petty and to preserve what is exemplary and rare. It is driven by the demand "that greatness shall be eternal" (UD 2, p. 68). It is informed by the methodological assumption that greatness has an enduring and intelligible look, that the enduring character of human excellence is accessible to the master historian and can be effectively transmitted by the historian's art. Dismissing the idea that history repeats itself endlessly without addition or subtraction at definite intervals, Nietzsche declares that monumental history properly rejects the demand for "absolute veracity" (*volle Wahrhaftigkeit;* UD 2, p. 70). Though haughtily indifferent to mapping the intricate skein of cause-and-effect relations determining events in history, the practitioner of monumental history does not thereby abandon truth as a standard. To the contrary, the explicit aim of monumental history is to exhibit the enduring truth about human excellence.[8]

Nietzsche is the first to acknowledge that because monumental history forgoes minute, painstaking analysis it risks becoming "free poetic invention" (UD 2, p. 70). Men of power and achievement, deceived by beautiful images of triumph and mastery torn loose from the actual dense web of cross-cutting causes and effects in which all deeds occur, may be tempted to reckless, disastrous adventures in rewriting the past and scripting the future. But the harm that monumental history can cause among great spirits is small, in Nietzsche's eyes, compared to the crimes perpetrated by weak, inartistic natures who arrogate to themselves a privilege for which they are unworthy. When the inept and the unfit, always for Nietzsche the vast majority, try to practice monumental history, they transform images of past greatness into idols to be worshipped rather than models to be emulated and surpassed. Indeed the weak multitude is the inexorable enemy of human nobility: the gods their monumental histories glorify freeze a single image of excellence as divine and absolute, sternly prohibiting fresh acts of human courage and strength (UD 2, pp. 71–72). Nietzsche's emphatic distinction between good and bad monumental history, between true and useful and false and disadvantageous images, affirms what he subsequently states plainly: that history serves life not when it promotes mere life but when it fosters the higher forms of life (UD 3, p. 75; UD 4, pp. 80, 82).

Whereas monumental history chronicles the exploits of and serves chiefly as a spur to action for outstanding individuals, antiquarian history belongs to "him who preserves and reveres" and addresses communities and traditions (UD 2, pp. 72–73). Antiquarian history serves life by teaching veneration of a people's or a nation's past; it infuses inherited customs, kin, and countrymen with solemn significance, providing present and future generations with knowledge of the conditions that served life in the past (UD 3, p. 73). Like monumental history, antiquarian history commits injustice against the past by distorting the historical record. This justified injustice ceases to be just only when the preservation of the old becomes an end in itself; then piety deteriorates into an insatiable, undiscriminating hunger for information about antiquity. Antiquarian history degenerates into antiquarianism when study of the past is divorced from service to the present. Antiquarianism undermines "higher life"; but even in the best case antiquarian history "paralyzes the man of action" by concentrating on the preservation of past forms of life at the expense of the creation of new forms (UD 3, p. 75).

The antidote to excessive antiquarian history is critical history. Critical history closely resembles the familiar scientific and scholarly study of history. A crucial difference is that critical history, like monumental and antiquarian history, has an explicitly ethical dimension. Critical history is properly employed to dissolve the claims that the past makes on the present so as to free "the man of action." The practice of critical history rests on a crucial theoretical assumption, call it a foundation, at once descriptive and normative:

> every past . . . is worthy to be condemned—for that is the condition of human things: human violence and weakness have always played a mighty role in them. It is not justice which here sits in judgment; it is even less mercy which pronounces the verdict: it is life alone, that dark, driving power that insatiably thirsts for itself. Its sentence is always

unmerciful, always unjust, because it has never proceeded out of a pure well of knowledge; but in most cases the sentence would be the same even if it were pronounced by justice itself. "For all that exists is *worthy* of perishing. So it would be better if nothing existed." (UD 3, p. 76)

Critical history mercilessly lays bare the violence and weakness, the errors and accidents, the aberrations and atrocities in which all human action is rooted. The danger of critical history is that it will demoralize men by revealing that what Nietzsche refers to as "first nature" *(erste Natur)*, that is character, is an unstable mix of vile elements. The danger is averted by summoning "a new, stern discipline" to fashion a second nature *(zweite Natur)* to replace the feeble original (UD 3, pp. 76–77). Although in this context Nietzsche uses the term *nature* to denote something essentially man-made and perishable, the nameless and vague standard which nevertheless condemns the "first nature" and governs the fashioning of the "second nature" has no identifiable maker and no apparent limits to its duration. Evidently, although human natures are artificial, the standards governing the making and the evaluation of human natures are not.

History serves the more exalted forms of life when a constantly varying mixture of monumental, antiquarian, and critical history is judiciously practiced; that means "always and only for the ends of life and thus also under the domination and supreme direction of these ends" (UD 4, p. 77). According to Nietzsche's diagnosis, however, the healthy relationship between life and history was ruined in nineteenth-century Europe by the transformation of history into a science or scholarly discipline (*Wissenschaft*; UD 4, p. 77). Science's inner compulsion to classify, order, and explain the world mechanically lets loose the floodwaters of history and washes away the unhistorical disposition.

Modern man, Nietzsche disgustedly declares, has become a "walking encyclopedia," stuffed to overflowing with the customs, art, philosophy, and religion of previous ages (UD 4, p. 79). Nietzsche's modern man, the original couch potato, is an overstimulated, passive, vacant spectator of all that has ever been. As a repository for the achievements of other cultures, modern man becomes incapable of "taking real things seriously" (UD 4, p. 79). Nietzsche's objection to the unrestricted reign of science is both moral and philosophical: too much truth about history saps vigor and drowns the truth about what is good for human beings.

In a culture ravished by the malady of history, "the great productive spirit" is compelled to turn against the "destructive and degrading" effects of the reigning pseudo-culture, and embracing the "divine joys of creation and construction . . . [he] ends as a solitary man of knowledge and satiated sage" (UD 4, p. 82).

But even great productive spirits are imperiled by the onslaught of history. History weakens the human capacity for awe, destroys the instincts, and distances human beings from real events in the world by insisting that "subjective depths" contain the key to all riddles (UD 5, pp. 84–85). This triumph of subjectivity all but ensures that "history does not make any personality 'free,' that is to say truthful towards itself, truthful towards others, in both word and deed" (UD 5, p. 84). And this loss of freedom or truthfulness toward oneself and others is, on Nietzsche's account, sharply at odds with what is good for human beings. Because of his firm ideas about the good and about human excellence Nietzsche can anticipate "a culture which corresponds to true needs [*wahren Bedürfnissen*] and does not, as present-day universal education teaches it to do, deceive itself as to these needs and thereby become a walking lie" (UD 5, p. 85).

Similarly, because of his firm ideas about the good and about human excellence, Nietzsche can see that the weak and self-deluded human character caused by oversaturation with history leads to the degradation of "the most truthful of all sciences, the honest naked goddess philosophy" (UD 5, p. 85). The advent of professional philosophy, the proliferation of institutionally supported reading, writing, and speaking about everything under the sun, is a consequence, Nietzsche asserts, of the historical sense run amok. Scholarship and criticism replace philosophy. The attempt to fulfill the "law of philosophy" in life and deeds is abandoned. Instead, scholars undertake the project of stuffing and mounting for public exhibition the well-preserved carcasses of once magnificent but now extinct philosophical doctrines (UD 5, p. 85). And critics overlook the works themselves to focus on the history of the author (UD 5, p. 87). The result is that scholarship and criticism only produce more scholarship and criticism; both are irrelevant at best and generally poisonous to right action.

The replacement of philosophy with scholarship and criticism harms life and paralyzes action by rendering them unworthy objects of investigation. Indeed, Nietzsche defines the degradation of modern man in terms of his rage for criticism. The critics' "critical pens never cease to flow, for they have lost control of them and instead of directing them are directed by them. It is precisely in this immoderation of its critical outpourings, in its lack of self-control, in that which the Romans call *impotentia*, that the modern personality betrays its weakness" (UD 5, p. 87). In response to the pathetic self-aggrandizement of scholars, bold measures are required to remind human beings of the "law of philosophy" and to make it possible for at least a few to live in accordance with it. The key is the right kind of education, a historical education provided by the "genuine historian."

The Genuine Historian

That the question of philosophy is no passing fancy but at the heart of Nietzsche's prescriptions for the right use of history is borne out by his brief but highly suggestive discussion of "objectivity" *(Objectivität),* "justice" *(Gerechtigkeit),* and the "striving for truth" (*Streben nach Wahrheit;* UD 6, pp. 88–89). Nietzsche denies that the quest for objectivity in modern historical studies arises from the desire to do justice since modern man lacks the requisite courage and stern will for just action. Justice, traditionally understood as the preeminent political virtue, has, for him, nothing to do with the fair distribution of resources, the remedying of injuries to body and property, or the promotion of the common good. Rather, his understanding of justice is more akin to an opinion advanced by Socrates—whom Nietzsche invokes as an authority in this context (UD 6, p. 88)—according to which justice is the health or right ordering of the human soul.[9]

Justice, "the rarest of all virtues," at once a moral and intellectual virtue, governs the desire for truth (UD 6, p. 88; also UD 5, p. 83).[10] Those who possess it are venerable because "the highest and rarest virtues are united and concealed in justice" (UD 6, p. 88). The just man, rare and solitary, is "the most *venerable* exemplar of the species man" (UD 6, p. 88). The truth that the just man seeks differs from both "cold, ineffectual knowledge" and effective instrumental knowledge. In service of the truth, the just man strives to reach a true judgment about humanity. Such a striving for truth is extremely rare: "The truth is that few serve truth because few possess the pure will to justice, and of these few only a few also possess the strength actually to be just" (UD 6, p. 89). The difficulty in serving truth has as much to do with the scarcity of virtue as with the inherent elusiveness of truth.

Serving truth differs from maintaining objectivity. Indeed, "objectivity and justice have nothing to do with one another" (UD 6, p. 91). Very often the claim of objectivity masks a political agenda or reflects a confusion of conventional norms with universal principles of judgment. Whereas justice requires distinguishing between what is grand and noble and what is mean and petty, objectivity, as Nietzsche sees the term used by modern scholars, refers to a principled neutrality toward all events and individuals (UD 6, p. 93). Objectivity so conceived is constitutionally unable to respect or report the truth about nobility and baseness. Accordingly, Nietzsche condemns modern man's objectivity because it springs from weak natures, fails to recognize crucial moral differences, treats unlike cases alike, and is oblivious to "what is worth knowing and preserving in the past" (UD 6, p. 94). Paradoxically, the problem with conventional objectivity is that it conceals or distorts the facts about the higher life.

In contrast to the injustice that nourishes modern man's objectivity, "a stern and great sense of justice," Nietzsche holds, is "the noblest center of the so-called drive to truth" (UD 6, p. 89). Whereas historical objectivity consists in reporting facts without judging or judging falsely, justice demands that history serve the goal of displaying what is high and rare. Whereas historical objectivity seeks general propositions, justice requires images of wholeness and beauty. Thus, the value of history "will be seen to consist in its taking a familiar, perhaps commonplace theme, an everyday melody, and composing inspired variations on it, enhancing it, elevating it to a comprehensive symbol, and thus disclosing in the original theme a whole world of profundity, power, and beauty" (UD 6, p. 93).

This weighty task belongs to "the genuine historian" (*der echte Historiker;* UD 6, p. 94). The genuine historian is both a knower and a creator whose comprehensive making or art is based on his universal knowledge. He "must possess the power to remint [*umzuprägen*] the universally known into something never heard of before, and to express the universal so simply and profoundly that the simplicity is lost in the profundity and the profundity in the simplicity" (UD 6, p. 94). Rich with

great and exalted experiences, "great historians" recover, correctly interpret, and beautifully express through their histories "the great and exalted things of the past" (UD 6, p. 94).

Thus the genuine or great historian is the supreme educator. But is
the supreme educator the highest type? Nietzsche proceeds to counsel
his readers: "Satiate your soul with Plutarch and when you believe in
his heroes dare at the same time to believe in yourself" (UD 6, p. 95).
Since Plutarch does not chronicle the careers of historians and artists
but rather celebrates political lives, the deeds of soldiers, statesmen, and
rulers, Nietzsche leaves unclear the rank of the genuine historian whose
heroism consists in recovering and chronicling the heroism of the past.

Nevertheless, the genuine historian shares with the highest types
found in Nietzsche's work, the superman and the philosopher of the
future, a passion and need for knowledge. For what justifies Nietzsche
in distinguishing the crimes against the truth perpetrated by modern
man's objective history from the omissions, embellishments, and fabrications crucial to the task of the genuine historian is superior knowledge
of a specific sort. Fabrications or lies about history are justified by the
service they render in fostering human excellence. And this service requires that history honor the truth in two decisive respects. First, useful
history must rest upon an unflinching recognition followed by a skillful
concealment of doctrines that Nietzsche considers true but deadly: "the
doctrines of sovereign becoming, of the fluidity of all concepts, types
and species, of the lack of any cardinal distinction between man and
animal" (UD 9, p. 112). Second, useful history must be informed by
human beings' "real needs" (*echten Bedürfnisse;* UD 10, pp. 122–123;
also UD 1, p. 66, and UD 5, p. 85). More boldly put, history serves life
well only on the basis of true knowledge of metaphysics and human
nature. Nietzsche's genuine historian is a lover of truth who transforms
history into art to educate noble natures and cultures.

Self-Knowledge and Self-Creation

Nietzsche's exploration of the right use of history is not merely theoreti-
cal; he also advances prescriptions for the right use of history in the
Germany of his day. One of the first truths that must be recognized if
Germany is to be rescued from the cultural philistinism to which, in
Nietzsche's view, his generation has sunk is "a *necessary truth:* the truth

that the German possesses no culture because his education provides no basis for one" (UD 10, p. 119). Whereas "Plato considered it necessary that the first generation of his new society (in the perfect state) should be educated with the aid of a mighty *necessary lie*," the first generation of a revitalized Germany must be educated in the necessary truth that it has been made sick by history (UD 10, pp. 118–119).

As a precondition for learning how to forget, the new generation "must taste this truth drop by drop, like a fierce and bitter medicine," and achieve the self-knowledge that it has been "ruined for living, for right and simple seeing and hearing," indeed, that it may not even be able any longer to find in itself "true life" (*wahrhaftiges Leben;* UD 10, p. 119). Before those who have been made sick by history can remake themselves they must unmake themselves, and before they can unmake themselves they must see how poorly their "first natures" (UD 3, pp. 76–77) have been made. And such an education presupposes a notion of right making and a standard governing the making of natures, a notion and a standard that are themselves intelligible and not made.

In the concluding passages of *Uses and Disadvantages* Nietzsche hopefully declares that the "malady of history" can be cured by the administration of the hard medicine consisting of the unhistorical and the suprahistorical (UD 10, p. 120). The former involves creating horizons to repel the ceaseless onslaught of what is transient, mortal, and devoid of inherent significance; the latter designates those powers "which lead the eye away from becoming towards that which bestows upon existence the character of the eternal and stable, towards *art* and *religion*" (UD 10, p. 120). The cure for too much history closely resembles the formula Nietzsche employed more than a decade later in his notebooks to describe the "supreme will to power," that is, "to stamp [*aufzuprägen*] Becoming with the character of Being" (WP 617).[11] A comprehensive understanding of the human condition reveals that "the eternalizing powers of art and religion" must combat the historicizing and reductivist powers of science for the sake of human excellence (UD 10, p. 120).

Science is the nemesis of art and religion because science's relentless quest for the historical determinants of actions and events reveals a world of endless flux or becoming and thereby "robs man of the foundation of all his rest and security, his belief in the enduring and eternal" (UD 10, p. 121). Scientific or objective knowledge must be harnessed in accordance with "a *hygiene of life*" (UD 10, p. 121). The restoration of health depends upon the very task Nietzsche assigned to the genuine historian: forming horizons and endowing existence with the character of eternity by means of edifying poems that take the shape of histories.

The poetic activity of the genuine historian depends upon studying and employing the past according to the "rule of life" (UD 10, p. 122). But how is knowledge of the "rule of life" acquired? As in the Foreword, Nietzsche asserts in conclusion that the study of ancient Greece provides an invaluable standpoint from which to discern the defects of the modern age. And he adds that ancient Greece also provides the teaching that is the foundation of health and the surest guide to the ends of life.[12] Modern man can become human again by heeding the injunction of the God at Delphi, "Know yourself" (UD 10, p. 122).[13]

Now broadly speaking 'Know yourself' is susceptible to two fundamental interpretations, one pointing outward and universal in scope, one pointing inward and focusing on the particular. Following a tendency more characteristic of Plato and Aristotle, 'Know yourself' may mean know the universal features that define a human being. Following a tendency more characteristic of Rousseau, romanticism, and modernism, 'Know yourself' could mean know the specific and original features that constitute your unique personality. Which is closer to Nietzsche's meaning?[14] Working against the subjectivist interpretation of 'Know yourself' is the fact that in *Uses and Disadvantages* Nietzsche sharply criticizes the cultivation and celebration of subjectivity as a symptom of modern decline (UD 4, pp. 80–81; UD 5, pp. 84–85). Speaking in favor of the universal interpretation is the fact that Nietzsche's description of Greek excellence depends on the distinction between real and apparent needs and on the importance of grasping the former so as to abolish the latter (UD 10, p. 122).

Nietzsche insists that modern man must do as the Greeks did: each must "organize the chaos within him by thinking back to his real needs" (UD 10, p. 123). Thus, he firmly grounds self-creation (organizing the chaos within) in self-knowledge (grasping one's real needs). Yet the knowledge of one's real needs does not come easily or naturally. Self-knowledge and hence self-creation depend—apparently everywhere and always—on specific virtues, prominent among which are honesty and strength and truthfulness of character (UD 10, p. 123). Virtue is necessary for identifying one's true or real needs and, once identified, for satisfying them.

A people whose self-creation is based on self-knowledge embodies the true or Greek conception of culture, that is, "the conception of culture as a new and improved *physis* [nature]" (UD 10, p. 123). The Greeks were able to create this new and improved nature, Nietzsche emphasizes, thanks to "the higher force of their *moral* nature [*sittlichen Natur*]" (UD 10, p. 123). Intellectual and moral virtue are the foundation of true culture, and philosophical virtue most of all: "every increase in truthfulness must also assist to promote *true* culture [*wahren Bildung*]: even though this truthfulness may sometimes seriously damage precisely the kind of cultivatedness now held in esteem, even though it may even be able to procure the downfall of an entire merely decorative culture" (UD 10, p. 123).

Nietzsche concludes by attributing marvelous powers to "true culture," an image of which he finds in Greek culture. He proclaims that true culture overcomes the distinction between inner life and outer conduct, does away with convention, and brings about a unanimity of life, thought, appearance, and will. These are thrilling and inspiring possibilities. Yet the very combination of moral and intellectual virtues that Nietzsche says underlies such a culture—honesty and strength and truthfulness of character—compels one to observe that Nietzsche does not sketch or analyze the structure of such a culture but rather only states its principle and its aspiration. Nor does he clarify the difficulty involved in treating *physis,* which is by definition above and untouched by human will, as the subject of human will; and he leaves uncertain how a higher moral nature can serve as the foundation of culture where culture is understood as the creation of a new nature. While it is clear by the end of *Uses and Disadvantages* that Nietzsche yearns for a perfect reconciliation of extremes, how that perfect reconciliation would look in practice remains extremely obscure.

Conclusion

There is a contest of extreme and rival opinions at the foundations of Nietzsche's ethics of history. Nietzsche himself does not overcome, within the confines of *Uses and Disadvantages,* the conflict between his opinion that values are created by human beings and imposed by them on a senseless world and his conviction that historical knowledge is possible and that the metaphysical structure of the cosmos and the rank order of types of human beings are intelligible. Whether what Nietzsche has left unreconciled can be reconciled by others is an open question. And whether Nietzsche effects such a reconciliation elsewhere, for example in his histories or *Thus Spoke Zarathustra* and *Beyond Good and Evil*, is an important question that cannot be answered without a careful analysis of those works. Meanwhile, the discovery of an unresolved contest of extremes in *Uses and Disadvantages* does not negate Nietzsche's achievement but rather constitutes a step in extricating it from the suffocating reverence to which it has been subject. *Uses and Disadvantages of History for Life* throws light on Nietzsche's grand attempt to reconcile philosophy and art in a good life by grounding the most admirable forms of making in the most comprehensive kind of knowledge.

Nietzsche's account of the right use of history suggests an underappreciated unity in his writings by raising the possibility that in his several histories Nietzsche wrote from the perspective, and assumed the responsibility, of the genuine historian. If the "genuine historian" fashions artworks in the light of true metaphysical knowledge and accurate understanding of true or real human needs out of raw materials drawn from history in order to educate toward human excellence, what might one expect to discover in studying Nietzsche's histories? It would, for example, be consistent with the hypothesis that Nietzsche writes history as a genuine historian to find that in reconstructing the origins, peak moment, and demise of Greek tragedy in *The Birth of Tragedy*, Nietzsche shows the role that the right or perfected form of art plays in making men wise; that in reconstructing the origins of our moral prejudices in *On the Genealogy of Morals*, he displays enduring and intelligible standards for praising, blaming, and ranking moralities; and that in reconstructing the origins of Christianity in *The Antichrist*, he brings to light the rank order of religious beings and religions.

Examination of *The Birth*, the *Genealogy*, and *The Antichrist*, I shall argue, vindicates the proposition that Nietzsche writes history governed by the assumptions, obligations, and ends that define the task of the "genuine historian." But where exactly does the genuine historian belong in the rank order? Where does he stand in relation to the highest type? Are the genuine historian's poeticized histories for the sake of the higher life the highest form of making or creativity that Nietzsche recognizes? To answer these questions it is necessary to view Nietzsche's histories in light of the two explicit accounts he provides of the highest type: Zarathustra's superman and *Beyond Good and Evil*'s philosopher of the future. First, however, it is necessary to view Nietzsche's histories in their own light.

2

The Ethics of Art:
The Birth of Tragedy

The dominant theme of *The Birth of Tragedy* is not artistic creativity, as is commonly supposed, but wisdom: how it is acquired, what it reveals, and its staggering impact on the individual who dares to lift its veil. This assertion is not contradicted by the fact that in the preface to the second edition of *The Birth of Tragedy*, Nietzsche's "Attempt at a Self-Criticism," Nietzsche calls attention to the proposition that "the existence of the world is *justified* only as an aesthetic phenomenon" and emphasizes that this thought is repeated several times in his book (BT ASC 5; BT 5, 24). The temptation is to understand Nietzsche's famous proposition as asserting that art, in the sense of individual creativity, is the fundamental human activity. Yet there is little warrant in his book for this understanding.

The fact is that in the key exposition of the proposition that existence is justified only as an aesthetic phenomenon, Nietzsche presents the individual, even the genius, as the passive medium, the unwitting tool through which a mighty god-like power, the "primordial artist of the world," expresses its creative will (BT 5). There, to the extent that Nietzsche describes a doctrine of self-making, he restricts it to a single god-like figure whose creative activity is the source of human activity. The consequence is to reduce the lives of flesh and blood human beings to "merely images and artistic projections for the true author" (BT 5). On this view, human beings receive their highest dignity not from making works of art but as works of someone or something else's art. Nietzsche's artists' metaphysics, taken at face value, deprives human beings of the goods—self-consciousness, autonomy, and creativity—modern philosophy most values.

The popular belief that Nietzsche champions the idea of self-making, central to the aesthetic interpretation of Nietzsche, is connected to a prominent debate occurring in the social sciences, humanities, and arts over whether the truth is made or discovered, invented or found. Nietzsche is commonly invoked as an authority for the view that what passes for knowledge is in fact constructed by the mind or some collectivity of minds to serve a range of often disguised human interests. What meaning there is in the world, according to this view, is placed there by human beings. On the question of whether truth is made or discovered, Nietzsche, according to the aesthetic interpretation, comes down on the side of those who believe that truth is made and invented.[1]

In fact, Nietzsche's account of the genesis and death of tragedy crucially relies on the opinion that the fundamental truth about humankind and the world is discovered, not made. Indeed, Nietzsche's central concern in *The Birth* is closely related to what Plato's Socrates referred to as the "old quarrel between philosophy and poetry" (*Republic* 607b). On the assumption that the truth is discovered, the question *The Birth of Tragedy* poses is whether art or philosophic thought is better suited to grasping and conveying knowledge about the human condition and the cosmos. And Nietzsche's clear answer is that art is better suited, and hence wiser than philosophy—or the dominant understanding of philosophy. This qualification is important because Nietzsche's attack on philosophy in *The Birth* in fact bolsters the claims of wisdom to guide life. Nietzsche argues in *The Birth* that the truth, or at least the most important truths about human nature and the metaphysical structure of the cosmos, can be known through tragic art which imitates or mirrors and transfigures nature.[2] His polemics against Socrates and his attack on the theoretical outlook notwithstanding, Nietzsche sets out in *The Birth* to answer the Socratic question concerning the best life; and the answer he proposes is in harmony with Socrates' conviction that the unexamined life is not worth living, or that human excellence depends on wisdom.

The preface Nietzsche wrote for the 1886 edition of *The Birth*, "Attempt at a Self-Criticism," emphasizes the book's ethical dimension.

Nietzsche begins by juxtaposing the grand military and diplomatic activity surrounding the Franco-Prussian War of 1870 to his solitary investigations of the meaning of Greek cheerfulness and Greek art, investigations brought to completion while he was "slowly convalescing from an illness contracted at the front" (BT ASC 1).[3] Comparing the peace attained at Versailles to the peace he attained with himself through figuring out why the Greeks, the best, most beautiful specimens of humanity, needed art, Nietzsche implies that private intellectual accomplishment ranks with military and diplomatic glory.

This corresponds to what he has to say in 1872 in the original preface dedicated to Richard Wagner. There, remarking on the "contemplative delight" in which his ideas were conceived, Nietzsche rejects "the contrast between patriotic excitement and aesthetic enthusiasm" (BT Preface). He insists that investigation of the birth of art among an ancient people, like waging war and negotiating peace, should be central to the life of a nation. Indeed, he argues that his questions about art constitute a pivotal encounter with a serious German problem central to German hopes. In opposition to the conventional contrast between art and the serious business of life, Nietzsche wants his readers to understand that nothing is more serious than understanding the significance of art because "art represents the highest task and the truly metaphysical activity of this life" (BT Preface). This conviction implies that if art is to be accorded its proper role in the life of the individual and the nation, its character must be discovered, its relation to other human activities must be determined, and its rank must be ascertained. Consequently, Nietzsche's efforts to establish the political urgency of questions about art results in a simultaneous elevation of knowledge. On his own account it is not art but contemplation or intellectual investigation that reveals art's uses and disadvantages.

Indeed, Nietzsche stresses in his later preface that the determination of the very "value of existence" was implicated in the questions he explored in *The Birth*. Recalling that he had wondered whether there was an "intellectual predilection," stemming from health, strength, and joy in life, for attending to the "hard, gruesome, evil, problematic aspect of existence" (BT ASC 1), he hints that the best, the strongest, and the most courageous Greeks proved their preeminence by creating tragic myths through which they came face to face with the terrible power of the Dionysian. And the best were brought to their knees by Socrates, the opponent of the tragic view, the theoretical man par excellence, the paradigm of the scholar and the scientist, who led a cowardly and duplicitous flight from truth.

Thus, right off the bat in his belated preface or postscript, Nietzsche portrays both art (the tragic myths of the Greeks) and philosophy (Socratic rationalism) as fundamental orientations toward the truth about the fundamental character of existence. And he implies that the superiority of the tragic myths stems from the fact that through them the Greeks bravely faced the ugly truth about existence, whereas Socrates' theoretical reason or science represented a cowardly ruse for evading and suppressing the terrifying truth about the human condition. Thus, Nietzsche's paradoxical argument is that by revealing the true character of existence art makes good on what theoretical reason or science promises but fails to deliver.

Without calling into question its basic argument, Nietzsche offers in his new preface several stinging criticisms of *The Birth:* the book was constructed out of immature personal experience; it was badly written, overwrought, and sentimental; it lacked "the will to logical cleanliness" and was "disdainful of proof"; it was too beholden to the forms of scholarship, to language drawn from Kant and Schopenhauer, to the authority of Wagner, and to misguided hopes for the rebirth of German culture (BT ASC 2, 3, 6). It is striking that these trenchant self-criticisms do not include doubts about the significance of the questions raised in the book or the general validity of the answers put forward. Indeed, Nietzsche emphasizes that what is enduring in the book is precisely the tasks undertaken: addressing a new problem, *"the problem of science itself"*; refining that new problem by *"look[ing] at science in the perspective of the artist, but at art in that of life"*; and discovering that to understand the Greeks and their art it is necessary to answer the question "what is Dionysian?" (BT ASC 2, 3). While criticizing the tone, the form, and the execution of his first book, Nietzsche affirms, from the vantage point afforded by fourteen years, the essential correctness of the book's fundamental assumptions, questions, and conclusions.

Of the many fundamental questions the book raises, none, according to Nietzsche, is graver than that of morality: "It is apparent that it was a whole cluster of grave questions with which this book burdened itself. Let us add the gravest question of all. What, seen in the perspective of *life*, is the significance of morality [*die Moral*]?" (BT ASC 4). As elsewhere in his writings, the perspective of life, for Nietzsche, is the perspective of the higher and highest forms of life. One could say that the gravest question of all for Nietzsche is the moral significance of morality, inasmuch as he seeks to determine the value or worth of morality, what it contributes to a strong, courageous, well-turned-out life.

What speaks against formulating Nietzsche's concern in terms of the morality of morality is a key ambiguity in his own use of the term "morality" that must be clarified at once. We can dispose of part of the confusion by recognizing that although for the most part he uses the term "morality" to designate forms of life he detests—as in Christian, democratic, herd, or slave morality—on occasion he uses "morality" in the ordinary sense as a general category referring to comprehensive schemes of right conduct.[4] The main point is that when Nietzsche attacks the "*moral* interpretation and significance of existence" (BT ASC 5), when he seeks to determine the "value of morality" (GM Preface 5, 6), and when he declares war on Christianity because it has waged war against "the higher type of man" by revaluing the "supreme values of the spirit as something sinful" (A 5), he speaks in the name of a higher morality or ethic, a particular vision of the best life.[5]

One must not be fooled by Nietzsche's tendency to use the term "morality" as a synonym for bad moralities into believing that he wished to abandon the language of praise and blame or that he rejected enduring standards governing human conduct. Despite his reputation as a champion of the view that ways of life are not susceptible to rational determination, Nietzsche reveals in his first book what was to be a career-long preoccupation with the constitutive features of human excellence. In contrast to the social scientist who as a matter of principle divides the world into hard facts and soft values and seeks to avoid mixing the scientific study of facts with the metaphysical inquiry into values, and equally in opposition to the liberal and postmodern pluralist who holds that there are a multiplicity of ways to be good, Nietzsche's primary interest in *The Birth* lies in the clarification of the one best life. In practice, Nietzsche writes as if questions concerning first principles and the greatest good can be clarified and indeed resolved by the human mind.

Nietzsche's "*antimoral* propensity," then, is rooted in a countermorality, an opposing ethic, an alternative conception of what is good, right, and fitting for a human being. Thus, his criticism of morality is in fact ultimately moral or, to avoid confusion, ethical. The ethics that informs Nietzsche's criticism of morality—the ethics of an immoralist (BGE 226; D Preface 4; EH IV 2–6)—may be glimpsed in what he says in *The Birth* to account for his silence about Christianity. What matters more to him than the accuracy of the artists' metaphysics that underlies his book is his implicit opposition to "the *moral* interpretation and significance of existence" (BT ASC 5). Viewing Christianity as "the most prodigal elaboration of the moral theme to which humanity has ever been subjected," he briefly sets forth an extravagant indictment of the practical and political consequences of the emergence of Christianity as the dominant religious force in European civilization (BT ASC 5).

The moral theme of Christianity is defined by appeal to absolute or transcendent values; ardent hostility to the instincts, passions, the sensible world, and to life itself; and belief in deliverance from the suffering of earthly life in a heavenly afterlife. "The *moral* interpretation and significance of existence" must be fought, Nietzsche declares, regardless of risk or consequence. The "will to decline" propagated by Christianity constitutes a mortal threat, "the danger of dangers" to the "fundamentally opposite doctrine and valuation of life—purely artistic and *anti-*Christian" expounded in *The Birth* (BT ASC 5).[6] What is suggested by Nietzsche's preface is confirmed by the core of his argument in *The Birth* in which he champions an ethics of art that is superior to its rivals because it is based on a more accurate understanding of the true or real needs of human beings and a more precise knowledge of the fundamental character of the cosmos in which they dwell.

The Artistic Nature of Man

Nietzsche introduces tragedy as a species of art. Tragedy is produced by the interplay between two contrasting principles or drives symbolized in Greek religion by the two "art deities," Apollo and Dionysus. Greek tragic drama, the pinnacle of art, is the outcome of the synthesis of the Apollinian art of sculpture, the form-giving art, and the Dionysian art of music, the passion-releasing art, after a long struggle for supremacy in which each seeks to become the ruling passion, the exclusive principle, of art and of existence.

Initially, Nietzsche views the Apollinian and Dionysian drives as corresponding to elementary, irreducible psychological or physiological states. He analogizes the contrast between Apollo and Dionysus to the distinction between tranquil dreaming and violent, uncontrolled intoxication, recalling, among other things, Socrates' account of the combination of sobriety and madness that impels the soul to philosophize (*Phaedrus* 244–257d). The Apollinian impulse to fashion soothing, radiant, and beautiful dream images thrives only in souls characterized by "that measured restraint, that freedom from the wilder emotions . . . that calm repose" (BT 1), which creates an enchanted fortress of illusions around the artist. Apollinian creativity demands a self-distancing from the tumultuous striving of the instincts and the harsh whirl of the waking world, an almost philosophical detachment that sustains an awareness of the distinction between reality and appearance.

In sharp contrast to the Apollinian artist's illusory dream-creations, the Dionysian artist gives ecstatic expression to his instincts and passions in his characteristic activity, the primal song, dance, and extravagant sexuality marking the ancient Dionysian festivals. Rather than forming a copy or imitation of the instincts and passions, the Dionysian artist unleashes his instincts and passions, freeing them to speak for themselves; he ceases to be a mere artist and becomes a living, breathing work of art. Whereas the Apollinian artist must be capable of escaping or detaching himself from the roaring push and pull of his instincts, Dionysian art demands the elimination of the gap between the instincts and the self.

Dionysian art, Nietzsche rhapsodizes, enhances human solidarity, overcomes man's alienation from nature, and renders visible the "mysterious primordial unity" (BT 1). Still more wonderful, the Dionysian artist's "paroxysms of intoxication" dissolve objectivity, or the capacity to stand apart, and engender a grandiose dream, a strange illusion: "he feels himself a god, he himself now walks about enchanted, in ecstasy, like the gods he saw walking in his dreams" (BT 1). Whereas the Apollinian artist fashions beautiful illusions to provide shelter from raging storms, the Dionysian artist surrenders his critical faculties and becomes the plaything of seething, wild forces.

Apollinian Wisdom and the Limits of Mythmaking

Both Apollo and Dionysus have their limits. The epitome of Apollinian culture, the Olympian gods, throws into sharp relief the limits of Apollinian mythmaking. Greek religion is a beautiful work of the imagination in which not only heroic deeds but "all things, whether good or evil, are deified" (BT 3).[7] Following the same procedure he later uses in the *Genealogy* and *The Antichrist*, Nietzsche investigates the human source of religious beliefs. "What terrific need was it," he asks, "that could produce such an illustrious company of Olympian beings?" (BT 3). The terrific need, it turns out, was rooted in a kind of metaphysical knowledge, closely related to the metaphysical knowledge that informs the right use of history by the genuine historian (UD 9, p. 112) and the insight that compels Nietzsche's madman to conclude that human beings must make themselves gods (GS 125).

Greek folk wisdom, according to Nietzsche, proclaimed the dismal knowledge that lay behind the Greeks' love affair with life:

> There is an ancient story that King Midas hunted in the forest a long time for the wise Silenus, the companion of Dionysus, without capturing him. When Silenus at last fell into his hands, the king asked what was the best and most desirable of all things for man. Fixed and immovable, the demigod said not a word, till at last, urged by the king, he gave a shrill laugh and broke out into these words: "Oh, wretched ephemeral race, children of chance and misery, why do you compel me to tell you what it would be most expedient for you not to hear? What is best of all is utterly beyond your reach: not to be born, not to *be*, to be *nothing*. But the second best for you is—to die soon." (BT 3)

Without questioning the demigod's evaluation of the human condition, Nietzsche asks how an infectious optimism, an overbrimming cheerfulness, a manly healthiness, epitomized by the Greek's savage and sensual myths, could emerge in full awareness of man's inherently miserable lot. His answer is that the need to esteem and love life, even in the face of the true but deadly wisdom of Silenus—the knowledge that the world is worthless and that human life is senseless—prompted the Greeks to seek relief from their suffering through the life-giving powers of the gods they made for themselves: "The Greek knew and felt the terror and horror of existence. That he might endure this terror at all, he had to interpose between himself and life the radiant dream-birth of the Olympians . . . It was in order to be able to live that the Greeks had to create these Gods from a most profound need" (BT 3).

The Greeks, according to Nietzsche, trembled at a world they rightly perceived to be inimical to human happiness, yet staunchly stood their ground. The Olympian gods represented a valiant response to an authentic and correctly perceived threat. Greek religion is an exquisite poem which spiritualizes the most profound and basic facts about existence—the worthlessness of the world and the senselessness of human life—and in the process of this beautiful representation of the ugly and terrifying, somehow not only renders life endurable but also endows it with a "higher glory" (BT 3). Creation springing from and skillfully concealing true insight is the Greeks' saving deed. By fashioning a poem about the gods based on true metaphysical knowledge and in the light of real human needs, the Greeks, to use terms Nietzsche subsequently employed in *Uses and Disadvantages,* proved themselves in their religious imagination to be genuine historians.

Yet Greek religion, according to Nietzsche, left something to be desired. If the function of Greek religious myth is to affirm life rather than to shrink from the disheartening incommensurability between human desire and the prospects for its satisfaction, then its deficiency is that Olympus towers above the Greeks, merely symbolizing the reconciliation of beauty and necessity. Although the Greeks provide in their gods an image of redemption, this image of supernatural powers and resplendent vices supplies, at most, an aesthetic or literary solution. And Nietzsche makes plain that that is not good enough. For "redemption through illusion" (BT 4) is an illusory or incomplete form of redemption: rescue from the terrifying meaninglessness at the core of life was achieved through Greek myth on life's fringes, in dreams. Apollo, unaided by Dionysus, imagines redemption but fails to confer it. Since redemption must occur not above or after but within life, and since Dionysus is the this-worldly deity par excellence, the Apollinian dreamer must join forces with the Dionysian reveler to satisfy the Greeks' powerful need to love life.

Dionysian Wisdom and the Limits of Intoxication

The "mysterious union of Apollo and Dionysus" stems from their intrinsic deficiencies; they are necessarily interdependent and "inwardly related" (BT 4). Apart, the Apollinian and Dionysian drives both prove incomplete and incapable of attaining satisfaction. It would, however, be an exaggeration to say, paraphrasing Kant, that the form-giving power of Apollo is, without Dionysus, empty and the passion-releasing power of Dionysus is, without Apollo, blind, because neither Apollo nor Dionysus exists in a pure form and neither can be entirely separated from the other.

As Nietzsche's analysis of the birth of the Olympian gods shows, the terrible wisdom of Silenus is the substratum of the Apollinian world of beauty and moderation. Apollo springs into action to erect a protective barrier against the "titanic and barbaric" instincts and the Dionysian knowledge of suffering. And just as Apollo draws strength from, indeed "could not live without Dionysus" (BT 4), Dionysus includes an Apollinian component. Whereas the Apollinian artist *re-presents* the passions by taming and adorning them, the Dionysian artist *re-produces* a copy of or echoes "the primal unity, its pain and contradiction," opening or surrendering himself to the very onslaught of the instincts the Apollinian artist seeks to keep at bay (BT 5).

The passions and instincts of the Dionysian artist serve as implements and raw material. He is simultaneously artist and work of art. To paraphrase Aristotle, in his artistic activity the Dionysian artist is, in a sense, the work of art produced. He imparts a shifting form to the disparate human drives; his Apollinian moment consists in displaying an image of basic human longings. However, having surrendered his subjective awareness, the intoxicated or maddened Dionysian artist is in no position or condition to appreciate his remarkable disclosures. Thus, just as the Apollinian artist creates an image of redemption but is not himself redeemed, the Dionysian artist is the source of wisdom about the human condition but is not himself wise.

Nevertheless, Apollinian and Dionysian art are not equal in regard to wisdom. The art of Apollo "paled before an art that, in its intoxication, spoke the truth" (BT 4). In the Dionysian states, "*Excess* revealed itself as truth. Contradiction, the bliss born of pain, spoke out from the very heart of nature" (BT 4). The Dionysian artist deserves to be considered a "world-historical genius" because the "primordial pain" embodied in his music is "a reflection of eternal being" (BT 5). The superiority of the Dionysian art of music to the Apollinian art of sculpture consists in nothing other than its power to exhibit the fundamental character of the cosmos.

The lyric poet whose art contained a "new germ which subsequently developed into tragedy" (BT 5) was on Nietzsche's view a kind of Dionysian artist, but not a subjective artist. Rather, and typical of the Dionysian artist, the lyric poet's passionate loves and hates became worthy of notice only insofar as they reflected the eternal character of being (BT 5). Indeed, in concluding his account of the lyric poet, Nietzsche provides a vivid description of the unity of the Dionysian artist, the object of his art, and the artistic activity itself, a vivid description that recalls Aristotle's notion of philosophical contemplation in which the intellect, the object of the intellect, and intellectual activity merge:

> Thus all our knowledge of art is basically quite illusory, because as knowing beings we are not one and identical with that being which, as the sole author and spectator of this comedy of art, prepares a perpetual entertainment for itself. Only insofar as the genius in the act of artistic creation coalesces with this primordial artist of the world, does he know anything of the eternal essence of art; for in this state he is, in a marvelous manner, like the weird image of the fairy tale which can turn its eyes at will and behold itself; he is at once subject and object, at once poet, actor, and spectator. (BT 5)

Like Aristotle's philosopher who blissfully participates in divinity through contemplation,[8] Nietzsche's Dionysian artist rises to the supreme heights in his artistic activity, merging with the uncreated "primordial artist of the world" (BT 5).

Art, for Nietzsche, is more philosophical than contemplation, and music, more adequately than the visual image, exhibits the natural order and its metaphysical foundations (BT 6).[9] Whereas Nietzsche regards language as inevitably interposing a distorting interpretation between the self and the world, music, he emphatically declares, stands in special relation to and is capable of symbolizing the cosmic order (BT 6).[10] Indeed, music, particularly that associated with Dionysian festivals, serves the cause of wisdom by revealing "the very heart of nature" (BT 4). And the heart that is revealed corresponds to Silenic wisdom, to the true but deadly doctrines that are the foundation for the genuine historian's activities, and to the revelations of Nietzsche's madman that are the grounds for the imperative to become god with which Zarathustra seeks to comply. As art is wiser or more philosophical than philosophy, music is wiser or more philosophical than language.[11]

The Dionysian artist, however, proves incapable of capitalizing on the hidden knowledge he incarnates. As the total embodiment of the "primal unity and primal contradiction" he provides a spectacle that displays the truth to a discerning observer, but he himself lacks discernment or even self-awareness. The Dionysian artist is possessed by, but not himself in possession of, the truth.[12] Whereas Apollo is, so to speak, all thought and no action, Dionysus is all action and no thought. Dionysian abandon and revelry, like Apollinian form-giving and mythmaking, fail to satisfy the acute human need for redemption. Greek tragedy, on Nietzsche's account, overcomes the failure of each by conferring a redemptive wisdom.

Tragic Wisdom as the Perfection of Human Nature

The final synthesis of Apollo and Dionysus in Greek tragedy represents the perfection of art and makes possible the perfection of human nature by giving the spectator a glimpse of the world as it really is while enabling him to live with this true but deadly knowledge. The perception of the valuelessness of human life that impelled the Greeks to create the Olympian deities, and the fantastic energies that flare up in Dionysian celebration, are harnessed by tragic drama and placed in the service of human excellence. The "tragic insight," the distilled content of Silenic wisdom, the debilitating doctrine that human life is "an endless stupid game," that man is a "plaything of nonsense," is transformed into redemptive wisdom. Tragic drama functions as a tinted lens or reflecting pool that permits indirect vision of the horrifying abyss. Nietzsche thus inverts Plato's parable of the cave, in which the seeker of wisdom escapes the dimly lit cave but must avoid gazing directly upon the sun to escape burning his eyes. Whereas Plato depicts the pursuit of knowledge as an ascent to dazzling heights, Nietzsche envisages the quest for truth as a descent to dreadful depths. For both, however, knowledge of the natural order seems to be the basis of human excellence.

Nietzsche traces the immediate origins of Greek tragedy to the tragic chorus. The chorus of primitive tragedy, the chorus of satyrs, created "a fictitious *natural state* and on it placed fictitious *natural beings*" (BT 7). These natural beings somehow embodied the "Dionysian wisdom of tragedy." By dispensing "with a painstaking portrayal of reality," tragedy brought to light the fundamental character of existence. The satyr chorus aroused the feeling in the Greek man of culture that he was in harmony with "the very heart of nature." Through a mysterious mechanism that depended upon the capacity of the satyr chorus to represent what is natural and what is metaphysical, and to identify the eternally unchanging reality that underlies the diversity of moral and political forms of life, tragedy redeems those who view it:

> The metaphysical comfort [*metaphysische Trost*]—with which, I am suggesting even now, every true tragedy leaves us—that life is at the bottom of things, despite all the changes of appearances, indestructibly powerful and pleasurable—this comfort appears in incarnate clarity in the chorus of satyrs, a chorus of natural beings who live ineradicably, as it were, behind all civilization and remain eternally the same, despite the changes of generations and of the history of nations. (BT 7)

What is only a delusion for tragedy's rivals—the ability to heal the wounds of existence—tragedy somehow actually achieves. The satyr chorus engenders profound knowledge and a worthy comfort by incarnating the permanent, immutable core of human nature. The satyr chorus does not project meaning upon the world; rather the satyr constitutes a singularly intelligible text which makes manifest the intelligible character of the world. The most interesting thing-in-itself—human nature—becomes clearly and distinctly visible in the figure of the satyr.

Tragedy yields ultimate metaphysical knowledge and brings comfort and a kind of redemption: "With this chorus the profound Hellene, uniquely susceptible to the tenderest and deepest suffering, comforts himself, having looked boldly right into the terrible destructiveness of so-called world history as well as the cruelty of nature, and being in danger of longing for a Buddhistic negation of the will. Art saves him, and through art—life" (BT 7). Tragedy generates a single, concentrated, and overwhelming moment of insight that mysteriously redeems the spectator by wounding him.[13] Its deadly and redemptive power lies in its capacity to pierce to the heart of things, to make manifest and represent the abysmal truth. Nietzsche artlessly describes "Dionysian man" as one who has "once looked truly into the essence of things"; who has *"gained knowledge"* of the "eternal nature of things"; who possesses "true knowledge" of "the horrible truth"; who, no longer able to take comfort even in the gods, "sees everywhere the horror or absurdity of existence." Suffering a nauseating wisdom, the spectator grasps not simply that "the time is out of joint," but that it is of the essence of time to be out of joint. Who but a lover of wisdom would willingly undergo such torment or require such treatment?

Tragedy transfigures and cures the ills it engenders in the spectator: "when the danger to his will is greatest, *art* approaches as a saving sorceress, expert at healing. She alone knows how to turn these nauseous thoughts about the horror or absurdity of existence into notions with which one can live" (BT 7). Art not only makes men wise but cures them of their wisdom: it promotes health like a vaccine that produces in the patient a mild case of the disease against which he is to be immunized. While effusive about tragedy's power to reveal the ugly truth and somehow make the spectator whole and healthy, Nietzsche says little about the beauty of tragedy or the pleasures derived from the creation of tragic drama. He is far more interested in art's capacity to reveal and conceal the fundamental truth than in the artist's ability to bring something brand new into existence.

Focusing on the ability of art to reveal the true nature of things, Nietzsche emphasizes that the dual-natured satyr featured in the tragic chorus serves as a clear image, uncorrupted by culture or civilization, of human nature, a being "who proclaims wisdom from the very heart of nature" (BT 8). The satyr, however, is more a mouthpiece for wisdom than a wise man. In contrast to the spectator of Greek tragedy and to Nietzsche the thinker, the satyr is ignorant of the wisdom it incarnates. But the wisdom the satyr incarnates seems to be indispensable to one who seeks wisdom, for the satyr chorus

> represents existence more truthfully, really, and completely than the man of culture does who ordinarily considers himself as the only reality. The sphere of poetry does not lie outside the world as a fantastic impossibility spawned by a poet's brain; it desires to be just the opposite, the unvarnished expression of the truth, and must precisely for that reason discard the mendacious finery of that alleged reality of the man of culture. (BT 8)

Art reveals the intelligible form of an original, abiding, and terrifying reality. The spectator of tragedy is precisely that subject before whom the world discloses its terrifying secrets.

Nietzsche further stresses the wisdom of art by using the traditional distinctions between nature and convention, the thing-in-itself and appearance, and what is eternal and what is perishable to explain the significance of tragic art:

> The contrast between this real truth of nature and the lie of culture that poses as if it were the only reality is similar to that between the eternal core of things, the thing-in-itself, and the whole world of appearances: just as tragedy, with its metaphysical comfort, points to the eternal life of this core of existence which abides through the perpetual destruction of appearances, the symbolism of the satyr chorus proclaims the primordial relationship between the thing-in-itself and appearance. The idyllic shepherd of modern man is merely a counterfeit of the sum of cultural illusions that are allegedly nature; the Dionysian Greek wants truth and nature in their most forceful form—and sees himself changed, as by magic, into a satyr. (BT 8)

Note the underlying agreement between Nietzsche's view of art and Plato's and Aristotle's understanding of the theoretical life: all agree that the ascent from opinion to knowledge of the world is the goal of man's worthiest activity.

Indeed, on Nietzsche's account, the great Greek tragic heroes were essentially philosophers whose suffering could be traced to their superior wisdom. Nietzsche interprets Sophocles' Oedipus as a mask for Dionysus, and Oedipus's bitter fate as further proof that knowledge of the natural order is both desirable and deadly (BT 9). Wisdom results in the agonizing estrangement from the dearest bonds of family and society: "the same man who solves the riddle of nature—that Sphinx of two species—also must break the most sacred natural orders by murdering his father and marrying his mother" (BT 9). Wisdom or knowledge of nature destroys happiness and transforms the knower into a wounded and miserable monster:

> Indeed, the myth seems to wish to whisper to us that wisdom, and particularly Dionysian wisdom, is an unnatural abomination; that he who by means of his knowledge plunges nature into the abyss of destruction must also suffer the dissolution of nature in his own person. "The edge of wisdom turns against the wise: wisdom is a crime against nature": such horrible sentences are proclaimed to us by the myth . . . (BT 9)

Similarly, Nietzsche's Prometheus, on the basis of his superior wisdom and propelled by a titanic desire to shoulder responsibility for the fate of humankind, defies the gods, brings man fire, and is punished for his defiance with eternal suffering (BT 9).[14]

As Nietzsche retells them, the stories of Oedipus and Prometheus teach that wisdom is the mark of human excellence, and that the price for such excellence is infamy and eternal pain. Despite his dismal portrait of the fruits of wisdom, Nietzsche gives no hint of wishing to back down from his identification of human excellence with a comprehension of the fundamental situation of human beings. One wonders whether wisdom inevitably shades into madness when pain becomes the measure of insight, for perfect knowledge would then seem to culminate in absolute torment, and supreme nobility would appear to manifest itself as utter degradation.

The Offense of Socrates

More grievous to Nietzsche than the wise man's suffering from wisdom is the victory of ignorance over wisdom. Accordingly, the death of tragedy in ancient Greece, the extinction of tragic wisdom, and the consequent "deep sense of an immense void" elicit from Nietzsche a mournful eulogy, strikingly anticipating his madman's proclamation of God's death (BT 11; GS 125). Nietzsche blames Euripidean drama and Socratic dialectics for sending tragedy to its grave. The former shifts tragedy's subject matter from the heroic, exalted theme of the consequences of wisdom for life to the commonplace civil affairs, mishaps, and comic entanglements of ordinary citizens; the latter brings tragedy before the bar of reason and finds the depiction of human life unconvincing because it defies rational articulation.

In the world of Euripidean drama the "everyday man" overran the heroes of tragic drama; instead of portraying the "grand and bold traits" of tragic heroes, Euripides' plays depict ordinary human beings with the "painful fidelity that conscientiously reproduces even the botched outlines of nature" (BT 11). The taste for the mundane triumphs over the taste for the rare; interest in the infinite variety of corruptions of human nature supplants fascination with the perfection of human nature. Euripides' dramas, on Nietzsche's interpretation, address the daily concerns of the common citizen and endorse the value of his business, public affairs, and humble pretensions to cultivation. And New Comedy, the child of Euripidean tragedy, glorifies "the cheerfulness of the slave who has nothing of consequence to be responsible for, nothing great to strive for, and who does not value anything in the past or future higher than the present" (BT 11).[15] The expanded horizon that Euripides' tragedy helps bring about results in a drastic narrowing of awareness of human nobility.

Nietzsche links Euripides' bringing the "masses onto the stage," including mass sentiments and norms, to the dramatist's misguided inclination to believe that "understanding was . . . the real root of all enjoyment and creation" (BT 11). The disadvantages of Euripides' art were rooted in the new form of understanding that Euripides championed. Yet the quarrel between tragic wisdom and Euripidean drama called into question not the primacy of wisdom but rather the content and the means to the acquisition of wisdom, for Euripidean drama embodied a claim about a rival kind of wisdom. The purest antithesis to tragic wisdom in *The Birth of Tragedy,* the demon or "deity that spoke through" Euripides, was the "Socratic tendency," a sham wisdom which "combatted and vanquished" tragedy (BT 12).

Nietzsche's nontraditional view of wisdom as Silenic wisdom, or knowledge of chaos, combined with his traditional opinion that wisdom is the foundation of human excellence, compels him to reevaluate the traditional veneration of Socrates. He defines the Socratic spirit as the impulse to subject phenomena to rigorous analytical scrutiny and to esteem speeches, deeds, artifacts, and nature exclusively with a view to their internal coherence and compliance with precise rational standards. And he condemns the Socratic spirit because it allegedly reflects a gross incapacity to see the world as it is, to comprehend what tragic wisdom makes visible. Thus, paradoxically, Nietzsche condemns *"aesthetic Socratism"* and its supreme standard—"To be beautiful everything must be intelligible"—on the grounds that such an outlook stems from ignorance and conceals the true character of existence (BT 12).

Nietzsche's characterization of Socrates as a kind of renegade poet concords with his treatment of Dionysian tragedy as an elevated form of philosophy. His depiction of the contest between poetry and philosophy as a grave struggle over competing interpretations of the meaning of human wisdom never calls into question that wisdom should determine conduct or be the object of human longing. His chief criticism of the theoretical man is that he chases after a counterfeit wisdom and conceals the truth about the human condition.

To study and criticize Socrates' alleged belief that there is a logos or rational structure to the world that is fully accessible to the human mind, Nietzsche adopts the same procedure that he employed to study the birth of Greek tragedy and that he later used to evaluate morality in the *Genealogy* and religion in *The Antichrist*. In each case he investigates the human need that supposedly spurs the creation of a comprehensive outlook on life. Yet he does not treat all comprehensive outlooks alike, debunking them by tracing them to their psychological or physiological sources. In particular, while he purports to discover that Socrates' belief in a rational order is a metaphysical illusion springing from an unnaturally strong desire to comprehend, the tragic insight apparently emerges from an unassailable perception of the human condition. Or at least a perception Nietzsche refrains from assailing.

The harmful effects of Socrates' belief in a rational order can be seen, according to Nietzsche, in Socrates' characteristic activity. Followed by young admirers, Socrates put statesmen, poets, and craftsmen to the test in the marketplace by examining them about their special skills. To the delight of his youthful companions, he routinely humiliated his respected interlocutors by revealing their inability to explain or give a theoretical account of their reputed excellence. On Nietzsche's account, Socrates discovers and decries the fact that the upstanding and respected Athenians knew "only by instinct." What Nietzsche discovers and decries is "the heart and core of the Socratic tendency" (BT 13), the elevation of discursive reason over instinctive action. In his characteristic activity, Socrates, according to Nietzsche, denigrates the instincts and subverts their legitimate authority to govern conduct.

Yet Nietzsche admiringly declares that Socrates possessed a negative instinctive wisdom. His daimonion—the instincts masquerading as a divine voice—spoke only to dissuade him from proceeding with a perilous course of action. Socrates is "truly a monstrosity *per defectum*" because his enormous instinctive powers were turned in the wrong direction (BT 13). Thus Socrates suffered from a crippling—and virulently contagious—inversion of the healthy or natural operations of the soul. In keeping with his assertion that the case of Socrates is not "open and closed," but "tremendously problematic," Nietzsche observes an admirable "natural power" in Socrates' theoretical urge, found only in "the very great instinctive forces." Socrates' logical instinct, although an "instinct-disintegrating influence," nevertheless reflected a prodigal, commanding drive.

Observing, with a hint of compassion, that Socrates, as a result of his impairment, is denied "the pleasure of gazing into the Dionysian abysses" (BT 14), Nietzsche maintains that Socrates wrongly believes that discursive reason is the path to wisdom. "Perhaps," Nietzsche speculates, "there is a realm of wisdom from which the logician is exiled? Perhaps art is even a necessary correlative of, and supplement for science?" (BT 14). Wisdom, then, would establish the right relations and division of labor between art and science by rendering visible the comprehensive domain in which art and science enjoy their characteristic prerogatives.

But science, discontent in its proper sphere of influence and blind to its own limits, seeks to be recognized as wisdom as such.[16] Nietzsche's account of tragedy's death at the hands of optimistic rationalism, which demanded a visible connection between right action and rational comprehension, shades into a contrast between two conflicting views of wisdom: the tragic and the scientific or theoretical. The decisive difference hinges upon divergent metaphysical presuppositions. Science rests upon "the unshakable faith that thought, using the thread of causality, can penetrate the deepest abysses of being, and that thought is capable not only of knowing being but even of *correcting* it" (BT 15). Though Nietzsche refrains from making the parallel explicit, the tragic perspective rests on an equally unshakable faith or claim to knowledge: music and especially tragic art, in contrast to speech and discursive reason, are capable of symbolizing and mirroring eternal being.

The faith underlying tragic wisdom presupposes, among other things, a fundamental disharmony between speech and being. Indeed, Nietzsche implies that it takes a Socrates to recognize the ultimate irrationality of the search for a rational order initiated by Socrates, and a *"Socrates who practices music"* to convey this "tragic insight" in an endurable form (BT 15). Thus, *The Birth* culminates in an anticipation of the revival of an old form of wisdom, a revival in which art reveals the human condition and in which right making is based on right knowing.

Although *The Birth of Tragedy* continues for another ten sections, Nietzsche's analysis of the contest between language and music, theoretical reason and art reaches its conclusion at the end of section 15. As is well known, Nietzsche came to regret writing sections 16–25. In turning from the past to the future, he anticipated a rebirth of tragedy and a renewal of German culture in the music of Richard Wagner. What he regretted, in particular, was having foolishly pinned his hopes on Wagner, who, it seems, he for a short time saw as "a Socrates who practices music." What is more, in Nietzsche's subsequent writings the idea that a transformation of the whole of society is possible or desirable recedes. Nevertheless, regrets and refinements of thought notwithstanding, *The Birth* is a unified work; Nietzsche's hopes for Germany's future rested on the same evaluation of music, art, theoretical reason, and wisdom as did his glorification of the Greeks' past.

Accordingly, Nietzsche deplores that Germany had become a "theoretical culture," having fallen under the spell of the belief that through science "all the riddles of the universe could be known and fathomed" (BT 18). It is precisely this optimistic delusion that conceals the "innermost and true essence of things" (BT 18). Recognizing this optimistic delusion as a delusion is a practical necessity inasmuch as the reform of culture must begin with insight into science's concealment of the innermost and true essence of things. With the tragic insight, Nietzsche explains,

> a culture is inaugurated that I venture to call a tragic culture. Its most important characteristic is that wisdom takes the place of science as the highest end—wisdom that, uninfluenced by the seductive distractions of the sciences, turns with unmoved eyes to a comprehensive view of the world, and seeks to grasp, with sympathetic feelings of love, the eternal suffering [*das ewige Leiden*] as its own. (BT 18)

In other words, the task of culture is to form individuals in the mold of Oedipus and Prometheus. What a society of such tragic seekers after wisdom and power would be like and how its citizens would govern themselves Nietzsche does not begin to spell out.

While in *The Birth* Nietzsche entertained the hope that Wagner would spearhead the creation in Germany of a tragic culture in which art would serve wisdom, in the later works in which he most fully expounds the character of the supreme type, he rejects the idea that the uniting of science or philosophy and art is the task of culture. The achievement of such a union becomes rather the task for single rare individuals, a superman or a philosopher of the future, who seeks to unite philosophy and art in himself. Nietzsche subsequently refines his understanding of the character of the rare individual, a "Socrates who practices music" (BT 15), one who combines philosophy and art at the highest levels by engaging in right making based on right knowing. And he thinks through more carefully the meaning of a reconciliation between philosophy and art in a world in which it takes tragedy to make men wise because knowledge of the fundamental character of existence is both desirable and deadly. In *Zarathustra* and *Beyond Good and Evil* it is not enough for the highest type to comprehend "the eternal nature of things"; he must also create and command it.

Conclusion

To what extent did Nietzsche stand by the ideas he expounded in *The Birth*? As I noted at the beginning of this chapter, in 1886, after *Zarathustra* and during the period in which he wrote *Beyond Good and Evil* and the *Genealogy,* Nietzsche explicitly criticized in his "Attempt at a Self-Criticism" the manner of presentation of his ideas in *The Birth,* while reaffirming their worth and the importance of the questions out of which they grew. Fourteen years after the fact, Nietzsche rejects the style but clings to the content of *The Birth.* Indeed, to a remarkable extent *The Birth of Tragedy* anticipates or embodies fundamental doctrines of his later thought and uses history in a manner consistent with the prescriptions he spells out in *Uses and Disadvantages* and his practice in subsequent histories.[17]

The seeds of the will to power, the death of God, nihilism, and the eternal return can be found in *The Birth.* The functions Nietzsche ascribes to Apollo and Dionysus anticipate the doctrine of the will to power inasmuch as these constituent drives of the self or soul create the protective myths known as moralities and unleash the energies that reveal the constructed character of tradition by making visible the true foundation of culture. Silenic wisdom and the tragic insight are variants on the discovery made by Nietzsche's madman and his Zarathustra that God is dead. The nausea induced by the knowledge that the cosmos is indifferent or hostile to human happiness anticipates the doctrine of nihilism according to which the highest values devalue themselves. The enviable Greek who receives the revelation of Silenus and through tragedy gazes upon the "horrible truth," yet thanks to the transfiguring powers of art retains his cheerfulness and love of existence, prefigures the superman and the philosopher of the future. And the belief that tragic wisdom yields metaphysical comfort by grasping and transfiguring the deepest layers of existence anticipates the transformative experience that lies at the heart of the doctrine of the eternal return.[18]

Moreover, a unity of method and intention connects *The Birth* to the *Genealogy* and to *The Antichrist,* and all three to the prescriptions for the right use of history set forth in *Uses and Disadvantages.* All three use ancient history as a means to clarify the rank order of desires, types of human beings, and forms of life; all three point to a conception of human excellence that places a premium on knowledge of the fundamental character of existence; and all three criticize the dominant forms of morality as deceitful and oppressive human artifacts on the basis of a rank order or ethical vision that appears to precede and stand judge over the creative activity of human beings.

Whether Nietzsche's account of the origins, the perfection, and the downfall of tragedy meets the standards of historical objectivity is an important question which I have not discussed. What should be clear by now is that it is of secondary importance whether tragedy actually came into being and perished in ancient Greece as he describes. For the truth Nietzsche wishes to teach concerns the fundamental relation between art, theoretical reason or science, and wisdom.

I have emphasized that Nietzsche glorifies tragedy as the highest form of art because it makes men wise, while paradoxically condemning the devotion to theoretical reason he attributes to Socrates because it rests upon a harmful superstition that turns men away from their true good. I have also pointed out that Nietzsche's account of the ethics of art is incomplete and open to question, for Nietzsche affirms but does not demonstrate that knowledge of chaos is possible and desirable, asserts rather than shows that tragedy provides metaphysical comfort by grasping and transfiguring the truth, and claims but does little to establish that the conception of reason and the world that he attributes to Socrates was wrong, or for that matter actually held by the historical or Platonic Socrates. In sum, Nietzsche's account of the genesis and death of tragedy points to but does not fully articulate or convincingly defend a conception of human excellence based on the wisdom of tragedy.

Still, the structure of his argument in *The Birth* is tolerably clear. No less than Socrates in Plato's *Republic*, and in strict accordance with the methodological strictures and substantive goals he subsequently outlines in *Uses and Disadvantages*, Nietzsche rigorously subordinates art to moral, political, and philosophical considerations, and above all to the conditions that allow those who are fit to attain and bear wisdom.

3

The Ethics of Morality:
On the Genealogy of Morals

Whether Nietzsche's account of the origins of our moral prejudices in *On the Genealogy of Morals* meets the standards of historical objectivity is an important question that cannot be responsibly avoided inasmuch as Nietzsche immediately forces the issue to center stage. On the one hand, Nietzsche takes pains in the preface to the *Genealogy* to emphasize the scholarly character of his genealogy and to insist that his findings about the origins and value of morality are vindicated by the superior new method that brought them to light. On the other hand, he not only declares his *Genealogy* a "polemic" in the text (GM Preface 2) but also gives it the subtitle "A Polemic."[1] Thus at the outset one is compelled to wonder about the polemical character of Nietzsche's genealogy, and about the rhetorical purposes that compel him to cloak his polemic in the authority of science and scholarship.

Speaking in the preface of "we knowers" and "us philosophers," Nietzsche apparently aims to correct his and his comrades' characteristic lack of self-knowledge by bringing to light "the *origin* of our moral prejudices" (GM Preface 1, 2). But he promptly reveals that the study of the origin of moral prejudices was instrumental to his primary concern: "What was at stake was the *value* of morality" (GM Preface 5). To determine the value of morality it is necessary to understand the origin of the conditions, political as well as psychological, under which men devised moral values. Thus, Nietzsche aims to undertake "an actual history of morality," that is, to discover "what is documented, what can actually be confirmed and has actually existed, in short the entire long hieroglyphic record, so hard to decipher, of the moral past of mankind" (GM Preface 7).

At least as he introduces it in the preface, genealogy appears to have little in common with the extravagant proclamations recently made depicting it as a new method of social inquiry embodying fundamental conceptual innovations. Genealogy, as Nietzsche introduces it, appears consistent with the official aims of a conventional historian—discovering through methodical investigation of the sources the origin or causes of specific beliefs and practices. And Nietzsche places genealogy in the service of a goal that is in harmony with traditional philosophy— determining the worth of rival ways of life.

The most influential spokesman for the popular view that genealogy represents both a new method of historical inquiry and a new substantive interpretation of morality is Michel Foucault. While Nietzsche's rhetoric lends support to the notion that genealogy disinters and brings to light hitherto unavailable historical insights, Foucault mythologizes the scientific and scholarly character of genealogy and fails to note, much less account for, the enormous gap dividing Nietzsche's account of genealogy from his practice of it. Indeed, the leaden seriousness of Foucault's account of genealogy obscures a crucial rhetorical feature of the three essays of the *Genealogy* to which Nietzsche calls attention: "Every time a beginning that is *calculated* to mislead: cool scientific, even ironic, deliberately foreground, deliberately holding off" (EH III, on GM).

Introducing his discussion of genealogy in "Nietzsche, Genealogy, History," Foucault declares, "Genealogy is gray, meticulous, and patiently documentary."[2] Yet the inspiring portrait that he proceeds to draw of the genealogist as the exemplary scholar is nonsense: if genealogy consists in the careful gathering of vast source material and patient attention to detail as Foucault says it does, then Nietzsche is no genealogist. For Nietzsche's genealogy is not gray. Inasmuch as Nietzsche reduces the whole complex and multifarious moral past of mankind to two competing moralities, it is closer to the truth to say that in practice his genealogy is painted in black and white. Nor is Nietzsche's genealogy meticulous. Inasmuch as he names no names, dates no events, and shows scant concern for details, variations, and anomalies, it would be more accurate to call his genealogy inspired guesswork, suggestive speculation, or a likely tale. And Nietzsche's genealogy, strikingly devoid of empirical evidence or scholarly apparatus, is anything but patiently documentary. Foucault's interpretation of Nietzsche's genealogy is not gray, meticulous, or patiently documentary, but rather a tall tale masquerading as a faithful and accurate restatement.[3] Foucault follows Nietzsche's lead by seeking to invest genealogy with an aura of scholarly and scientific legitimacy that it does not merit. But by reading Nietzsche's myth both literally and selectively Foucault compounds the difficulty of understanding Nietzsche's mythmaking.

Another reading of Nietzsche's *Genealogy* is called for, a reading that is more attentive to what Nietzsche says about his procedure, how he actually proceeds, and the gap between the two. To begin with, Nietzsche's genealogy, though it purports to emulate their rigor, differs markedly in purpose from the sciences and critical scholarship. Nietzsche's genealogy is not value free; indeed, it affirms an order of rank governing desires, states of the soul, and forms of life. As I remarked in Chapter 2, one must not be misled by Nietzsche's confusing tendency to equate morality with Christian, herd, or slave morality into concluding that he renounces interest in and abandons investigation of human excellence. Nothing could be farther from the truth. In the preface he contends that the reason morality, or slave morality, is the "danger of dangers"—and all three essays bear out the contention—is that it thwarts the attainment of and indeed conceals from view "the *highest power and splendor* actually possible to the type man" (GM Preface 6).

The aim of genealogy is not precise historical explanation but rather precise understanding of human excellence, or, speaking loosely, the moral significance of moralities.[4] The two of course are not disconnected, as Nietzsche himself makes clear in *Uses and Disadvantages* where he calls for a judicious blend of the different kinds of history. One use of historical explanation in the *Genealogy* is to expose the false claims and harmful effects of slave morality. But one of slave morality's false claims revolves around metaphysical first principles (the belief in God and a supersensible world), and one of the harms caused by slave morality is the dispiriting of the higher type of man. As it turns out, the true metaphysics according to which the slave's belief in God is seen as false, and the right conception of human beings in light of which the higher types may be distinguished from the lower, are themselves

not determined by genealogy but rather determine Nietzsche's understanding of the scope and purpose of genealogy.[5] To the extent that
Nietzsche's genealogy pursues the historical record, it uses familiar tools
and techniques turned on an object previously kept off-limits from critical scientific and scholarly inquiry. It is part critical history, with a special emphasis on the origins, unleashed on the sacred precincts of morality; but primarily it is a form of monumental history, devised to
display the character of human excellence. Overall, and like *The Birth*
and *The Antichrist*, it serves the pedagogical purposes of a genuine
historian.

It can be difficult to separate the monumental history from the critical history in Nietzsche's *Genealogy*. The revealing fact is that despite
Nietzsche's promise or boast to uncover the actual history of the origin
of moral prejudices, he displays, in his capacity as a genealogist, little
interest in establishing the historical veracity of his account of the origins of morality. Nietzsche leads the reader to believe that he will discipline his rhetoric and confine his gaze to the demonstrable facts, but he
openly proclaims his *Genealogy* a polemic, and in practice he subordinates rigorous scholarship to inspired re-creation. While he plainly intends the *Genealogy* to at least roughly approximate the actual unfolding
of history, in execution his genealogy constitutes the creation of an illus-
trative myth or poem.[6] That does not mean that the chief claims of
the *Genealogy* are subjective or arbitrary. Again displaying his implicit
agreement with Aristotle that poetry is more philosophical than history,
Nietzsche poeticizes history the better to bring out the truth about the
origins, and thereby the nature, of our moral prejudices.[7]

Thus, in opposition to the prevailing view that in his *Genealogy*
Nietzsche has established or elaborated a new mode of moral and historical inquiry, and notwithstanding his own boasts, Nietzsche, in fact,
subordinates the study of history to the study of psychology, or the nature of the human soul. He returns to what he regards as the origins or
the prehistory of morality and writes a loosely historical narrative to
uncover and reestablish the set of moral valuations or standards that he
believes accurately reflect the real rank order of drives, souls, and forms
of life. Indeed, the origins Nietzsche is primarily concerned with are
neither historical nor social and political but rather the conditions
within the soul that determine the actions both of those who give the
original names to values and of those who revalue the original valua-

tions. Consistent with the methodological strictures and basic presuppositions of history that he lays out in *On Uses and Disadvantages,* Nietzsche judges noble morality and slave morality on the basis of opinions about the cosmos and the true or real needs of man.

What Is Noble and What Is Slavish

Nietzsche briskly introduces the first of the three essays that compose the *Genealogy* with a vague reference to pioneering studies of the origin of morality carried out by certain unnamed English psychologists (GM I 1). He swiftly shifts focus from the results of the Englishmen's investigations to the wants and desires that motivated their inquiries, dictated their methods, and rendered them apparently obtuse to the moral implications of their findings. He observes that the historical and scientific method practiced by the English systematically traces morality—the pride of man's intellectual and spiritual life—to what is passive, involuntary, or mechanistic in behavior.

Such scientific explanations, Nietzsche asserts, eradicate the distinction between man and brute and may be most instructive for what they reveal about the character of the researchers who produce them. Initially, he does not dispute the Englishmen's findings; he takes issue with their motivations for digging up dirt and condemns them for failing to draw the proper conclusions about conventional morality from what he regards as their explosive revelations.[8] In short, he attempts to determine the worth of the English psychologists' doctrine by understanding its origins. He thus introduces the allegedly new genealogical approach not as Descartes unveiled his new method, with the articulation of a set of rules for its sound application, but by means of a demonstration of the insights yielded by its application to the practices of his rivals.

Maintaining the focus on the Englishmen's moral intentions, Nietzsche proposes two alternative explanations of the Englishmen's motives for conducting investigations that seek to locate the origins of morality in subrational sources. First, their degrading hypotheses about the roots of morality may stem from an angry desire to retaliate against mankind for shattered dreams and tarnished hopes. Nietzsche envisages a range of unsightly motives, from the mistrust of "disappointed idealists," to hostility against Christianity, to "a lascivious taste for the grotesque, the painfully paradoxical, the questionable and absurd in existence" (GM I 1). Alternatively, he speculates that the scientific reduction of morality to animal desire and mechanical causality may reflect the intentions of stout-hearted, great-souled men courageously tracking down and articulating the dismaying, repellent, hitherto well-concealed facts. Such men will have "trained themselves to sacrifice all desirability to truth, *every* truth, even plain, harsh, ugly, repellent, unchristian, immoral truth.—For such truths do exist" (GM I 1).

Introducing genealogy by performing one on his rivals, Nietzsche does not dissolve the meaning of morality or repudiate truth as the goal of intellectual inquiry. Just the opposite: in calling attention to the moral intentions in which the scientific study of morality originates, he sharply distinguishes between despicable and admirable motives and places an uncompromising devotion to facing ugly and immoral truths at the center of respectable genealogy. The genealogist, like the spectator of Greek tragedy and the genuine historian, must be able to recognize and endure true but deadly doctrines.

Nietzsche moves rapidly from casting doubt on the Englishmen's findings by raising questions about their motives to flatly proclaiming their theories of the origins of morality false owing to a methodological flaw he calls unhistorical thinking. This flaw consists in projecting onto other cultures and periods one's own moral sensibilities and categories. The thinking of the English historians of morality, like that of all philosophers, is "*by nature* unhistorical" (GM I 2). Nietzsche asserts that it is precisely his possession of the "historical sense" that distinguishes him from all previous philosophers (GM I 2: see also BGE 224; TI "Reason in Philosophy" 1). By "historical sense" he seems to mean the capacity to understand the past free from modern prejudices and preconceptions. Far from affirming the essential subjectivity and time-bound character of all knowledge, the "historical sense" is a virtue that enables one to achieve an objective suprahistorical and transcultural understanding.[9]

The English, on Nietzsche's account, investigated the historical origins of the concept "good" or "good actions" by imagining a set of social relations in the distant past that conformed to their rigid, preconceived notions about morality. Key concepts figuring prominently in the contemporary English moral vocabulary, such as utility, habit, and altruism, were read into the elementary and primitive encounters between human beings. The English, Nietzsche contends, committed a related error when they studied contemporary behavior: current English practices and usages were passed off as timeless human traits or basic, universal features of language. The English unwittingly gazed across time and over their borders through the distorting lens of their own moral convictions.[10]

In contrast to the Englishmen, whose results are tainted by their perspective, Nietzsche claims to have discovered man's original moral valuations and political relations; his own gaze, he boldly assumes, is unclouded, and his own perspective, he firmly believes, reveals the basic qualities of and the true relations among men. After having brought the dangers of perspectival distortion to the awareness of the reader, he embarks on his examination of the history of morality implicitly denying that his genealogy is vitiated by any ontological or practical obstacles inhering in his own perspective. Indeed, Nietzsche's critique of morality and his practice of genealogy are incompatible with doctrines of radical perspectivism and radical historicism, including some of his own extreme declarations on the subject.[11] In practice, he exudes a boundless confidence that he has penetrated to the brute and decisive facts about morality.

Nietzsche ascribes to the English psychologists the view that the concept "good" originally referred not to the actor but to the benefit enjoyed by the person who was the object of an action. Eventually those who benefited attributed goodness to the initiator of beneficial actions. This resulted in the establishment of selfless deeds as the model of praiseworthy conduct. Nietzsche judges this vaguely utilitarian theory of the origins of moral evaluation as historically untenable and psychologically absurd. Something quite different, he contends, actually transpired: "the judgment 'good' did *not* originate with those to whom 'goodness' was shown! Rather it was 'the good' themselves, that is to say, the noble, powerful, high-stationed and high-minded, who felt and established themselves and their actions as good, that is, of the first rank, in contradistinction to all the low, low-minded, common and plebeian" (GM I 2).

"Good" was originally born of the pathos of nobility and distance. Yet if what is noble is good, then Nietzsche's unabashed attribution of nobility to those who "seized the right [*Recht*] to create values and to coin names for values" suggests that the antithesis of good and bad antedates its appearance in language. Those who created the original values seem to combine nobility in the sense of social and political status and nobility in the sense of personal excellence. The "noble, powerful, high-stationed and high-minded" who gave the original names to things not only exercised "the lordly right [*Herrenrecht*] of giving names" but appear on Nietzsche's account to have deserved to possess that right. Their aristocratic value judgments were in his eyes good value judgments; they were the "highest rank ordering, rank defining value judgments" (GM I 2).

Although Nietzsche does not address it, the question arises whether the original "good" was good because it was created by those who were noble, or whether the "good" was created by those who were noble because it was good. Either way, by saying that the judgment "good" was invented by those who were noble Nietzsche indicates that nobility was not invented but a designation of rank that preexisted the rightful designators. Since the distinction between nobility and baseness, between highminded and plebeian, presupposes some conception of the good, Nietzsche's examination of the origins reveals that in the beginning the judgment "good" reflected what indeed was good. In other words, he implies that the "noble, powerful, high-stationed and high-minded" coined words for and crystallized in language natural distinctions among men that were already embodied in the original relations of political life.

In addition to his freewheeling reconstruction, devoid of reference to a specific historical situation and meant to refute the English hypothesis about the genesis of morality, Nietzsche invokes a philological argument to provide historical evidence to substantiate his account of the origins of morality. As in *Uses and Disadvantages,* where he claimed that his knowledge of the past enabled him to break from the disabling prejudices of the present (UD Foreword), so too in the *Genealogy* he asserts that classical scholarship provides him with the key to evaluating "the danger of dangers" (GM Preface 6) or morality: "The signpost to the *right* road was for me the question: what was the real etymological significance of the designations for 'good' coined in the various languages?" (GM I 4). But Nietzsche's philological evidence is amazingly thin. He maintains that the utilitarian equation of "good" with "useful" or "unegoistic" is contravened by a survey of the evolution of "good" in various languages:

all led back to the *same conceptual transformation*—that everywhere "noble," "aristocratic" in the social sense, is the basic concept from which "good" in the sense of "with aristocratic soul," "noble," "with a soul of a high order," "with a privileged soul" necessarily developed: a development which always runs parallel with that other in which "common," "plebeian," "low" are finally transformed into the concept "bad." (GM I 4)

It is noteworthy that in connecting nobility of social and political status to nobility of soul Nietzsche omits any documentary evidence, presenting only the fruits, the "fundamental insight" that emerged from his studies of ancient etymologies. Moreover, he does not acknowledge the problems inherent in, much less defend, the controversial assumption that conceptual transformations recorded in language accurately reflect actual empirical moral and political relations. His heart is plainly not in the effort to carry out "an actual history of morality" based on what can be documented and confirmed (GM Preface 7). This is worth emphasizing, not to condemn Nietzsche for failing to meet the standards of a conventional historian, but to see more clearly that he practices history as a genuine historian and therefore seeks through his histories to lay bare not the historical record but the truth about human excellence.

Although the concept "good" originally reflected social and political preeminence, the noble man's power over others was the most visible sign of a still more fundamental character trait. Singling out the ancient Greek vocabulary as evidence, Nietzsche argues that the typical character trait by virtue of which the political aristocrats felt themselves to stand over and apart from the common man was the self-perception that they were the real, the actual, or the truthful (GM I 5). Thus a primitive form of probity spawns the original and by implication healthy or good notion of "good."

At all times nobility is bound up with truthfulness, but over time the kind of truthfulness that characterizes nobility changes. The first nobles are truthful in that they act instinctively and spontaneously, without guile. Their deeds truly reflect their desires. At a later stage the nobles are truthful in the sense that they tell the truth. Finally, after the original nobility falls from political power, truthfulness comes to mean nobility of soul and "becomes as it were ripe and sweet" (GM I 5). Note that

Nietzsche suggests a disharmony between the ripest forms of truthfulness and nobility and the exercise of political power by indicating that the political demise of the noble class corresponds to the full flowering of the noble individual. This tension between human excellence and political preeminence goes to the heart of his *"quiet* problem" (GM I 5), which concerns the value or danger of morality.

To determine the value of morality, Nietzsche proceeds to examine a few more basic human types. The priestly type is an intermediate character, between the noble man and the slavish man; he holds a ruling position, but he rules in the interest of slavish values. The Jews, the priestly caste *par excellence,* occupy a pivotal role in Nietzsche's genealogy, curiously akin to Socrates' role in *The Birth of Tragedy* (BT 13–15; also TI "The Problem of Socrates" 5, 7, 11), as villains whose deformed virtues reflect a measure of their greatness. Although essentially unhealthy, the priestly aristocrats made man an interesting animal, superior to other beasts, by giving depth to the human soul and making it evil (GM I 6; indeed, the priestly aristocrats, in spite of their sickliness, also make possible the "great health" and the "supremely self-confident mischievousness in knowledge" that goes with it; GM II 24).

Unfit to cross swords with their rivals, the Jews commit an "act of the *most spiritual revenge*" (GM I 7). When menaced by the physical or military superiority of the knightly aristocracy, the Jews, on Nietzsche's account, resorted to the classic form of slave warfare—psychological warfare—to hang on to their privileged political position. Deploying their religious teachings for a far-reaching political purpose, they inverted and denatured aristocratic values. They devised a new moral code by substituting blessedness for happiness; and what the Jews understood as blessed was precisely what the noble man disdained to acknowledge—the weak, the sick, the oppressed. At the same time, the Jews vilified and designated as sinful the elements or signs of earthly happiness—power, beauty, prosperity. As a result of this epic smear campaign, all forms of exuberant self-affirmation were reinterpreted as wicked or sinful. Nietzsche's indignation mounts with every brushstroke he adds to his portrait of the original "revaluation of values." Indeed, he practically denounces as wicked or sinful that "Jewish hatred—the profoundest and sublimest kind of hatred, capable of creating ideals and reversing values, the like of which has never existed on earth before" (GM I 8).

What begins with the Jews achieves world historical significance in organized Christianity, a kind of Judaism for the people. Speaking quite generally—for Nietzsche's argument remains almost entirely unencumbered by historical or documentary evidence—the slavish man and his way of thinking attain power propelled by *"ressentiment,"* the angry desire to punish and surpass those who are better or more powerful. *Ressentiment* takes hold when a disparity arises between a man's longing and the outcome of his striving. All men, by nature apparently, seek the uninhibited expression of their desires in deeds (GM I 10, 11, 16). Physical weakness, mental sloth, and ingrained cowardice bar the vast majority from attaining satisfaction. Constant frustration deforms the original human longings. The slavish man's "creative deed" (GM I 10) consists in inverting and negating the noble man's values. Slave morality is fundamentally reactive and derivative, but phenomenally effective; its massive success consists in inducing the aristocrats to accept its valuations and play by its rules. Whereas the noble man is marked by truthfulness, the slavish man deceives himself and thrives by promulgating lies. In the slave revolt the wrong conception of good comes to prevail by means of a ghastly trick; it is as if a chess player, facing checkmate, were to convince his opponent that the object of chess is to lose your pieces and surrender your king.

Nietzsche acknowledges that both the noble and the slave mode of valuation result in a falsification of the world. But the slavish "sin against reality" is on his account far graver:

> When the noble mode of valuation blunders and sins against reality, it does so in respect to the sphere with which it is *not* sufficiently familiar, against a real knowledge of which it has indeed inflexibly guarded itself: in some circumstances it misunderstands the sphere it despises, that of the common man, of the lower orders; on the other hand, one should remember that, even supposing that the affect of contempt, of looking down from a superior height, *falsifies* the image of that which it despises, it will at any rate still be a much less serious falsification than that perpetrated on its opponent—*in effigie* of course—by the submerged hatred, the vengefulness of the impotent. (GM I 10)

The creative deed of the slaves is bad because it involves a falsification of what is higher and deserving of respect. Faithfulness to a rank order independent of human making and willing elevates, on Nietzsche's account, the act by which the noble man gives names over the slaves' creative revaluation of values.[12]

The trademark tactic the slavish men use to insinuate their values among the noble class is to make rational, critical self-examination respectable. Whereas noble men had no need to justify their happiness, slavish men established rational justification as an indispensable support to happiness (GM I 10). On Nietzsche's view, the demand for rational justification obfuscates the real grounds of action and human excellence. The moral imperative to scrutinize the motives and reasons for actions arises only when action is hampered and deprived of a natural outlet. The widespread practice of demanding reasons for actions, Nietzsche holds, is largely responsible for fostering the hesitation, moderation, and calculation that corrupted the noble class's behavior and characterizes the slavish man.

Nietzsche's understanding of the decline and fall of the noble morality at the hands of slave morality reflects the critical distinction between the "good and bad" of the former and the latter's "good and evil." The similar vocabulary the rival moralities use to designate the fundamental moral antithesis obscures a decisive difference. The noble type spontaneously think of themselves and their way of life as good, and as a minor matter, an afterthought, refer to the "common man" as "bad." "Bad" is ascribed in a loose, offhand fashion; it means "not us," "them," or "not of noble character." The predicates lack bite; they express indifference rather than hatred, detachment rather than anxiety. Whereas the noble man begins with a positive affirmation of his own strength and well-being, the slavish man's first thought is a negative judgment directed against nobility, strength, and well-being. The slave's original valuation consists in slapping the label "evil" on the health and happiness of the noble man (GM I 11). Whereas the noble man's "good" is a spontaneous invention that reflects the goodness of his spirit, the slavish man's "good" is a makeshift conceptualization that reveals his sordid desire to blunt the noble man's power.[13]

According to Nietzsche's unforgiving reconstruction, the slavish man's frustrated desires and swelling ambitions impel him to devise rights, promulgate laws, elaborate principles of justice and equality, and preach charity to make the world safe for the meek, the poor, and the oppressed.[14] According to Nietzsche's genealogy, the rule of law, liberal protections for the individual, and democratic justice and equality are tools of oppression. But these elements of bourgeois morality are not, as some suppose, an effort by the strong to oppress the weak; rather, from Nietzsche's perspective, they are vicious weapons in an all-too-successful war waged by the weak many against the strong few.

In section 13, among the most influential in the *Genealogy,* Nietzsche provides an analysis of one of the key tactics by which the slaves win the war they wage against the strong and healthy: establishing as a regulative norm the fiction that a person can be separated from and held accountable for his deeds. Yet Nietzsche's argument on behalf of the claim that "'the doer' is merely a fiction added to the deed" (GM I 13) is very weak. Moreover, it contradicts fundamental elements of his genealogy.

Nietzsche begins innocently enough. In a parable caricaturing the Gospels, he identifies the motive that impels the weak to label strength a vice and self-restraint good: "That lambs dislike great birds of prey does not seem strange: only it gives no ground for reproaching these birds of prey for bearing off little lambs" (GM I 13). The motivation for the lambs' valuation is, Nietzsche indicates, understandable, but he makes clear that their judgments should carry no weight for the birds of prey. Nietzsche suggests that Christian morality is a perfectly intelligible case of wishful thinking: those poorly endowed to obtain happiness in this world invent a scheme of morality that vindicates their suffering, and condemns strength and well-being as evil.

Nietzsche moves swiftly from psychological motivation to moral censure. But his moral censure is obscured by a faulty theoretical argument. He asserts that it is absurd for the lambs to condemn the birds of prey for their predatory behavior and to demand that they desist. The condemnation and the demand rest on a mistake, he says, a conceptual error concerning the relation between force and will, that is, an incorrect idea about metaphysics promoted by "the seduction of language," that encourages the drawing of an absurd distinction between an actor and his acts.

Whereas we speak of a flash of lightning as if lightning were one thing and the flash another, Nietzsche insists that lightning is nothing but the flash we see in the sky. Extending this line of reasoning, he suggests that it is false to the phenomena to separate strength from the expression of strength; it is absurd to imagine a "neutral substratum behind the strong man," a subject, self, or soul that is *free* to express strength or not to do so." But is it? Nietzsche introduces a far-reaching metaphysical thesis to explain why the strong man is not free and should not be held accountable for the exercise of his strength: "there is no such substratum; there is no 'being' behind doing, effecting, becoming; 'the doer' is merely a fiction added to the deed—the deed is everything" (GM I 13). Yet there are very good reasons to doubt Nietzsche's categorical pronouncement about the ultimate constitution of things and its significance, according to him, for moral and political life.

First, it does not follow, from the uncontroversial assertion that a lightning flash is not the result of a subject, that human beings lack selfhood or agency. Nietzsche's analogy does not suffice as an argument. And precisely what is needed Nietzsche does not supply: a reason to believe that the analogy between lightning flashes and strong human beings is sound. Second, and more significant, at crucial junctures Nietzsche's genealogy rests upon the very distinction between doer and deed that he claims in section 13 is an absurd and harmful invention of slaves.

Consider, for example, three important remarks from section 10:

The slave revolt in morality begins when *ressentiment* itself becomes creative and gives birth to values; the *ressentiment* of natures that are denied the true reaction, that of deeds, and compensate themselves with an imaginary revenge . . . (GM I 10)

. . . and they [the "well-born"] likewise knew, as rounded men replete with energy and therefore *necessarily* active, that happiness should not be sundered from action. (GM I 10)

To be incapable of taking one's enemies, one's accidents, even one's misdeeds seriously for very long—that is the sign of strong, full natures in whom there is an excess of the power to form, to mold, to recuperate, and to forget. . . . (GM I 10)

Nietzsche's distinction between true reactions or deeds and the imaginary revenge marking the slave revolt presupposes that the slave can be separated from and blamed for his misdeed. Moreover, the knowledge typical of the noble mode of valuation that "happiness should not be sundered from action" implies that the character of action is in part under the control of the agent inasmuch as action may be ill-advisedly sundered from happiness. And finally, the ability of strong natures to actively forget their misdeeds rests upon the notion that there is a self, subject, or soul, distinct from its deeds and greater than their sum, that can stand apart, fashion, and judge its acts.

Nietzsche's genealogy presupposes the distinction between doer and deed in other crucial respects. Although he associates the very idea of accountability with slave morality, Nietzsche clearly holds the slaves accountable for promulgating slave morality, for domesticating man, and for debasing culture (GM I 11; III 14). And he continues to ascribe nobility to the "birds of prey" even when they prove susceptible to the stratagems of the lambs and ingloriously fall from power. Thus, he separates the slaves from their deeds by blaming them for poisoning the noble types, and he separates the nobles from their deeds by continuing to honor their nobility despite their humiliating defeat. None of this is very surprising in light of the fundamental defect in Nietzsche's claim that the slavish man invents the distinction between doer and deed, a distinction grounded in the ability to stand apart from one's deeds or self-consciousness: the invention of self-consciousness already presupposes self-consciousness or the ability to stand apart from one's deeds.

Furthermore, the very victory of the lambs that Nietzsche laments proves what he momentarily appears to deny, namely, that strength can be redirected, inhibited, or bottled up. Asking strength to show self-restraint is not absurd in the sense that it is contrary to logic, a confusion of grammar, or metaphysically impossible. Rather, and consistent with Nietzsche's overall argument, he regards restraining strength as depraved because it produces "the diminution and leveling of European man" (GM I 12) and prevents the cultivation of healthy human beings. His real criticism is that it is wrong, unjust, indeed a crime against the order of rank for the weak slaves to use cleverness and guile to defeat the powerful nobility.

If there were no "being" behind doing, if the doer were merely a fiction added to the deed, if the deed were everything, then it would be just as absurd for Nietzsche to condemn the lambs for disarming and taming the birds of prey as it was, on his account, for the lambs to condemn the birds of prey. If Nietzsche were right that the doer may not be separated from the deed, then one would have to say that it is only a seduction of language that seduces Nietzsche into blaming the lambs for their deceit, for separating them from their counterfeiting of ideals as if they were free to do otherwise. Nietzsche's manifest sympathies for the defeated nobility and his fierce antipathy toward the victorious slaves are intelligible only in terms of the key idea for which he holds the slaves accountable: that the doer is more than his deed.

Nietzsche concludes the first essay with a rousing declaration that a hierarchy of moralities does exist. Exhibiting his tendency to paint in black and white, he asserts that "The two *opposing* values 'good and bad,' 'good and evil' have been engaged in a fearful struggle on earth for thousands of years" (GM I 16). But at this point he introduces an important nuance. Although slave morality has noble morality on the defensive almost everywhere, in some places the conflict is undecided, and in those places, or within those natures, a third possibility, a "higher nature" based on a mix of noble and slave qualities, presents itself. Where the struggle between master and slave morality persists, "one might even say that it [the struggle] has risen ever higher and thus become more and more profound and spiritual: so that today there is perhaps no more decisive mark of a *'higher nature'* [*höheren Natur*], a more spiritual nature [*geistigeren Natur*], than that of being divided in this sense and a genuine battleground of these opposed values" (GM I 16). Inasmuch as the typical character trait of the noble man was a kind of truthfulness (GM I 5) and the characteristic deed of the slave was a creative revaluation of values (GM I 10), the implication of Nietzsche's genealogical analysis is that some union of truthfulness and creativity forms the basis for the achievement of the "*highest power and splendor* actually possible to the type man" (GM Preface 6).

Anticipating one of the very misconceptions of his thought which prevails today, Nietzsche makes clear his fundamental concern with human excellence by emphasizing that *Beyond Good and Evil,* a dangerous slogan because it advocates a rejection of conventional morality, "does *not* mean 'Beyond Good and Bad'" (GM I 17). Imploring the reader to resist confusing the criticism of slave morality with the criticism of all forms of human excellence, he poses a stark choice between the well-being of the majority, or the slavish mode of valuation, and the well-being of the few, or the noble mode of valuation. As I have noted, the right choice for Nietzsche depends on restoring a truthfulness exemplified by noble morality and exercising a creativity characteristic of the slavish man. The crucial unanswered question at the end of the first essay is how Nietzsche can blend the noble trait of truthfulness with the creativity that he ascribes to slaves so as to accomplish "the future task of the philosophers: this task understood as the solution of the *problem of value,* the determination of the *order of rank among values*" (GM I 17).

Genealogy presupposes but also calls into question the possibility of determining the rank order of desires, human beings, and forms of life. The dilemma that reverberates in Nietzsche's *Genealogy*—and throughout his thought—is how to justify the rank order within the horizon of his own teaching that all orders of rank or tables of values are creations of the human will. The second and third essays of the *Genealogy* restate this dilemma from different angles but do not resolve it.

Conscience, Justice, and Human Excellence

In the second and third essays Nietzsche contributes to the effort to determine the rank order of values by clarifying the character of justice and the problem of truth. His *Genealogy* remains throughout what it was in the first essay, a form of edifying poetry that contributes to "the solution to the *problem of value,* the determination of the *order of rank among values*" (GM I 17) by bringing to light the true human needs and the actual character of the cosmos.

In the second essay, "'Guilt,' 'Bad Conscience,' and the Like," Nietzsche reiterates the position that he adopted in the preface that morality is the real problem regarding man and the genuine subject of his genealogy. He proposes to determine the nature of man by exploring how man became able to recognize and honor moral demands: "To breed an animal *with the right to make promises*—is not this the paradoxical task that nature has set itself in the case of man? Is it not the real problem regarding man?" (GM II 1).

Morality presupposes the ability to make and keep promises; and the practice of promising presupposes the capacity to take responsibility for one's actions. Exercising responsibility depends on thinking in terms of cause and effect and distinguishing necessity from chance. On Nietzsche's view, human beings did not always think in theoretical terms that justified promise-making and validated promise-keeping. It falls to genealogy to uncover "the long story of how *responsibility* originated" (GM II 2). This task is undertaken in light of the larger aim of evaluating the goodness of promise-making and responsibility-taking, or the value of morality.

Nietzsche finds as the "ripest fruit" of the cruel process by which human beings came to hold themselves responsible an enviable human type,

> the *sovereign individual,* like only to himself, liberated again from morality of custom, autonomous and supramoral (for "autonomous" and "moral" are mutually exclusive), in short the man who has his own independent, protracted will and the *right to make promises* [*versprechen darf*]—and in him a proud consciousness, quivering in every muscle, of *what* has at length been achieved and become flesh in him, a consciousness of his own power and freedom, a sensation of mankind come to completion. This emancipated individual, with the actual *right* to make promises [*wirklich versprechen darf*], this master of a *free* will, this sovereign man—how should he not be aware of his superiority over all those who lack the right to make promises and stand as their own guarantors of how much trust, how much fear, how much reverence he arouses—he *"deserves"* all three—and of how this mastery over himself also necessarily gives him mastery over circumstances, over nature, and over all more short-willed and unreliable creatures? (GM II 2)

With the emergence of the "emancipated individual," there also appears another type, an impostor who illegitimately arrogates to himself the right and responsibility for promises. By what signs may the one who is entitled to make promises be distinguished from him who "promises without the right to do so"? The man with the right to make promises bears an identifying mark: such a one unites "the extraordinary privilege of responsibility," "rare freedom," and "power over oneself and over fate" in a "dominating instinct" (GM II 2). The emancipated individual reveals his character by calling his dominating instinct, the instinct that enables him to secure freedom, conscience (GM II 2).

Nietzsche not only links the conscience of the emancipated individual, which is the "highest, almost astonishing, manifestation" (GM II 3) of conscience, to what is highest and worthiest in a human being; he also links what is highest and worthiest to torture and cruelty. The right to affirm oneself is grounded in conscience; conscience presupposes the capacity for memory, a stable identity, and a self or soul whose actions are to some degree regular and calculable. Memory and a stable identity over time, however, are achievements, not gifts from nature or providence (although the capacities for memory and a continuous character are gifts, not achievements). Memory, according to Nietzsche, is developed by means of terrifying and cruel (especially religious) rituals that painfully imprint the basic demands and fundamental prohibitions of social life on selves dominated by unruly desires (GM II 3). Although he does not undertake the investigation or offer a shred of empirical evidence, Nietzsche avers that examination of "our former codes of punishment" reveals that collective, civilized life depends upon violently compelling human beings to view themselves as agents, forcing them to maintain a stable self-identity, and disciplining them to remember their actions and claim responsibility for them.

But this form of cruelty, he also makes clear, is inescapable preparation for the advent of the emancipated individual. Indeed, the primitive practices out of which the emancipated individual emerged also constitute the origins of all intellectual and moral achievements (GM II 3). Blood and cruelty of course do not guarantee the production of human excellence. Cruelty in itself is neither good nor bad, but rather good or bad with respect to the end it serves. Memory, education, law, freedom, conscience, indeed discipline and formation of character are all forms of cruelty, that is, the forcible repression, rechanneling, and retraining of desire and passion. For Nietzsche the primary end for which cruelty must be exercised is the attainment of human excellence, and the second essay makes clear that human excellence depends upon a cruel if highly refined conscience. The third essay reveals that the most refined conscience is the intellectual conscience.

Previous genealogists of morals, Nietzsche argues, utterly failed to distinguish the conscience that governs the emancipated individual from "that other 'somber thing,' the consciousness of guilt, the 'bad conscience'" (GM II 4). Just as "beyond good and evil" does not signify the transcendence or abandonment of ethics, so too Nietzsche's criticism of the bad conscience does not imply the rejection of all forms of conscience. Indeed, just as Nietzsche's effort to go beyond good and evil is motivated by a severe notion of what is good, so too his critique of the bad conscience stems from the austere dictates of the good or intellectual conscience. He says of previous genealogists that because of their ignorance of ancient history, their slovenly tendency to confuse their own experience and knowledge of modern history with experience and history as a whole, that is, their lack of intellectual conscience, "it stands to reason that their results stay at a more than respectful distance from the truth" (GM II 4). But the former genealogists of morals stay at a more than respectful distance not only from historical truth but from knowledge of the rank order of the kinds of conscience and the ends of human life. It is this knowledge about human excellence, and not a theoretical innovation or a breakthrough in historical method, that distinguishes Nietzsche's new genealogical understanding of conscience.

Conscience is connected to justice through human excellence. But the dominant notion of justice, Nietzsche believes, obscures this connection. The naive, old-style genealogists connected the origins of the "sense of justice" to the punishment of criminals. They believed that the original thought behind punishment was that those who disobey the law deserve punishment because they were free to obey. Nietzsche's famous counterargument is that the punishments authorized by conventional morality for breaking promises and behaving unjustly had their origins rather in the pleasure derived from inflicting pain and the enjoyment that comes of watching others suffer (GM III 4). This violent and cruel form of compensation, Nietzsche asserts, determined the original legal relations between creditors and debtors. Justice, on this account of the origins of morality and punishment, might seem to be totally conventional or socially constructed, entirely a creature of human desire or will. Yet this is not how Nietzsche sees it. One of his primary convictions is that justice, or rather justice in a higher sense, a sense identified with the spirit and judgments of the strong, healthy individual, stands judge over the bad conscience and condemns conventional morality.

In section 11 Nietzsche dwells upon the nature of justice *(Gerechtigkeit)*. He begins by explicitly rejecting the idea that the origin of justice lies in the sphere of *ressentiment* (GM II 11). *Ressentiment* flourishes among those who feel aggrieved and hate what they imagine to be the source of their pain. Justice, however, is slandered when it is equated with *ressentiment* and its political expression, the vengeful and reactive drive to secure equal rights.[15] What many today call social justice is more or less what Nietzsche condemns as *ressentiment*. Speaking "for truth's sake," he declares that the home of justice is far from reactive feelings. Rather the "spirit of justice" in its original form denoted spiritual health, and spiritual health signified the capacity to judge truly:

When it really happens that the just man [*der gerechte Mensch*] remains just even toward those who have harmed him (and not merely cold, temperate, remote, indifferent: being just is always a *positive* attitude), when the exalted, clear objectivity, as penetrating as it is mild, of the eye of justice and *judging* is not dimmed, even under the assault of personal injury, derision, and calumny, this is a piece of perfection and supreme mastery on earth—something it would be prudent not to expect or to *believe* in too readily. (GM II 11)

Of course, the same prudence that proclaims supreme mastery rare also cautions against concluding that it is nonexistent. Justice, in the sense of seeing the world unfalsified, without prejudice, is, according to Nietzsche's account, a moral and intellectual virtue that combines courage and good conscience.[16]

On Nietzsche's view it was the just or comparatively just man who, first and for the longer part of history, instituted and administered higher law *(Recht)*. The original forms of founding and legislating aimed to impose "measure and bounds upon the excesses of the reactive pathos" (GM II 11). In other words, early forms of civilization complied with the demands of justice by cruelly containing and effectively controlling reactive feelings. The most effective means, according to Nietzsche, by which the active, strong, healthy, and noble sought to discipline and govern the reactive and sickly was the establishment of sacred standards or a higher law *(Recht)* through the institution of humanly made or positive law *(Gesetz)*. Nietzsche asserts that the higher law or right *(Recht)* must be a creature of humanly made or positive law *(Gesetz)* and that the idea of *Recht* "*in itself* is quite senseless" because "life operates *essentially,* that is in its basic functions, through injury, assault, exploitation, destruction and simply cannot be thought of at all without this character" (GM II 11).

The thesis that higher law is a creation of human law seems to lend support to the opinion that on Nietzsche's view morality is socially constructed. Yet the fact remains that he presents justice *(Gerechtigkeit)* as the standard which governs the correct application of cruelty and the establishment of a higher law through positive law to regulate the lower passions. Although he asserts that what appears to be higher law or right is in fact originally determined by human law, Nietzsche judges both *Recht* and *Gesetz* in terms of *Gerechtigkeit*. Moreover, since the right to lay down law belongs on his account to the "stronger, nobler, more courageous," it follows that the distinctions between strength and weakness, nobility and baseness, and courage and cowardice preexist both law-making and value-creating. In opposition to, rather than as the consummation of, the drift of modern philosophy, Nietzsche's account of the origins of bad conscience and law recognizes and rests upon a standard independent of the will—he calls it justice—that determines the goodness or badness of desires, souls, and forms of life.

Though less explicitly than in his account of the origins of higher law in positive law and positive law in justice, Nietzsche's judgments concerning the uses and disadvantages of the "bad conscience" also rely upon a definite conception of the human good. He displays a pronounced ambivalence about the bad conscience, regarding it as the "most uncanny and most interesting plant of all our earthly vegetation" (GM II 14) but also as the "gravest and uncanniest illness" (GM II 16). The bad conscience results when human beings, forced to live within society under peaceful conditions, are deprived of the natural outlets for their creaturely desires (GM II 16). When the strong desires to inflict cruelty and achieve mastery are turned inward they receive expression as self-inflicted cruelties, prominent among which is the will to self-mastery. Since self-mastery is the mark of the emancipated individual, it is fair to conclude that the bad conscience is also the bridge to a higher form of existence.

There would be no bad conscience, and hence no self-mastery, were it not for those who sought mastery over others by founding states. Although Nietzsche admiringly describes the founders of states as "the most involuntary, unconscious artists there are" (GM II 17), he makes clear that state-making is the precondition for, but of lower rank than, self-making. Art is always a matter of imposing form. Founders are artists because they form packs of wild human beings into political entities; they create something new and grand by bending and molding recalcitrant material into an ordered whole (GM II 17). Though themselves free of the bad conscience, the artist-founders are responsible for the bad conscience, inasmuch as they instill it among the subjects and citizens as a necessary device, an instrument of political control, that enables people to live together in society through the discipline or cruel repression of their predatory instincts.

Curiously, the instinct for freedom or mastery that impels artist-founders to go out and forge herds of human beings into a political order is precisely the instinct that the artist-founders seek to control in individuals; they discipline the people to internalize the instinct for freedom in order to secure the stability of the state (GM II 18). But just this instinct for freedom or power, when internalized, impels a man to take himself as the object or raw materials that must be ruthlessly remade and mastered.[17] The bad conscience becomes on Nietzsche's account "the womb of all ideal and imaginative phenomena" (GM II 18) and as such the precondition and impetus to the higher forms of self-making. The bad conscience "is an illness as pregnancy is an illness" (GM II 19), and like pregnancy it is an expression of fertility that brings into existence new forms of life.

What standards govern a healthy birth or right self-making? Nietzsche gives some hints in the final sections of the second essay. Knowledge is a crucial precondition for right self-making, particularly the combination of disbelief in the Christian God and repudiation of conventional morality. Nietzsche's declaration that "Atheism and a kind of *second innocence* belong together" (GM II 20) indicates that disbelief in God ought to issue in a freedom from the forms of restraint or guilt characterizing conventional or Christian morality. Although this is to the good, atheism, or disbelief in the Christian faith, is far from the last word on the human significance of gods and conscience. This is because there are noble uses for gods and a higher form of conscience. Indeed, Nietzsche offers the Greek gods as an example of how well-made gods, which reflect nobility and represent the deification of the animal in man, can preserve freedom of the soul and ward off the bad conscience (GM II 23).

Just as gods, despite the pernicious role they have played in promoting the bad conscience, when well-used can combat the bad conscience, so too, guilt, although it has been associated with self-deception and self-torture, can contribute to the cultivation of human excellence. Nietzsche envisages a reversal in which strong spirits would feel guilty over having felt the bite of the bad conscience toward "the *unnatural* inclinations," a bite sanctified by conventional Christian morality (GM II 24). In sum, Nietzsche's criticism of the bad conscience does not require the repudiation of external moral standards; to the contrary, he advances an alternative understanding of right and wrong that prescribes what higher human beings should feel guilty about. In opposition to the slavish mode of valuation that has succeeded in linking guilt to the highest powers and attainments of the human spirit, Nietzsche advocates a revaluation which restores respect for excellence by linking guilt to that which obstructs the achievement of the "*highest power and splendor* actually possible to the type man" (GM Preface 6).

The revaluation of conventional values requires a higher type of man, a type with a spirit that is severe and respectful toward itself, accustomed to heights, capable of solitude, confident and playful in its knowledge, in short, embodying what Nietzsche calls "*great health*" (GM II 24). Although he doubts that such a one exists or could exist in his weak and enervating age, he boldly assigns to this higher type of man, "the *redeeming* man of great love and contempt, the creative spirit" (GM II 24), the divine task of redeeming reality. And he emphasizes that the capacity of the "redeeming man" to redeem reality, that is, to save it from both Christianity and nihilism, rests on the redeeming man's superior and comprehensive knowledge of reality (GM II 24). Genealogy thus shows the necessity for but does not itself provide an account of the redemption of reality or the comprehensive knowledge on which that redemption is based. But Nietzsche does not therefore leave his reader with no place to turn. For in the *Genealogy,* at the close of the second essay, he proclaims that Zarathustra, and Zarathustra alone, is free and endowed with the strength to teach about the "redeeming man" (GM II 24–25).

Ascetic Ideals and the Problem of Truth

In the third essay Nietzsche abandons all pretense to writing rigorous history. The rhetoric of science and scholarship gives way to that of the physician of the soul. And the genre shifts from history to literary commentary. In the preface he had asserted that the third essay was an illustration of the exegesis of an aphorism (GM Preface 8). The aphorism in question comes from *Zarathustra* and deals with the dispositions demanded by wisdom: "Unconcerned, mocking, violent—thus wisdom wants *us;* she is a woman and always loves only a warrior" (GM III 1). And indeed the climactic theme of the third essay is the wisdom or self-knowledge of the genealogist.

The ascetic ideal has meant many things to many people. The best way to understand its history is in terms of a nonhistorical "basic fact of the human will" (GM III 1), namely that "*it needs a goal*—and it will rather will *nothingness* than *not* will" (GM III 1). As with conscience, Nietzsche judges the ascetic ideal in light of the goals it serves.

And just as Nietzsche saw a connection between conscience and the emancipated individual, so too he links ascetic ideals to independence. One cannot learn from an artist about the meaning of ascetic ideals because artists are dependent creatures always serving some morality, philosophy, or religion (GM III 5). The best place to discover the higher meaning of the ascetic ideal is in "a genuine *philosopher*" (GM III 5). Genuine philosophers view chastity, and by extension ascetic ideals, as providing "so many bridges to *independence*" (GM III 7). The solitude secured by ascetic ideals, likened by Nietzsche to a desert, represents liberation from servitude to the demands of family and political life (cf. Z I "On the Three Metamorphoses"). When philosophers pay homage to the ascetic ideal they honor the independence they conceive as the condition for human excellence and affirm the philosophical life as the highest life (GM III 7). Indeed, so great is the impiety of the philosophers that they believe the ascetic ideal, properly conceived and executed, brings about a cheerful asceticism, combining a freedom and elevation that makes them, as it were, divine (GM III 8). Thus the ascetic ideal in the highest sense, the philosophical sense, serves an ethics of self-deification.

The three great vows of the ascetic ideal are poverty, humility, and chastity (GM III 8). They belong to the severe conditions in which not only philosophers but all "great, fruitful, inventive spirits" flourish (GM III 8). As he proceeds to elaborate the worthy uses of ascetic ideals, however, Nietzsche keeps his sights trained on philosophers. Philosophers are averse to dependence; they avoid everything having to do with the present, with political life, with romantic love, and even with friendship. Guided by the motto "he who possesses is possessed" (GM III 8), and driven by a supreme and lordly desire for truth, the philosopher refrains from presenting himself as a martyr to truth, and even avoids using the word *truth*. This avoidance does not stem from an aversion to truth but, quite the contrary, reflects a kind of love that recoils from the degradation through common usage that the word *truth* has suffered (GM III 8; see also BGE 230, 295). Devotion to truth compels philosophers to maintain a respectful reticence toward the object of their devotion.

Concluding that philosophers have been drawn to the ascetic ideal because it promotes the supreme form of flourishing, Nietzsche emphasizes that the supreme form of flourishing or spirituality relies upon unspiritual and unphilosophic experiences and practices (GM III 9). Every achievement in the realm of the spirit has been "paid for by spiritual and physical torture" (GM III 9). Thus the characteristic ambition of a philosopher "to build a *new heaven*" is typically grounded "only in his *own hell*" (GM III 10). A contest of extremes rages in and energizes the philosopher's soul.

Like all things the ascetic ideal can be misused. Whereas for philosophers the ascetic ideal serves as a stimulus to the highest forms of life, in the hands of priests it becomes a weapon deployed against life (GM III 11). The conflicting uses to which the ascetic ideal may be put reflect low and high elements within man himself. Although or rather because man "is *the* sick animal," he is also restless, daring, and disposed to great experiments with himself, a creature who strives for ultimate mastery (GM III 13; see also A 14). A combination of extremes, man is at one and the same time an exceedingly "courageous and richly endowed animal" and "the most imperiled, the most chronically and profoundly sick of all sick animals" (GM III 13). Ascetic ideals that enable man to overcome his natural sickness, display his courage, and exercise his rich endowment are well used; ascetic ideals that cause man to indulge in or exacerbate his essential sickness represent an abuse.

Under the tutelage of ascetic priests, sickliness has become ever more normal among mankind. Expressing fear that the "rare cases of great power of soul and body" are facing extinction (GM III 14), Nietzsche rails against the sick and weak because they corrupt the healthy and strong, posing a massive threat to the cultivation of human excellence (GM III 14). The dangers the sick pose to the healthy, which have reached epidemic proportions in the modern era, are not unique to any one historical epoch, but an almost ineliminable aspect of social and political life, at work in every family, organization and commonwealth (GM III 14). Like Aristotle, Nietzsche finds a basic conflict at the root of collective life; but whereas for Aristotle that conflict was between the poor and the rich (*Politics* 1290a30–1292a37), for Nietzsche it is between the sick and the healthy. And Nietzsche's opinion is far more deeply entangled with metaphysics than is Aristotle's. For whereas Aristotle's universal judgment is a generalization from experience,

Nietzsche's universal judgment is a generalization rooted in speculations about the permanent standards defining the health and sickness of the human soul.

Writing in dread of the prospect that he will be a witness to the final poisoning and extinction of the healthy by the sick, Nietzsche returns to the analysis of *ressentiment* developed in the first essay, restating that the main weapon of the weak is to induce the strong to embrace a false rank order of values. From the loudly trumpeted concern with rigorous historical investigation designed to reveal the origins of moral prejudices, he arrives at an undisguised exhortation, couched in the moral language of "ought" and the political language of "right," to defend the higher forms of human life from the lower:

> But no greater or more calamitous misunderstanding is possible than for the happy, well-constituted, powerful in soul and body, to begin to doubt their *right [Recht] to happiness* in this fashion. Away with this "inverted world"! Away with this shameful emasculation of feeling! That the sick should *not* make the healthy sick—and this is what such an emasculation would involve—should surely be our supreme concern on earth; but this requires above all that the healthy should be *segregated* from the sick, guarded even from the sight of the sick, that they may not confound themselves with the sick. Or is it their task, perhaps, to be nurses or physicians?
>
> But no worse misunderstanding and denial of *their task* can be imagined: the higher *ought* not to degrade itself to the status of an instrument of the lower, the pathos of distance *ought* to keep their tasks eternally separate! (GM III 14)

By this point Nietzsche also appears to have dropped the pretense *to determining* the rank order of values as announced in the first essay. For he appears *to know* plainly what the rank order is, and with this knowledge firmly in hand, he now presents his goal as determining how to protect the vulnerable but worthy higher types from enervating exposure to the ruthless but worthless multitude of mankind.

Respect for the intellectual conscience is central to Nietzsche's task. Where religions, including Christianity, remain "true to the facts"—as in the doctrine that redemption cannot be achieved through the exercise of moral virtue—he applauds them (GM III 17). But for the most part Christianity is bad and false, based on self-deception, thwarting self-knowledge not only among the weak but worse, among the strong.

Modern man, under the influence of Christianity, has moralized the world, interpreting it according to false and debasing metaphysical and ethical notions.

Characteristically, Nietzsche's objection is not to lying itself but to dishonest and harmful lies, lies based on and encouraging self-deception (GM III 19). To promulgate "a real lie, a genuine resolute, 'honest' lie," a lie of the sort Nietzsche says one could receive instruction on from Plato, it would be necessary for modern man to know himself better (GM III 19). Lies based on self-knowledge are legitimate, even useful, but modern man, Nietzsche explains, lacks both the honesty and the courage for self-knowledge. Analysis of characteristically Christian and modern forms of self-deception leads Nietzsche, in the final sections of his *Genealogy*, to turn to fundamental questions about the meaning of science and the problem of truth. Or rather he returns to these questions, for the knower's self-knowledge was the problem with which he began the *Genealogy* (GM Preface 1, 2).

Modern systematic scholarship, though appearing irreligious and a victorious rival to the ascetic ideal, is in fact *"the latest and noblest form of it"* (GM III 23). Scholars and scientists misunderstand their actual motives for pursuing knowledge and the real value of the knowledge they acquire (GM III 23). Although for most of its practitioners scholarship serves as a vehicle for avoiding painful self-knowledge and hiding from hard truths, there remain, among the philosophers, scholars, and scientists, some "last idealists of knowledge," who pride themselves on their unbelief and their opposition to the ascetic ideal (GM III 24). Nietzsche has great respect for these devoted opponents of religious belief even as he stresses that their opposition itself reflects a kind of faith. They are "unconditional on one point—their insistence on intellectual cleanliness" (GM III 24).

Paradoxically, the "last idealists" are unconditionally opposed to unconditional beliefs. This paradoxical devotion to knowledge, which Nietzsche acknowledges as his own, is itself rooted in the ascetic ideal and tightly bound up with the healthy or good conscience; for the hard, heroic free spirits who repudiate the ascetic ideal do so on the basis of the intellectual conscience, the most spiritualized form of the ascetic ideal (GM III 24). Thus the repudiation of the ascetic ideal by free spirits is at the same time an affirmation of it.

Free spirits are very free, but not fully free because they lack full self-

knowledge, in particular the knowledge that their intellectual conscience is rooted in a questionable faith, a faith in the truth. The slogan
of real freedom of spirit, according to Nietzsche, was found among an
eleventh-century Islamic sect, the Assassins: "Nothing is true, everything is permitted" (GM III 24). With this perspective, he asserts, "the
faith in truth itself was *abrogated*" (GM III 24).

But was it? Does not the Assassins' slogan represent a gain in self-
knowledge and an achievement in the pursuit of knowledge about morality? What is it but the intellectual conscience, that is the faith in truth
itself, that compels some to face up to the hard truth that nothing is
true and recognize its implications for life? Granting Nietzsche's assertion that free spirits are governed by the intellectual conscience and that
"it is precisely in their faith in truth that they are more rigid and unconditional than anyone" (GM III 24), is not the further demand that this
faith be questioned, is not the quest to grasp the truth about the theoretical status and moral value of faith in the truth, the ultimate expression
of ascetic virtue as understood by the philosopher?

Nietzsche merges the perspective of the genealogist on the value of
truth with that of the philosopher and the practitioner of gay science.
He refers the reader to the fifth book of *The Gay Science* and specifically
to section 344, "How we, too, are still Pious," to clarify his paradoxical
assertion that to deny that philosophy rests on a faith stands philosophy
and truth on their heads (GM III 24). The "metaphysical faith" on
which philosophy rests—emphatically including Nietzsche's gay science
and his genealogy—derives from "the Christian faith, which was also
Plato's, that God is truth, that truth is *divine*" (GM III 24, quoting
GS 344). True, the divinity or fundamental importance of truth, "is becoming ever more unbelievable" (ibid.). But this process, by which the
truth becomes unlovable by being loved too well, is animated by the
view or faith that truth is the one thing needful. Calling the goodness
of truth into question is the latest and highest expression of the service
of truth and hence a reaffirmation that truth is good.

It is precisely because Nietzsche himself continues to place a premium
on truth that he feels compelled to bring to light a question that he
maintains has lain hidden in the blind spot of scholarship, science, and
all previous philosophy, a question about the value of the will to truth
that animates these disciplines. Once "faith in the God of the ascetic
ideal is denied," when God is known to be dead, "*a new problem arises:*

that of the *value* of truth" (GM III 24). What begins in the attempt to determine the value of morality by identifying its origin culminates in the imperative to question the value of truth. This imperative is nothing other than the will to be truthful about what truth is, and as such is, in Nietzsche's *Genealogy*, the highest form of the ascetic ideal. Indeed, Nietzsche's practice of genealogy reveals itself as an instance of the effort to be truthful about the truth and hence as an exemplary expression of the ascetic ideal.

"Unconditional honest atheism," the quality Nietzsche admired in Schopenhauer, his ideal of the philosopher (GM III 5; see also SE 1, 2, 3, 8, pp. 127, 136, 139, 185), is driven by the will to truth (GM III 27). But "unconditional honest atheism" is also among the most spiritual and final expressions of the ascetic ideal because denying oneself belief in God is denying that which has hitherto elevated human existence. Rejecting belief in God, just like questioning the value of truth, reflects the creed, "No more lies!" Ironically, the Christian God and Christian morality perish from their very own "training in truthfulness." Things stand differently, however, in regard to the philosopher and his way of life because the philosopher, in whom the will to truth comes to consciousness as a problem, achieves a decisive gain in self-knowledge and thereby makes progress in satisfying his ruling passion.

But what does the genealogist or philosopher do on the basis of his newly gained self-knowledge? The *Genealogy* does not say, but it does declare that an answer can be found in *Thus Spoke Zarathustra* (GM II 25).

Conclusion

No two approaches to political philosophy might seem more dissimilar and at cross-purposes than a characteristically modern investigation into the genesis of moral beliefs or prejudices and the quest, typical of ancient philosophy, to articulate what is noble, just, and good. Generally speaking, the former sees moral values as rooted in a particular historical epoch and made by human beings; the latter relies upon metaphysical speculation and knowledge of human nature to clarify the permanent standards of human conduct. Nietzsche's genealogy combines the two approaches. Although he proudly flaunts his supposedly highly developed "historical sense" as the key to his own genealogy of morals, his chief criticisms of morality in the *Genealogy* rest upon an appeal, more typical of the philosophy of Plato and Aristotle than of modern philosophy, to notions of nobility, the soul's health, and the just man.

While slave morality, on Nietzsche's view, must be debunked by being traced back to its lowly origins in crippled human passion, noble morality is vindicated by being shown to spring from robust, well-constituted souls. Nietzsche's genealogy presupposes that nobility, the health of the soul, and justice are not socially constructed but rather that standards of human perfection and corruption preexist their articulation in language and their embodiment in social and political institutions. Nietzsche evaluates morality and political life in terms of their promotion or obstruction, expression or distortion of human excellence. His peculiar use of history in fact contravenes the historicist thesis that the grounds of morality are artifacts inextricably tied to a contingent clime and time: Nietzsche in effect argues that human health or the rank order of values that determines what is good and bad has one look throughout history.

This is not to deny but rather to affirm the ambiguity in Nietzsche's account of the ethics of morality and the conflict between the fundamental elements that constitute his practice of genealogy. Just as the first essay in the *Genealogy* reveals his ambivalence toward morality based on reflections about truthfulness and creativity, and the second essay exhibits his ambivalence toward conscience based on reflections about autonomy and justice, so too the third essay shows his ambivalence toward ascetic ideals based on a conception of human excellence that places philosophy at the top of the rank order. The *Genealogy*'s criticism of slave morality and modernity is inextricably bound up with a vision of the good. The first essay defends a higher kind of morality, the second champions a higher form of conscience, and the third honors a higher type of ascetic ideal. Nietzsche himself emphasizes that to erect a new ideal one must first tear down old ideals; what his account of the ethics of morality in the *Genealogy* demonstrates is that he tears down old ideals by availing himself of higher ideals.

It should not be thought that Nietzsche's view that the human soul acquires depth in history through *ressentiment,* the bad conscience, and ascetic ideals contradicts the thesis that his genealogy crucially relies upon nonhistorical standards of human excellence. Rather, his view that slave morality, the bad conscience, and ascetic ideals brought something new into the world—the soul or self with its depths and doubts, its right to make promises, and its spiritualization of cruelty—indicates, among other things, that the original nobility were deficient in some crucial respect and therefore did not occupy the highest rank.

In fact, what the original nobility lacked, in spite of their truthfulness, was knowledge. Their truthfulness was based on a fundamental ignorance of the real condition of human beings, that is, they lacked complete knowledge of metaphysics and the true needs of humankind. The noble mode of valuation was deficient because it did not recognize the true but deadly doctrines informing the practice of the genuine historian; the Dionysian tragic wisdom that is the reward of Greek tragedy; indeed, the knowledge stemming from the coming to self-consciousness of the ascetic ideal that faith in the truth calls into question the very convictions upon which it rests. These closely related insights appear to have entered the world, according to Nietzsche's *Genealogy*, through the momentous activities of the priests and the slaves, that is, through those who were moved by *ressentiment,* suffered from the bad conscience, and honored ascetic ideals.

Indeed, the standpoint from which Nietzsche writes the *Genealogy*, a book for knowers that poeticizes the history of morality to clarify the character of human excellence, partakes generously of both the truthfulness marking the noble mode of valuation and the creativity prominently at work within the slavish mode of valuation. Nietzsche's *Genealogy* is edifying poetry because its sweeping narratives about great men and dastardly villains are based on and intended to illuminate metaphysics and true or real human needs. Accordingly, genealogy is a prime example of right making based on right knowing. Although genealogy provides an education in the ethics of morality that contributes to a new rank order of values, it neither displays nor exemplifies the highest rank. For that, according to the *Genealogy* itself, one must turn to Nietzsche's *Zarathustra*.

The enthusiasts who portray Nietzsche's genealogy as a pioneering method of social inquiry misrepresent his purpose and obscure his practice. Although he introduces genealogy as a more scholarly and more rigorously historical method than previous attempts to understand morality, in practice, his genealogy is inspired reconstruction that exploits the appearance of historical veracity to win a hearing for its claims about the higher and lower types of human beings. Genealogy,

Nietzsche's distinctive approach to the history of morality, is openly partisan and designed to determine and to display the value of moralities and the rank order of values. Like history and art, genealogy in Nietzsche's hands is a vehicle for exhibiting human excellence and depravity so as to defend the former against the perennial menace of the latter.

4

The Ethics of Religion:
The Antichrist

Unlike his first two book-length histories, Nietzsche's third and final major history, *The Antichrist,* has enjoyed little acclaim or attention. This neglect is significant because *The Antichrist* would seem to command a place of distinction as the first and only completed part of Nietzsche's planned four-part work, *Revaluation of All Values.*[1]

Whatever the reason for the silent treatment,[1] it is noteworthy that *The Antichrist* has little to offer in the way of support for doctrines popularly associated today with Nietzsche's name. Speculations, radical or otherwise, about perspectivism and human agency, the death of metaphysics, the indeterminacy of language, and the pervasive and inescapable role that willful, manipulative interpretation play in judgment are lacking. Nor does Nietzsche introduce new doctrines. Rather, old opinions about religion, morality, nature, and truth, crucial to the arguments made in *Uses and Disadvantages, The Birth,* the *Genealogy,* as well as elsewhere attain unprecedented prominence in *The Antichrist.* In short, Nietzsche teaches in *The Antichrist,* as in his two earlier histories, that there is a rank order among human beings; that the standards governing history, art, morality, and religion are neither made nor imagined but rather discovered and comprehended; and that human excellence demands a solitary, suprapolitical life based on a clear-eyed grasp of the human condition.[2]

In *The Antichrist* Nietzsche also puts aside the promise, announced but never carried out in the *Genealogy*, to undertake an investigation of actual, documentable history. In *The Antichrist* he eschews the pretense to rigorous historical study while insisting even more strongly that he has identified not only the actual psychological drives and real human needs that produce religious belief but also the rank order that determines the worth and dignity of these drives and needs. His tirade against Christianity in *The Antichrist*, like his friendly praise of Buddhism, his unconventional and highly stylized portrait of Jesus, his depiction of the law of Manu as a model framework for organizing a healthy society, and his examples of nobility in history, exhibit his standards of praise and blame with an unnerving simplicity and clarity. Just those opinions around which so much contemporary scholarship has congregated drop out of sight. In particular, his celebrated ideas about perspectivism and the human or social construction of reality fade into the background as Nietzsche, undertaking one of the tasks announced in *Genealogy* (GM I 17), elaborates a relatively well-defined rank ordering governing desires, human beings, and forms of life.

It is in the light of this rank-ordering that he savagely condemns Christianity for having, under the tutelage of the lowest-ranking human instincts and longings, shamelessly falsified the world. In view of his vehement attacks on Christianity throughout his writings, one cannot help wondering whether scholars have turned a deaf ear to *The Antichrist* not because they disapprove of Nietzsche's hyperbolic language nor because they object to his scorn for Christianity, but rather because they were offended by the specific reason he repeatedly affirms in *The Antichrist* for hating Christianity. For those who see Nietzsche as first and foremost a teacher of perspectivism, an advocate of the relativity of all outlooks, a revolutionary opponent of the conviction that truth is a valid object of human desire, the arguments of *The Antichrist*, which evaluate religions in terms of their conformity to a metaphysical order and the degree to which they support true or real human needs, are likely to appear worse than useless.

In fact, it is not the ruling themes in *The Antichrist* that are anomalous, but rather the balance of power among longstanding rivals for preeminence among Nietzsche's ideas. While one would be hard-pressed to find a single major idea trumpeted in *The Antichrist* that is not well represented throughout Nietzsche's other writings, those of Nietzsche's characteristic opinions that depend upon the assumption that knowledge is made, not discovered, take a back seat.

To take an important example: it is not through creativity that Nietzsche's heroes in *The Antichrist* distinguish themselves but rather through their superior courage in venturing to the perilous outer bounds of human knowledge. Examples of exceptional human beings whose great deed consists in self-creation or who seek to remake the social and political world in their own image are conspicuous by their absence. Creativity of course is not entirely absent from *The Antichrist.* The leading creators in *The Antichrist* are the makers of religions, and religions are the primary forms of artwork. Yet Nietzsche does not apply aesthetic but rather ethical standards to the evaluation of religions, strictly judging them on the basis of the knowledge they embody about the world and human nature and the knowledge they make possible for those who live under their sway. In *The Antichrist,* he views religion as a form of art but he keeps art under the supervision of philosophy. Right making based on right knowing practically defines, for Nietzsche, the fashioning of virtuous or "moraline-free" religion.

The Vices and Sins of the Theologians

In accordance with his habit, Nietzsche briefly sketches in the preface to *The Antichrist* the proper character of his intended reader. In contrast to a work like Marx's *Communist Manifesto,* which aims at the widest possible readership, Nietzsche declares of *The Antichrist* that "This book belongs to the very few" (A Preface). So few are those for whom he intends his book that he reproaches himself for having once entertained the idea that there were worthy readers among his contemporaries. Echoing Zarathustra's lament amid the crowd in the marketplace that he was not the "mouth for these ears" (Z Prologue 5), Nietzsche writes *The Antichrist* secure in the knowledge that he is not "one for whom there are ears even now" (A Preface).

Nevertheless he knows what qualities are necessary for those who would benefit from his message. The center of gravity in the catalogue of longings and virtues he ascribes to his "right readers"—severe, uncompromising honesty, contempt for and independence from political life, care for truth undiluted by considerations of use or safety, courage for forbidden, unasked questions, reverence or love for oneself and un-conditional freedom before oneself—is the dedication to the advancement of fearless thought (A Preface). In *The Antichrist*, as in his previous histories, Nietzsche understands human excellence, which he speaks about in terms of power, fitness, Renaissance virtue, *virtù*, and moraline-free virtue (A 2), as the strength to seek out and bear harsh, repellent, unchristian truth (GM I 1), to acquire and endure wisdom about the real character of existence (BT 3, 7, 9), and to live with and create on the basis of the true but deadly doctrines that define the place of human beings in the world (UD 6, 9, 10).

He begins by emphasizing the immense distance that sets him and his ilk apart from the rest of humanity (A 1). Citing Pindar on the legendary race that dwelled in the icy wastelands at the ends of the earth—"Neither by land nor by sea will you find the way to the Hyperboreans"—Nietzsche calls himself, as well as his proper companions and right readers, Hyperboreans.[3] Or better, super-Hyperboreans. For he says that his own happiness lies beyond the Hyperboreans' frozen wastelands. Speaking not as a brazen explorer setting out on a dangerous expedition but rather as a seasoned and savvy home-coming hero, he proclaims, "We have discovered happiness, we know the way, we have found the exit out of the labyrinth of thousands of years" (A 1). Unlike his madman and in contrast to Zarathustra, both of whom declare that *determining* a new way in the aftermath of the death of God is their problem, Nietzsche, in *The Antichrist*, boasts of a happiness and fundamental insight *already* attained.

Cringing at the inevitable comparison between his new happiness and the happiness modern man presumptuously believes he has achieved, Nietzsche declares that it was precisely modernity and all its sickness, laziness, and general uncleanliness from which he recoiled and sought escape (A 1). Insisting that modernity's "happiness of the weakling" must be resisted at all costs (A 1), he grounds that resistance in a boldly proclaimed ethic:

> What is good? Everything that heightens the feeling of power in man, the will to power, power itself.
>
> What is bad? Everything that is born of weakness.
>
> What is happiness? The feeling that power is *growing*, that resistance is overcome.

Not contentedness but more power; not peace but war; not virtue but fitness (Renaissance virtue, *virtù*, virtue that is moraline-free).

The weak and the failures shall perish: first principle of *our* love of man. And they shall even be given every possible assistance.

What is more harmful than any vice? Active pity for all the failures and all the weak: Christianity. (A 2)

Yet Nietzsche's plain language is deceptively plain. The crucial terms in his list of fundamental axioms or first principles lack self-evident definitions. Shall we understand power as referring to preeminence in hand-to-hand combat, the rule over one's passions, the governance of great kingdoms, or perhaps knowledge of the intelligible character of the world? How shall we distinguish what heightens the *feeling* of power from what actually heightens power? Is weakness a physical, moral, or intellectual vice? What counts as resistance overcome? What obstacles are necessary and immovable and which can be dissolved or conquered by human powers? And what is the connection between power and love of man? The hard question is not whether Nietzsche invokes a conception of the human good, but rather concerns what is presupposed and demanded by the conception of the good that he does invoke.

One demand, at least in Nietzsche's eyes, is waging war against Christianity or what amounts to the same thing for him, morality. Like Christianity, Nietzsche teaches that the love of man issues in moral imperatives. Yet whereas for Christianity love of man obliges one to feed the hungry, clothe the naked, and give shelter to the homeless, for Nietzsche love of man demands unsentimental extermination of "the weak and the failures." And the weak and the failures for Nietzsche are the vast majority. Although he admires Christianity for the organizational genius it displays in willing, breeding, and attaining its favored type, "the domestic animal, the herd animal, the sick human animal—the Christian" (A 3), he rejects what he regards as the Christian conceit that mankind as a whole is getting better and better. He counters that "'progress' is merely a modern idea, that is, a false idea" (A 4). True excellence, he observes, has never been anything more than a fortunate accident. The attainment of human excellence, that is, of "a *higher type,* which is, in relation to mankind as a whole, a kind of superman," is on his view exceedingly rare but apparently always and everywhere possible (A 4).

The higher type, hitherto a result more of luck than of planning, faces, Nietzsche believes, an unprecedented peril in the form of modern

Christianity. Siding "with all that is weak and base, with all failures," Christianity has perpetrated a destructive revaluation of values: "it has corrupted the reason even of those strongest in spirit by teaching men to consider the supreme values of the spirit as something sinful, as something that leads into error—as temptations" (A 5). Christianity's revaluation stands the true rank order of values on its head, promulgating a decadent doctrine in which weakness brazenly proclaims itself strength and strength is scorned as sin.

Christianity and modern morality exalt pity. Pity, or compassion for the downtrodden, is harmful because it saps the energy and strength of the healthy and well-constituted and preserves what is ripe for destruction, the multitude of weaklings and failures (A 7). What may seem a crude Social Darwinist vision of political life is in fact deeply aristocratic. Pity, according to Nietzsche, is the practice of nihilism, not because it disables the instincts that preserve life, but rather because it enervates the instincts that seek an increase in true or real power (A 7). Whereas pity may be good for the survival of the species, it is definitely a catastrophe for the higher types. Nietzsche's war on Christian pity, waged on behalf of those who are victimized by it, is rooted in his understanding of spiritual health. Prompted by his love and wisdom, he once again appeals to the notion of the philosopher as a physician, proclaiming the imperative to excise the cancer ravaging the body politic in order to save not the soul of the body politic but his own soul and the souls of his fellow Hyperboreans (A 7).

The true philosopher-physician must oppose the whole of inherited philosophy because it is sick with theologians' contaminated blood (A 8). But first he must see the plague as it is and diagnose its calamitous effects. From Nietzsche's point of view, self-styled free thinkers such as the natural scientist and the physiologist reveal their own corruption by their failure to condemn or even discern the corruption around them. Although prizing knowledge, they lack the priceless knowledge of the basic requirements of human excellence.

Nietzsche shows how much he prizes knowledge through his zealous condemnation of the crimes that theologians commit against it. The theologians' "perspective," according to him, is "distorted," "dishonest," and "faulty" (A 9). Moreover, the theologians' instinct to lie is systematic, pervasive, and diabolical: "it is the most widespread, really *subterranean,* form of falsehood found on earth" (A 9). It is also thoroughly predictable: "Whatever a theologian feels to be true *must* be false: this is almost a criterion of truth ... whatever is most harmful to life is called 'true'; whatever elevates it, enhances, affirms, justifies it, and makes it triumphant, is called 'false'" (A 9). Like Nietzsche's Plato (BGE Preface), his theologians do violence against the truth, making her look ridiculous by standing her on her head (cf. BGE 220). The malevolent motive that compels the theologians to abuse the truth is the desire for power. And what is wrong with that? Simply that the theologians, nihilists who wish to bring longing to an end, long for the wrong kind of power, a political power that reflects a weak soul that cannot face up to the hard facts about life.

Nietzsche also criticizes Kantian philosophy as a bad lie. As a kind of secularized Christian faith, Kant's philosophy retains Christianity's major vice, the falsification of the world in the interest of the exaltation of the wrong values. Observing that "the Protestant parson is the grandfather of German philosophy," Nietzsche (himself the son and grandson of Protestant parsons) lays the blame for Kant's philosophy or "*insidious theology*" at the doorstep of Kant's German education and heritage (A 10). He accuses Kant of mendaciously fabricating a realm, beyond the prying eye and clumsy grasp of reason, where truth and morality are united. In so doing, according to Nietzsche, Kant straitjackets reason and denigrates reality, reducing our world, that is, the sensible, cultural, and political world, to the debased status of mere appearance. As a philosopher, Kant was, in Nietzsche's eyes, sincere but inept; but as a moralist he turned out to be, in Nietzsche's view, a catastrophe.

Nietzsche condemns Kant's moral philosophy more strongly than his metaphysics not because he regards morality as more important than truth but rather because he regards nothing as more important than the truth about how one should live. Against the Kantian doctrine that virtue consists in obedience to a universal and impersonal law, he puts forward the hard-won truth about virtue that it "must be *our own invention, our* most necessary self-expression and self-defense" (A 11). Like the moral law according to Kant, virtue according to Nietzsche must be self-given. Virtue, according to Nietzsche, is especially necessary in lying well. Unlike Kant, who rejected all lying in principle, Nietzsche advocates a virtuous use of truth and lies. The trouble with Kantian moral philosophy is that it lies about the worth of lies, poisoning the truly virtuous by undermining their belief in their right to lie.

Although authorized to lie, the truly virtuous are distinguished by their intellectual integrity or conscience. This they share with a few skeptics, "the decent type in the history of philosophy" (A 12). Invoking "the most basic requirements of intellectual honesty" (A 12), Nietzsche maintains the necessity of separating philosophical inquiry from morality. Or better, he insists that the ethics of philosophical inquiry is independent of and sits in judgment over conventional morality (see also GS 344; GM III 24–27).

Thus, there is a fundamental and insuperable conflict between those who seek truth and the priestly type who consider it their sacred task to improve mankind by articulating redeeming moral visions. By contrast, real freedom of spirit, the rare fruit won by cultivating the most basic requirements of intellectual honesty, demands "nothing less than a 'revaluation of all values,' an *incarnate* declaration of war and triumph over all the ancient conceptions of 'true' and 'untrue'" (A 13). Thus, the revaluation of ancient conceptions of "true" and "untrue" depends on the conviction that intellectual honesty is a higher good.

Nietzsche knows that his cause or crusade—to articulate and redeem knowledge of the human good—faces terrifying odds: he fears that all of human history is against him, and believes that at every turn the dominant morality of his day distorts or suppresses hard truths about the human condition and human excellence. Although he recognizes that seeking the truth makes him a kind of defiant outlaw, he insists that such defiance stems from a form of modesty. Although modesty is ordinarily deemed the gentlest of social virtues, his kind of modesty, he says, has "offended men's taste longest of all" (A 13). While it strikes the official religious or political authorities as a presumptuous and subversive refusal to profess allegiance or worship in the prescribed manner, his modesty arises, Nietzsche asserts, out of the simple duty of intellectual conscience that requires one to know the facts about that before which one is asked to kneel.[4]

The modesty that keeps Nietzsche from bending his knee before the Christian God and conventional morality is uncommonly demanding (A 14). It requires that he deny what the theologians teach—that man is created by God—and reject what German Idealism proclaims—that man emerges out of the unfolding of Spirit in history; it dictates that man be understood as an animal, the most bungled and the sickliest, the one who has strayed most dangerously from his instincts, and yet also the most interesting; it counsels the repudiation of the will as a discrete faculty and insists on nothing but mechanistic interpretations of man; and finally, it commands the rejection of all versions of human perfection that denigrate the senses and the body (A 14). Nietzsche's modesty is more an intellectual than a moral virtue; it does not govern his relation to others but rather constitutes his relation to the truth.

Modesty, in Nietzsche's sense, is precisely what Christianity, in his judgment, lacks. In fact, Christianity offers an ambitious, self-certain, and dreadfully wrong picture of the world, a picture in which "neither morality nor religion has even a single point of contact with reality" (A 15). The whole of Christian doctrine is based on imaginary causes, imaginary effects, imaginary beings, an imaginary natural science, an imaginary psychology, and an imaginary teleology (A 15). It is not the involvement of imagination that arouses Nietzsche's ire, but rather the emancipation of the imagination from governance by the intellect or the intellectual conscience. Accordingly, he explains that the Christian "*world of pure fiction* is vastly inferior to the world of dreams insofar as the latter *mirrors* reality, whereas the former falsifies, devalues, and negates reality" (A 15).[5] As in *The Birth*, he evaluates artistic activity in terms of the truth it conveys. He condemns Christianity not because it is a poem or work of the imagination but because it is a hateful poem that violates philosophical justice by falsifying and denigrating reality.

More generally speaking, Nietzsche's immoralism receives expression in *The Antichrist* as a severely demanding and highly restrictive ethic of religion that subordinates creativity to knowledge by making knowledge about the dominant role that creativity has played in the history of religion a crucial precondition of human excellence. Christian priests, weak and impoverished men serving weak and impoverished people, create a weak and impoverished God. Slandering this world and lying about the next, Christianity represents "the deification of nothingness, the will to nothingness pronounced holy!" (A 18). Like every religion, Christianity is a species of artistic invention and therefore subject to the standards of art. But the standards of art are ethical. The god that Christianity has created is bad poetry, a disgrace to the "*creator spiritus* in man" (A 19) because of the morality it teaches, one in which "all cowardices and wearinesses of the soul, find their sanction!" (A 19).

Praising and blaming the comprehensive and historically influential works of art called religions on the basis of how well they embody and provide instruction in human perfection, Nietzsche reveals that religion, among the highest forms of art, is justified only as a moral phenomenon. By collapsing the distinction between religion and poetic invention, by depicting religion as a grand artistic genre, and by evaluating religion in terms of the contribution it can make to the cultivation of human excellence, his critique of religion clarifies the high moral significance he attaches to art. His rationalistic and moralistic critique of religion exhibits, writ large, the rationalism and moralism of his evaluation of art.

Religious Beings as a Higher Type of Man

The Antichrist features two religious beings whom Nietzsche singles out as teachers and heroes of the spirit—the Buddha and Jesus. What is noteworthy is Nietzsche's explicit standard for praising the religious life: intellectual integrity or respect for reality. Although all religion is invented by man for his own use, Buddhism and the life Jesus led are more useful inventions or artworks than Christianity because they are based on respectable understandings of the human condition and satisfy true or real human needs.

Anticipating a predictable but mistaken contrary inference, Nietzsche expresses the hope that his "condemnation of Christianity has not involved me in any injustice to a related religion with an even larger number of adherents: *Buddhism*" (A 20). Buddhism is not simply the opposite of Christianity, for like Christianity it is a nihilistic religion. But Buddhism is nihilism with a remarkable difference. Whereas Christianity interprets reality in terms of sin and evil, Buddhism calls suffering by its true name (A 20). Buddhism is a respectable form of nihilism because it respects reality.

The nihilistic inclination within Buddhism, according to Nietzsche, is rooted in two physiological facts or character traits: excessive sensitivity to pain and an exaggerated preoccupation with concepts and logical procedures (A 20). Yet these weaknesses of body and spirit do not lead to the telltale feelings of *ressentiment*. Buddhism does not counsel escape from suffering, as does Christianity, by malevolent falsification of the world. Rather, Buddhism teaches escape from suffering through self-mastery and the maintenance of a strictly controlled social world and environment. Devotion, fanaticism, and the belief in other worlds, as well as the restless, churning ambition of the soldier, ruler, and artist, are strictly forbidden. Buddhism is honest about its goals and successful in attaining them: "Cheerfulness, calm, and freedom from desire are the highest goal, and the goal is *attained*. Buddhism is not a religion in which one merely aspires to perfection: perfection is the normal case" (A 21). Although a distinctly undionysian religion, hostile to great creators and great rulers alike, Buddhism earns Nietzsche's admiration because it goes a long way (though not the whole distance) toward satisfying the demands of the intellectual conscience.

Buddhism furnishes the critic of Christianity with an example of a comparatively healthy religion that throws into sharper relief Christianity's specific evils. While Nietzsche emphasizes that Buddhism cannot lay claim to achieving the highest form of human perfection, Christianity, he asserts, gives expression to the lowest class instincts and is the means by which the lowest political classes seek salvation (A 21). Whereas Buddhism seeks to calm and satisfy the desires, Christianity despises the body. Whereas Buddhism counsels moderation and prescribes ideas that soothe or cheer, Christianity teaches "cruelty against oneself and others," hatred for those who are different, and especially "hatred of the *spirit* of pride, courage, freedom, liberty of the spirit" (A 21). Whereas Buddhism avoids intoxicants and is marked by a serene sobriety, Christianity is marked by gloomy and exciting notions. Whereas Buddhism is concerned with the amelioration of pain and the perfection of the individual, Christianity seeks to inflict pain, to make sick, to enfeeble, and to tame.

Yet the most important difference from Nietzsche's point of view between Buddhism and Christianity, two great decadent religions, concerns Buddhism's superior capacity for respecting the truth and avoiding lies. Buddhism, he emphasizes, "is a hundred times colder, more truthful, more objective. It is no longer confronted with the need to make suffering and the susceptibility to pain *respectable* by interpreting them in terms of sin—it simply says what it thinks: 'I suffer'" (A 23). Though Buddhism may fall short of the supreme human perfection, Christianity wages a ruthless and relentless campaign against bodily health and spiritual independence. Though Buddhism does not tell the whole truth, Christianity promulgates lies and deranges the respect for truth.

Indeed, Christianity, on Nietzsche's view, reflects the perfection of the shameful Jewish instinct to flee from and suppress the natural order of things. Judaism, the predecessor and propagator of Christianity, like Christianity and Buddhism, represents an instance of the imagination put in the service of life, but in opposition to rather than in the service of the higher forms of life. In order to survive, the Jews paid what Nietzsche regards as a vastly excessive price:

> this price was the radical *falsification* of all nature, all naturalness, all reality, of the whole inner world as well as the outer. They defined themselves sharply *against* all the conditions under which a people had hitherto been able to live, been *allowed* to live; out of themselves they created a counterconcept to *natural* conditions; they turned religion, cult, morality, history, psychology, one after the other, into an incurable *contradiction to their natural values*. (A 24)

The priestly type in Judaism as well as in Christianity gains power and extends his dominion by "making mankind *sick* and in so twisting the concepts of good and evil, true and false, as to imperil life and slander the world" (A 24). The Jewish and Christian reinterpretation of human affairs in terms of God's will is, according to Nietzsche, "that most mendacious device of interpretation, the alleged 'moral world order'" (A 25). The huge irony is that Jesus, the historical link between Judaism and Christianity, exemplifies in Nietzsche's eyes a form of life in which redemption is achieved without appeal to a transcendent moral order. And Nietzsche's portrait of Jesus as a man who achieves eternity within time takes on heightened significance in view of the fact that "the fundamental conception" of *Thus Spoke Zarathustra*, the doctrine of the eternal return (EH III, on Z, 1), is centrally concerned with loving eternity.[6]

What is of chief concern to Nietzsche in studying Jesus' life is "the *psychology of the Redeemer*" (A 28). Nietzsche scoffs at the notion that his interest has anything in common with the breakthroughs in philological-historical criticism of the Gospels achieved by David Strauss and his like. Though once attracted to Strauss's scientific demonstrations of the contradictions in which the Gospels abound, he now finds such studies "mere scholarly idleness" (A 28). The goal of studying the life of Jesus as told by Scripture—in keeping with the task of a genuine historian, at least in regard to monumental history—should be neither to discredit nor to vindicate Scripture's fidelity to historical fact, but rather to determine "*whether* his type can still be exhibited at all, whether it has been 'transmitted'" (A 29). Of course Nietzsche can discount the relevance of historical-philological criticism because he shares the fundamental premise of all such investigations: that Scripture is a literary work or artifact. This, however, does not lead him to depreciate the biblical narratives because, for him, poetry is an important vehicle for exhibiting the truth about human excellence.

The glad tidings that Jesus wished but ultimately failed to teach concern, on Nietzsche's interpretation, not another world but this world: "True life, eternal life, has been found—it is not promised, it is here, it is *in you:* as a living in love, in love without subtraction and exclusion, without regard for station. Everyone is the child of God—Jesus definitely presumes nothing for himself alone—and as a child of God everyone is equal to everyone" (A 29). For Nietzsche's Jesus, the experience of eternity is real, open to all, and attainable in earthly existence irrespective of politics and social station.

Yet all was not well with Jesus and his teaching. Nietzsche stresses the connection between Jesus' doctrine of redemption through eternal life and his hypersensitive instincts. Jesus' longing for "a merely 'inner' world, a 'true' world, an 'eternal' world," is satisfied through a rejection of the solid world of custom, politics, and religious tradition (A 29) and is rooted in two instincts: first, *"the instinctive hatred of reality,"* and second, *"the instinctive exclusion of any antipathy, any hostility, any boundaries or divisions in man's feelings"* (A 30). These instincts reflect a physiological reality, an extreme capacity for suffering and a hypersensitivity to contact with or resistance from the external world. Yet these instincts also make possible a superior perspective on morality, politics, and religion.

Despite the misunderstandings of Jesus' own uncomprehending disciples, who transformed him into a priestly fanatic (A 31),[7] Jesus' "glad tidings," Nietzsche emphasizes, represent a form of redemption that promises the attainment of eternity in the here and now. Although Jesus' doctrine that the kingdom of heaven belongs to the children implies that the price of eternity is a kind of infantilism of the spirit (A 32),[8] and despite Jesus' aversion to and hatred of reality, Jesus is, in Nietzsche's eyes, a higher type of man. For owing to his disabilities, he becomes an involuntary skeptic and a kind of "free spirit" doubting and gaining emancipation from many things deserving of doubt and unworthy to hold him: "he does not care for anything solid: the word kills, all that is solid kills. The concept, the *experience* of 'life' in the only way he knows it, resists any kind of word, formula, law, faith, dogma. He speaks only of the innermost: 'life' or 'truth' or 'light' is his word for the innermost—all the rest, the whole of reality, the whole of nature, language itself, has for him only the value of a sign, a simile" (A 32).

The skepticism of Nietzsche's Jesus results in his emancipation or exile not only from convention but also from every kind of formal knowledge and culture, from tradition and learning, from every form of political and practical attachment (A 32). He is skilled at living on high mountains not because he sees "the wretched ephemeral babble of politics and national self-seeking *beneath*" himself (A Preface) but because he is incapable of seeing them at all. Since Nietzsche's Jesus lives of necessity on high mountains, and since his aversion to reality was given, not chosen, his involuntary skepticism also renders him a kind of captive or slave.[9]

Jesus' innocent isolation from ordinary life, his instinctive disregard for external trappings, finds expression in a deeply ambiguous kind of self-deification, for in his doctrine "Sin—any distance separating God and man—is abolished" (A 33). Nietzsche's Jesus, like his Buddha, achieves a kind of blessedness or satisfaction. Again, like the Buddha, Jesus does so not as warrior, ruler, or artist, but in a withdrawn, self-sufficient sphere, the spiritual content of which Nietzsche leaves obscure. Thus Jesus' real significance for mankind, according to Nietzsche, has little to do with the theological role imposed upon him by Paul and promulgated through organized Christianity. It has everything to do with his own single-minded, utterly egoistic, inward-looking exercise in self-deification. Rather than teach a faith, Jesus showed how to experience eternity within the confines of finite human life; he became almost more than human by overcoming the spirit of revenge, by achieving a "superiority *over* any feeling of *ressentiment*" (A 40). Without faith in a personal God or speculations about a transcendent order, Jesus attains a kind of perfection. His legacy to mankind is his life as a model of the good life. And living before the birth of the Christian God, Jesus can serve as a model of how one can make oneself godlike for those who live in the aftermath of the death of God.

Yet Jesus' doctrine of redemption, still more than organized Christianity, blatantly negates appearance, draining the everyday world of sense and significance. If Nietzsche is correct that it is up to free spirits to grasp the church as "this embodiment of mortal hostility against all integrity, against all *elevation* of the soul, against all discipline of the spirit, against all frank and gracious humanity" (A 37), then it becomes difficult to maintain his distinction between Jesus and the Church. For it is hard to see how the legacy of Nietzsche's Jesus to mankind, his indiscriminate, passionless love of all, arising out of physical weakness and an eccentric spirituality and culminating in a radical detachment from practical life, bespeaks integrity, elevation, discipline, or humanity. Nietzsche's Jesus—much like his Zarathustra—achieves a kind of redemption through loving eternity, a kind of redemption that, more radically than the organized Christianity that Nietzsche opposed, makes a mockery of the active, engaged, and this-worldly life.

On Truth and Lies in an Unholy and a Holy Sense

Whereas Nietzsche's Jesus goes some way toward respecting the intellectual conscience, Nietzsche's Christianity relentlessly betrays it. The key Christian inference—"'Faith makes blessed: *hence* it is true'" —is itself not a proof but rather an untestable hypothesis about the fruits of faith (A 50). Reductively construing the proposition "faith makes blessed" as meaning that faith gives pleasure, Nietzsche insists that pleasure yields no proof of truth. To the contrary, invoking the experience "of all severe, of all profoundly inclined spirits," and distinguishing between the pleasurable and the truthful, he declares that devotion to the truth requires a terribly severe discipline:

> At every step one has to wrestle for truth; one has had to surrender for it almost everything to which the heart, to which our love, our trust in life, cling otherwise. That requires greatness of soul: the service of truth is the hardest service. What does it mean, after all, to have *integrity* [*Rechtshaffenheit*] in matters of the spirit? That one is severe against one's heart, that one despises "beautiful sentiments," that one makes every Yes and No a matter of conscience. (A 50)

Nietzsche is satisfied of the falsity of Christianity on the basis of his opinions about human perfection, according to which the quest for the truth is seen to be a terrible trial and at the same time the one thing needful. Rejecting the useful and the pleasant as criteria for determining the human good, he indicates that service of the truth is not only the hardest service but also the most painful and disadvantageous. Thus, while repudiating the idea that the capacity of a belief to give pleasure counts in favor of its claim to be true, he indicates that ugly opinions that require great renunciation have a presumption in their favor. The crucial point is not that Nietzsche's ethics of religion, like organized Christianity, rests on a non-evident premise or faith, but rather that the content of Nietzsche's ethics places service of truth and intellectual integrity first.

Accordingly, he condemns as contemptible Christianity's aversion to knowledge and the disciplines through which knowledge is attained.

> Another sign of the theologian is his *incapacity for philology*. What is here meant by philology is, in a very broad sense, the art of reading well—of reading facts without falsifying them by interpretation, without losing caution, patience, delicacy, in the desire to understand. Philology as *ephexis* in interpretation—whether it is a matter of books, the news in a paper, destinies, or weather conditions, not to speak of the "salvation of the soul." (A 52)

The service of truth also compels him to attack Christian martyrs for the immeasurable harm they do to the cause of truth by encouraging the false inference that a belief for which someone gives his life must be true (A 53). Offering the ultimate sacrifice, however, is, for Nietzsche, a vulgar substitute for the intellectual integrity and the long, arduous labors necessary to acquire even small truths. Yet if the service of truth is the hardest service, if service of truth requires resisting with all one's might the seductive proposition that faith makes one blessed, then it would seem that Nietzsche is in fact in agreement with the Christian martyr that the truth belongs to him who endures the greatest loss for truth's sake.[10] Accordingly, the real dispute between Christian service and the service of the truth does not concern whether the truth is good or whether it is preferable to life, but rather turns upon what the truth is about the best life.

The service of truth, as Nietzsche understands it, requires the rejection of the Christian—and in another sense perspectivist—idea of a truth that is fundamentally personal and unique. He emphasizes that grasping the truth depends upon virtue or specific excellences of spirit: "Truth is not something which one person might have and another not have: only peasants and peasant apostles like Luther can think that way about truth. One may be sure that modesty, *moderation* in this matter, becomes greater in proportion to the degree of conscientiousness in matters of the spirit" (A 53). Moderation in knowledge and conscientiousness in matters of spirit point toward skepticism. And, invoking Zarathustra as a model, Nietzsche asserts that greatness of spirit consists in a freedom from conviction achieved by means of a powerful, inexhaustible skepticism (A 54). Whereas the great spirit may temporarily make use of convictions in order to attain a greater freedom, the man of conviction, that is, the believer or the party man, depends on a few convictions, "a strict and necessary perspective in all questions of value" for orientation and decision (A 54). The "great passion" of the skeptic employs the intellect to dissolve convictions that pass within its orbit; yet to the extent that great skepticism also rests on vital convictions about the goodness of truth, skepticism too is exposed to the danger of hardening into a kind of dogmatism.

Thus the great skeptic, the opponent of conviction, is still subject to the temptations, dangers, and pathologies that always accompany fidelity to conviction. And the greatest danger or pathology is fanaticism, exemplified for Nietzsche in the figures of Savonarola, Luther, Rousseau, Robespierre, and Saint-Simon (A 54), men who began as subverters of authority only to become authorities themselves. Wherever inclination or opinion has hardened into conviction, one should, Nietzsche warns, be prepared to encounter a fanaticism that spoils the conscience and impairs the intellect for questions of truth and falsity, a fanaticism that prefers demagoguery to cool and reasoned discourse, and that vents itself in passionate denunciations of conventional morality and apocalyptic or utopian visions of a transformed humanity. In contrast, the true skeptic recognizes that skepticism is based on a conviction, but this recognition of course cannot guarantee that his conviction that serving the truth is good will not itself rigidify so as to deprive him of the capacity to be skeptical about the bases of his skepticism.

Indeed, convictions are more dangerous than lies, or rather convictions are the most dangerous form of lie, for they are lies for which one is ready to suffer, condemn, punish, kill, and be killed (A 55; cf. HH 483). Whereas the convictions of "the party man" or partisan are deplorable precisely because they are always believed in, the lies promulgated by the priests and theologians are tolerable insofar as the priests and theologians do not believe them, but use them to good purpose. Indeed, good politics requires "priestly or philosophic-priestly rule"

(A 55) in which wise religious leaders conjure illusions and contrive convictions for the discipline of the party men or common believers. Nietzsche's account of the law of Manu in sections 56–57 provides a vivid illustration of such priestly lies placed in the service of the truth.

Politics and Natural Right

Although his portraits of Buddhism, Jesus, and his "right readers" suggest that human excellence is achieved outside of politics, Nietzsche introduces a caste system, the ancient Hindu law of Manu, as a well-constituted political order that serves human excellence.[11] Apparently unconcerned with historical accuracy or proof, but complying with the imperative that he believes imposes upon the critic of Christianity the task of making Christianity look contemptible, he introduces the law of Manu to reveal "the greatest contrast of ends" (A 57).

Nietzsche insists that, whereas Christianity teaches political equality, the law of Manu embodies the opposite and correct understanding that inequality is sanctioned by nature and the basis for all healthy, well-constituted political orders. The law of Manu is not identical to the best political order, but rather, as in Alfarabi's account of the virtuous regime, is an instance of a best order that is capable of being realized through a variety of religious codes.[12] Unconstrained by the need to piece together complicated and contingent historical material, and uninterested in the details that distinguish the law of Manu from other religions, Nietzsche is free to sketch those dimensions of the law of Manu—or to supply it with features—that conform to reason and nature and constitute the basis of all healthy political orders.

The law of Manu "originates like every good code of laws" in the summation and codification of centuries-old experimentation and experience (A 57). Consequently, the founding lawgivers neither create freely and spontaneously nor probe their own inner depths searching for materials out of which to create a blueprint, bearing their unique signature, for the remaking of political society. Rather, the lawgivers are priests and theologians—very much unlike the Buddha or Jesus—who organize and refashion inherited customs, rituals, and beliefs in view of what they, as discerning readers of history and human nature, determine has turned out well and what badly in the experience of their people.

The lawgiver, reminiscent of Nietzsche's genuine historian, must conceal the multi-layered origins of the law from those subject to it. By means of a "holy lie" the lawgiver brings to an end "further experimentation, a continuation of the fluid state of values, testing, choosing, criticizing values *in finitum*" that characterizes the birth and early history of a people (A 57). Thus the spirit of innovation and experimentation, the life-blood of Nietzsche's great spirited skeptic, is poison to the healthy political order. The anti-skeptical spirit that must dominate in the healthy political order is secured by the indispensable devices of revelation and tradition, or more precisely by tales or myths told about the gods and ancestors. A revealed law, Nietzsche maintains, is by definition divine, whole, perfect, and beyond human reason. A traditional law, believed to have been observed from time immemorial, hallowed by untold generations, steeped in mystery, and carried forward by the inertia of tradition, overwhelms questions, doubts, and inclination for change. A "higher reason" obliges the priests to promulgate a law supposedly authored by God or gods and vouched for by tradition in order to severely limit the use of reason by the public.

Moreover, higher reason demands that observance of the law become automatic, because automatic observance of the law perfects reliance on the instincts in all walks of life. Instincts disciplined by law, Nietzsche rhapsodizes, are "the presupposition of all mastery, of every kind of perfection in the art of life" (A 57; see also BGE 188). While one might imagine a variety of uses to which a holy lie could be put, for Nietzsche the holy lie embodied in the law of Manu (as in all good codes of law) has as its general aim to render obedience unconscious and habitual. Obviously, though, what is true of the vast majority cannot be true of the priestly promulgators of the holy lie: the few who supervise the production of unconscious, habitual, and well-regulated behavior among the many must discipline themselves to undertake daring deeds and must grasp the higher reason that sanctions their holy lies.

A holy or noble lie differs from cynical manipulation, vulgar deceit, and partisan propaganda because it conforms to a "higher reason." The law of Manu, and the lie on which it is based, are rational in the sense that they reflect and are sanctioned by "a *natural order*, a natural lawfulness of the first rank, over which no arbitrariness, no 'modern idea' has any power" (A 57). The supreme requirement this natural order imposes is the establishment of a caste system reflecting three distinct types of human beings: "Nature, not Manu, distinguishes the pre-eminently spiritual ones, those who are pre-eminently strong in muscle and temperament, and those, the third type, who excel neither in one respect nor in the other, the mediocre ones—the last as the great majority, the first as the elite" (A 57).

The highest caste, according to Nietzsche *"the fewest,"* represents "happiness, beauty, and graciousness on earth" (A 57). Those belonging to the highest caste, "the most spiritual men," those who "find their happiness where others would find their destruction," who take joy in self-conquest, and who play with burdens that would crush others, find neither happiness nor joy in governing. They are more like self-absorbed and playing gods, more like Nietzsche's Buddha and Jesus, than like philosopher- or priest-kings. It is the second class, the "guardians of the law," who maintain order and security, staffing the military and exercising political power. The highest instantiation of the political man, the king, arises out of the second or guardian class. Yet the king, as "the highest formula of warrior, judge, and upholder of the law," remains the faithful deputy of the highest class (A 57). Owing to their profound aversion to political life and lack of inclination and knowhow to promulgate a holy lie, Nietzsche's Buddha and his Jesus would seem to fit in quite naturally at the top, above those who practice politics, among the few, the playing gods.

The task of classification of souls is simplified by Nietzsche's insistence that the variety of types of souls is fundamental, enduring, and severely limited: "The order of castes, the *order of rank,* merely formulates the highest law of life; the separation of the three types is necessary for the preservation of society, to make possible the higher and the highest types. The *inequality* of rights [*Rechte*] is the first condition for the existence of any rights at all" (A 57).[13] The third class, composed of the mediocre, the decent, the civilized, and the educated, provides the broad base on which the few play their dangerous and exhilarating games. Nietzsche leaves little room for doubt concerning the scope of the lowest class. It includes not merely the working class and the agricultural class, but the educated and professional classes as well. The lowest and largest class of Nietzsche's healthy society embraces Hegel's universal class and indeed the entire bourgeois world.

Nietzsche anticipates and explicitly rejects the supposition that natural endowments or capacities are significantly malleable or socially constructed, and that society is at fault for or can correct mediocrity: "To be a public utility, a wheel, a function, for that one must be destined by nature: it is *not* society, it is the only kind of *happiness* of which the great majority are capable that makes intelligent machines of them. For the mediocre, to be the mediocre is their happiness, mastery of one thing, specialization—a natural instinct" (A 57). The necessity inhering in the natural variety and distribution of human souls, and not, as some have argued, mistaken assumptions about the requirements and internal dynamics of mass industrial society,[14] justifies, on Nietzsche's view, a caste society.

For Nietzsche, no amount of technological progress, redistribution of wealth, or political reform would alter the demand of justice for a caste society. This is because on his view it is not membership in the laboring class that produces narrow, mediocre souls. For him, widespread mediocrity is an observable fact about the natural types of man, and his argument is that a tripartite class structure in a well-constituted political order gives each of the three basic types the work and satisfaction for which it is best suited. This is not, however, to claim that Nietzsche's account of the healthy political society, with its bold metaphysical assumptions, is free from controversial economic and empirical assumptions. It isn't, but repudiation of these peripheral empirical assumptions does not alter his central argument about the rank order of natural types.

Nietzsche maintains that mediocrity as such ought not to be censured, in part because every high culture needs the labor and productive power of the masses to support the spiritual adventures of the few. His insistence that the exceptional human being should treat the mediocre with greater tenderness than he treats himself or his peers does not reflect respect but is rather a practical judgment stemming from considerations of enlightened self-interest: the stability of political society and the happiness of the few depend upon preserving the "worker's sense of satisfaction with his small existence" (A 57). Yet, at the same time, Nietzsche emphasizes that the worker's sense of satisfaction is not illusory, but well suited to the inclinations and capacities of his soul. Those who undermine the worker's sense of satisfaction with his work and circumscribed existence, who encourage him to envy and desire the privileges and prerogatives of the higher and highest, who instill in him new demands and aspirations, the most destructive of which is the aspiration for equal rights, commit the double harm of depriving high culture of its foundation and robbing the multitude of men of their chief source of pleasure and the ground of their sense of self-worth.

The obvious parallels that link Nietzsche's healthy political order to the city that Plato's Socrates sketches in the *Republic* should not obscure key differences.[15] Nietzsche and Socrates are in agreement that the political community must be divided into three hierarchically ordered classes with the wisest in the position of supreme power, the guardians defending, and the masses laboring; that a lie is necessary for founding and maintaining the just city; and that nature furnishes a standard for ordering political society. Yet while Socrates sacrifices the happiness of the highest or philosophical class by imposing upon them, contrary to their wish to philosophize, the duty to govern the city (*Republic* 419–421c, 519c–520d), Nietzsche's healthy political order secures the happiness of the few by releasing the most spiritual from political responsibility and handing over political rule to the second-ranking class, the "guardians of the law." Whereas Socrates' city is constructed in strict accordance with justice, Nietzsche's healthy political order is elaborated subject to the requirements of human excellence. Thus, whereas Socrates sacrifices the happiness of the most excellent human beings to justice, Nietzsche holds that justice requires the sacrifice of everything else to the happiness or cultivation of "the higher and the highest types" (A 57).

To avoid misunderstanding let me state the obvious: Nietzsche's account of the law of Manu is historically dubious and a threadbare, distasteful blueprint for politics. It is nonetheless of interest as a statement of his opinions about the rank order of human types. Nietzsche's utopia gracefully accommodates exalted beings—like his Buddha and his Jesus—who flourish in the rarefied regions above politics. Viewing political life in light of "imagined republics and principalities," he shows the enormous gap between the political options that the modern world offers and what nature and reason require from politics, and he teaches that in the best political order the best type of human being is neither attracted to political life nor bound to govern.

Nobility in History

In the final sections of *The Antichrist* Nietzsche pays brief tribute to a select company of cultures and individuals that, in opposition to Christianity, have embodied noble values. These include the ancient Greeks, the Roman Empire, Epicurus and Lucretius, Islam, the Renaissance, and Cesare Borgia (A 58–62). What he finds to celebrate in these exemplars of nobility, and not only or most interestingly in the philosophers among them, is either intellectual virtue or the services rendered to intellectual virtue.

For example, although he emphasizes that the Roman Empire built its social organization in the grand style and *sub specie aeterni*, Nietzsche portrays Roman excellence in government as dependent upon a robust philosophical temperament. It was the loss of intellectual virtue caused by contact with Christianity, he insists, that resulted in Rome's decline and fall. Knowing just where to strike, Christianity "sucked out of each single one the seriousness for *true* things and any instinct for *realities*" (A 58). And when he despairs that the "whole labor" and the "whole meaning" of the ancient world have been lost, the squandered legacy he mourns is an ethos distinguished above all by the cultivation of intellectual virtue:

> All the presuppositions for a scholarly culture, all scientific *methods*, were already there; the great, the incomparable art of reading well had already been established—that presupposition for the tradition of culture, for the unity of science; natural science, allied with mathematics and mechanics, was well along on the best way—the *sense for facts*, the last and most valuable of all the senses, had its schools and its tradition of centuries. Is this understood? Everything *essential* had been found, so that the work could be begun. . . . (A 59)

Nietzsche measures the progress and decline of antiquity, as he judged Christianity, Buddhism, and Jesus, in terms of intellectual integrity.

The Renaissance represents for Nietzsche a last, failed opportunity in the fateful contest between noble values and Christian values (A 61). He gleefully holds aloft the blasphemous image of Cesare Borgia as pope as the symbol of the lost chance to abolish Christianity and secure the triumph of noble values. Considered out of context, his elevation of a brutal military adventurer to leadership of Christendom could appear to be a decisive glorification of the warrior-king. Yet he does not present Cesare Borgia as pope as the epitome of human excellence, but rather as the event that could have abolished Christianity and prevented the cowardly dishonesty that German Protestantism excelled in instilling

(A 62). Borgia as pope could have made possible a form of excellence he himself did not embody. Indeed, the distance between Borgia—a violent, ruthless, ambitious man of war and conquest—and the profoundly antipolitical lives lived by the Buddha and Jesus corresponds to the distinction between the "guardians of the law" who fight and rule and "the few" who occupy the highest caste in Nietzsche's healthy society (A 57). In Nietzsche's hands, Cesare Borgia as pope points to the political conditions for, but not the actual attainment of, human excellence.

Conclusion

The Antichrist, the last of Nietzsche's histories, rewards study. In it Nietzsche prominently displays the standards he consistently applies throughout his histories to praise and blame art, morality, and religion. As in *The Birth* and the *Genealogy*, in *The Antichrist* he subordinates the acquisition of exact historical knowledge to the examination of the truth about human excellence.

Nietzsche's histories exhibit coherence and continuity, manifested less in questions answered than in questions raised, less in disputes settled than in fundamental and unresolved tensions brought to light. The unanswered questions and unresolved tensions point to the core of Nietzsche's thought. In *The Birth* he asserts but does not explain how Greek tragedy reveals knowledge of the essence of things and bestows metaphysical comfort. Presenting his *Genealogy* as a prelude to the urgent task of establishing a new rank order of values, he diagnoses the evils of *ressentiment* but offers little indication of how the disease is to be vanquished. And in *The Antichrist*, he severely judges and ranks religions and religious types with regard to their conformity to a natural ethical order for which he fails to give the slightest philosophical justification. These closely related difficulties are rooted in the contest between his conviction that the creation of values is a human being's highest act and his conviction that comprehending the conditions which make creativity essential to human flourishing is the basis of human perfection. Although Nietzsche's histories vividly display the contest of extremes in his thought, they do not contain a satisfactory account of the outcome of this contest.

In sum, Nietzsche's histories, like those of his "genuine historian," presuppose true metaphysical knowledge and accurate understanding of true or real human needs. Like the "genuine historian," Nietzsche aspires to fashion poems about human excellence from raw materials drawn from history to educate great spirits. But who or what is a great spirit? This is perhaps the most important incompletely answered question in his histories. To adequately address it one must turn from Nietzsche's histories to the two formidable accounts he offers of the supreme human type: Zarathustra's superman and the philosopher of the future anticipated in *Beyond Good and Evil.*

II

THE HIGHEST TYPE

... Zarathustra is more truthful than any other thinker. His doctrine, and his alone, posits truthfulness as the highest virtue ...

Ecce Homo

Oh, how should I not lust after eternity and after the nuptial ring of rings, the ring of recurrence?

Never yet have I found the woman from whom I wanted children, unless it be this woman whom I love: for I love you, O eternity.

Zarathustra, "The Seven Seals"

Love is the state in which man sees things most decidedly as they are not. The power of illusion is at its peak here, as is the power to sweeten and transfigure. In love man endures more, man bears everything. A religion had to be invented in which one could love: what is worst in life is thus overcome—it is not even seen any more.

The Antichrist

5

The Beginning of Zarathustra's Political Education: *Thus Spoke Zarathustra* (Prologue)

Nietzsche's efforts to come to terms with the moral significance of the death of God, its uses and disadvantages for life, lead to the foundations and the peak of his thought. In criticizing the teaching of philosophy in the universities of his day, he announced his criterion for determining the authority of a philosophical teaching: "The only critique of a philosophy that is possible and that proves something, namely trying to see whether one can live in accordance with it, has never been taught at universities: all that has ever been taught is a critique of words by means of other words" (SE 8, p. 187).[1] Nietzsche, as nowhere else, puts his philosophy to the test in *Thus Spoke Zarathustra*.[2] By dramatizing the attempt to live the highest kind of life, Zarathustra's speeches and deeds clarify the severe and radical practical implications arising from, and the theoretical defects inhering in, Nietzsche's fundamental convictions.[3]

To be sure, *Zarathustra* is a work marred by a diffuse plot, repetitive speeches, and obscure images. Yet Nietzsche himself vouched for its unique significance, declaring it his most profound and farsighted work.[4] I believe that this judgment is fair, for *Zarathustra*, more relentlessly than his histories and *Beyond Good and Evil*, reveals the obstacles to supreme mastery demanded by Nietzsche's new ethics. Indeed, the tale told in *Thus Spoke Zarathustra* constitutes a grave indictment, from the point of view of convictions that Nietzsche himself cherished, of his own ideas about the relation between knowledge, freedom, and mastery in the attainment of human excellence.

In studying Zarathustra's speeches and deeds common sense dictates what fascination with Nietzsche's multifarious style may obscure: Zarathustra's shortcomings, errors, and setbacks should be examined and placed in perspective no less than his merits, insights, and triumphs. Consideration of the vices he betrays in deed is as important to reaching a reasoned evaluation of his teaching as is an investigation of the virtues he praises in speech. His atrocious ineptitude as an orator and his disappointing quest for disciples beg for consideration alongside his brave repudiation of the need for followers and companions and his slashing polemics directed against the lusterless lives of those living in the twilight of Christianity. One must fully appreciate the desperate and immoderate character of his efforts to articulate a doctrine of secular redemption, not merely applaud his Herculean quest to liberate the creative will. Finally, mindful of Zarathustra's disconcerting suggestion that being a poet he lies too much (Z II "On Poets"), one must be wary of taking his assertions, observations, and visions at face value. His credentials and character must be established rather than assumed. So severe and encompassing is his criticism of humanity, so bold and all-embracing is his promise of superhuman splendor, so demanding is the new regimen he teaches, that Zarathustra himself must be held to the highest standard.

This is more than fair since the highest standard is Zarathustra's standard. The highest standard, as Zarathustra conceives it, depends upon the courage to face the world as it really is. Zarathustra cherishes honesty—a virtue at once moral and intellectual—because it is an indispensable prerequisite to knowing and achieving what is great (Z IV "On the Higher Men" 8). Or as Nietzsche puts it in restating Zarathustra's self-understanding:

> . . . Zarathustra is more truthful than any other thinker. His doctrine, and his alone, posits truthfulness as the highest virtue [*Tugend*]; this means the opposite of the cowardice of the "idealist" who flees from reality; Zarathustra has more intestinal fortitude than all other thinkers taken together. To speak the truth and to *shoot well with arrows,* that is Persian virtue [paraphrasing Zarathustra in Z I "On the Thousand and One Goals"].—Am I understood?—The self-overcoming of

morality out of truthfulness; the self-overcoming of the moralist, into his opposite—into me—that is what the name of Zarathustra means in my mouth. (EH IV 3)

And, to repeat, the task of truthfulness in philosophy, the only critique of a philosophy that is possible and proves anything, according to Nietzsche, is trying to see whether one can live in accordance with it (SE 8, p. 187). *Thus Spoke Zarathustra* is the most philosophical of Nietzsche's works because it displays most vividly the kind of life demanded by the supreme form of truthfulness about morality.

Evaluation of Zarathustra's practical teaching hinges upon distinguishing between the prodigious significance he audaciously attributes to his new dispensation and the recurring setbacks, self-delusion, and misery that dominate his adventures. There is a discrepancy between Zarathustra's claims to wisdom and his exhibition of foolish, reckless, and hysterical behavior. There is a disproportion between his hopes for a new kind of man and his ill-fated efforts to recruit and instruct potential supermen. There is a disparity between the freedom from the past he announces as his goal and the ineliminable limitations on freedom that he stumbles against as he attempts to empower the creative will to command time. And there is a fateful imbalance between the weight the doctrine of the eternal return can bear and the actual work he assigns to it. One betrays Zarathustra, much in the manner of his fawning disciples, by failing to distinguish his seductive boasts from his actual achievements, his grandiose promises from his genuine accomplishments.

The glaring gap between expectation and experience, speech and deed, and theory and practice pervading *Thus Spoke Zarathustra* constitutes a decisive clue to the meaning of Zarathustra's doctrine and the significance of Nietzsche's achievement. The conclusions of theory and the lessons of experience converge in Zarathustra's tragicomic adventures. The incoherence that undercuts Zarathustra's teaching is, in Nietzsche's philosophical poem, magnified, brought to life, and infused with a human sense. A major consequence of Nietzsche's decision to explore fundamental questions of moral and political philosophy through the medium of drama is to produce a vivid image of the disintegration of judgment, the loss of dignity, the estrangement from human ties, the sacrifice of intellectual integrity, and the victimization by an insatiable pride that result—regardless of the fundamental nobility of the original impulse—when the will is assigned the ruling position in the soul. It must immediately be added that the bankruptcy of the will's rule would be neither vivid nor compelling were it not for the intellectual conscience that drives Zarathustra to make himself a god.

I cannot say that Nietzsche himself understood *Thus Spoke Zarathustra* exactly as I interpret it, that is, as a searing criticism of the structural defects contained in the very foundations of Zarathustra's quest for supreme knowledge, freedom, and mastery. Who can look into Nietzsche's mind? We each may, however, explore the work that Nietzsche has left us. I do maintain that my reading is governed by the drama and overall structure of *Zarathustra* and consistent with Nietzsche's most striking claims about the relation between *Zarathustra* and his other works. In addition, my account identifies metaphysical and ethical themes that, as I argued in earlier chapters, are central to Nietzsche's histories. And my account shows how the contest of extremes that unfolds in those histories is pushed to a more fundamental level in the work that Nietzsche himself claimed as his most profound and farsighted. Finally, as I shall show in Chapter 9, my account of Zarathustra's abandonment of his "highest hope" is strongly supported by Nietzsche's discreet abandonment in *Beyond Good and Evil* of his second conception of the highest type, the philosopher of the future.

On my reading, the striking achievement of *Thus Spoke Zarathustra* is to exhibit a coherent and persuasive picture of the incoherence and unworkability of Zarathustra's highest hopes. Whether Zarathustra comes to realize fully the incoherence and unworkability of his new ethics is difficult to say on the basis of what he says and does. But uncertainty on this question does not entail ambiguity everywhere.[5]

Whether Nietzsche deliberately sought to show through his art the failure of Zarathustra's aspiration to bring into being a new kind of man who makes himself the master of his world by commanding the greatest things must remain open to question. However that question is answered, attention to the overwhelming indications of the text gives rise to a compelling picture of the dire consequence for moral and political life stemming from Zarathustra's teaching as well as the fatal theoretical difficulties that afflict his account of human excellence. Like the alcoholic who steadfastly denies his addiction while the evidence of his disease abounds in decreased production at the office, deteriorating relations with friends, and the breakdown of his family, Zarathustra deludes himself about his highest hopes in such a way as to reveal the roots and consequences of his delusion. Although he refuses to view his devastating practical setbacks as a reflection of a flawed theoretical understanding, his debacle in the market place, frequent histrionics, prolonged association with unworthy disciples, quickly forgotten union with eternity, and absurd posturing and dealings with the higher men constitute, according to Nietzsche's own standard as set forth in *Schopenhauer as Educator* and reaffirmed by Zarathustra, a devastating judgment against Zarathustra's new ethics.

But this is by no means the whole story. For it is precisely the devastating judgment that *Thus Spoke Zarathustra* issues against Zarathustra's "highest hope" that vindicates the philosopher in Zarathustra. It is Zarathustra's hatred of the lie in the soul, inseparable from his intellectual conscience, that transforms his praise of creativity into an unrivaled exhibition of the inhumanity and the betrayal of wisdom which the exaltation of the creative will demands.

Zarathustra's devotion to the truth is a kind of higher piety.[6] Because his rebellion is bound up with that which he rebels against, Zarathustra should be seen as a member of the moral and philosophical tradition that he excoriates and seeks to overcome. Contrary to the dogma of the new school of Nietzsche interpretation that depicts Nietzsche as having broken radically with traditional morality, religion, and philosophy, the pathos of Zarathustra's quest becomes intelligible only in the light of the traditional doctrines he powerfully evokes and on which his own exhortations and aspirations depend. By emphasizing the traditional dimension in *Thus Spoke Zarathustra* I do not, however, seek to portray Nietzsche as essentially a reactionary. Nor do I wish to deny the revolutionary dimensions of Zarathustra's hopes and promises. Like his creator, Zarathustra is both reactionary and revolutionary. Accordingly, my aim is to draw attention to the fundamentally antagonistic elements that lie at the foundations of his doctrine.

Zarathustra's Descent

Zarathustra is a teacher whose origins are shrouded in mystery. For the reader, his life begins when he leaves his home at the age of thirty and goes up alone into the mountaintop cave for ten years during which he "enjoyed his spirit and his solitude" (Z Prologue 1). We learn little about his childhood, upbringing, or adult life. Until part IV we have hardly any idea about his appearance, although in a related matter Nietzsche held that a key to unriddling the mystery of Socrates was grasping the significance of Socrates' physical ugliness (TI "The Problem of Socrates" 3, and "Skirmishes of an Untimely Man" 19, 20).

Is Zarathustra an exception to Nietzsche's own rule that physical beauty and bodily health reflect good character? Or is it rather that we are deprived of what Nietzsche himself regards as information critical to the evaluation of Zarathustra? And what of Zarathustra's lineage and descent? Was he the scion of a well-to-do family or born into poverty? What of his youth, his education, his journeys, his amorous adventures? What books has he read and loved? What need prompted him to sever all connections with civilization for ten long years? How does he feed and shelter himself? What recommends him as a herald? On the basis of what authority does he teach? Has his word been vouched for by signs and miracles? Has he performed brave deeds, overcome formidable obstacles, or received the endorsement of wise teachers?

The customary ways in which we recognize that somebody has a claim to wisdom or deserves our ear are not readily apparent in Zarathustra's case. Moreover, we are forbidden or prevented from investigating the origin and development of his teaching by the silence surrounding his past.[7] Whereas Nietzsche's typical practice in his histories is to investigate the need that engenders beliefs about morality and religion, in *Zarathustra* the text points away from Zarathustra's origins and development, creating a man without a history.[8]

Zarathustra "enjoyed his spirit and his solitude, and for ten years did not tire of it" (Z Prologue 1). His self-imposed exile from practical and political life, from companions and books,[9] was neither a trial in the wilderness nor a painful self-sacrifice, but rather a confident, deliberately sought spiritual adventure. But what kind of spiritual adventure? So little is revealed about the character of Zarathustra's activity that it is difficult to say whether or to what extent he was engaged in reflection on things eternal or introspective examination focused on his own distinctive memories, passions, and hopes.[10]

We do quickly learn, however, that Zarathustra's solitude has at last become burdensome. It is a prompting of the heart rather than a conclusion of the mind that impels Zarathustra, after ten good years, to return to society, in search not of friends but of students and disciples. Stepping before his cave, claiming for himself a position at the center of the sun's world, he addresses the glowing heavenly body with a mixture of reverence and presumption:

> You great star, what would your happiness be had you not those for whom you shine?
>
> For ten years you have climbed to my cave: you would have tired of your light and of the journey had it not been for me and my eagle and my serpent.
>
> But we waited for you every morning, took your overflow from you, and blessed you for it.
>
> Behold, I am weary of my wisdom [*Weisheit*], like a bee that has gathered too much honey; I need hands outstretched to receive it. (Z Prologue 1)

In this revision of Plato's allegory of the cave, cave and sun now both occupy heights above political life.

Zarathustra confesses to the overrich sun his envy for its glory and his wish to emulate its happiness. Although the sun appears to be self-sufficient, inasmuch as its movement and its light do not depend on the admiration or presence of human beings, Zarathustra, presumptuously comparing his ambitions and wisdom to those of the sun, insists that the sun, like him, is in need of companions, or if not companions grateful admirers who bask in its warmth and reflect its brilliance. The sun's magnificence is confirmed or validated, he implies, by those whom it benefits. His insinuation that the sun, contrary to appearances, is not self-sufficient leads into Zarathustra's acknowledgment of his own dependence, his disclosure of his weariness with his wisdom and a confession of his need for others to receive wisdom from him.

But can Zarathustra's characterization of the "great star," arising as he acknowledges it does from weariness and envy, be trusted? Whereas Zarathustra articulates his own neediness, the sun's alleged neediness must be articulated by Zarathustra. Moreover, the sun's movement and light are not subject to change on account of the opinions of human beings. What appears to distinguish the sun is precisely its independence, and its lack of need for human recognition. What terrific need then compels Zarathustra to begin his descent by deflating the sun and bringing it down to earth, to vindicate the significance of his own need to shine for others by projecting it on to the "great star"?

Unlike the sun, which looks up to no other object, Zarathustra looks up to the sun as his model. His decision to imitate the sun by "descend[ing] to the depths" is not driven by the dictates of theoretical or practical reason, nor by duty or compassion, nor again by considered reflections on right conduct, but by a need, by the desire to fill an emptiness, to receive external confirmation of the worth of his wisdom. Whereas Plato's Socrates suggested that the philosophic life, characterized by self-sufficiency, was the most pleasant life, and that therefore the philosopher had to be persuaded and compelled against his inclination to return to the cave to rule the political community (*Republic* 520d, 586e), Zarathustra, displaying great eagerness to teach, to unburden himself of his wisdom, comes to experience the self-sufficient life as intolerable. He seeks to instruct others because he wishes to alleviate his painful loneliness and gratify his vanity. His ambition is to become a revered teacher by sharing his knowledge and if necessary foisting it upon others, heedless of their desires and interests, indifferent to what they hunger for, unconcerned about what foods will nourish their souls and which will poison them.

Zarathustra's wish "to become man again," his very human desire to be honored among men, reflects a lack of self-sufficiency that separates him fundamentally from the "great star" he aspires to emulate. Moreover, his desire for recognition of his peculiar wisdom reflects, as his own adventures soon reveal, his shortsightedness, for an element of his wisdom consists in the knowledge that the multitude of men are blind to human excellence (Z Prologue 3, Z I "On the New Idol"). Having grown fatigued with futilely reaching toward the highest, Zarathustra, oblivious of the cost, the requirements, and the obstacles, seems bent on obtaining a second-best form of satisfaction. And with consummate finesse he portrays this concession to weakness and need as a token of his magnanimity and wisdom.

Descending from the Olympian remoteness of his mountaintop, Zarathustra encounters an old man, a kind of holy man or saint who lives alone in the forest. The old saint, like Zarathustra an outcast from society, recognizes him and notes a dramatic change in his bearing. Once a humble seeker, Zarathustra now projects a menacing pride; formerly, he carried "ashes to the mountains"; now, he appears as one who would threaten the people by bringing "fire into the valleys" (Z Prologue 2). The saint, an imperfect judge of character, exaggerates the people's hostility and Zarathustra's volatility. Failing to see the disgust that weighs Zarathustra down, he attributes to Zarathustra a purity and freedom from disgust belied by Zarathustra's envy of the sun and soon to be discredited by his vengeful condemnation of the last man (Z Prologue 5).

Appearing to mistake Zarathustra for the man Zarathustra wishes to become, the saint admonishes him to proceed with caution because he understands that Zarathustra has "become a child," implying a liberation that comes from a new innocence but also a vulnerability rooted in an unspoiled naivete. Like Zarathustra—and like Jesus—the old saint views the child as a symbol of spiritual awakening,[11] and thus is led to ask Zarathustra why, in view of his transformation, he wishes to return to society only to be once again dragged down by human pettiness. Zarathustra's answer—"I love man"—reveals that he shares a passion with the old man. Yet the old saint who had once loved man was compelled by his disappointments to try to love God. Conversely, it seems that profound disappointment in his love for God, or what is highest, has caused Zarathustra to search for love among men.

But Zarathustra's love for man is called into question by the revision he immediately offers of his explanation for bringing an end to his solitude: "Did I speak of love? I bring men a gift."[12] Since gift-giving may be prompted by ambition, self-aggrandizement, and the like, the saint advises Zarathustra that what the people, who really wish to perpetuate their condition of humble need and unthinking servitude, really need is someone to lighten their load and ease their burden in life. He admonishes Zarathustra to adopt a kind of prudence whereby the giver confers to the beneficiary what is appropriate to the beneficiary's needs and capacities. But in response to the saint's entreaty to do no more than fulfill the people's humblest needs by giving them alms, Zarathustra declares that he is not poor enough to give alms. He refuses to aid the people in assuming a beggarly posture, but he does not protest that the saint has misperceived the true needs of the people nor does he declare that the people actually require the gift of knowledge that he wishes to bestow.[13] Agreeing with the saint's low assessment of the people, he declares himself unable to provide for such impoverished needs. Thus Zarathustra acknowledges that as a teacher he thinks more of himself than of his students.[14]

The saint then voices concern about Zarathustra's safety, explaining that people are naturally inclined to distrust bizarre characters, hermits like Zarathustra and himself, who ask too many questions and boast of strange new doctrines. Again, Zarathustra neither questions the saint's characterization of the people nor denies the saint's reiteration that he possesses an explosive gift. The two seem in agreement that the people are rightly wary of a hermit's treasures. Whether out of concern for the people or for Zarathustra, the saint admonishes Zarathustra to "see to it that they accept your treasures," that is, to tailor his gift to the people's capacities and requirements. But Zarathustra has made up his mind. His haughty insistence on giving the people what suits him rather than what they need indicates a contempt for the people themselves, a lack of the art of rhetoric, and a questionable practical wisdom.

Convinced that Zarathustra cannot make himself understood to the people, the saint bids him to stay in the forest. But Zarathustra is not tempted. Reacting with surprise when the saint, explaining the pleasures of his solitude, says that in the forest he sings, laughs, cries, and hums and thus praises God, Zarathustra wonders, "Could it be possible?" Revealing the foundations of the wisdom he wishes to present to the people as a gift, he exclaims to himself, "This old saint in the forest has not yet heard anything of this, that *God is dead!*"

Although Zarathustra seems to know divine matters plainly, he appears confused about human matters. For his initial misjudgment of the saint demonstrates an incapacity to discern whether his interlocutor belongs among those who share his precious knowledge. Lacking the knowledge of human character to discover promptly a sympathetic interlocutor's fundamental commitments in a face-to-face conversation, how likely is it that Zarathustra has the ability to gauge the effects of a new teaching on the people? Undaunted by his error in judgment and respectful of the saint's comforting illusion and simple piety, Zarathustra displays rare compassion by deliberately refraining from informing the saint that God is dead. Indeed, he shows vastly greater consideration for the religious illusions of the pious saint than for the conventional beliefs of the ordinary citizens he soon meets.

Zarathustra's Debacle

Reminiscent of Nietzsche's madman, Zarathustra heads straightaway for the marketplace, where he introduces a radical new philosophy

(Z Prologue 3; GS 125). The madman proclaimed a catastrophe for the human spirit brought on by the death of God; and he also envisaged a new task and opportunity for human beings who grasped the significance of God's death, that of becoming gods by inventing festivals of atonement and sacred games (GS 125). Zarathustra echoes the madman's apocalyptic pronouncement by holding forth on two hitherto unknown and extreme human types that come on the scene when God dies: "the superman,"[15] an image of supreme achievement, and "the last man," a portrait of supreme degradation. The crowd Zarathustra addresses, however, has not gathered to be educated, but to be entertained. They have come to watch a spectacular stunt, a death-defying tightrope performance. Although he wishes to teach the crowd to be spiritual tightrope walkers risking their lives for the sake of knowledge and spiritual purification rather than spectators gawking at a daredevil overhead, Zarathustra ends up by making a spectacle of himself.

He begins his speech or sermon to the people at fever pitch, unleashing a torrent of words, assailing his audience with extreme implications of his radical doctrine that God is dead. He ferociously condemns the people's happiness, morality, virtue, and religious beliefs in the apparently sincere hope that his message will be appreciated, applauded, and taken to heart. It is not particularly surprising that the people should respond to his zealous speech with blank stares and jeering. But who is to blame for this failure to communicate? Consistent with his self-confessed limitation, his admission that he lacks the poverty to give alms (Z Prologue 2), Zarathustra refuses or is unable to meet the people part way by adapting his rhetoric and demeanor to their opinions and needs. Like Nietzsche's madman, who confessed to himself that he proclaimed his message before the people whom he addressed were prepared to hear it, Zarathustra appears in need of learning that there is a disproportion between the knowledge about human excellence he wishes to teach and the intellectual and moral capacities of those he seeks out as his students.

His first words are dogmatic pronouncements about what man is and far-reaching demands about what he should become: "*I teach you the superman.* Man is something that shall be overcome. What have you done to overcome him?" (Z Prologue 3). The superman is the end or goal of man, the species' specific perfection. The superman differs more from the ordinary man than does the ordinary man from an ape. Advancing a crude version of the Darwinian account of the origins of man, Zarathustra affirms that man developed out of the worm and through the ape to his present condition. But man, he insists, can transcend his humanity by fanning the flames of the "great contempt." The great contempt is the appropriate or worthy response to the contemptible character of human existence. Most lives, according to Zarathustra, are marked by "poverty, filth, and wretched contentment" that defile the highest of which man is capable. One does not blame an ape for behaving like a beast, but one does denounce brutishness—or civility, moral reasoning, and decency—in a being who is made for, or can make himself, better. Zarathustra's speech presupposes that human beings possess a nature and a dignity, whatever their origins, that not only elevates them above apes but above humanity as hitherto known. Accordingly, Zarathustra rapidly proceeds to relegate virtually all pleasures and ideals traditionally understood as human to the category of the brutish.

Yet there is a highly traditional cast to Zarathustra's condemnation of tradition; his revaluation of the Christian meaning of heaven and earth is enmeshed in traditional theological categories and philosophical assumptions.[16] For example, although he avoids stating precisely in what human wisdom consists, he characterizes the wisest as "a mere conflict and cross between plant and ghost." His caricature of the view common to the biblical (and Platonic) understanding that a human being is composed of two elements of quite different rank—body and soul—reveals a dependence on traditional doctrines that he means to put behind him. Moreover, his entreaty to his brothers to abandon "otherworldly hopes" and to *"remain faithful to the earth"* reflects a reversal, not a repudiation, of the distinction between heaven and earth (Z Prologue 3).

Indeed, Zarathustra continues to operate within the parameters of the Christian tradition inasmuch as he holds that sinning still exists although he knows that God is dead, for at the very least "sin" implies transgression of commandments, order, or laws not of the individual's own making. But how can sin persist when God is dead, and consequently the underlying reality that makes sin a violation has been refuted or overcome? Unfazed by these difficulties, Zarathustra solemnly intones that "To sin against the earth is now the most dreadful thing, and to esteem the entrails of the unknowable higher than the meaning of the earth" (Z Prologue 3). Regarding "the meaning of the earth" as fundamentally stable, self-subsistent, and knowable, he declares his preference for the real and permanent against the imaginary and fleeting.

Indeed, just as Christianity asks men and women to sacrifice what they desire in this life for the sake of rewards in heaven, Zarathustra asks the townspeople to make the supreme sacrifice for the sake of "the meaning of earth." A man's "greatest experience" occurs when he learns to despise his own happiness, reason, and virtue. Zarathustra condemns the people as "polluted streams" not only because they fall dreadfully short of excellence, but also because, lost in the pursuit of phantasms of happiness, reason, and virtue, they are entirely oblivious to their despicable condition. The people are mediocrities who no longer value or understand the difference between mediocrity and excellence. They have ceased to hunger for or comprehend transcendence and to despise or recognize mediocrity. As a confirmation of Zarathustra's low opinion of the people, when he evokes the advent of the superman in charged terms of lightning and frenzy, the people badly miss his meaning: a voice from the crowd asks him to produce the tightrope walker whose performance had brought them to the marketplace—and all the people laugh.

Zarathustra is amazed. But is it not his amazement that is amazing?

Zarathustra's heralded powers of speech and his striking evocation of the superman neither agitate nor inspire the people. It is tempting to attribute his icy reception to the people's obtuseness. Yet would a shrewd or prudent teacher persist in haranguing an inattentive audience? Although his rhetoric is thoroughly ineffective as a means for presenting his gift of wisdom to the people, his ineffective rhetoric reflects the character of his wisdom. Caught by surprise when the people crudely interpret his metaphors for the superman in light of the circus entertainer they expect, Zarathustra appears to have failed to take his criticism of fellow human beings seriously. While his frenzy does not disturb the people's intellectual and moral slumber, their slumbers feed his frenzy.

Why does Zarathustra choose the marketplace to introduce a radical critique of the way of life centered around the marketplace? And what need impels him to resume his speech where he had broken it off, in spite of his acknowledgment that he cannot make his teaching comprehensible to the people? What irresistible impulse goads him to persist in his hopeless, self-defeating task? Zarathustra appears temporarily blind to the fact that to endear himself to the people he must debase himself by popularizing his teaching. Impossibly, he wants to gain the adoration of the very object of his poisonous denunciations. He both despises the multitude and craves the fame that is theirs alone to confer.[17] He depends on the people for their recognition of his teaching that all dependence is depraved.

Resuming his exhortation, Zarathustra stresses the connection between danger and perfection. Great pain and great renunciation are, for him, the precondition for great lives, that is, for lives that overcome what is human in man. Reciting a kind of prophecy foretelling the advent of a new type of being, he proclaims that man is an incomplete being, a dangerous inbetween, neither beast nor superman (Z Prologue 4; cf. BGE 62). This means that the goal of a human life is determined by the fact that human beings are essentially incomplete, lacking a goal. Being a bridge and not an end, human beings require a goal appropriate to their open-ended character. That goal is the superman. Revealing the teleological dimension of his call for the transcendence of man, Zarathustra urges the people to adopt the superman as their end or telos, to devote their lives to the establishment of his reign on earth.

Frenetic motion and intense, dissatisfied yearning characterize the states of the soul Zarathustra loves (Z Prologue 4). Accordingly, he establishes the intensification of pain and suffering as a man's cardinal duty and a visible token of his election. Loving the man who agonizes over his sense of incompleteness, Zarathustra regards the ability to suffer the human condition as a touchstone of excellence. Excellence is promoted by seeking spiritual danger, tottering on the edge of the abyss, swinging from one intense desire and inevitable disappointment to another equally intense and ill-starred desire. The chaos in a man's soul is, for Zarathustra, like a badge of honor that separates men in the order of rank.

His view is a forerunner of the popular opinion that the intensity of the *Angst* it harbors is a reflection of a soul's depth and capacity for spiritual insight. Agitation is more estimable than equanimity because in light of the infinite causes of agitation, equanimity must reflect superficiality and ignorance, a blindness to the real precariousness, fluidity, and impermanence of the things human beings cherish.[18] Zarathustra's praise of agitation in the soul thus is rooted in controversial metaphysical views and reflects strong opinions about true or real human needs. The exaltation of agitation and the concomitant depreciation of equanimity are grounded in the view that conventional morality and bourgeois civilization frustrate the higher task proper to a being who lacks but needs an end—and that task is making an end for himself.

The eventual emergence of the superman depends upon the practice of virtue in the present. Zarathustra conceives of virtue as a form of self-love. Self-love is necessarily the love of an incomplete self, the self's love of its unresolved and painful longings. Such virtue is properly an addiction and a catastrophe. Loving virtue insofar as it causes or amplifies alienation and anxiety, Zarathustra teaches that the way to overcome alienation and anxiety is to exacerbate them and take them beyond the limit. Only by seeking out a life-and-death struggle, by confronting its own greatest danger, can a self transcend the wretched contentment for which conventional moral and political life prepares it. Few virtues are good, but one is best of all for concentrating one's energies into a single, pure, consuming force (Z Prologue 4).

Dionysian images, marked by explosive energy and a rhetoric of extremes, abound as Zarathustra exhorts the crowd to shoulder the crushing burden of transforming their everyday lives into nothing less than a justification of existence. Reserving his love for those who, throwing caution to the wind, renounce all else in order to prepare the advent of the superman, he declares that reason must become a hungry lion, voracious and bestial; virtue and justice should set the soul ablaze; pity ought to dictate the supreme sacrifice made by Jesus. The object of Zarathustra's hope and love must possess superhuman or divine powers inasmuch as he "justifies [*rechtfertigt*] future and redeems [*erlöst*] past generations." Having assigned divine prerogatives and responsibilities to those who make the superman their goal, Zarathustra closes his first speech with a dramatic prophecy that links the superman to heavenly wonders and implies that he himself is a kind of prophet: "Behold, I am a herald of the lightning and a heavy drop from the cloud; but this lightning is called *superman*" (Z Prologue 4).

To his continued amazement, Zarathustra's vision of the redeeming man-god elicits still more laughter from the crowd. He naively wonders whether he must adopt the shrill sermonizing rhetoric of conventional religious leaders to capture the crowd's heart (Z Prologue 4). The irony is that while rejecting the content of conventional piety he has already adopted, but with poor results, the terms, the pose, and even something akin to the aim of the priests he denounces. Like a parody of an itinerant preacher, he seeks to redeem a fallen world and save lost souls, but unlike the Christian priests and theologians he condemns, he finds no takers for his message of redemption.

The mocking laughter in response to his exhortation to serve the superman prompts Zarathustra to "speak to them [the people] of what is most contemptible." Wounded by the contempt showered upon him, he repays like with like; he retaliates by hurling at the people a vision of their ultimate degradation, "that is the *last man*" (Z Prologue 5). With this act of revenge, Zarathustra once again seems bent on misunderstanding the people. For he proceeds as if the people he condemns as weak and paltry could possess the powers of comprehension to discern, or the strength of character to acknowledge, an image of themselves in his devastating portrait of the last man.

The last man whose image Zarathustra flings at the people is the antithesis of the superman and therefore, like the superman, an extreme. Whereas the superman symbolizes the transcendence of the human condition, the last man is marked by the absence of higher aspirations; he is little more than a well-fed and self-satisfied beast. Incapable of imagining, much less striving for worthy goals, the last man is almost subhuman because he is numb to wonder and shame alike.

Inasmuch as his will is weak and shriveled, the last man is decidedly inferior to the slavish man whose religion of love, according to the *Genealogy*, arises from a seething hatred of health and nobility. Whereas the slavish man is consumed with envy for the power he lacks and wants, and is prepared to will nothing rather than not will, the last man, knowing neither ambition nor yearning, wants for nothing and scarcely wills. Whereas the slavish man despises what is good and reveres what is poisonous and corrupting, the last man cannot muster the energy for judgment. Whereas the slavish man, remembering the taste of freedom, yanks recklessly at his chains, the last man meekly obeys orders and is content to avoid causing a disturbance. Whereas the slavish man chomps at the bit, the last man obeys like a domesticated plow animal. The last man is more despicable than the slave, for the slave, consumed with envy and driven by corrupted passions, at least manifests the life of the will, still kicking.[19]

The last men form a society of sad sacks who believe that they exemplify the supreme achievements of the human spirit. Perfectly pleased with themselves, the last men regard themselves as second to none: "We have invented happiness," say the last men, and they blink. And indeed, the last men are inventive or creative in their way, bringing into existence a new and matchlessly degraded form of life. But their invention is based on ignorance of themselves and their world. Indeed, failing to see their reflection in Zarathustra's words, the crowd interrupt him and clamor for him to turn them into "these last men," desiring the very fate from which he had hoped to save them.

It is a doleful sight when the people ask Zarathustra to turn them into the insipid last men. Yet it is more than a touch pathetic that Zarathustra should advertise his new teaching in the marketplace, allowing himself to be humiliated by the crowd's rejection and incited by their mocking to lash out with a stupefying picture of their future. His frustration betrays a distorted perception of his own rhetorical gifts and a striking incapacity to draw practical conclusions from his basic convictions; for it is precisely his diagnosis of "the last man" that explains the people's inability to comprehend the contemptible character of the last man's life.

The conclusion of his speech on the last man marks a change in Zarathustra's orientation. He sadly realizes that his education in solitude has made it impossible for him to address the people effectively. Before he can adopt a new course of action, though, a spectacle overhead commands attention (Z Prologue 6). No sooner does the tightrope walker commence his performance than a motley-clothed jester dances out upon the rope, mocking and reproaching him "in an awe-inspiring voice" for venturing where he does not belong and for blocking the way of his superior. Then, contemptuous of the tightrope walker's safety, the jester leaps over his head, causing the acrobat to lose his balance, or his will, and to plummet to the ground.

The description of the tightrope walker's plunge into the marketplace recalls the account Nietzsche's madman furnishes of man's spiritual fall into the swirling abyss resulting from the revelation of the death of God

(Z Prologue 6; cf. GS 125). The tightrope walker evokes the death-defying adventures or "limit experiences" that Zarathustra sees as necessary to the discipline of the superman. As Zarathustra kneels beside him, the tightrope walker, maimed and mortally wounded, regains consciousness and states that the jester who tripped him was the devil and that the devil will now drag him to hell. Zarathustra, however, denies the reality of the devil and hell, God and heaven. Yet in assuaging the dying man's fear that he will be sent to the devil by proclaiming that the Christian vision is illusory, Zarathustra at the same time robs him of his highest hope. Drawing the moral implications from Zarathustra's dogmas, the dying tightrope walker says that if Zarathustra is right about the nonexistence of the devil and the mortality of the soul, then death is not fearful and life is not valuable.

According to the tightrope walker's reasoning, if heaven and hell do not exist, then human beings do not differ from beasts and therefore are not accountable for their actions: everything is permitted, nothing is punished, and human life is meaningless. Yet because it is the loss of meaning in human existence that strikes the greatest terror in Zarathustra's heart, he abruptly rejects the tightrope walker's inference. The tightrope walker's life was not contemptible but praiseworthy, Zarathustra hastens to affirm, because the tightrope walker dared to leave his tower and, heedless of the consequences, attempted to cross over. Ignorant of that goal for which he risked his life, he accepted his vocation although fraught with danger.

The tightrope walker, however, had not said that his life was contemptible, but that lacking divine supports human life was simply a species of animal life and therefore devoid of moral significance. It was Zarathustra who declared that merely animal life is contemptible. Thus Zarathustra permits himself to invoke traditional categories of praise and blame while repudiating the traditional support of such moral judgments. These complexities notwithstanding, the dying man expresses his gratitude to Zarathustra, and Zarathustra, admiring the man for having made danger his vocation, promises to bury him with his own hands. Although he displays compassion and admiration for the tightrope walker, Zarathustra's calm, approving demeanor while he witnesses his public humiliation and fatal fall reflects Zarathustra's opinion, stressed in the opening speech on the superman, that no cost is too great to pay for bringing about the superman's way of life.

A New Truth

Zarathustra's mounting frustration and the crowd's growing hostility compel him to leave the marketplace. Yet his public humiliations prove instructive. Before the prologue ends he declares that he has beheld "a new truth" (Z Prologue 9; see also Z IV "On the Higher Men" 1). Henceforth he will abandon the hope of educating the people and will devote himself to educating hermit-creators and "whoever still has ears for the unheard of" in the steps necessary to become a superman: "Living companions *I need,* who follow me because they want to follow themselves—wherever *I want*" (Z Prologue 9, emphasis added). Still focusing on his own needs and wants, Zarathustra now needs and wants to lure away a few rather than convert or redeem the herd. And the character of his motive, the quality of the redemption, and the degree of independence he truly wishes for his companions are called into question by his insistence that those who rebel must submit to his needs and wants.[20] The fear that Zarathustra has become merely a more selective seeker after admirers is reinforced in parts II and III by the hapless crew of worshipful disciples who gather around him.

In fact, Zarathustra's inability to overcome his concern with the opinion of the people, though he is chastened and in possession of "a new truth," is already in evidence. He proclaims his desire to antagonize the people and arouse their wrath. No longer wishing to be a shepherd to the herd, he declares his desire "to be called a robber by the shepherds" (Z Prologue 9). Yet his wish to be recognized as a criminal shows that despite his decision to confine his pedagogical efforts to the few he has not yet emancipated himself from the desire for honor among the many. If he cannot achieve fame as a hero, he will at least bask in the limelight as an outlaw. Thus his dramatic repudiation of his ambition to educate the people reflects his continuing dependence upon them.

Zarathustra's "new truth" involves the realization that his good consists in creativity. Creativity, or the ethics of creativity, places the creator in opposition to the political authorities, for the man most hateful to "the good and the just"—that is, ordinary, conventional citizens—is "the man who breaks their tables of values, the breaker, the law breaker; yet he is the creator" (Z Prologue 9). But what is it that Zarathustra's creator creates? And why can't the creator break the hold of conventional values over himself without breaking the table of values for "the good and the just"? What is to prevent the creator from emancipating himself from the bonds of conventional morality while leaving intact the vulnerable cluster of opinions, customs, and norms that sustain social and political life? Is it that the act or education by which the true creator comes to see through the values that dominate in his society requires that he strip away the aura of legitimacy of those values for the rest of society? Or rather, does such value-smashing represent a gratuitous act of violence? Must the destruction that precedes and accompanies creation be political destruction?

Political life could be seen as a precondition for the superman's development, just as a parents' household and authority equip children ultimately to leave home and establish an independent life. More important, one might confine boldness and originality to the realm of thought and private affairs while functioning in society as a law-abiding citizen. This describes Kierkegaard's knight of faith, who, despite his extraordinary spiritual life, appears in public indistinguishable from an ordinary citizen, the conduct of Socrates' philosopher in imperfect regimes, and the life of the free spirit and the philosopher as Nietzsche occasionally depicts them.[21]

This, however, is not Zarathustra's way. In the prologue, he maintains a desire for public recognition of his radical ambitions. Along with his aspiration to attain an unprecedented height, he yearns for the satisfaction of having others know that his insight into what is needed exceeds that of all others. Therefore, he is compelled to make an exhibition of his prowess. Subsequently, he will come to understand that his radical ambition requires the repudiation of all forms of dependence, including the dependence on having others recognize his freedom from dependence. In the meantime, echoing the jester, he makes his goal the sole good: "To my goal I will go—on my own way; over those who hesitate and lag behind I shall leap. Thus let my going be their going under" (Z Prologue 9). Heedless of the consequences of his action for the rest of society, Zarathustra views the expounding of his vision of human excellence to those who have ears to hear it as his first responsibility and sole task.

Zarathustra's last speech in the prologue, like his first, takes place in the presence of the sun. Whereas in the first speech he declared his envy for the sun's happiness and proclaimed that his own wisdom was ripe for distribution, he now proclaims his devotion to his animals, the eagle and the serpent, the proudest and the cleverest (klugste) animals under the sun (Z Prologue 10). Lowering his sights from the heavens, he says that his animals are his friends and maintains that there is a harmony between his pride and his cleverness. He spots his eagle "soar[ing] through the sky in wide circles" with his serpent coiled around its neck. This strange alliance has an ominous aspect, for cleverness so situated is both dependent upon and a mortal threat to pride. Announcing that he has found men more dangerous than animals and that he now wishes to be led by his strangely related serpent and eagle, Zarathustra seems to vindicate the counsel of the old saint in the forest who told him to prefer animals in the forest to other men. Yet Zarathustra's animals embody a threat of their own.

Zarathustra's pride seems no longer bound up with teaching and giving but rather with the attainment of greater knowledge: "That I might be more clever! That I might be clever through and through like my serpent" (Z Prologue 10). The sight of a serpent coiled around the neck of his eagle flying round and round, this image of cleverness as a circling circle, evokes the eternal return but with a menacing edge, for cleverness is carried aloft by external powers, a hostage to the whims of pride.[22] And this powerful suggestion that cleverness is both dependent upon and a threat to pride augers a fateful defect dwelling in Zarathustra's highest hope.

Conclusion

We learn about a teacher both from the ideals he reveres and from those he reviles; and we gain knowledge from studying his vices as well as his virtues. In the prologue, where Zarathustra is driven by a desire to teach people how they should live in light of his discovery that God is dead, his failings are as noteworthy as is his new vision. His practical incompetence and political ineptitude are manifested in his rhetorical failures and his misapprehensions about how the people will react to his radical teaching. His seething contempt for and violent denunciation of ordinary lives reflect a tendency to judge political life in terms of prodigiously high standards. And his uncompromising individualism, embedded in his vision of a radical transcendence of conventional notions of happiness, reason, and virtue, presses toward the radical depreciation of all forms of political life and the severance of the connection between politics and human excellence.

Zarathustra's depreciation of politics is neither accidental nor incidental. It is steadily intensified in parts I and II as he moves toward his surreal reconciliation with eternity at the end of part III. To anticipate: Zarathustra's conception of the superman severs the connection between the highest life and the requirements of political community by its extreme exaltation of the will. The effort to extend one's will forces individuals apart into worlds of their own making. Indeed, Zarathustra's ethics of the creative self clashes with the very idea of the human being as a social and political animal. The demand for total mastery, the quest for unconditioned creativity, the uncompromising aspiration to expand the domain of what is one's own creation to the limits, undermines the common life that makes politics, friendship, and love possible. Men and women retain only an abstract humanity in common when they are charged with the endless, thankless task of increasing the scope of their self-legislation until their command is complete.

Zarathustra's superman reflects an ethical vision that transcends Left and Right by radically denigrating political life as a whole. From Zarathustra's perspective, the dreams of universal brotherhood and particularist community alike entrap the rare individual in stultifying prisons produced and maintained by forces external to his will. Part I of *Thus Spoke Zarathustra* encourages the hope that liberating forms of life created by rare individuals for single occupancy are possible and desirable.

6

The Ethics of Creativity:
Thus Spoke Zarathustra (Part I)

Part I of *Thus Spoke Zarathustra* gives an account of "the way of the creator." Solemn denials that Nietzsche articulates a positive moral vision and elaborate theoretical arguments as to why he could not or would not crumble before the fact that Nietzsche's Zarathustra does spell out a new ethics. This ethics does not consist of rules of right conduct but is a specific form of life to which those who would be creators must conform. The way of the creator includes an understanding of the highest possibilities of the human spirit, a distinctive notion of virtue, and a frank account of the proper role in the good life of the state, romantic love, and friendship.

Zarathustra's new ethics is addressed to rare human beings capable of proving themselves worthy of the discovery that God is dead by making themselves gods. The speeches in part I show that spiritual excellence so understood requires the relentless and systematic stripping away of every political and human attachment. The path to the superman, however, does not end with the transcendence of political life. The speeches in parts II and III reveal that the ascent from man to superman requires not only overcoming all forms of dependence on other human beings but also surmounting every external power that conditions the will and thereby limits self-mastery. Inasmuch as Zarathustra conceives of the creator as one who makes his own will a law (Z I "On the Way of the Creator"), his new ethics should be seen as a radicalization of the characteristically modern doctrine according to which the good is equated with freedom and freedom is understood in terms of living under laws that one makes for or gives to oneself.[1]

Following in the footsteps of political philosophy as it is traditionally understood, Zarathustra seeks to articulate the distinctive and enduring features, or nature, of human beings in order to determine how such creatures should best live. His audacious and outlandish conclusion, that to live well human beings must make themselves gods, is rooted in fundamental convictions typical of Nietzsche's thought. Like Nietzsche's madman, Zarathustra knows that God is dead; and in full agreement with the madman, he believes that as a consequence of the discrediting of a moral order inhering in nature, prescribed by reason, or given by God it has become imperative, for human beings who are able, to become gods themselves. Human beings can make themselves gods by fully liberating the creative will. Subject to what he has authorized, formed, or willed, Zarathustra's creator lives in accordance with what is at one and the same time an ethics of creativity and an ethics of self-deification.

Zarathustra's new ethics comes to light in his efforts in part I to teach it to others. Many of his speeches are aimed at inducing certain gifted men[2] to adopt a heretofore untried, obscure, and terribly harsh way of life. He admonishes his interlocutors to repudiate the moribund happiness and desiccated beliefs that have comprised Christian bourgeois civilization and to assume the severe demands and undergo the exacting sacrifices that lead to the attainment of human excellence as he newly interprets it. The severe demands and exacting sacrifices point resolutely away from politics: dedication to the task of self-perfection requires of the superman, among other things, complete dissolution of the bonds that tie him not only to the larger political community but to family and friends and in the end, to all human beings.[3]

Thus Zarathustra's new ethics contains an answer to the famous question raised by Aristotle in book III of the *Politics* (1276b16–1277b30) concerning the relation between the good man and the excellent citizen. Whereas Aristotle taught that the good man and the excellent citizen coincide only in the best regime, the regime dedicated to virtue, Zarathustra's account of the way of the creator indicates that the good man and the excellent citizen constitute utterly opposed types, and thus the superman cannot find a home in any city. Speaking quite generally, Aristotle, and Plato too (*Republic* 496a–e, 592a), recognized an inherent tension between the philosophical life and the good citizen's life that did not preclude the philosopher living as a peaceful, law-abiding citizen within an imperfect city, privately benefiting his friends while pursuing the highest or philosophical life. In contrast, according to Zarathustra, the highest human life brooks no compromise or reconciliation with the political community. Zarathustra enlarges the gulf between virtue and politics to unbridgeable proportions. As Zarathustra comes to understand him, the superman stands opposed to all forms of social and political life. The comparative absence in *Thus Spoke Zarathustra* of speeches devoted to the traditional themes of politics is not an oversight but a consequence of the ethics of creativity. Zarathustra does not provide a new politics *because* of his interpretation of the ethical significance of political life. The metamorphosis from man to superman dictates the overcoming of human beings' existence as social and political animals and thereby renders the care for and the organization of political society trivial pursuits.[4]

Part I of *Thus Spoke Zarathustra* shows, among other things, how Zarathustra's denigration of politics follows from his extreme elevation of the goal of humanity. This extreme elevation is thrown into sharp relief by his first speech, the parable "On the Three Metamorphoses," in which he presents a metaphoric description of the stages through which a vaguely defined elect few ascend to spiritual excellence by purging themselves of prejudice and delusion. The knowledge and purity such spirits attain requires severe solitude and results, says Zarathustra, in rendering the self master of its world. Such mastery requires a kind of virtue. In fact, Zarathustra imparts a new meaning to the old notion of virtue as he sets forth the specific kind of excellence that liberates and empowers the creative will. Mastery also involves a whole way of life. Accordingly, in a variety of speeches Zarathustra clarifies the life of the creator by expounding the purpose of the state, romantic love, and friendship. These speeches reveal an insuperable contradiction between the one best life and any and all forms of political life.

Zarathustra's speeches manifest a grim unity. For all practical purposes, he completes his praise of the superman as a creator by the end of part I. Why then does Nietzsche continue to unfold Zarathustra's saga? My view is that definite philosophical reasons compel Zarathustra to carry forward his quest: dissatisfaction with his new ethics prompts him to keep talking and searching. The fruitful question is what inadequacy of the creative life does he bring to light in part I that impels him to persist in his quest to articulate the character of human excellence. What dragon or demon harasses and haunts him, eventually forcing him to embrace the delusive doctrine of the eternal return?

From the beginning, Zarathustra's exaltation of the will, his effort to free the will from all that holds it fast, his ambition for the creator to remake the world in his own image, turns out to be a manifestation of a restless desire for transcendence or eternity. Because he understands creativity in terms of the full liberation and supreme empowerment of the will, Zarathustra's exhortation to cast off the fetters of all illegitimate constraints is entangled with the doctrine that all restraints on the will are illegitimate. Creativity, for Zarathustra, requires freedom from the need for others and is completed in mastery of the most basic forms of necessity, for all forms of necessity illegitimately diminish the will's sovereignty. The ethics of creativity, radically thought through, reveals itself to be not the antithesis of the yearning for permanence and transcendence but rather a monumental effort to satisfy that yearning by securing eternity entirely by means of one's own powers. Whether the supreme type is conceived of as the self-legislating source of all human values, as in part I of *Zarathustra,* or as the impassioned thinker and master of the eternally recurring selfsame reality, as in later parts, his vocation entails the renunciation of community and tradition, law and political obligation, family, romantic love, and friendship.

A Parable on the Superman

The first speech of part I, "On the Three Metamorphoses," an overture sounding many of the fundamental themes in *Zarathustra,* offers an allegorical account of how "the strong reverent spirit that would bear much" becomes first a camel, then a lion, and finally, in its ascent to the loftiest heights, a child.[5] Although the parable appears to depict the discrete and necessary stages that lead to the overcoming of morality, in fact, the spirit's development is at every stage both motivated and constrained by the intellectual conscience, a kind of higher morality. Each of the spirit's basic transformations is the consequence of an apparent gain in understanding. On closer inspection, however, it turns out that each advance rests upon a dogmatic and dubious claim to metaphysical knowledge that serves the spirit's prodigious pride and demanding will. The upshot of Zarathustra's parable is that the achievement of ultimate freedom in which the spirit, reborn as a child, utters "a sacred 'Yes' and 'wills his own will,'" motivated as much by a desire for truth, however harsh and ugly, as by a desire for harsh and ugly truth, rests on dogmatic foundations. In this, Zarathustra's parable foreshadows the judgment his speeches as a whole offer about the origins of the ethics of creativity and the fate of the ambition to self-deification.

The strong, reverent spirit first appears as a humble and pious camel displaying unswerving devotion to a single task.[6] It seeks out teachers who can instruct it in "what is most difficult" (Z I "On the Three Metamorphoses"). Owing to its dreadful character, the pursuit of knowledge is what is most difficult. This emphasis on knowledge notwithstanding, the spirit's choice of mentors is dictated by an implicit and unexamined belief about which human type possesses wisdom; indeed, this initial choice seems to constitute the spirit's first test. Beseeching certain "heroes" to disclose to it how to exult in its strength, the spirit seems willing—indeed anxious—to undergo a litany of deprivations and humiliations. Exhibiting a powerful predisposition to identify strength with the capacity to bear ugly truths, the spirit that would bear much, to prove its valor, would it seems be compelled to create terrifying visions and dreadful images if they did not already exist.[7]

Though putting a question to the heroes about what is most difficult, the spirit does not so much as pause for an answer before it proposes a number of its own, evidently untutored interpretations of the humiliations, deprivations, and estrangements that reveal and build strength. Defining heroism in terms of the capacity to endure gruesome trials for the sake of repugnant knowledge and ugly truths, Zarathustra's parable seems to rest on the presupposition that the knowledge most worth possessing is intrinsically odious and nauseating.

In a remarkable series of metaphors, the "strong, reverent spirit that would bear much" envisages the brutal training reserved for it in its incarnation as a camel. The spirit, not merely prepared for the worst but actively seeking it, quickly confirms its deep-rooted intuition that truth is not splendid but sordid, not a cure but an affliction, not empowering but enervating. One wonders, however, whether the spirit's intuition about where to look for truth does not drastically bias its findings. Indeed, one has only to imagine the crushing impact on Zarathustra's "spirit that would bear much" were it to discover that the waters of truth were crystal clear lakes rather than "filthy waters" inhabited by repellent reptiles; or if it had feasted on the delicious fruits of knowledge rather than suffered hunger from nibbling on the paltry fare of "the acorns and grass of knowledge"; or if knowledge enabled it to acquire noble friends rather than resulting in friendship "with the deaf, who never hear what you want"; or if knowledge proved an enchanted forest and a delight to the eyes rather than a path to "the loneliest desert." Zarathustra's spirit thrives and depends for his deepest satisfactions on the concrete encounter with repellent realities.

The spellbinding images of a ghastly world in which "for the sake of the truth" one renounces the things and beings one cherishes almost obscure the fact that they are uttered as parts of questions put by the spirit rather than as findings confirmed by experience or reason. The spirit's vision of knowledge, friendship, truth, and love is asserted rather than argued. And although hypothetical, its understanding of the world is quickly absolutized and made the ground for a new and higher form of spirit. Not only is the outcome of the spirit's quest determined by the unexamined conviction that knowledge is abysmal, but Zarathustra's conception of who is to count as a worthy spirit is inevitably conditioned by the same dogma. Reminiscent of the fact that his own past is shrouded in secrecy, Zarathustra omits to explore the upbringing, education, and experience that mold a spirit capable of asking dangerous questions and inclined to the conclusions that evidence spiritual excellence and reveal knowledge's bitter harvest. Thus, the stage that was to show the strong spirit's submission to tradition instead reveals its attachment to nontraditional convictions congenial to its disposition. While the content of the convictions of Zarathustra's spirit is radical, the failure to expose those radical convictions to critical reflection is all too traditional.

The spirit as camel initiates the overcoming of tradition by first submitting to it. But the pious camel's discovery—or the confirmation of its preconceived notion—that the tradition to which it submits is tainted and untenable, though a difficult burden to bear, is neither the greatest discovery nor the most difficult burden. A greater confrontation awaits the spirit as it moves from challenging particular moral traditions to confronting the very idea of morality or a moral order before which the will must bow. That confrontation calls for a kingly courage and strength.

Compelled to seek out the extreme, the spirit abandons political life
as it speeds into "its desert." "In the loneliest desert" the spirit becomes
a lion, a hunter and beast of prey, the king of beasts, who seeks to "conquer his freedom" and become "master in his own desert" by defeating
"the great dragon." Whereas the camel finds particular moral traditions
dismally wanting, the lion battles the very idea of morality itself, represented in Zarathustra's parable by the great dragon called "Thou shalt."
Although the imperative "Thou shalt" evokes the Ten Commandments
and hence Judaism and Christianity, Zarathustra presents "Thou shalt"
as the paradigmatic form of moral utterance. The dragon who proclaims "Thou Shalt" stands in the way of the lion who, wishing to make
its will supreme, says "I will."

To attain "ultimate victory" the spirit must win absolute freedom,
which it comes to identify with absolute mastery. Since freedom and
mastery depend on the outcome of its battle with the dragon, the lion's
desire "to fight with the great dragon" is not itself a manifestation of
freedom or freely undertaken. Indeed, because the lion is constrained
by the desire for freedom and mastery to do battle, the question arises
as to what forces shaped its opinions about freedom and mastery. Does
the spirit seek freedom because it sees through the claims to transcendent foundations made by all moralities and uncovers their human
sources, or is the spirit driven to define morality as a contingent, man-
made system in order to satisfy its prodigious appetite for freedom? In
fact, the dogmatic assumptions that underlie the tests proposed by the
spirit as camel continue to determine its self-understanding as a lion.
Although its right to freedom is based on its purportedly superior
knowledge about the character of morality, the lion's insatiable longing
for freedom fetters it to a dogmatic certainty concerning the absolute
illegitimacy of all morality. And, paradoxically, this dogmatic certainty
is coupled with a claim to embody a higher ethic.

The dragon utters a stark challenge to the lion in the barren desert:
"All value has long been created and I am all created value." With curious credulity, the lion straightaway accepts the dragon's claims to be an
awful foe, a creature of exalted stature. But is it wise, or consistent with
the sacrifices the spirit as a camel endured for "the sake of the truth," to
trust the audacious claims of a mortal enemy?[8] Care for the truth dictates asking, as the lion does not, whether the dragon is a worthy enemy.
Whatever the reason for the lion's pious acceptance of the dragon's por-

tentous boast, the lion seems to have a stake in puffing up its adversary, in investing him with grandeur and grave significance. Would it not be a crushing blow, imperiling the worth of the spirit's labors, to discover at the climactic moment that the dragon who purported to stand for all value was instead an overblown, smoke-billowing impostor who stood for only some values?[9] Perhaps more difficult than confronting the dragon in the desert would be the demoralizing failure to find a worthy or proper enemy.[10]

The great dragon, representing the essential lie of conventional morality, is a worthy opponent inasmuch as it engages the regal lion's finest qualities. Since, however, the dragon fulfills a vital function in the realization of the spirit's aspirations, and because Zarathustra's tale alerts us to the human propensity for creating moralities, it is necessary to ask whether the lion in fact has surreptitiously created a formidable foe that does it honor. Would not questioning the dragon's spectacular claims be a greater test of strength than accepting them at face value? Is the courage that unconditionally affirms the collective illegitimacy of all forms of morality more splendid or noble than the courage called for in acknowledging a permanent doubt about rival moralities, and hence confronting the truth of, or within, each?[11]

The spirit's vested interest is powerful and clear.[12] If freedom is the human good, and freedom is understood as independence from constraints, external and internal alike, then either all constraints can be overcome or the good is unattainable. The question is whether the purported discovery of the artificial character of all morality spawns the moral imperative to acquire freedom, or rather whether in an attempt to justify a monstrous appetite for the good of freedom the spirit is driven to think away the claims of morality. In either case, the desire for untrammeled self-assertion is formed by imperatives arising from sources other than the self. The dragon, an intransigent foe of the will's desire for empowerment, proclaims: "Verily, there shall be no more 'I will.'" Yet in spite of the dragon's menacing overtones, Zarathustra's parable exudes optimism. There is no tragic conflict between the will's highest demands and morality, for the spirit can dissolve the conflict, bringing an end to the reign of ignorance and error by discovering the truth about morality, namely, that it is a nonbinding myth devoid of sanctions.

The victory of the lion's "I will" over the dragon's "Thou shalt" appears to entail the final discrediting of a natural, rational, or divinely revealed moral order. Still, the lion's victory relies upon the supposed discovery of a universal truth, namely, that the origins of morality lie in human beings. In harmony with Nietzsche's madman who found in the death of God the opportunity and the need to invent "festivals of atonement" and "sacred games," the new understanding of the origins of morality won by the spirit brings about the chance to exercise "the right [*Recht*] to new values." These new values redeem the world inhabited by the self that makes them. Thus Zarathustra's parable, like Nietzsche's parable of the madman, teaches that the only worthy response to the death of God and the collapse of traditional morality is to seize the powers that were previously thought to be the special prerogative of God.[13] But whereas Nietzsche's madman does not go beyond declaring the imperative to self-deification, his Zarathustra actually seeks to provide an account of the discipline by which one may become a god.

Zarathustra's ethics of self-deification presupposes the distinction between the sacred and the profane. His parable reveals that the resolute campaign directed against what was historically loved as most sacred does not require, indeed cannot survive, the rejection of the sacred as such. For in assigning the lion the task of proclaiming a "sacred 'No' even to duty," he attributes to the lion the power and the obligation to maintain perpetual vigilance against the illusion and caprice of conventional morality. In other words, Zarathustra affirms the sacred responsibility to renounce and eradicate false notions of the sacred.

Moreover, contrary to its aspirations, the lion fails to win freedom from the imperatives of morality as such. For although the old tablets are shattered, they are replaced with new ones upon which are engraved solemn commandments: Thou shalt sacrifice what is most dear for the sake of the truth; Thou shalt be free; Thou shalt revere reverence; and Thou shalt utter a sacred yes by willing your own will. The lion's apparent defeat of the dragon reveals itself as a stunning victory for morality, or the spirit's higher morality, inasmuch as right and obligation are conspicuously at work throughout the spirit's transformations and in its highest instantiation. Since the idea of the sacred persists and indeed is regenerated in the final metamorphosis of the spirit, the dragon, the symbol of morality, lives on and prospers in the spirit's heart.

Although blessed with an iron will and ferocious courage, the lion is unable to reap the fruits of its victory. Although the lion has won the freedom that is a prerequisite to the creation of "new values," Zarathustra declares that the lion is incapable of generating a new creed and thus is denied the greatest good. Apparently, the heroic virtues that enabled the spirit to overcome the old values and the old understanding of morality bar it from assuming "the right to new values."

The greatest good, toward which the spirit from the first has been ascending, the assumption of the right to the creation of "new values," is reserved for the spirit become a child. The surpassing merit of Nietzsche's decision to have his Zarathustra adopt the child as symbol for the supreme achievement of the spirit is that it dramatizes the deep ambiguity inhering in the good understood as pure creativity. On the one hand, the child reflects an extreme independence from morality and tradition. On the other hand, the child is also a dependent creature: fragile and vulnerable, weak and helpless, selfish and slavishly dependent, incapable of benefiting from the lessons of the past. A child's horizon is both unbounded and closed; its activity is context-free because its undeveloped intellect cannot retain or grasp the contours of any context. Zarathustra's striking image suggests that the spirit's finest hour is marked by a loss of consciousness, a drastic narrowing of awareness, and a radical break with previous experience.[14]

Thus the strong, reverent spirit would seem to lose itself and make a supreme sacrifice in achieving self-perfection, since the courage, pride, and capacity for reverence that characterize the spirit during its quest seem to evaporate at the very moment of the quest's fulfillment. Accordingly, total escape from tradition and history may prove a Pyrrhic victory. Can a child perform noble acts or dream of wholeness? Can a child strive for something great or stand alone? What of the child's instinct for rank and capacity for reverence—identifying marks, according to Nietzsche, of the noble soul (cf. BGE 263, 287)? Indeed, is not the child the antithesis of the spirit capable of discharging its strength and imposing its image on the world (cf. BGE 13, 203, 211)? What is clear is that the spirit's final stage culminates neither in the equanimity and wisdom of the sage nor in wild and frenzied Dionysian revelry. The question is whether the spirit's peak moment—entailing the freedom and innocence, but also the simplemindedness and helplessness of the child—is distinguishable from an infantilization of the spirit.

While Zarathustra's image brings to light an ominous defect in his conception of the supreme excellence, he does not yet take this defect to heart. Evoking the child's powers with venerable terms, he advances a prophetic description of the child-creator that simultaneously invites comparison to the omnipotent biblical God, creator of the heavens and the earth, and to Aristotle's conception of an impersonal divinity: "The child is innocence and forgetting, a new beginning, a game, a self-propelled wheel, a first movement, a sacred 'Yes.' For the game of creation, my brothers, a sacred 'Yes' is needed . . ." (Z I "On the Three Metamorphoses"). In the form of the child-god, Zarathustra's spirit becomes the pristine origin of movement and the primal source of meaning, a self-sufficient and self-determining master of its world.

But Zarathustra's intermingling of biblical imagery with vocabulary drawn from Aristotelian metaphysics complicates matters. The notion of "a new beginning" and the idea of what is "sacred" evoke the God of Genesis who creates the world *ex nihilo* at a discrete moment in time and whose creations are holy because he is holy. The "self-propelled wheel," reflecting uniform motion around a stationary center, and "a first movement" conjure up Aristotle's eternally selfsame divine intellect that imparts motion to the sensible world. It is not necessary to enter into the venerable debate, which reached peak intensity during the Middle Ages, concerning the ultimate compatibility of belief in the biblical God with acceptance of Aristotelian metaphysics, and in particular the critical conflict between the biblical view that the world was created in time and the Aristotelian view that the visible world is eternal. It is enough to observe that Zarathustra's complete indifference to the perplexing relation between divinity as understood by biblical religion and divinity as understood by Greek philosophy, reflected in his cavalier mixing of disparate elements rooted in conflicting traditions to create an image of the supreme human type, intensifies misgivings concerning his child-god. Not only is the synthesis of conflicting elements of extremely doubtful theoretical viability but each of the individual elements would seem to have been previously discredited, drawn as each is from traditions undercut by the lion's triumph over the dragon.

Combining the creativity of the biblical God and the reflexivity of Aristotle's divine being, the child rises to divinity insofar as he possesses a purified, uncorrupted will that makes its own activities the object of its exertions and insofar as by commanding himself he commands the whole of which he is a part: "the spirit now wills his own will, and he who had been lost to the world now conquers his own world." The child-god becomes the child-king through an act of self-creation and self-sanctification that simultaneously creates and sanctifies the world as a whole.

But if all values are created, the decisive question becomes why creativity and self-sanctification are deemed valuable and good. The teaching that the will and its offspring lack value unless value is self-imparted appears to give rise to an infinite regress: if the source of the will's value is the will's willing itself, what is the source of the value of the will's willing itself, that is, of the willing that wills the will? More sharply put, what conditions Zarathustra's exaltation of unconditioned creativity? And by what signs can a self-willed will be recognized? How can one who claims to have "conquer[ed] his own world" be sure that he is more than a madman who proclaims himself a god? Zarathustra's ordeal with the eternal return in parts II and III helps answer these questions by elucidating the manner in which a will could achieve absolute sovereignty. In particular, his ordeal clarifies the insuperable obstacles to making one's will a supreme law by showing that it is necessary to abandon wisdom in order to persuade oneself that one has become a god.

The Purpose of Virtue

Zarathustra's attack on conventional morality and political life is noteworthy both for its ferocity and for its form. Effectively radicalizing the young Marx's radical call to undertake the "ruthless criticism of everything existing,"[15] the mature Nietzsche puts in the mouth of the mature Zarathustra a battle cry that extends beyond the realm of ideas, if not demanding, at least sanctioning the ruthless annihilation of everything existing.[16] Zarathustra subordinates all considerations of justice to the production of the highest type; more precisely, he views the discovery, education, and preservation of the highest type as the sole demand of what is right and good. Although throughout his career Nietzsche flirts with the notion of a perfect political order that has as its highest and sole aim the creation of genius, Zarathustra is driven to repudiate political hopes and programs as he thinks through the requirements of the ethics of creativity. The logic of his new ethics compels Zarathustra to abandon the task of remaking society, and ultimately even to reject the narrow goal of serving others by acting as the herald and midwife to the superman. He discovers that founding, legislating, and ruling, at least in the political sense of these terms, constitute neither integral activities nor practical necessities of the good life. For Zarathustra's supreme type, politics is an unnecessary evil.

Zarathustra's repudiation of politics is grounded in his conception of virtue. "On the Teachers of Virtue" begins with a speech given by a sage whom Zarathustra has sought out on the basis of his reputation for speaking well "of sleep and of virtue." According to the sage, virtue has primarily functioned as a system of imperatives designed to mute desire and to induce an anemic tranquillity. The function of morality and religion, he explains, has been and still is to promote political order by serving as an opiate for the masses.

Although he recognizes that the sage is endowed with an enviable rhetorical skill, Zarathustra contemptuously dismisses him as a fool. In spite of the fact that Zarathustra is frequently regarded as denouncing his contemporaries for their obliviousness to the nihilistic outlook of the age, in this candid moment of private reflection—Zarathustra is engaging in a heart-to-heart talk with himself—he levels a different accusation against the preachers of virtue. Instead of criticizing the preachers of virtue for failing to take stock of the realities of nihilism, he attacks them for basing their religious ideas on a false belief in the metaphysical reality of nihilism: "And verily, if life had no sense and I had to choose nonsense, then I too should consider this the most sensible nonsense" (Z I "On the Teachers of Virtue").

At this juncture, Zarathustra's attack on conventional morality springs neither from a repugnance at consorting with the masses, nor from a distaste for the sage's style, nor finally from jealousy at the sage's legion of disciples. Adhering to the strictures elaborated in "On the Three Metamorphoses" dictating that moral judgments be purged of aesthetic and sentimental considerations, Zarathustra rejects the sage's teaching because it is based on a mistaken understanding of the world. Christian virtue is a reasonable response to nihilism, but the nihilistic interpretation of the world, Zarathustra indicates, is unreasonable. He concedes that if the meaning of human life were wholly elusive, then the preachers of virtue would be justified in teaching their life-denying creed; indeed, he declares that in such circumstances it would be sensible to follow them.

What, then, is the correct interpretation of human life that is blotted out by the sage's extravagantly pessimistic understanding? Zarathustra reveals that once he was a victim of the powerful delusion that the preachers of virtue have yet to escape, namely, that human well-being depends on the assumption that the ordinary sensible world somehow reflects a supersensible will or design (Z I "On the Afterworldly"). Thus Zarathustra found himself assaulted by the same hostile forces that overcame Greek tragedy, reaffirming Nietzsche's assertion in his first book that Socrates represents "the one turning point and vortex of so-called world history" (BT 15).

The turning point in his private confrontation with this formidable viewpoint, Zarathustra reveals, came when he realized that the hidden creator-god he aspired to discover was not a compelling interpretation of the world as it really is, but rather a wish or prayer that he had created for himself to alleviate his suffering. This discovery freed him from his self-made superstition. Having been set free by his gain in self-knowledge, and having generalized from his private disappointment to the discovery that all gods are "man-made," he "invented a brighter flame" for himself (Z I "On the Afterworldly"). Thus, he boldly pro-claims that not merely his god and heaven but all gods and afterworlds are false beliefs induced by human suffering and despair, and he pro-ceeds to make this knowledge, the knowledge that God is dead, which is a claim about the world based on his self-knowledge, the premise of his reinterpretation of virtue. He connects the lies about heaven and the delusions about Being to weary and suffering bodies, and he grounds the truth about the lies perpetuated about heaven and the delusions promulgated about Being in healthy bodies.

Both truth and lies ultimately originate in the ego. The same ego that creates lies and delusions, that projects value onto things, is itself valu-able because it is honest and speaks the truth:

> Indeed, this ego and the ego's contradiction and confusion still speak most honestly of its being—this creating, willing, valuing ego, which is the measure and value of things. And this most honest being, the ego, speaks of the body and still wants the body, even when it poetizes and raves and flutters with broken wings. It learns to speak even more honestly, this ego: and the more it learns, the more words and honors it finds for body and earth.
>
> A new pride my ego taught me, and this I teach men: no longer to bury one's head in the sand of heavenly things, but to bear it freely, an earthly head, which creates a meaning for the earth. (Z I "On the Afterworldly")

The ego is both creative and truthful, proclaiming the truth about the primacy of its own creativity.[17]

Zarathustra's discovery of the real character of the ego gives rise to not only a "new pride" but also a "new will" (Z I "On the After-worldly"). The new pride teaches men to reject the lie of heaven and to freely create a meaning for the earth. The new will teaches men to affirm the creating, valuing, willing ego. Free or virtuous creativity is rooted in knowledge of the ego's creativity and authority. Zarathustra emphasizes that willing is elevated by being grounded in knowledge about the heavens and the real character of the ego and that such knowledge arouses great hostility: "Many sick people have always been among the poetizers and God-cravers; furiously they hate the knower [*den Erkennenden*] and that youngest among the virtues, which is called 'honesty' [*Redlichkeit*]. They always look backward toward dark ages; then, indeed, delusion and faith were another matter: the rage of reason was godlikeness, and doubt was sin" (Z I "On the Afterworldly").

Although he condemns the poetizing and God-craving practiced by the many sick people, Zarathustra condemns neither poetizing nor the reasonableness of seeking to imitate God. Indeed, he advocates a poetizing guided by the virtue of honesty and rooted in the knowledge proclaimed by the ego so that human beings can give up their unreasonable worship of God and proceed to the higher task of making themselves gods.

The "awakened and knowing" honestly grasp the real character of body and soul and understand the relation between them (Z I "On the Despisers of the Body"). The reason of the body, Zarathustra says, is more reasonable than the wisdom of the spirit or soul. Although he conceives of the soul as an aspect of body, Zarathustra understands the body in terms that recall the traditional conception of the soul: "The body is a great reason, a plurality with one sense, a war and a peace, a herd and a shepherd. An instrument of your body is also your little reason, my brother, which you call 'spirit'—a little instrument and toy of your great reason" (Z I "On the Despisers of the Body").

The body, like the traditional soul, is a unity that hosts difference, an entity that both commands and obeys, and an intelligible structure including but not exhausted by reason. Those who despise the body are misguided but respectable inasmuch as contempt is a precondition for reverence (cf. Z Prologue 4). Those who feel contempt for the body need only come to understand that contempt too is a form of creativity, an expression of the willing and valuing ego, in order to break free from created, otherworldly heavens so that they may satisfy their real needs by self-consciously creating heaven on earth. But this emancipation of creativity from hatred of the body requires virtue.

The virtue in question must be uniquely one's own and an "earthly virtue" that seeks the good because the good is known to be self-created (Z I "On Enjoying and Suffering the Passions"). Virtues are really children of the passions. Rejecting the ancient doctrine of the unity of the virtues, Zarathustra argues that self-knowledge is advanced by the fomenting of a war within the soul or spirit among the many virtues that contend for dominance and lust for total mastery. On the view that the passions ought to be incited to a fever pitch, Zarathustra urges his "brother" to become a battleground on which conflicting desires are deliberately polarized and emboldened to seek supremacy to the point where they come into lethal combat with one another. Thus, he adapts Hobbes's dismal depiction of the war of all against all as an ennobling regulative ideal for the soul's experience of its heterogeneous desires and needs. The contest among individuals for honor and supremacy that Nietzsche asserted "is necessary to preserve the health of the state" (HC, p. 36; see also BGE 158) is transformed by Zarathustra into a ruthless war waged among the passions and virtues for domination of the soul.

The goodness of this agonizing contest, this rarefied restlessness within the soul, stems from the fact that the very acts that constitute the self's triumph over the routine and the given—the creation of artifacts, images, and values—inevitably become new instruments of enslavement. Zarathustra envisages a self that resembles a Kafkaesque convict, constantly engineering prison breaks only to find, just beyond the loathsome gray walls from which he has escaped, a larger, more odious, higher-security prison of his own making. Self-making for Zarathustra is a terrifying responsibility because its presupposition seems to deprive one of a principle for calling a halt to the process. The necessity of overcoming all traces of political life is but one fearful consequence of Zarathustra's identification of virtue with self-making.

Nevertheless, Zarathustra's revaluation of virtue remains within the domain of the traditional conception of virtue it presumes to supplant, inasmuch as Zarathustra openly and unabashedly relies on a definite opinion about a human being's essential capabilities, distinguishing attributes, and highest task. This can be seen in a famous speech in which he asserts on the basis of his observations of "many lands and many peoples" that every people's conception of good and evil originates in its will to power (Z I "On the Thousand and One Goals").[18] He sets forth a seemingly objective, universal, and necessary law, namely, that every people establishes as holy what it finds rare and difficult, and fixes as good what enables it to rule and surpass its neighbors. Although opinions about the holy and the good differ vastly from people to people, the origin of these opinions is invariant.

This universal invariance, of course, cannot be established by empirical observation, however thorough. Nor does Zarathustra claim to so establish it. The logic of justification differs from the logic of discovery. Although he traces his discovery of the will to power to his observations, he vindicates his observations by advancing a theoretical understanding of man, at once descriptive and normative, that functions exactly as does a conception of human nature in traditional political philosophy:

> Verily, men gave themselves all their good and evil. Verily, they did not take it, they did not find it, nor did it come to them as a voice from heaven. Only man placed values in things to preserve himself—he alone created a meaning for things, a human meaning. Therefore he calls himself "man," which means: the esteemer.
>
> To esteem is to create: hear this, you creators! Esteeming itself is of all esteemed things the most estimable treasure. Through esteeming alone is there value: and without esteeming, the nut of existence would be hollow. Hear this, you creators! (Z I "On the Thousand and One Goals")

Esteeming and creating on the basis of the knowledge that man is essentially an esteemer and creator is the pinnacle of virtuous activity. As Zarathustra's remarks on the state, romantic love, and friendship make clear, the creator's path to the pinnacle must leave politics and other people far behind.

The Purpose of the State

Generally speaking, Nietzsche condemns the modern state for its implacable hostility to human excellence. Although Nietzsche did occasionally entertain the hope for, and sketch the image of, a radically aristocratic political order exclusively dedicated to promoting the highest forms of human flourishing,[19] Zarathustra's ethics grants no place to politics in the best life. It is important to observe that Zarathustra takes scarcely any notice of the practical and material requirements for sustaining the life devoted to human excellence. But this neglect is only one aspect of the fundamental tension in his ethics between political life and the best life. Indeed, his scattered remarks on law, the state, and the marketplace stress the fatal danger that political life poses to the best life.

Zarathustra's instrumental view of law, and the end he wishes the law to serve, are on display in his indictment of the "pale criminal." It is conventional to read "On the Pale Criminal," a speech that speaks of guilt and punishment and the manner in which conventional authorities make healthy men feel guilty about their red-blooded desires, as an anticipation of Freud. What such readings tend to miss is the practical significance for Zarathustra of the real relation between convention and human excellence, or law and real human needs.

For Zarathustra, crime and punishment derive their legitimacy from their capacity to justify and strengthen those who are fit to pursue the best life. Untroubled by the pale criminal's commission of robbery and murder, Zarathustra deplores the fact that the pale criminal's reason corrupts his original innocent impulse to kill in cold blood. In contrast to Dostoevsky's Raskolnikov, who comes to learn that even in the most favorable circumstances a human being who tries to play god by committing premeditated murder must suffer guilt in order to be redeemed from his crime, Zarathustra convicts his pale criminal for sullying an otherwise admirable deed by feeling guilt for the blood he spills. Instead of proudly declaring that robbery was a substitute for the murder for which he truly thirsted, the pale criminal shows himself unworthy of the original admirable impulse to violence by confessing that he accidentally murdered in the process of a robbery. His contrition, his bending his judgments to the moral prejudices of society, betrays the honest voice of his desires.[20] By accepting society's guilty verdict, the pale criminal submits to and participates in the conventional slandering of the body and desire.

Not only does Zarathustra denounce the people for weakening the pale criminal's resolve, but reaffirming the judgment he declared in the prologue that it is better to perish than live in wretched contentment, he declares his hope that the people themselves might perish from a criminal madness (Z I "On the Pale Criminal"). His avid praise of theft and murder for sport, and his eagerness for mass hysteria and destruction, reflect not only a contempt for the conventions that implement fundamental prohibitions of moral and political life but also exhibit the conviction that such fundamental prohibitions are themselves both conventional and unwise.

Zarathustra's contempt for convention and law is the outward and impious face of a higher piety. This higher piety emerges as he expands his attack on modern political institutions to include condemnation of the modern state for fatally impairing the development of the virtuous man. In "On the New Idol" he deplores the fact that the modern state is seen as the embodiment of God's will on earth (see also SE 4, p. 148). Assuming the role of the true prophet, he zealously denounces the state as a monstrous impostor peddling a false conception of redemption to the people. Enthusiastic devotion to the modern state, he declares, has come to assume the central role in people's lives formerly occupied by religious belief. Yet the nation-state, contrary to its seductive slogans, does not redeem; instead, it mutes the deep human need for redemption. Of course, in condemning the state as a modern idol Zarathustra borrows a chapter from a book he has been instrumental in consigning to the flames.

Like Marx, Zarathustra views the state as the opiate of the masses. However, on Zarathustra's view, this opiate is not fabricated and administered by an economically ascendant class to forestall discontent among an oppressed laboring class. Rather, the multitude seduces and conquers the natural elite by persuading them to accept base and enervating democratic mythologies that sanctify compassion, equality of rights, and the brotherhood of man. Capitalism and liberal democracy, on Marx's view the bane of the working class, represent for Zarathustra a decisive victory for the multitude of humanity. The real beneficiaries of the emergence of the modern nation-state are not, as Marx argued, the wealthy bourgeois property owners who, in order to satisfy their "wolfish hunger for profit," deploy the organs of the state to wring the last drop of surplus value—and life—from the vast class of wage laborers. Instead they are the weak and downtrodden themselves, who induce the state to sustain and care for them by providing food, shelter, rights, and entitlements. The state thereby not only straitjackets the "great souls" but squanders its limited resources that ought to be directed to cultivating the best type (see also GM III 14–15; A 8).

The modern state is marked by universal education, the diffusion of information through mass media, and the desire for acquisition, all of which lack, from Zarathustra's perspective, any saving graces. He holds that the comforts, conveniences, and supposed advantages provided by the modern state represent contemptible forms of pleasure and sanction a false, poisonous freedom. Indeed, genuine freedom is undermined by the political or legal freedom that is the hallmark of modern liberal democracies. He announces that it would be preferable to allow the "all-too-many," the "superfluous," to waste away and die rather than to permit the satisfaction of their needs to hamper the development of the well-constituted men of "rich hearts" (see also WP 373). But he is not bereft of compassion: his heart goes out to the handful of rare and gifted souls oppressed and dehumanized by the modern state. The form of domination in the modern state oppressing Zarathustra is the subjugation of the needs of the few to the requirements of the many.

Zarathustra does not, however, despair of the possibility of attaining freedom in the modern world, precisely because he severs the connection between freedom and the modern state. The "leap to freedom" of which only "great souls" are capable is a leap beyond the state: "Only where the state ends, there begins the human being who is not superfluous: there begins the song of necessity, the unique and inimitable tune." "A free life," as he envisages it, requires an abandonment of politics to make possible a reconciliation with necessity.

His understanding of the bitter antagonism between the interests of the few and the many leads Zarathustra to conclude in his next speech, "On the Flies in the Marketplace," that the health of the best men is imperiled in all forms of political society. He radicalizes the already extreme antagonism he has found between human excellence and political life: whereas in the previous speech he had admonished his brothers to seek solitude to escape from the specific dangers posed by the modern state, now he reveals that the first step outside of solitude places one squarely within the marketplace. He thereby implicitly denies, contrary to speculations Nietzsche entertains elsewhere, that a superior individual could construct an enclave or citadel in society, perhaps in association with others, sealed off from the invisible, poisonous stings of the people's jealousy for the lofty and rare (see, e.g., BGE 25, 26; HH 235).

The flight to solitude comes to appear not merely as a contingent response to the specific dangers that arise within the modern state but as a necessary withdrawal from political life rooted in the ethics of the creative will. Embedded in Zarathustra's assessment of the dangers that confront creators is not only the hardhearted view that the well-endowed are free from the obligation to care for the less fortunate, but also a remarkable confession of the essential vulnerability of the rare and gifted soul. Though Zarathustra avoids it, his speech provokes the disturbing question: what kind of delicate creature is this potential superman who allows himself to be driven from society by flies?

The Purpose of Romantic Love

Whereas the state can never be more than a hindrance to human excellence, the ethics of creativity assigns romantic love and friendship important though exclusively instrumental roles. In "On Chastity," Zarathustra affirms his preference for living alone, outside the city, and hence his freedom from the desires that are best or only satisfied in the company of others. He identifies as the greatest menace of city life, worse even than "to fall into the hands of a murderer," lying in the arms of a woman. Scorning those who identify sexual intercourse as the highest pleasure, he qualifies his condemnation by distinguishing between innocent and corrupt desire. He does not employ this distinction to defend sexuality springing from innocence but to identify the circumstances under which chastity is a virtue: namely, when chastity is effortless, accompanied by grace and prankishness, and results in the spiritualization of desire. And he connects the spiritualization of desire to the pursuit of knowledge. It is the knower, one who loves truth beyond considerations of utility, for whom he advocates as the true eroticism a sensual asceticism in which the desire for truth is as strong and intoxicating as the desire of a healthy body for another. Zarathustra's conviction that sexual desire represents a lowly form of eros that is elevated in the longing for and pursuit of knowledge reflects the powerful Platonic streak in his understanding of human excellence.[21]

In "On Little Old and Young Women," Zarathustra confides his troublesome "little truth" about woman to a "little old woman" utterly devoid of sexual charms. Though Zarathustra, who lives as a hermit, is a particularly unlikely expert on romantic love, and though his chosen interlocutor appears ill-suited to illuminate his way, the old woman prevails upon Zarathustra to share his teaching about woman. Zarathustra's major insight is that woman's chief task and highest hope is to serve not men in general but rather "the real man" *(der echte Mann).* She does this by providing recreation for the real man or rare soul, and by engaging in procreation for the purpose of rearing supermen. Woman's happiness is entirely subordinated to or equated with the realization of the dream of the superman. Born to serve, woman is relegated to the status of instrument or plaything, bereft of rights and prerogatives.

Although Zarathustra indicates that woman is by nature unfit to create and command, he is no simple misogynist. The nongifted man is consigned to a decidedly more slavish status than woman. In contrast to the woman who becomes the lover of a "real man," the slavish man lacks an essential function and hence is expendable. Zarathustra's teaching about woman's crucial instrumental task, however objectionable, reflects Nietzsche's consistently espoused view that morality and politics derive their sole justification from their capacity to serve a single goal— the production of the highest type—whether under the name genius, superman, or philosopher of the future.

Zarathustra condemns noninstrumental love, especially that form of romantic love which culminates in marriage, because it brings about the surrender of heroic ambitions and results in the lover's debasing loss of independence (Z I "On Child and Marriage"). He rejects the idea that marriage is the most desirable form of life for the vast majority, or, more precisely, he views the vast majority as unworthy to participate in so holy a rite as marriage. Second to none in investing marriage and child-rearing with gravity and vital importance, he indicates that the desire for marriage and children is common, but the entitlement exceedingly rare. In the light of his higher piety Zarathustra comes to understand marriage as a sacred undertaking for the rearing of the superman, and he is led to denounce as desecrations the vast majority of actual marriages.[22]

Zarathustra sees marriage and love as means to a higher ideal: love is "merely an ecstatic parable . . . a torch that should light up higher paths" (Z I "On Child and Marriage").[23] Indeed, the best of loves for another human being is a mere stepping-stone to a blissful solitude: one has not really learned to love well until one overcomes the need to love another. Zarathustra's conception of friendship is no less chilling in its uncompromising rejection of the dignity of political and practical life; but like his understanding of marriage it is a consistently drawn consequence of the ethics of creativity.

The Purpose of Friendship

Readers have been tempted both to romanticize Zarathustra's vision of friendship and to cast it in Aristotelian terms. The fear that life in the modern state withers the will of great souls, and the teaching that romantic love plays an essentially instrumental role in the best life, do not by themselves preclude an exalted notion of friendship. Friendship rooted in mutual dedication to the acquisition of virtue may flourish precisely at the point where human beings overcome lower-ranking desires and break free from illusory allegiances. Yet friendship on this crudely Aristotelian model encounters a perplexing problem noted by Aristotle: does the actual possession of virtue, in contrast to its pursuit, conflict with the preservation of friendship (see *Nicomachean Ethics* 1159a1–12)? Does the achievement of virtue render the friend superfluous, an oppressive burden impeding the exercise of virtue? Is there room at the peak for the companion without whom climbing the rugged mountain would have been impossible?[24]

The answer hinges upon how one understands the hierarchy of ends and the virtues which serve them. For example, Aristotle envisaged a highest activity, theoretical contemplation, the object of which could be shared without being diminished or altered. In contrast, the "new will" Zarathustra introduces, spurred on by a "new pride," seeks to become a law unto itself. It is diminished when shared because what is shared, the product of a cooperative venture, is no longer purely self-made. Thus Zarathustra's radically instrumental doctrine of friendship is another inexorable and fearful consequence of his effort to invest the creative will with absolute sovereignty.

In "On War and Warriors" Zarathustra likens himself to a general and bids his brothers to live a "life of obedience and war," the aim of which is neither material gain nor political power but rather conquest in the realm of knowledge. Indicating that his great love compels him to proclaim the truth to his best friends who are at the same time his best enemies, he distinguishes saints of knowledge from warriors of knowledge. The saints possess truth and are superior to the warriors who struggle to gain it. Sainthood, however, is made possible by those who place their lives on the line to carry the banner of knowledge forward. In contrasting his vision with the Christian—"War and courage have accomplished more great things than love of the neighbor"—Zarathustra confirms a passion they share by urging upon his brothers a religious war or crusade for knowledge.

While "the good war that hallows any cause" can be fought against almost anybody, the best war is fought against the worthy enemy, that is, the strongest, proudest, most severe kind of human being. The worthy enemy is also the best friend because he confers the greatest benefit by posing the most formidable challenge. Friends show their mutual devotion in clashing head on. It is not that friendship culminates in a battle to the death, but rather that the battle that constitutes real friendship results in the combatants' emancipation from the need for friendship: perfect friendship enables one to achieve perfect solitude.

In "On the Friend" Zarathustra considers the nature of friendship from the perspective of the "hermit." Just as he obtained expert testimony on love from an unerotic, old woman, he seeks counsel on friendship from a friendless man. He learns that only he who thoroughly knows and loves solitude, only he whose reverence compels him to test and oppose the one he admires, is worthy of friendship. The hermit confesses that the friend offers a respite from his grueling, endless introspection. At best, the friend serves as a reflection of high hopes, a powerful spur to renewed experiments in self-liberation, culminating in the liberation from the need for friends. But as with Zarathustra's conception of marriage, the true form of friendship is entirely instrumental.

To be sure, Zarathustra can speak beautifully of the importance of restraint and discipline in a friendship, capturing a critical moment in the dialectic of closeness and distance that binds friends:

> You do not want to put on anything for your friend? Should it be an honor for your friend that you give yourself to him as you are? But he sends you to the devil for that. He who makes no secret of himself, enrages: so much reason have you for fearing nakedness. Indeed, if you were gods, then you might be ashamed of your clothes. You cannot groom yourself too beautifully for your friend: for you shall be to him an arrow and a longing for the superman. (Z I "On the Friend")

But Zarathustra captures only a moment of friendship, for he does not prize the friend for what he is but for what he reflects, and the fearful extreme to which he takes the insight that we strive to make ourselves beautiful in order to honor our friends is that it is forbidden to display weakness or need in the friend's presence. While Zarathustra is keenly aware of the gulf that, again and again, reasserts itself between friends, he seems unable to account for the moment of intimacy and melting of barriers in friendship. It is not merely that for Zarathustra the friend is compelled to choose between friendship and self-perfection, but that one learns through battle with the friend to achieve perfection by overcoming the need for friendship.

In "On Love of the Neighbor" Zarathustra assails the debased relationship that has come to pass for friendship. He views love of the neighbor, the Christian form of friendship, as arising from the need to flatter vanity and forget weakness and failure. He contends that, under the guise of fulfilling the pious injunction to love one's neighbor, people satisfy an array of ignoble longings for approval, honor, and power. This spurious form of friendship reflects a flight from assuming responsibility for one's deeds. Echoing the prophet Amos (Amos 5:21), Zarathustra declares his disgust with the people's festivals. In opposition to "the love of the neighbor" he introduces, as the true festival, love of "the friend." But the fact remains that he describes a bond utterly devoid of tenderness and compassion. The friend is esteemed because he represents an image and promise of the superman's perfection. Indeed, Zarathustra believes that loving the friend is identical to loving what is farthest away, because the friend's purpose is precisely to symbolize unachieved freedom and mastery. The friend, like woman, is a catalyst, a goad, a disposable torch which illuminates the way, but which must be unsentimentally abandoned even before it burns out.

Thus Zarathustra's glorification of friendship intensifies rather than qualifies the radical egoism that he teaches. Associating the blossoming of freedom with the growth of solitude, he solemnly declares that freedom is the prerogative of a few souls possessing "a new strength and a new right [*ein neues Recht*]" (Z I "On the Way of the Creator") to escape from their yoke.[25] One component of the yoke is the need for other human beings. The crushing weight of solitude is likely to break all but the rarest souls. While the crushed and broken will return to their friends, those with the strength and the right will somehow transform the burden of solitude into new opportunities for higher expressions of the creative will.

Identifying the way of the creator with the way of the lover (Z I "On the Way of the Creator"), Zarathustra suggests that the epitome of love is the creator's self-love. Friendship—love directed outward—serves to prepare the creator for the most authentic expression of love, self-love, a love concentrated sharply inward. Zarathustra's creator is the paradigm of selfishness, turning the "twosomeness" of friendship into a "onesomeness," since friendship becomes for him a model for the spirit's intercourse with itself.

In a stunning aphorism in *Beyond Good and Evil,* Nietzsche declared that "Love of *one* is a barbarism for it is exercised at the expense of all others. The love of God, too" (BGE 67). The argument of part I of *Thus Spoke Zarathustra* emphatically teaches that self-love is exercised at the expense of all others. From the perspective of the judgment Nietzsche offers in *Beyond Good and Evil,* Zarathustra must be viewed as equating the highest and at the same time only worthwhile form of friendship and love, the creator's self-love, with absolute barbarism.

Conclusion

One frequently hears, both from those who come to praise Nietzsche and those who come to bury him, that he is a critic who lacks a positive teaching and has nothing to say about politics. That view is deeply mistaken. Nietzsche's Zarathustra teaches a new ethics that calls for a radical denigration of political life, a consuming contempt for ordinary human beings, and a form of utopian individualism that relentlessly overturns every human attachment that stands in the path of the creator—and every human attachment does so stand. Premature moral indignation or a patronizing refusal to take seriously Zarathustra's "new pride" and "new will" blurs the fundamental issue. Part I of *Thus Spoke Zarathustra,* predominantly optimistic, appears to complete Zarathustra's account of the way of the creator. The fruitful question is what deficiency of the creative life obliges Zarathustra to persist in his quest to articulate the content and contours of the highest life and ultimately to live it. To paraphrase Nietzsche, what terrific need compels Zarathustra to dream the dream or endure the nightmare of the eternal return?

Answering that question requires tracing the "new speech" that comes to Zarathustra in part II (Z II "The Child with the Mirror"). This new speech leads to his agonizing recognition of and bitter struggle with the necessities beyond politics that continue to hold the will fast. And his speeches and deeds in parts II and III reveal how the internal demands of the ethics of creativity compel him to seek and finally to embrace the corrupt metaphysical comforts supplied by the eternal return. In sum, Zarathustra's attempt to respect the imperatives arising on the way of the creator by making his will a law unto itself brings more fully to light the self-deification that is the crowning imperative of the ethics of creativity.

7

The Lust for Eternity and the Pathos of Self-Deification: *Thus Spoke Zarathustra* (Parts II and III)

Parts II and III of *Thus Spoke Zarathustra* feature the curious emergence of the doctrine of the eternal return. In *Ecce Homo*, Nietzsche identifies Zarathustra as the teacher of the eternal return, "that is of the unconditional and infinitely repeated circular course of all things" (EH III, on BT, 3). And he emphasizes that the eternal return is the "fundamental conception" of *Thus Spoke Zarathustra* (EH III, on Z, 1).[1] Examination of Zarathustra's speeches and deeds bears out Nietzsche's judgment. But the eternal return is fundamental to *Zarathustra* much as the San Andreas Fault is a basic part of the California coastal region. Zarathustra's invention, embrace, and abandonment of the eternal return reflect a massive subterranean structural weakness in his ethics of creativity. The eternal return does not fulfill or redeem his hopes for overcoming man. To the contrary, his humiliating surrender to his lust for eternity discredits the good—a self-made god—to which the ethics of creativity summons. Yet the defeat of Zarathustra's aspiration to self-deification proves a triumph for Nietzsche's art and thought. For by showing that the ethics of creativity requires Zarathustra to command eternity, and that Zarathustra must abandon his beloved wisdom to make himself believe that eternity can be made subject to his will, Nietzsche's *Thus Spoke Zarathustra* exposes the vain and debasing ambition that underlies Zarathustra's highest hopes.

The dubious origins of Zarathustra's conception of the eternal return have been inadequately observed. There is a strong tendency, supported by Nietzsche's explicit statements, to view the eternal return as the centerpiece of his prescriptions for life, the glittering crown of his revaluation, the exquisitely carved capstone of Zarathustra's teaching. Commentators, rightly impressed by Nietzsche's insistence on the fundamental importance of the eternal return, have gone to great lengths to show that the doctrine is coherent and workable, as, for example, a theory of literary self-creation,[2] a kind of gentle bourgeois hedonism,[3] a practical test of one's ability to affirm one's life,[4] and a doctrine that brings redemption by paradoxically both "let[ting] beings be" and "giv-[ing] them a new center of gravity."[5]

Zarathustra's confrontation with eternity does mark the high point of Nietzsche's meditations on the ethics of creativity. But placed in dramatic and argumentative context, the doctrine of the eternal return comes to light not as the vindication of the ambition to emancipate the creative will fully, but as a decisive rebuke to that ambition. Zarathustra's vision of the eternal return is a hypothesis about the fundamental structure of the world put in service of a scheme for empowering the will so that it can become a law unto itself. Both the corrupt motivation for the hypothesis and the incoherence of the final scheme are intelligible on the basis of Zarathustra's speeches and deeds. And understanding the origins and unworkability of the eternal return clarifies the causes and consequences of Zarathustra's failure to achieve godlike mastery.

Heidegger points the way to understanding the significance of the eternal return in *Thus Spoke Zarathustra*. He sees the eternal return as one of Nietzsche's "decisive thoughts," a statement of Nietzsche's fundamental metaphysical position. At first glance, Heidegger argues, the eternal return renders freedom both superfluous and impossible. Indeed, in the last analysis the doctrine remains entangled in the tension between freedom and necessity that bedeviled the metaphysical tradition that the eternal return was devised to overcome. Heidegger, however, goes beyond the doctrine's conceptual difficulties to probe the ambition that drove Nietzsche to embrace it. Interpreting *Thus Spoke Zarathustra*, he asks provocatively whether the eternal return is "a form of ill will *against* sheer transiency and thereby a highly spiritualized spirit of revenge?"[6]

Heidegger's question is a deliberate provocation, for Zarathustra regards the spirit of revenge as his archenemy. And the spirit of revenge

is closely related to the passion of *ressentiment*, which, according to
Nietzsche's analysis in the *Genealogy*, combines an envy of superior
forms of strength and beauty with the pursuit of power by means of
the ruse of revaluing weakness as strength and strength as weakness.
Heidegger's incisive suggestion is that the eternal return, the aim of
which is to redeem man from the spirit of revenge, reflects the supreme
or most spiritual expression of revenge.

In fact, Heidegger's analysis restates and elaborates Zarathustra's own
confession in the speech "On Redemption" that the form of revenge
from which he suffers—"the will's ill will against time and its 'it was'"—
is the supreme form or real meaning of revenge (Z II "On Redemption"). Following Heidegger who follows Zarathustra, I shall argue that
Zarathustra's supreme effort to overcome revenge embodies the supreme form of revenge. This conclusion is not opposed to what Zarathustra says and does, but is rather dictated by Zarathustra's speeches
and deeds.[7] But whereas Heidegger believes that the error of Nietzsche
and his Zarathustra was to remain within the grips of metaphysical
thinking, and that a more radical form of thinking can find its way to a
location beyond revenge, I draw the lesson from *Zarathustra* that the
attempt to extinguish or transcend revenge altogether—whether in the
effort to will the past or to overcome metaphysics—reflects an abiding
enslavement to the spirit of revenge. For what is the ambition to surpass
the human, if not a confession of hatred for the human condition?[8] And
what is hatred, according to Nietzsche, if not the resentment of a weak
and needy soul?

The doctrine of the eternal return completes Zarathustra's teaching
about the superman or the highest type. While Zarathustra does not
mention the eternal return in the prologue or elsewhere in part I, and
while the term "superman" eventually drops out in parts II and III
where the eternal return moves to the center, the two are nevertheless
intimately related.[9] Indeed, the eternal return is prefigured early on, and
the attainment of the supreme form of human excellence remains Zarathustra's goal even after he puts the term "superman" aside. In the prologue, Zarathustra entertains the political hope of transforming the lives
of the people through his new teaching about the death of God and the
superman. But his failure in the marketplace teaches him that his task
is not to teach many but rather to instruct the few creators. Later in
part I, having abandoned his political hopes, he expounds an ethics of

creativity which calls for the systematic emancipation of the creator's will from all forms of practical dependence. But in part II he makes the crucial discovery that there are other and still more fundamental forms of dependence.

To liberate creativity from the grip of necessity, Zarathustra attempts to discover or create an interpretation of the moment that allows for a form of willing in the present that confers mastery over the past and future. The doctrine of the eternal return, which affirms that all events are inextricably bound together, could seem to fit the bill. For to master the moment under the conditions posited by the doctrine of the eternal return would be to master the whole. But Zarathustra fails to confront squarely the fact that the eternal return, if true, absolutely precludes the genuine or free acts of will that would allow for mastery of the moment. The wrenching irony of Zarathustra's adventures is that the eternal return, the very doctrine meant to salvage the freedom of the creator and empower the creative will, results in a form of eternal imprisonment seldom dreamed of in previous philosophies.

The "new ways" he goes and the "new speech" that comes to Zarathustra at the beginning of part II (Z II "The Child with the Mirror") culminating in the mawkishly effusive professions of love for life and eternity concluding part III, spring from a brave insight into the basic limitations on the creative self, but end sadly in a humiliating crumbling of philosophical will. Zarathustra's "new ways" and "new speech" present a profound modification of the way of the creator, a modification necessitated by the discovery that creativity must become absolute mastery if the will is to enjoy free rein.

The quest for absolute mastery is motivated by the internal demands of the ethics of creativity, and is also bound up with Zarathustra's very human neediness. The first ominous notes are sounded in his opening monologue with the sun, in which his envy for the sun's self-sufficiency and his own need for the people's recognition distort his estimation of his wisdom. "On the Adder's Bite" is a pivotal speech because it hints that it is under the influence of the poison of the spirit of revenge that Zarathustra devises the means for overcoming revenge. Increasingly the fiery preacher yields to the diffident, brooding, sickly wanderer, tormented by the intolerable feeling that he is unequal to the task at hand. In his bleakest hours, a series of nightmares assail Zarathustra; these ghastly visions introduce the eternal return. Equally menacing are the insipidly cheerful interpretations of his nauseating visions that his disciples obsequiously offer their master.

The decisive moment in Zarathustra's convalescence comes when he ecstatically proclaims at the conclusion of part III his "lust after eternity and after the nuptial ring of rings, the ring of recurrence" (Z III "The Seven Seals"). His Dionysian elation may suggest a final triumph over the spirit of revenge. Yet the cheerful or reverent interpretation of his reconciliation with eternity, which mirrors his disciples' pathetic credulity, disintegrates under the questioning that Nietzsche mandates as a requirement of the intellectual conscience (GS 2) and that is required by the truthfulness that Nietzsche proclaims as Zarathustra's distinctive virtue (EH IV 3). In fact Zarathustra's ecstasy is not achieved through a heroic transformation of the ugly into the beautiful; rather, it is accomplished by Zarathustra's adoption of his disciples' debasing practice of prostrating themselves before the ugly and, in willful disregard of the testimony of their intelligence, exalting it as if it were beautiful. This ignominious betrayal is reflected in the drastic physical deterioration Zarathustra has suffered when he makes his first appearance in part IV. It receives its most astonishing expression when Zarathustra is dragged down to the level of the higher men he professes to loathe and scandalously joins them in an act of ass-worship (Z IV "The Ass Festival").[10]

The Need for Freedom and the Spirit of Revenge

The speech "On the Adder's Bite" presents Zarathustra as a passive victim poisoned by a common animal. Nestled in among speeches criticizing the hypocrisy of the "good and just," praising hardness, celebrating extravagant passion, and envisaging a superhuman freedom from the need for other human beings is an episode showing Zarathustra fatigued by the midday sun, sheltering himself under a shady tree, covering his face with his hands to create a double-layered shield from the bright light and scorching heat. But the transformation of the sun into an oppressor is not the sole noteworthy transformation of a friend into a foe. Whereas in the prologue Zarathustra wishes to be led by his eagle, "the proudest animal under the sun," and the serpent, "the cleverest animal under the sun" (Z prologue 10), in his present adventure the adder, a venomous snake, becomes Zarathustra's mortal enemy, purporting to poison him with what the adder, which comes from a family known for its cleverness, promises are deadly consequences.

The adder's bite causes the sleeping Zarathustra to cry out in pain. Expressing his gratitude to the adder for waking him because his "way is still long," Zarathustra's gracious response suggests either that his wisdom is still incomplete or that his mission remains in some crucial respect unfinished. The adder responds simply in sadness: "my poison kills." Undaunted, Zarathustra bravely replies, "When has a dragon ever died of the poison of a snake?" But his claim to possess a special immunity to the adder's poison is belied by a certain vulnerability revealed in his choice of words. In "On the Three Metamorphoses," the "great dragon" represented the moral outlook, the symbol of mankind's duplicitous efforts to pass off artificial moral codes as the work of nature, God, or universal reason. The image with which Zarathustra chooses to describe himself suggests that it is, of all things, the spirit of morality that enables him to withstand the adder's bite. Moreover, as his subsequent interpretation of his encounter with the adder makes clear, the adder itself also symbolizes the conventional moral outlook. Thus, what Zarathustra presents as that aspect of character which serves as the source of his immunity to the adder's poison—his dragon-likeness— testifies to the presence of the adder's poison within his system. This prefigures his momentous confession in the decisive speech "On Redemption," that he is the victim *par excellence* of the spirit of revenge (Z II "On Redemption").

To his disciples who ask him about the moral of his encounter, Zarathustra delivers a sermon that reinforces the suspicion that the adder symbolizes the spirit of revenge. Zarathustra's immoral moral concerns the meaning of morality and justice. He indicates that his own gracious reaction to the adder's bite is an example of how wrongs and misfortunes must be embraced as further opportunities for the expression of strength, and he provides edifying maxims so that others can follow his example. In general, he rejects the justice that loves to condemn and punish, and favors instead a justice understood as "love with seeing eyes" *(sehenden Augen)*. Such justice does not consist in seeing what others need or what is their due and giving it to them. Rather, as Zarathustra proclaims, "I give each my own." His justice consists in seeing what is *his* own and giving it to others in order to benefit himself, suggesting not overrichness and an excess of strength but weakness that cannot look beyond one's own needs.

Indeed, in conclusion Zarathustra stresses a kind of incapacity for overcoming peculiar to hermits. Himself a hermit, he warns against injuring hermits because they do not forget or forgive. Thus although he proudly replied to the adder that he was invulnerable to its poison, and although he presents his encounter with the adder as a paradigm for responding to what he later calls the spirit of revenge, he reveals that as a hermit he possesses a special vulnerability to the poison of revenge.

Like Adam and Eve, who were awakened from their blissful innocence, had their eyes opened, and were expelled into human history as a result of the snake's machinations, Zarathustra has his eyes opened by the adder's bite and becomes aware that his "way is still long." Like Adam and Eve, who acquired moral knowledge thanks to the snake's interventions, Zarathustra is prompted by the adder's bite to offer lessons on the morality of revenge. Yet the evidence steadily mounts that Zarathustra is not, as he claims, invulnerable to the adder's poison, but vengeful, as he declares hermits to be. As the spirit of revenge persistently bedevils him in his struggle to articulate the formula that will secure the emancipation of the creative will, Zarathustra's need or desire for a radically free creative will reveals itself to be an offspring of the spirit of revenge.

In the first scene of part II, having abandoned his efforts to teach and lead and after many years of renewed seclusion in his cave, Zarathustra suffers a gruesome dream. Looking into a mirror carried by a child, he sees peering back at him a laughing devil. Later, he equates the devil with the spirit of gravity (Z II "The Dancing Song"). Yet rather than viewing the image in the mirror as the devil or spirit of gravity within, he interprets the dream as a sign that his "*teaching* is in danger," distorted by his enemies, who have caused those dearest to him to be ashamed of his gift. He feels compelled to leave his solitude to defend his honor, restore his endangered "teaching," and recover his lost friends (Z II "The Child with the Mirror"). But there is a discrepancy between the beneficent motivation that he explicitly proclaims and the immense need that shines clearly through. Like a slow-motion replay of the prologue, the opening scene of part II highlights the crucial move whereby Zarathustra revalues a selfish impulse as generosity and traces his dependence on others to his own spiritual abundance.

It is Zarathustra himself who reveals that his return to mankind is prompted primarily by concern not for others but for himself; that he must once again descend not to give to others what they need but to give others what he needs them to have. In the grips of a feverish egoism and a "wild wisdom" that have made his cave a prison, he invokes violent erotic imagery to describe the love that compels him again to forsake his solitude:

> My impatient love overflows in rivers, downward, toward sunrise and
> sunset. From silent mountains and thunderstorms of suffering my soul
> rushes into the valleys.
>   Too long have I longed and looked into the distance. Too long have
> I belonged to loneliness; thus I have forgotten how to be silent. Mouth
> have I become through and through, and the roaring of a stream from
> towering cliffs: I want to plunge my speech down into the valleys. Let
> the river of my love plunge where there is no way! How could a river
> fail to find its way to the sea? Indeed, a lake is within me, solitary and
> self-sufficient; but the river of my love carries it along, down to the
> sea. (Z II "The Child with the Mirror")[11]

Whereas earlier Zarathustra stressed the self-sufficiency and self-love of the creator (Z I "On the Way of the Creator"), he now presents himself as a lover enduring a painful separation from his beloved. His principal metaphor for his love—a powerful water flow pulled irresistibly downward by gravity—suggests that his love for his teaching and his friends, like his love for eternity, stems from and is dominated by his deadliest enemy, the spirit of revenge, who sometimes goes by the name the spirit of gravity.[12]

This venture forth from his solitude, Zarathustra declares, differs from his last: "New ways I go, a new speech comes to me; weary I grow, like all creators, of the old tongues. My spirit no longer wants to walk on worn soles." The "wild wisdom" that dictates his "new ways" and "new speech" will, he warns, frighten even his friends. Soon enough it will frighten even Zarathustra himself as he proceeds to probe the nature of the obstacles above and beyond politics that keep the creative will from becoming a law unto itself.

One such obstacle, apparently already overcome by Zarathustra, is God and gods. In Zarathustra's view creators must be knowers, and what they must know is their obligation to create for themselves the world in which they dwell (Z II "Upon the Blessed Isles"). You cannot become a god if God or other gods rule the world. So in a moment of monumental hubris, straining the capacities of the syllogism, and confusing a deep longing with a decisive proof, Zarathustra declares it a necessity that gods are merely fictitious on the grounds that an actual god would be an unbearable source of envy to him:

> But let me reveal my heart to you entirely, my friends: *if* there were gods, how could I endure not to be a god! *Hence* there are no gods. Though I drew this conclusion, now it draws me . . .
>   Willing liberates: that is the true teaching of will and liberty—thus Zarathustra teaches it . . . Away from God and gods this will has lured me; what could one create if gods existed? (Z II "Upon the Blessed Isles")

Note the structure of Zarathustra's argument: Whereas Nietzsche's madman argued from the death of God to the imperative to become gods, Zarathustra argues from his own desire to become a god to the death or nonexistence of God and gods. Drawn by conclusions and lured by drives, Zarathustra is compelled by his own tyrannical need for absolute mastery to utter his rejection of God and gods. By decreeing that what is antithetical to his happiness cannot be true, he betrays the very presumption Nietzsche often denounced as a vice at the root of conventional morality and religion (D 90; BGE 39; GM I 1; A 53). More stunning is the bizarre twist that Zarathustra's syllogism gives to his critique of religion: disbelief in God and gods no less than belief in God originates in envy.[13]

God represents an insufferable affront to Zarathustra's pride as creator and thinker,[14] an intolerable limitation on his will, a major obstacle to achieving the good as he understands it. Equating God with the idea that what is real is uniform and unchanging in nature, Zarathustra quickly adds that the idea of the permanent or the eternal is "only a parable." But he rejects the idea of God not on the grounds that it is merely a parable but because it is a harmful parable or poem. Although, in Zarathustra's view, "the poets lie too much," they do not lie enough in the right way about the right things: "It is of time and becoming that the best parables should speak: let them be a praise and a justification of all impermanence" (Z II "Upon the Blessed Isles").

The creator's weighty task is to praise and justify all impermanence or becoming. Accordingly, Zarathustra regards creation as nothing less than "the great redemption from suffering, and life's growing light." But to accomplish redemption and justify impermanence the will must be free: "Willing liberates: that is the true teaching of will and freedom—

thus Zarathustra teaches it" (Z II "Upon the Blessed Isles"). Linking willing to creating, Zarathustra scorns those who wish to bring an end to willing. But not all willing is equally efficacious. In what does the willing that liberates consist? It consists, according to Zarathustra's concluding remarks in "Upon the Blessed Isles," in perfecting the beautiful image of the superman that lies imprisoned within man.

This emancipation or perfection depends on a kind of virtue: "Oh, my friends, that your self be in your deed as the mother is in her child—let that be *your* word concerning virtue!" (Z II "On the Virtuous"). The use of the mother's love to illustrate the nature of self-love exhibits the radical implications of Zarathustra's revaluation. By taking the most tender, natural, and inviolable human relationship and adopting it as a model for a man's attachment to his own virtue or deeds, he appropriates a form of love exhibiting the selfless devotion of the lover and the total need of the loved one to sanction an unconditional love of self.

Despite the radically self-regarding character of his conception of virtue, Zarathustra's heart is not devoid of feeling for others. It is precisely his enemies, the priests, who command his respect and arouse his compassion:

> They are evil enemies: nothing is more vengeful than their humility. And whoever attacks them, soils himself easily. Yet my blood is related to theirs, and I want to know that my blood is honored even in theirs . . .
>
> I am moved by compassion for these priests. I also find them repulsive . . . (Z II "On Priests")

His compassion for the priests compels him to wish that "someone would yet redeem them from their Redeemer!" Held in chains by "false values and delusive words," the priests require knowledge to set them free. Until freedom is attained, the moral differences among men amount to nothing: "Never yet has there been a superman. Naked I saw both the greatest and the smallest man: they are still all-too-similar to each other. Verily, even the greatest I found all-too-human" (Z II "On Priests"). Inasmuch as Zarathustra's blood, by his own admission, is related to that of the priests, it is proper to conclude that he remains, like the smallest man, unfree and that he shares the priests' most distinctive characteristic, their unparalleled vengefulness.[15]

Pursuing the connection between religion and the spirit of revenge,

Zarathustra likens "preachers of *equality*" to tarantulas who corrupt the soul by infecting it with the poison of revenge. The priestly equation of justice and virtue with equality reflects "the tyrannomania of impotence." Weakness and envy combine in the revenge-poisoned soul to declare that all are equal. This declaration is not just, but uses the language of justice to shame and incapacitate truly virtuous souls. Anticipating that his own teaching will be misperceived as egalitarian, Zarathustra emphatically rejects this error in understanding: "I do not wish to be mixed up and confused with these preachers of equality. For, to *me* justice speaks thus: 'Men are not equal.' Nor shall they become equal! What would my love of the superman be if I spoke otherwise?" (Z II "On the Tarantulas").[16]

On Zarathustra's view, the distinction between the greatest and smallest must be maintained if he is to vindicate his love for the superman. This love necessitates cleansing the chief poison from men's souls "for *that man be redeemed from revenge,* that is for me the bridge to the highest hope, and a rainbow after long storms" (Z II "On the Tarantulas"). Zarathustra seeks to overcome the Christian notion of redemption not by overcoming the very need for redemption but by championing a rival notion of redemption. The question as to who will redeem Zarathustra, the herald and precursor of the redeemer, must be asked with especial urgency since in the conclusion to "On the Tarantulas" he anticipates that his soul will "whirl with revenge" as a result of his having been bitten by his "old enemy," the tarantula. His fear of what he might do compels him to ask his friends to tie him down. And this acknowledgment of the need to take precautions against powerful temptations is revealing. For Zarathustra's concluding vow that he will "never dance the tarantella," like his boast of invulnerability to the adder, is quickly belied by his own words. Fast on the heels of his vow of immunity to the tarantula's poison follow painful confessions of weakness and need culminating in his revelation in "On Redemption" that his is the true form of revenge.

Zarathustra's anger and despair bubble to the surface in three personal songs of lament.[17] In "The Night Song," the coming of darkness awakens his profound craving for love. As he gives expression to long-suppressed desires and festering wounds, sublime hopes emerge along with ugly impulses. Frustration of the erotic desire to give engenders a cruel, vengeful desire to hurt those who refuse to receive:

They receive from me, but do I touch their souls? . . . I should like to hurt those for whom I shine; I should like to rob those to whom I give; thus do I hunger for malice. To withdraw my hand when the other hand already reaches out to it; to linger like the waterfall, which lingers even while it plunges: thus do I hunger for malice. Such revenge my fullness plots: such spite wells up out of my loneliness. My happiness in giving died in giving; my virtue tired of itself in its overflow. (Z II "The Night Song")

The poison of revenge seems to have penetrated to the deep recesses of Zarathustra's heart. The teacher who proclaimed that he was bringing redemption from the plague of revenge appears to be stricken with an advanced case. Sunk in poverty, consumed by envy, and racked by hunger for revenge—and his praise of solitude and his attack on the rabble notwithstanding—Zarathustra confesses to a blazing desire to be loved by other souls and a hatred of the people for refusing to thank him for his gift. As he comes into focus as an unrequited lover aching for reconciliation with his beloved, his contempt for the people becomes ever more indistinguishable from bitter recriminations hurled in desperate grief at the impassive object of his heart's longings.

In "The Dancing Song," Zarathustra reveals that his love for life and wisdom is more fundamental than his love for the people. He chances upon a company of lovely, light-footed girls dancing in a secluded meadow (Z II "The Dancing Song"). Now an onlooker of "godlike dances"—as opposed to one in whom a "god dances" (Z I "On Reading and Writing")—Zarathustra, with his heavy-footed presence, like a surrogate for his archenemy, the spirit of gravity, brings the dancing to an abrupt halt. In an effort to persuade the graceful girls to return to their dance, he volunteers to mock the spirit of gravity with a godlike dance of his own. But instead of fulfilling his promise, he ironically becomes the object of life's mocking speech.

Declaring that she is "a woman in every way," life chastises Zarathustra for committing the common error of treating what he has yet to fathom as unfathomable, and ridicules him for acting like all "virtuous men" by imposing on her his virtues—profundity, faithfulness, eternity, mysteriousness. Angry and jealous, his "wild wisdom" attacks Zarathustra for his love for life: "You will, you want, you love—that is the only reason why you *praise* life" (Z II "The Dancing Song"). Zarathustra acknowledges to himself his exclusive love for life. But that does not mean his desire for wisdom is weak. To Zarathustra life and wisdom, both personified as ravishing women, "look so similar." And while both resemble a coy, dangerous enchantress, his wisdom is especially alluring and elusive:

> Oh yes wisdom! One thirsts after her and is never satisfied; one looks through veils, one grabs through nets. Is she beautiful? How should I know? But even the oldest carps are baited with her. She is changeable and stubborn; often I have seen her bite her lip and comb her hair against the grain. Perhaps she is evil and false and a female in every way; but just when she speaks ill of herself she is most seductive. (Z II "The Dancing Song")

Reminiscent of Cleopatra and her power over Antony, wisdom and life hold an irresistible fascination over Zarathustra.[18] His reveries, however, prove short-lived. His song concludes with lovers estranged: he rejects wisdom's advances and life spurns his professions of devotion. The tension or contest between life and wisdom remains unresolved. As sadness engulfs Zarathustra, echoes of the madman's grief-stricken queries rise from the surrounding woods: "Why? What for? By what? Whither? Where? How? Is it not folly still to be alive?" (Z II "The Dancing Song"; see also GS 125). After two trips to the mountaintop and two journeys among men, Zarathustra's despair reveals that he has yet to invent the sacred games that his parable "On the Three Metamorphoses" (like Nietzsche's parable of the madman) presents as an imperative arising from the death of God. At this juncture, not even the hope of the superman brings comfort.

Memories well up in the forlorn Zarathustra. Estranged from friends, life, and wisdom, he recalls his first love and its bitter end (Z II "The Tomb Song"). Pronouncing a eulogy over the murdered "visions and apparitions" of his youth, he recalls that as a young man he was "fashioned for loyalty ... and for tender eternities," a dreamer longing to appreciate all beings as divine and see all days as holy. The fresh recollection of his agonizing loss of belief, love, and eternity provokes him to declare a curse against his enemies. Ascribing infinite sanctity to his hopes, he declares his loss of "the visions and dearest wonders" of his youth a greater misfortune than "any murder of human beings." What success he attained estranged him from his friends: "And when I did what was hardest for me and celebrated the triumph of my overcomings, then you made those who loved me scream that I was hurting them most." In his grief he blames his enemies for causing him an anguish which his own analysis in part I indicates has its roots instead in the fundamental conflict inhering in the way of the creator between the pursuit of perfection and the preservation of friendship.

Bearing the wounds of a frustrated religiosity, Zarathustra acknowledges his inability thus far to cure himself by transforming his sorrows into a blessing and gift. Although his "highest hope" is as yet "unspoken and unredeemed," he has not yet renounced the highest. He proclaims that he was able to survive the terrible losses of his youth thanks to his hard, invulnerable will. Indeed, he hints that his will is still capable of restoring his unredeemed visions and wonders. This redemption entails recovering the experience of eternity, making all things divine, and seeing all days as holy. The fulfillment of Zarathustra's highest hope would thus seem to combine two ideas he has previously associated with the spirit of revenge: the idea of eternity and the rage to see all things as fundamentally equal, albeit equal in their divinity or holiness. Indeed, the ethics of creativity which culminates in the ambition to bestow or will an eternal significance on all things turns out to be the supreme leveling doctrine.

The ambition to create a world he can revere is in Zarathustra's view something that he shares with the wise, although the wise do not see things in quite this way (Z II "On Self-Overcoming"). He attacks the wisest for ascribing special purity to the desire for truth when in fact such a desire reflects a lust to rule, to compel reality to "yield and bend," to make it "smooth and serve the spirit as its mirror and reflection." The will to truth is an imperfect expression of the will to power inasmuch as it reflects the desire by the wise to create a rational world order which they can revere. But is this creation free and praiseworthy?

Zarathustra answers this question by appealing to "the way of all living things" (Z II "On Self-Overcoming"). The self, like all living things, must obey. But either it can obey forces external to its own will, such as nature, reason, or chance, or it can obey itself. The form of obedience in which the self heeds its own commands is superior; and it is identical to making the will a law unto itself. A will that heeds its own commands must be simultaneously legislator, executor, judge, and subject. With this insight Zarathustra suggests that he has "crawled into the very heart of life and into the very root of its heart." Combining his previous assurance that the will liberates (Z II "On the Blessed Isles") with his new teaching that the will should both command and obey, one can say that creativity as Zarathustra understands it consists in both justifying impermanence with parables and willing one's own will. It turns out that the idea of willing one's own will is the parable by which Zarathustra attempts to justify impermanence.

Parables of Becoming and the Justification of Impermanence

Still uncertain as to what precisely is required of him (Z II "On Great Events"),[19] Zarathustra hears a soothsayer's doctrine which "touched his heart and changed him." This doctrine is a nihilistic interpretation of the death of God: "'All is empty, all is the same, all has been!'" (Z II "The Soothsayer"). Whereas in the prologue Zarathustra found the death of God exhilarating and liberating, now, as if to seek escape from the soothsayer's suffocating interpretation of the human condition, he sinks into a deep sleep. However, he suffers a terrifying nightmare. Later, he relates to his disciples his dream of a graveyard at midnight in which he is a passive, helpless onlooker to stock elements from a Gothic horror story. In this dream, as gates creak and birds shriek and the wind howls, a black coffin spews forth thousands of sinister, mocking children's faces. Zarathustra is overwhelmed and thrown to the ground.

When Zarathustra finishes retelling his dream, the disciple whom he "loved most" steps forward and volunteers an interpretation of the nightmare. This interpretation illustrates nothing so much as the disciple's slavish mind. For his obsequious account denies Zarathustra's fear and trembling, casting Zarathustra as the hero of the dream, overcoming death with laughter, bringing forth new wonders, and vanquishing all enemies. Sure that his dream has a meaning and unhappy that his disciple has failed to discern it, Zarathustra rejects his disciple's idealizing and apologetic interpretation. Disappointed, he insists on the need to "atone for bad dreams." Siding with the soothsayer's despairing prophecy over the disciple's optimistic reading, he passes over his disciples and calls the soothsayer to eat and drink by his side.

Zarathustra moves directly from affirming the soothsayer's prophecies to exploring the nature of redemption. Whereas one might expect that a speech of his entitled "On Redemption"[20] would comprise various vehement attacks on the fundamental religious desire for a happiness that transcends worldly injustice and misfortune, instead, one finds that redemption, in Zarathustra's view, is the one thing needful.[21] Feeling himself crippled as a result of the painful sight of deformed human beings everywhere he looks, Zarathustra declares that in a crucial respect the past does not differ from the present; everywhere he sees only "fragments and limbs and dreadful accidents—but no human beings." Owing to the huge gap, everywhere apparent, between what men are and what the ethics of self-deification requires them to become, life among men is for Zarathustra a living Hell, a waking nightmare.

Zarathustra views escape from this Hell or redemption as the work of a completely solitary individual. Reaffirming the connection between creativity and willing and linking both to redemption, he defines redemption in terms of making the past subject to the creative will: "To redeem those who lived in the past and to recreate all 'it was' into a 'thus I willed it'—that alone should I call redemption. Will—that is the name of the liberator and joybringer; thus I taught you, my friends" (Z II "On Redemption"). The imperative to will the past and redeem those who lived in it does not reflect a concern on Zarathustra's part for the suffering and injustice that mark human history. Untouched by the plight of other human beings, he aims to view the pervasive suffering spanning the landscape of human existence as necessary, and to make his own will the source of that necessity. He does not wish to moralize an ugly necessity, but rather to command that necessity so as to make his own will sovereign and free.

Can the will accomplish the awesome task of redemption? In contrast to his optimistic teaching in "On the Three Metamorphoses" that the will can will itself and proclaim a sacred affirmation of the world, Zarathustra now declares, presumably in the light of lessons he has learned during his wanderings, that the will's dominion is severely circumscribed:

> But now learn this too: the will itself is still a prisoner. Willing liberates; but what is it that puts even the liberator himself in fetters? "It was"—that is the name of the will's gnashing of teeth and most secret melancholy. Powerless against what has been done, he is an angry spectator of all that is past. The will cannot will backwards; and that he cannot break time and time's covetousness, that is the will's loneliest melancholy. (Z II "On Redemption")

The past exercises a cruel and tyrannical dominion over the will in the present. If the will cannot subjugate time, it remains conditioned by, and hence in the thrall of, an external or foreign power. Even after breaking free of the forms of political or practical dependence, the creative will, Zarathustra now grasps, remains enslaved to the same sovereign that rules the people he reviles.

This new knowledge of the last obstacle that stands between the creative will and liberation engenders a consciousness of slavery and a slavish consciousness:

> Willing liberates; what means does the will devise for himself to get rid of his melancholy and to mock his dungeon? Alas, every prisoner becomes a fool; and the imprisoned will redeems himself foolishly. That time does not run backwards, that is his wrath; "that which was" is the name of the stone he cannot move. And so he moves stones out of wrath and displeasure, and he wreaks revenge on whatever does not feel wrath and displeasure as he does. Thus the will, the liberator, took to hurting; and on all who can suffer he wreaks revenge for his inability to go backwards. This, indeed this alone, is what *revenge* is: the will's ill will against time and its "it was." (Z II "On Redemption")

Willing to brook no equals, Zarathustra imperiously imputes to himself, the one who best understands the will, the supreme and only genuine form of revenge. Consequently, the figures presented in Nietzsche's books normally thought of as epitomizing the slavish consciousness—Euripides, Socrates and theoretical men, Jews and Christians, democratic egalitarians, socialist agitators, and university professors—must be understood as studies of revenge in an inferior or diluted form, and hence, as inferior or diluted studies of revenge. Inasmuch as Zarathustra attempts to achieve liberation through willing time, *Thus Spoke Zarathustra* is perhaps the supreme case study of the supreme form of revenge. The most far-reaching implications of revenge on the grand scale may stem from what Zarathustra identifies as its defining symptoms: desperately grasping after foolish notions of redemption and, out of deep frustration, furiously attacking innocent beings. For with this analysis of the origins of revenge and its characteristic symptoms, Zarathustra may have provided the explanatory framework that makes intelligible both his own peculiar and protracted attempt to obtain redemption through the elaboration of the doctrine of the eternal return, and his fear and loathing of the multitude of humanity.

If the will is to be free, it must subjugate the meaningless flow of the dreadful series of incidents and accidents that constitute the past and bring them under its exclusive authority. If the past is indeed an immovable stone, if the yoke of the past cannot be thrown off by an act of the will, then a mockery is made of the sacred new beginning Zarathustra imagines as the child's birthright in "On the Three Metamorphoses." Rejecting previous doctrines of redemption that required the will to submit to various interpretations of necessity, Zarathustra reiterates that the creative will comes into its own by willing or commanding the past: "I led you away from these fables when I taught you, 'The will is a creator.' All 'it was' is a fragment, a riddle, a dreadful accident—until the creative will says to it, 'But thus I willed it.' Until the creative will says to it, 'But thus I will it; thus shall I will it'" (Z II "On Redemption").

While Zarathustra proceeds to lament that what he has taught has not yet been spoken, the reader is compelled by what Zarathustra himself has taught about redemption to wonder whether as one who knows himself to be a prisoner of the past Zarathustra is not bound to make himself foolish by inventing a foolish and comforting illusion of redemption. Since Zarathustra has an enormous interest in discovering how to empower the will to "will backwards," the doctrine of the eternal return, the teaching that empowers the will to redeem itself by enabling it to will backwards, becomes a source of fundamental interest and keen suspicion. The reader is obliged to wonder along with Zarathustra, "Who could teach it also to will backwards?"

Part II concludes with Zarathustra recounting another nightmare vision. Cowering before his "angry mistress" who demands "without voice" that he return to his solitude and assume the responsibility "to command great things" (Z II "The Stillest Hour"), he cries in meek protest that he is frightened by what is demanded of him. Commanding great things, he confesses, involves a kind of knowledge beyond his strength, a knowledge, he lets it be known, by which he is not worthy to be broken. Although in his immediately previous speech he ridiculed the ignorance of "the good and the just" about what is great, worrying that even the highest men will call his superman devil (Z II "On Human Prudence"), Zarathustra now appears to manifest the very mark of the higher man—terror at what excellence demands.

The silent voice continues to flog Zarathustra with criticism. When he bemoans the people's mocking rejection of his teaching, the voice replies that although he deserved to be rejected the rejection was of little consequence. Preaching to the people is a petty thing while what matters is commanding great things. By restricting himself to teaching the superman, Zarathustra evades his obligations. Although he thinks that he cannot command because he lacks "the lion's voice for commanding," he is told in his dream that what is necessary is that he "become a child and without shame." Since the child, according to Zarathustra's own parable (Z I "On the Three Metamorphoses"), is the highest incarnation of the spirit, Zarathustra, in effect, is blamed for dodging the imperative to become the superman by teaching its significance to others.

Indeed, it is a serious error to absolve Zarathustra of responsibility for fully imagining or paving the way for the superman on the grounds that he is merely the superman's teacher, herald, or advocate.[22] In fact, he is the teacher of the superman who is compelled by the force of his teaching to renounce the safety of mere advocacy and to make himself a god in accordance with the demands of his new ethics. Attempts by commentators to insulate Zarathustra from responsibility for living up to the highest demands of his ethics overlook the fact that Zarathustra recognizes the authority of the imperative to command great things and reluctantly seeks to carry it out.

But Zarathustra is not yet ready. His "awesome mistress" bears down on him and demands that he return again to his solitude. Against his will, he joylessly heeds the order to return to his cave. Ironically, his groveling submission to a nameless authority reflects the very incapacity for commanding that he has inveighed against and renders suspect his fitness to command great things. The conclusion of part II thus dramatizes Zarathustra's fall from the heights from which he spoke when he commenced his sojourn among humankind in the prologue. With his dignity battered and his pride wounded, Zarathustra weeps bitterly. Shrouded in guilt and shame, like an upbraided child aware that he has misbehaved and deserves his punishment, he takes leave of his friends and retreats into his solitude.

The opening speech of part III finds Zarathustra climbing mountains, his hour of truth, at the same time his moment of greatest peril, at hand. He expressly anticipates confronting his "final peak," his "hardest path" and his "loneliest walk" (Z III "The Wanderer"). His extreme formulations give the impression of a man facing an inexorable curse, yet (much as Nietzsche responded to the demon's account of existence;

GS 341) he discerns in the heart of the curse an opportunity for obtaining an eternal blessing. The "hour" speaks to him:

> Only now are you going your way to greatness! Peak and abyss—they are now joined together.
>
> You are going your way to greatness: now that which has hitherto been your ultimate danger has become your ultimate refuge. (Z III "The Wanderer")

Zarathustra's way to greatness appears to require the reconciliation of the extremes that confront him. Up to this point, he explains, his knowledge and his experiences, even his mountain-climbing and his wanderings, have primarily concerned himself. Now, he realizes, he must attain a more comprehensive form of knowledge. To become a true knower he needs the hardness to look away from himself, to look beyond what most see and to discover "the ground and background of all things." The knowledge to which he aspires as a true knower is so comprehensive, he realizes, that to attain it he must reach a peak from which all that he once looked up to he must see beneath him.

With this recognition of the need to attain a divine perspective, Zarathustra's "ultimate loneliness" begins. Emphasizing the unity of the extremes, he indicates that the path to the heights leads through the "deepest depth." This prospect leaves him melancholy and bitter, aware that in his lonely pursuit of the heights he faces a special danger, "the danger of the loneliest" which is "love of everything if only it is alive." If love is the special danger of the loneliest, then the end of part III, which finds Zarathustra in love and alone and lusting after eternity, would suggest that he falls victim to "the danger of the loneliest," and hence fails to attain his "ultimate peak."

Zarathustra's "vision of the loneliest," which appears in the next speech, "On the Vision and the Riddle," constitutes a pivotal account of his understanding of eternity, a decisive moment in his attempt to identify the conditions under which the creative will can attain redemption by commanding the past. Zarathustra's most elaborate nightmare exposes the illicit sleight of hand that enables him to stare inexorable necessity in the face and call it freedom and mastery.

After two days spent in silent sadness on a ship bound for the blessed isles, "the ice of his heart broke" enabling Zarathustra to relate his riddle, "the vision of the loneliest," to sailors whom he characterizes as "bold searchers" and "researchers," men who love adventure and danger and prefer guessing to deducing.[23] The vision begins with Zarathustra climbing up the side of an eerie, desolate mountain, the air heavy with gloom and death. Perched on his shoulder is a gruesome creature he identifies as "the spirit of gravity, my devil and archenemy" who exercises a malignant form of thought control over him: "he sat on me, half dwarf, half mole, lame, making lame, dripping lead into my ear, leaden thoughts into my brain." In view of Zarathustra's encounters with the adder and tarantula, and in light of his confession that priestly blood flows through his veins, one is compelled to consider the extent to which his encounter with the dwarf betrays a poisoned perspective. And more immediately one is forced to wonder how rapidly the dwarf's leaden poison spreads, what its symptoms are, and whether there is a remedy to counteract the toxin with which the fiendish monster contaminates Zarathustra's mind.

Like the lion whose courage enabled him to confront the dragon for "ultimate victory," Zarathustra courageously squares off against the dwarf, declaring a showdown: "'Stop, dwarf!' . . . 'It is I or you! But I am the stronger of us two: you do not know my abysmal thought. *That* you could not bear.'" Apparently forgetting that the dwarf had been poisoning his mind—or exhibiting signs of the poison's swift dissemination—he solemnly declares that he is free to make a clean break with his companion, who, he adds for good measure, is incapable of bearing his "abysmal thought."

From out of nowhere a gateway suddenly appears. In the ensuing conversation, the two opponents present apparently rival interpretations of the metaphysical significance of the gateway. Although Zarathustra claims victory, the contest appears to vindicate the dwarf's interpretation. According to Zarathustra's solemnly intoned interpretation, the gateway represents a vision of the moment, time, and eternity:

> Behold this gateway, dwarf! . . . It has two faces. Two paths meet here; no one has yet followed either to its end. This long lane stretches back for an eternity. And the long lane out there, that is another eternity. They contradict each other, these paths; they offend each other face to face; and it is here at this gateway that they come together. The name of the gateway is inscribed above: "Moment." But whoever would follow one of them, on and on, farther and farther—do you believe, dwarf, that these paths contradict each other eternally?

Past and future offending each other offend or dishearten the creator because their discontinuity, reflecting the past's imperviousness to the human will, thwarts the creator's effort to make his will sovereign and free. Zarathustra's first interpretation of the moment suggests not an eternal return of the same but an eternal unfolding of the unprecedented. Apparently, the flow of time is devoid of form or structure, apart from the fact that all moments equally represent the meeting of an essentially unrelated past and future. Seen in this way, the unrecoverable past which must be willed if the will is to be sovereign and free mocks the quest for total mastery and freedom. No wonder Zarathustra has been filled with dread: if the moment, time, and eternity are constituted as he at present conceives them, then his hopes for liberation and redemption by the creative will are in vain. But at this darkest moment, teetering on the brink of the abyss, he discovers metaphysical comfort by embracing a new interpretation in which time is constituted by a definite, rational, and redeeming structure.

Indeed, his enemy, the spirit of gravity, incarnated as the gruesome dwarf, turns out to be Zarathustra's angel of mercy, providing him with an alternative interpretation of the moment which he swiftly adopts as his own. "'All that is straight lies,' the dwarf murmured contemptuously. 'All truth is crooked; time itself is a circle.'" The dwarf's opinion appears to be a nutshell description of eternity understood as eternal return. Zarathustra, however, angrily denounces the dwarf's interpretation as a flight from the awful truth: "You spirit of gravity . . . do not make things too easy for yourself! Or I shall let you crouch where you are crouching, lamefoot; and it was I that carried you to this *height*."

Why does Zarathustra regard conceiving of time as a circle as making things too easy? And too easy for whom? These questions take on heightened significance in view of the fact that subsequently Zarathustra calls himself "the advocate of the circle" (Z III "The Convalescent" 1) and sings of his "lust after eternity and after the nuptial ring of rings, the ring of recurrence" (Z III "The Seven Seals"). Indeed, his initial indignation should not be allowed to obscure the critical fact: Zarathustra promptly embraces the interpretation of eternity as a circle or ring, an interpretation that is introduced by his deadliest enemy and that he initially rejects as a cowardly deceit.[24]

In the blink of an eye Zarathustra becomes the unwitting disciple of the spirit of gravity, a spokesman for the spirit of revenge. He silences the dwarf, encouraging the impression that he has rejected the dwarf's understanding and resumed the elaboration of his original interpretation of the moment. Yet he proceeds to develop the dwarf's description of the moment as a necessary aspect of a single infinitely repeating or circular process:

> Behold . . . this moment! From this gateway, Moment, a long eternal lane leads *backward:* behind us lies an eternity. Must not whatever *can* walk have walked on this lane before? Must not whatever *can* happen have happened, have been done, have passed by before? And if everything has been there before—what do you think, dwarf, of this moment? Must not this gateway too have been there before? And are not all things knotted together so firmly that this moment draws after it *all* that is to come? Therefore—itself too? For whatever *can* walk—in this long lane out *there* too, it *must* walk once more.
>
> And this slow spider, which crawls in the moonlight, and this moonlight itself, and I and you in the gateway, whispering together, whispering of eternal things—must not all of us have been there before? And return and walk in that other lane, out there, before us, in this long dreadful lane—must we not eternally return?" (Z III "On the Vision and the Riddle" 2)

Immediately after denouncing the idea that time is a circle, Zarathustra advocates a vision in which eternity is a kind of self-repeating ring. This stunning about-face, this embrace of a view which only a moment before he characterized as making things too easy, does indeed constitute the affirmation of a sham solution, prompted by the spirit of revenge, to the problem of willing backward.

Zarathustra's original notion of the moment as the vertex of two rays leading in different directions imposed absolute limits on the will's capacity to will backward and command time. For willing takes place in the present and is directed to the future. As such, willing could have no influence on the past—at least on most interpretations of time and eternity. But Zarathustra's adopted interpretation of eternity, by maintaining the essential continuity of past and future in the moment, implies that a genuine assertion of the will in the present, an affirmation of the moment, simultaneously affirms and conquers the past and future. For if all things are knotted firmly together, then mastery of any moment would result in mastery of the whole; if all things are knotted firmly together, then successfully willing the moment becomes the supreme expression of the will to power.

But is mastery of or willing of the moment possible under the conditions established by Zarathustra's doctrine of eternity? A genuine act of will presupposes a modicum of initiative, some form of freedom for acting upon and altering the world. Yet, if the will is knotted together firmly with all things, its freedom is illusory. If it is unfree then its pretensions to mastery are a vain delusion. Although it could appear as a solution to the problem of willing backward, the doctrine of eternal return abolishes the possibility of willing altogether. Concerning this conundrum the lame and lame-making dwarf, the spirit of gravity, the parent of revenge, offers no comment. Indeed, he does not speak again. There is no need since he has acquired, in Zarathustra, an eloquent spokesman.

Although Zarathustra boasted of his own courage as he stepped forward to face the dwarf (Z III "On the Vision and the Riddle" 1), and accused the dwarf of cowardice that would prevent him from confronting Zarathustra's "abysmal thought," it is Zarathustra who blinks, confessing his fear of his own thoughts and what lies behind them. It is unclear what causes him greater distress: the threat to the freedom of the will posed by his interpretation of eternity, or the anguish sparked by the awareness that he has fallen under the spell of the spirit of revenge, betraying his intellect to redeem his will.

The vision of the gateway vanishes as Zarathustra, trapped between nightmares, uncertain whether he is waking or dreaming, is suddenly confronted by another terrifying image:

> A young shepherd I saw, writhing, gagging, in spasms, his face distorted, and a heavy black snake hung out of his mouth. Had I ever seen so much nausea and pale dread on one face? He seemed to have been asleep when the snake crawled into his throat, and there bit itself fast. My hand tore at the snake and tore in vain; it did not tear the snake out of his throat. Then it cried out of me: "Bite! Bite its head off! Bite!" Thus it cried out of me—my dread, my hatred, my nausea, my pity, all that is good and wicked in me cried out of me with a single cry. (Z III "On the Vision and the Riddle" 2)

In yet another reenactment of the poisoning depicted in "On the Adder's Bite," "On the Tarantulas," and a moment before in his encounter with the dwarf, Zarathustra comes to the rescue of the gagging shepherd. Powerless to remove the snake with his own hands, he is prompted by his hatred, nausea, and pity—the most vengeful reactions—to cry out his counsel to the snake's victim.

Here Zarathustra breaks off his retelling. No longer addressing his disciples—who in the past have gravely disappointed him by slavishly interpreting his doubts, weaknesses, and hysteria as symbolizing mastery of self and world[25]—Zarathustra invites the "bold searchers" and "researchers" on board the ship to guess the meaning of his "vision of the loneliest." But he promptly usurps the sailors' role by supplying the requested interpretation, an interpretation that reaffirms the link between the highest man and the most vengeful man, and the necessity for the high to pass through the depths:

> *What* did I see then in a parable? And *who* is it who must yet come one day? *Who* is the shepherd into whose throat the snake crawled thus? *Who* is the man into whose throat all that is heaviest and blackest will crawl thus?
>
> The shepherd, however, bit as my cry counseled him; he bit with a good bite. Far away he spewed the head of the snake—and he jumped up. No longer shepherd, no longer human—one changed, radiant, *laughing!* Never yet on earth has a human being laughed as he laughed! O my brothers, I heard a laughter that was no human laughter; and now a thirst gnaws at me, a longing that never grows still. My longing for this laughter gnaws at me; oh, how do I bear to go on living! And how could I bear to die now! (Z III "On the Vision and the Riddle" 2)

Zarathustra tempts his listeners to believe that the gagging shepherd overcomes the supreme nausea by metamorphosing into a superhuman being. But darkness and utter mystery now surround the process by which this dazzling metamorphosis takes place. Zarathustra's vision of a radical transformation from the depths of degradation to the peak of splendor strains credulity. One excellent reason for skepticism is the scandal of his disciples, who are distinguished by their servile credulity, their tendency to understand his craven cowering and disabling despair as signs of freedom and mastery. To avoid following in the ignominious footsteps of the disciples, whom Zarathustra himself rebukes and finds contemptible, one must ask whether a persuasive account has been or can be offered of the gagging shepherd's transformation into a radiant being. The basic demands of the intellectual conscience and the truthfulness that, according to Nietzsche, Zarathustra's doctrine prizes as the highest virtue (EH IV 3), compel one to probe whether Zarathustra's vision of a glorious transformation is not a deceitful interpretation of his response to the dwarf's challenge. And Nietzsche's and his Zarathustra's guiding interest in the base motives that impel human beings to falsify the world, inventing moralities and religions that enable them to love and attain power, encourages one to consider what end such a deceit might serve.

In fact, Zarathustra's "vision of the loneliest" leaves him with "riddles and bitterness in his heart" (Z III "On Involuntary Bliss"). On a lonely sea voyage he struggles to come to grips with the meaning of his devastating visions. While silently conversing with his conscience he reaffirms that he is required as the teacher of self-perfection to perfect himself. He understands his perfection, his final overcoming of his abysmal thought, as requiring "the final overbearing, prankish bearing of the lion" (Z III "On Involuntary Bliss"). And this is noteworthy for what it leaves behind. For what has become of the child, the highest form of the spirit?

While no longer equating perfection with becoming a child as in "On the Three Metamorphoses," Zarathustra does speak of caring for his children. The striking implication is that he has begun to retreat from the highest demand imposed by the ethics of creativity. This implication is somewhat offset by the fact that he confesses not only to "trembl[ing] with godlike desires" for heaven but also that his longings have always and primarily been for the "bright heaven" (Z III "Before Sunrise"). And he does claim that he has served these "godlike desires" by restoring Chance, "the most ancient nobility of the world . . . to all things" (Z III "Before Sunrise"). Presenting himself as a redeemer, Zarathustra proclaims that his restoration of Chance redeems all things and makes them free. But his teaching that "no 'eternal will' wills," or that God is dead, culminated in a demand that a finite will command time and master eternity. Although his yearning for the "bright heaven" may remain as strong as ever, Zarathustra has yet to produce an account of self-deification that does not call into question the very aspiration to overcome humanity that springs from his understanding of the needs of the human spirit in the wake of God's death.

Inventing Sacred Games: A Debasing Euphoria

After a new round of wanderings among humankind, Zarathustra heads for his cave. His return home serves as an occasion for a reprise of his major ideas and aspirations (Z III "On Old and New Tablets"). Suffice it to say that neither man nor Zarathustra's uncommon repugnance to man has undergone any serious alteration in the wake of his traumatic illness and his voyage of recuperation.

After reliving old glories, reaffirming his rejection of the present, and reasserting fabulous promises for the future as if they had lost none of their luster, Zarathustra at last reaches his cave. Despite his homecoming, his work is far from over, for his "abysmal thought" remains untamed. At home, Zarathustra, whose behavior is compared to that of a madman (Z III "The Convalescent" 1),[26] lets loose a bloodcurdling bellow causing his animals, his only remaining companions, to flee. Calling himself godless and speaking as "the advocate of life, the advocate of suffering, the advocate of the circle," he summons his "abysmal thought." Yet despite his long period of preparation and training, the approach of his abysmal thought triggers a massive wave of nausea that knocks him unconscious—and he "long remained as one dead" (Z III "The Convalescent" 2).

In contrast to his previous collapse, on this occasion, neither in his deathlike coma nor during the seven days of feverish consciousness that follow is Zarathustra beset by nightmares. His mind appears to have produced effective defenses. His return to health is depicted in the form of an allegory evoking the biblical story of the creation of the world with motifs from Christian theology thrown in for good measure: Zarathustra recovers in seven days; he awakes in a fragrant garden; he delights in a rose apple; and he has become the new shepherd to placid sheep robbed from their old shepherd. The cause of his convalescence is unclear. Is it "some new knowledge" as his animals suspect? Or rather a hidden reservoir of strength that enables him to triumph over the spirit of revenge? Or is his recovery rather a triumph for the spirit of revenge, as he follows his disciples in revaluing his infirmity as a show of power?

A dreamlike atmosphere dominates in Zarathustra's garden. Almost immediately after he has rebuked the sunny interpretation of his convalescence offered by his animals by insisting on the awesome power of words to deceive—"Are not words and sounds rainbows and illusive bridges between things which are eternally apart?"—his animals turn the eternal return into a hackneyed jingle, a harmless nursery rhyme:

> "O Zarathustra," the animals said, "to those who think as we do, all things themselves are dancing: they come and offer their hands and laugh and flee—and come back. Everything goes, everything comes back; eternally rolls the wheel of being. Everything dies, everything blossoms again; eternally runs the year of being. Everything breaks, everything is joined anew; eternally the same house of being is built. Everything parts, everything greets every other thing again; eternally the ring of being remains faithful to itself. In every Now, being begins; round every Here rolls the sphere There. The center is everywhere. Bent is the path of eternity." (Z III "The Convalescent" 2)

This insipidly cheerful interpretation of the eternal return echoes the dwarf's assertion that "All truth is crooked; time itself is a circle" (Z III "On the Vision and the Riddle" 2). And Zarathustra's casual and good-natured ridicule of the animals' version of his teaching as a hurdy-gurdy song parallels his initial rejection of the dwarf's vision. But it is important to notice that he listens to his animals as he lies "still weary of this biting and spewing, still sick from my own redemption." True, one must be skeptical of the animals' version of Zarathustra's doctrine of eternity inasmuch as Zarathustra derides it as hurdy-gurdy song. Yet perhaps his doctrine of redemption and eternity deserves to be presented as a hurdy-gurdy song. After all, it was Zarathustra himself in "On Redemption" who declared that in seeking to overcome the past the will that knows itself to be enchained wills foolishly.

Explicitly equating convalescence with triumph over nausea, Zarathustra identifies himself with the gagging shepherd in "On the Vision and the Riddle" as he relates how "that monster crawled down my throat and suffocated me. But I bit off its head and spewed it out." However, having saved himself from death by suffocation, did Zarathustra disgorge all the snake's poison? The fact of his continued suffering, in particular his suffering from his own redemption, suggests that he did not. He recounts, in particular, two sources of his suffering: a "great disgust with man" and, echoing the judgment pronounced by the soothsayer, that "All is the same, nothing is worth while, knowledge chokes." Zarathustra thus seems to suffer from a moral repugnance to mediocrity and to be weighted down by a metaphysical grievance arising from insight into the ultimate structure of the cosmos.

In fact, the moral repugnance and the metaphysical grievance are intimately related. The metaphysical barriers to absolute liberation serve as an absolute leveling force, a metaphysically grounded radical egalitarianism: "Naked I had once seen both, the greatest man and the smallest man: all-too-similar to each other, even the greatest all-too-human. All-too-small, the greatest!—that was my disgust with man. And the eternal recurrence even of the smallest—that was my disgust with all existence. Alas! Nausea! Nausea! Nausea!" (Z III "The Convalescent" 2). Not the mere return of the smallest man, but the return of the greatest man as kith and kin to the smallest man stokes the fires of Zarathustra's torment. It is in view of the interpretation of the human condition as set forth in "On Redemption" that his insistence on the resemblance of the greatest to the smallest may be understood. For according to his analysis the will of the greatest, like that of the smallest, is held in chains by the past; hence, the greatest as well as the smallest is uncreative, enslaved, and impotent.

Having set his sights so terribly high, Zarathustra finds himself in agreement with Hobbes (*Leviathan*, ch. 13) that the equality of human beings based on weakness is a more essential moral fact than the existence of various forms of inequality or excellence. But in contrast to Hobbes, for Zarathustra, a teacher dedicated to establishing a new order of rank and articulating the supreme form of excellence, the recognition of mankind's equality grounded in weakness must be poisonous. Indeed, it was Zarathustra himself who proclaimed that he did "not wish to be mixed up and confused with these preachers of equality. For, to *me* justice speaks thus: 'Men are not equal.' Nor shall they become equal! What would my love of the superman be if I spoke otherwise?" (Z II "On the Tarantulas").[27] Indeed, Zarathustra should not be mistaken for the preachers of equality. In spite of his wishes and the teachings of justice, Zarathustra, by virtue of his teaching about will, eternity, and the spirit of revenge, must rather be seen as the high priest among them. For it is Zarathustra's doctrine that annihilates the distinction between the greatest and the smallest and thus establishes an equality between the superman and the last man.[28]

Like the human disciples before them, Zarathustra's animals lack the ears to hear the cry of distress rising from the belly of his being. They attribute his disgust to a bad dream from which he will wake to greet a glorious new day. Rather than rebuking his animals for their ingratiating interpretations, as he did his disciples for theirs, Zarathustra credits them with having understood that his convalescence involves an invented comfort: "How well you know what comfort [*Trost*] I invented for myself in seven days! That I must sing again, this comfort and convalescence I invented for myself. Must you immediately turn this too into a hurdy-gurdy song?" (Z III "The Convalescent" 2).[29] It is a mark of Zarathustra's weariness and resignation that he bemoans the haste with which his animals popularize his invented comfort, but is powerless to defend a better view. He thereby acquiesces in the burlesque of his doctrine of eternity.

Urged by his animals to forget his doubts, to embrace his destiny as the teacher of the eternal return, and to sing along with them, Zarathustra listens impassively as they proclaim his new dogma, which reflects a purely deterministic understanding of the world:

Behold, we know what you teach: that all things recur eternally, and we ourselves too; and that we have already existed an eternal number of times, and all things with us. You teach that there is a great year of becoming, a monster of a great year, which must, like an hourglass, turn over again and again so that it may run down and run out again; and all these years are alike in what is greatest as in what is smallest; and we ourselves are alike in every great year, in what is greatest as in what is smallest. (Z III "The Convalescent" 2)

Only a moment before, Zarathustra had admonished the animals for their foolishness; now they are writing his script:

"Now I die and vanish," you would say, "and all at once I am nothing. The soul is as mortal as the body. But the knot of causes in which I am entangled recurs and will create me again. I myself belong to the causes of the eternal recurrence. I come again, with this sun, with this earth, with this eagle, with this serpent—*not* to a new life or a better life or a similar life: I come back eternally to this same, selfsame life, in what is greatest as in what is smallest, to teach again the eternal recurrence of all things, to speak again the word of the great noon of earth and man, to proclaim the superman again to men. I spoke my word, I break of my word: thus my eternal lot wants it; as a proclaimer I perish. The hour has now come when he who goes under should bless himself. Thus *ends* Zarathustra's going under." (Z III "The Convalescent" 2)

To these prophetic words Zarathustra has no reply. The process of his "going under," initiated in the opening scene of the prologue, concludes with the by-now-familiar collapse. He lies down in stillness, abandoned even by his serpent and his eagle, locked in comforting conversation with his soul.[30]

The final speeches of part III record these ecstatic reveries, the product of the comatose prophet's feverish imagination, in which Zarathustra experiences himself as having attained a redemptive reconciliation with eternity. Yet the ecstatic joy with which he silently proclaims himself triumphant reveals a broken man. He confesses that he is utterly enthralled by the matchless seductress, life, "whose coldness fires, whose hatred seduces, whose flight binds, whose scorn inspires" (Z III "The Other Dancing Song" 1). Driven to frenzy by his Cleopatra, he so completely imagines life as a ravishing woman that, returning to advice he received from the old woman in part 1, he declares that he will master life with his whip. But it is embarrassingly plain, from life's poised, coy reply stating that the two lovers must learn to live together, who has the upper hand, who commands and who obeys.[31]

Like a desperate lover, Zarathustra confesses his absolute and in effect abject devotion to life, his willingness to make what, from the point of view of his own doctrine, is the ultimate sacrifice: "And we looked at each other and gazed on the green meadow over which the cool evening was running just then, and we wept together. But then life was dearer to me than all my wisdom ever was" (Z III "The Other Dancing Song" 2). Dearer to Zarathustra than friends, honor, dignity, or even the intellectual conscience that Nietzsche praised so extravagantly and the truthfulness he insisted was prized by Zarathustra as the highest virtue, is life and the myth of redemption that makes life bearable.[32]

As Zarathustra replaced his disciples and the dwarf, he now becomes his own buffoon and barrel organ reveling in a hurdy-gurdy song of pleasure, contentment, and eternal salvation:

> Oh, how should I not lust after eternity and after the nuptial ring of rings, the ring of recurrence?
> Never yet have I found the woman from whom I wanted children, unless it be this woman whom I love: for I love you, O eternity.
> *For I love you, O eternity!* (Z III "The Seven Seals")

Under the holy name eternity, one discerns in Zarathustra an extreme and destructive tendency.[33] Who can fail to be reminded by the spectacle

of this lustful preacher of eternal salvation of Zarathustra's own devastating observation about the impact of romantic love on the quest for
truth: "This one went out like a hero in quest of truths, and eventually
he conquered a little dressed-up lie. His marriage he calls it" (Z I "On
Child and Marriage")?[34]

Contrary to Nietzsche's subsequent promises, Zarathustra sacrifices
his intellect (BGE 23). Driven by poisoned passion and passionate resentment against the limits imposed by necessity on his will, he abandons his wisdom so that he can love life better by taking a blissful leap
into the arms of eternity.[35] And the gravity of his betrayal stems not only
from his insistence on the preciousness of honesty (Z IV "On the Higher
Men" 8), but also from the fact that Nietzsche tells us that it is precisely
Zarathustra's doctrine, in contrast to the mendacity of Christianity, that
"posits truthfulness as the highest virtue" (EH IV 3). The way of the
creator does not culminate in the restoration of human dignity but
rather finds its peak moment in a scandalous union with eternity, built
of desperate lies and degrading lust, dwarfing all previous formulas for
revenge.

Conclusion

Nietzsche regarded Zarathustra as the teacher of the eternal return
(EH III, on BT, 3) and regarded the eternal return as the fundamental
conception of *Thus Spoke Zarathustra* (EH III, on Z, 1). Indeed, parts II
and III of *Thus Spoke Zarathustra* provide the most sustained treatment
of the eternal return in Nietzsche's writings. What begins in a craving
for absolute mastery and becomes entangled in the need for absolute
freedom comes into focus through visions and nightmares and is ultimately transformed into a comforting and redemptive metaphysical
fiction. But the comfort and the redemption are costly. The argument
and action of *Zarathustra* powerfully suggest that the eternal return
must be understood as a reactive thought, a reflection of weakness, indeed, the brainstorm and child of the spirit of revenge. Zarathustra's
embarrassing, melodramatic, and finally preposterous betrothal to eternity in the final speech of part III marks the climax of his self-deception
and humiliation. Imagine his revulsion when on his wedding night he
delicately lifts his bride's lacy white veil only to see the crooked, tooth-
less smile of a withered, misshapen hag.

Since the doctrine of the eternal return provides the missing piece in the quest to achieve a godlike affirmation and godlike self-sufficiency that Zarathustra assigns to the superman, it is important to recall the specific defect in his original account of the ethics of creativity. The ethics of creativity is based on the metaphysical knowledge that God is dead. This means that all moral values, religious beliefs, and philosophical doctrines, all conceptions of good and bad, have in fact been created by human beings. Zarathustra might have concluded that nothing is true, everything is permitted. Instead he discovers an ethics of creativity that views most everything as worthless and only one thing as needful. That one thing, the highest and sole worthy goal of a good life, is the absolute liberation and the supreme empowerment of the creative will. Absolute freedom and supreme power are achieved in the highest type, a being who conquers his own world by making his will a law unto itself.

By stages, Zarathustra discovers that the naked will is stymied in its efforts to free itself fully from the grips of necessity and to achieve the unqualified freedom necessary for the exercise of unconditioned creativity. In the first stage, he methodically emancipates the creator from moral and political dependence. But, as is foreshadowed throughout the prologue and part I and brought to articulate awareness in part II, morality and politics do not exhaust the forms of necessity, and the state, romantic love, and friendship do not cover the varieties of dependence. Try as the will might to escape all that holds it fast so that it can command the greatest things, irreversible time proves an unrelenting master. Ingeniously, Zarathustra realizes that the will can restore its supremacy by bringing the intrinsic, bedrock constraints that time—understood both as the burdens of the past and the laws of causal necessity—imposes on all beings under its sovereignty. Spinoza, who Nietzsche believed shared his tendency "to make knowledge the most *powerful passion*" (letter to Franz Overbeck, 30 July 1881, in L, p. 177), and whom he honored as a predecessor and kindred spirit, was wrong from the perspective of the ethics of creativity to think that knowledge of necessity brought freedom. For freedom to be preserved in the teeth of necessity, necessity must be made subject to the will.

But willing or commanding necessity is easier said than done. There is a thin line between making a virtue out of necessity and rationalizing weakness by calling it strength, or attempting to overcome enslavement by renaming it freedom. What distinguishes the mastery of necessity from the mere or mad assertion of mastery? The doctrine of the eternal return represents Zarathustra's understanding of the conditions for the possibility of willing or mastering the most comprehensive forms of necessity. As I have argued, Zarathustra cannot meet those conditions: his attempt to overcome his humanity by mastering necessity discloses that contrary to the hopes for self-deification inscribed in the ethics of creativity, some forms of necessity are invulnerable to even the strongest wills.

Thus Spoke Zarathustra puts on epic display the contest of extremes in Nietzsche's thought as it chronicles Zarathustra's attempt to effect a reconciliation between knowing and making at the highest, most comprehensive level. The character of the reconciliation at which Zarathustra aims is concisely set forth in one of Nietzsche's unpublished notes:

> To impose upon becoming the character of being—that is the supreme will to power.
>
> Twofold falsification, on the part of the senses and of the spirit, to preserve a world of that which is, which abides, which is equivalent, etc.
>
> That *everything recurs* is the closest *approximation of a world of becoming to a world of being:*—highpoint of the meditation. (WP 617)

In fact, the supreme form of the will to power, as it comes to light in *Thus Spoke Zarathustra,* does indeed consist in falsifying the world by imposing upon the meaningless flux of events the shape of eternal necessity. Zarathustra's bogus reconciliation with eternity, the low point of his ordeal, is the high point of Nietzsche's thought experiment. For Zarathustra's ordeal shows that the fulfillment of the moral imperative to self-deification, which Nietzsche's madman derives from the death of God and from which Nietzsche's Zarathustra infers God's death, requires a staggering self-delusion, a base lie.

Zarathustra achieves a union with eternity by bestowing a false and degrading reality on the cosmic fiction of the eternal return. His parable of becoming is not beautiful and does not justify impermanence. His dream of redemption and its purported attainment in the love of eternity reveal a yearning for and faith in transcendence more Platonic than Nietzsche's Plato in its grandiose and categorical pronouncements about the ultimate constitution of things, and in the tidy, blissful redemption that it promises the believer. It is thanks to Nietzsche's art and the intellectual conscience with which he endows his great protagonist that one can see in Zarathustra's reconciliation with eternity a higher swindle, a counterfeiting of transcendence, an immense philosophical ruse, a tyrannical desire on a cosmic scale to have one's cake and eat it too.

Zarathustra shows that the highest and most comprehensive form of right making based on right knowing is tantamount to godlike mastery. By revealing that absolute mastery is impossible he provides practical motivation and theoretical justification to reevaluate the interpretation of the human condition that gave rise to the ethics of creativity and its debasing moral imperative to transcend the human condition by making oneself a god.

8

Retreat from the Extremes:
Thus Spoke Zarathustra (Part IV)

Part IV, the concluding and longest in *Thus Spoke Zarathustra,* appears
to add little to Zarathustra's account of the ethics of creativity and its
supreme demand that human beings make themselves gods. Nietzsche
wrote that the fourth part of *Zarathustra* comes after *Zarathustra* is fin-
ished, serves as a "sublime finale," and is an intermission between *Zarathustra* and works to come.[1] Nevertheless, part IV contributes to an understanding of Zarathustra's account of the best life. For his descent into
farce is in part a consequence of his failing to fulfill, or live in accordance
with, the superhuman requirements imposed by his new ethics. And
since on Nietzsche's view the only test of a philosophy that is worthwhile
and proves anything is whether one can live in accordance with it (SE 8,
p. 187), it is pertinent to explore the kind of life Zarathustra lives in the
wake of his sham reconciliation with eternity.

Part IV functions as a kind of epilogue following Zarathustra, a weary
teacher despairing of discovering or creating a healthy, upright soul, as
he indulges his new interest in diseased and suffering souls. In particular, he becomes intrigued with the pathology epitomized by "the higher
man." This victim of overreaching, whose ambition exceeds his grasp
and whose critical faculties surpass his creative powers, discerns vulgar-
ity, hypocrisy, and wretched contentment in the contemporary manifestations of culture, politics, and religion. The higher man, however, lacks
the power to create for himself a higher form of life; he becomes, as a

result of his supposedly true insight, one more enfeebled casualty of the times. He is a kind of great man who, because he "suffers from the deficiencies of his age more acutely than do smaller men" (SE 3, p. 145), is, as much as the last man, a child of the modern dispensation that Zarathustra excoriates.

Part IV chronicles the farcical, surreal encounters of the prematurely aged Zarathustra with the higher men; it culminates with the bizarre banquet Zarathustra throws in honor of his odd company of social outcasts, physical cripples, and grotesque misfits. There is much parody and black humor in this part; the important question is what causes Zarathustra to become a party to and complicit in the higher men's debasing behavior. Indeed, Zarathustra appears a shadow of his former self, ministering to and obsequiously ingratiating himself with other shadows. Part IV presents an excruciating spectacle calling to mind a washed-up champion prizefighter, a pale image of his glory days, absorbing blow after blow, just barely sustained on his feet by an inextinguishable pride. In the role of host to the higher men, Zarathustra is revealed to be neither superman nor prophet, but a kind of higher man himself, morbidly hostile to the prevailing social and political arrangements in the name of a vague notion of transcendence that his own convictions forbid him to embrace.[2]

Having boasted of overcoming pity, Zarathustra joins the higher men in an act of ass-worship and unwittingly becomes, for a moment, thoroughly pitiful. All the more impressive, therefore, is his final renunciation of drunken songs (Z IV "The Sign") to which, Zarathustra acknowledges, he temporarily fell victim, and to which his companions and admirers remain captive. Zarathustra's new sobriety reveals that all higher men do not attain equal heights. Although Nietzsche brings Zarathustra's saga to an end before the implications for the good life of this new sobriety come into view, I shall suggest that the perspective of *Beyond Good and Evil*, the perspective of a free spirit, embodies this new sobriety.

The price of Zarathustra's terrible bargain with the devil consummated in part III is immediately visible in the first scene of part IV, writ large in his newly white hair and the yellowing and darkening his body has undergone since his ostensible convalescence and reconciliation with eternity.[3] While he boasts of honey coursing through his veins, his body dramatically testifies to inner decay. Even his usually fawning animals remark that he appears to be in a "dreadful mess" (Z IV "The Honey Sacrifice").

Zarathustra's sorry state points to the crucial transition marked by part IV. Whereas from the moment of his return to mankind in the prologue he had focused on the extremes, the supreme type and the most contemptible man, he now proclaims a fascination with intermediate types, a wish to become a fisherman in the "abysmal rich sea" of the world, "a sea full of colorful fish and crabs" (Z IV "The Honey Sacrifice"; cf. Matthew 4:19). Boasting that he is "the most sarcastic of all who fish for men," Zarathustra seems to have tacitly abandoned the things that transcend man: the superman; the utterance of a "sacred Yes"; the need to make of the will a law unto itself; the obligation to "command great things"; the craving for redemption from time; the will to love and master eternity. Once having zealously sought the superhuman, Zarathustra now turns to examining "the human world, the human sea," to using his "best bait" to "bait the queerest human fish" (Z IV "The Honey Sacrifice").

Nevertheless, the "queerest human fish," the higher men, are related to the superman. Inasmuch as each of the higher men is a seeker of excellence, the vision of the superman looms over part IV. No longer, however, as a promise unfulfilled and a goal not yet reached, but as a promise denied and goal that cruelly mocks those who seek it. The special contribution of part IV is to bring to light the sad practical consequences that befall those who try to live in accordance with Zarathustra's ethics of creativity. Not least of those is Zarathustra himself.

The Higher Men

Weighed down by a heavy happiness and no longer a commanding presence, Zarathustra determines, some time after his supposed reconciliation with eternity, that the time for him to descend from his mountain is still far in the future, and he thus resolves to make his teaching known only to those who ascend to his heights. His first visitor is not long in coming. As he sits lost in thought outside the entrance to his cave, he is startled by a strange shadow that he spots lying next to his own (Z IV "The Cry of Distress"). The second shadow belongs to the soothsayer, the proclaimer of the great weariness who, just as in part II, comes bearing ill tidings that command Zarathustra's attention. Speaking with an overflowing heart, the soothsayer warns Zarathustra that soon "waves of great distress and melancholy" will carry him away. Not only the soothsayer's prophecy of Zarathustra's impending emotional chaos but his mere presence in Zarathustra's hitherto impassable heights indicates that Zarathustra is no longer sovereign in his own realm. The sacred boundaries he had sought to erect on his mountain (Z III "On Old and New Tablets" 19) have been breached.

As Zarathustra and the soothsayer speak, a blood-curdling cry of distress, the cry of the higher man, resounds from the abysses surrounding Zarathustra's cave. This cry is the occasion for the soothsayer to announce and for Zarathustra to concur in the judgment that "pity"—concern with human distress—is Zarathustra's final sin and test. Filled with dread, perhaps reminded of his many shrieks of horror and hideous nightmares attending his attempt to redeem the world through the exercise of his creative will, Zarathustra listens patiently as the soothsayer condemns his heights for containing "no mines of happiness or treasure rooms or new gold veins of happiness" (Z IV "The Cry of Distress"). He does not protest the soothsayer's accusation that he has failed to fill the void created by the death of God and that he has been unable to create for himself the golden and glowing happiness for which he yearns and which he understands to be required by his new ethics.

But Zarathustra does vigorously deny the soothsayer's concluding contention that "all is the same, nothing is worth while, no seeking avails, nor are there any blessed isles any more." Against this catechism of despair, he boldly affirms that blessed isles do indeed exist. Just as in the prologue Zarathustra was the lone voice proclaiming the death of God, he now is the last to maintain belief in a divine realm. Despite his shattering setbacks and the impact of his profound disappointments, to which his withered body gives arresting testimony, Zarathustra clings to a belief in a sacred goal for human life. But he has lost his single-minded dedication. Instead, he assumes responsibility for insuring the safety of the unredeemed higher man who has wandered into his realm.

Not an hour after Zarathustra has embarked on his search for the higher man, he spots two flamboyantly adorned kings driving a laden ass (Z IV "Conversation with the Kings"). He rudely wonders aloud how one ass can serve two kings. The kings indicate that propriety prevents them from speaking about this embarrassing problem in public;

noting but not flustered by Zarathustra's lack of tact, they reveal that it is precisely good manners and conventional decency from which they have sought to escape. They are in flight from a decadent society where the nobility are no better than the "gilded, false, painted mob." Their sense of rank has been offended by the withering of the capacity to make moral distinctions. In their kingdom, "Nobody knows how to revere any longer."

Like Zarathustra, the kings are plagued by nausea arising from the ascendancy of the rabble. And also like Zarathustra, they are in search of the higher or highest man. Evidently unaware of who they themselves are and the nature of him whom they seek, the kings wish to install the higher man as a ruler in the belief that he represents society's last best hope. Apparently the superman, a being too pure for political rule, does not figure in their reformist plans. But Zarathustra refrains from rebuking the kings for aiming too low and does not admonish them to occupy themselves exclusively with giving birth to the superman. Although he admits to having formerly been indifferent to kings, he illustrates his new attachment to the human world by declaring his delight with the kings' wisdom and inviting them to be guests at his cave.

The spirit of farce is heightened as Zarathustra, continuing along his way, inadvertently steps on an ill-tempered man lying stretched out and concealed in a swampy valley (Z IV "The Leech"). Confusion arises as to who is to blame and who has invaded whose realm. Sovereignty in Zarathustra's realm is now open to dispute. The grotesque swamp-dweller, whose arm is bloody and leech-bitten, calls himself the "conscientious in spirit" and claims Zarathustra, whom he calls "the great leech of conscience," as his teacher. The conscientious in spirit contends that he follows Zarathustra in making a strict and narrow form of intellectual conscience his special virtue. But for Zarathustra's new acquaintance, knowledge, identified with certainty, is a kind of foolhardiness that levels all distinctions:

> Rather know nothing than half-know much! Rather be a fool on one's own than a sage according to the opinion of others! I go to the ground—what does it matter whether it be great or small? whether it be called swamp or sky? A hand's breadth of ground suffices me, provided it is really ground and foundation. A hand's breadth of ground—on that one can stand. In the conscience of science there is nothing great and nothing small. (Z IV "The Leech")

Like the doctrine of the eternal return, which obliterates the distinction between the greatest and the smallest, the conscience of science, when elevated to a ruling impulse, effaces every moral difference. Thus the conscientious in spirit, whose compulsive quest for certain knowledge compels him to forsake not only human society but also simple human dignity, does appear to be Zarathustra's pupil. Accordingly, Zarathustra treats him fondly, inviting him to be his "dear guest" at dinner that evening.

Zarathustra then chances across a spastic old man sprawled on the ground who "kept looking around with piteous gestures, like one abandoned and forsaken by all the world" (Z IV "The Magician" 1). Showing signs of consciousness, the old magician, utterly cut off from society, suffering his solitude as an agonizing hardship, recites a poem heavy with despair. His verses describe the torment he feels as the plaything and victim of a cruel, mysterious, unnameable God. Repelled by the song's shameless display of self-pity, and finally unable to restrain himself, Zarathustra rains blows on the old man, denouncing him as a liar, counterfeiter, and wicked magician.

The magician, a transparent mask for Richard Wagner,[4] confesses to Zarathustra that he long aspired to create images of great human beings for the public, but eventually came to realize that the artistic representation of greatness constitutes an evasion of the task of making oneself great. This aspiration to greatness, combined with the magician's recognition of his failure to achieve it, earns Zarathustra's respect. Yet not realizing that his recognition serves as another evasion of the obligation to make himself great, the magician obsequiously declares that he seeks Zarathustra because he believes him to be "one who is genuine, right, simple, unequivocal, a man of all honesty, a vessel of wisdom, a saint of knowledge, a great human being" (ibid. 2). But Zarathustra immediately disavows any such grand achievement. He reinforces the interpretation that his apparent triumph over nausea in the conclusion to part III was fraudulent by denying having ever glimpsed a great human being, and by mockingly declaring that only a fool could still believe in the possibility of distinguishing between great and small.

Zarathustra's next encounter is with a religious figure (Z IV "Retired"), a tall man in black with a gaunt, pale face in whom he immediately notes a resemblance to "the tribe of priests." Oddly, given his admission that his blood is related to theirs (Z II "On Priests"), Zarathustra wonders what a priest would be doing in his realm. He curses the old man and seeks to slip past him unnoticed. But the old man sees him and promptly reveals their kinship.

The frail priest is a seeker,[5] a seeker of "the last pious man," whom he seems to identify with the saint in the forest whose blissful worship of God Zarathustra had refused to disturb by revealing that God was dead (Z Prologue 2). The old man, calling himself "the last pope," explains that he formerly believed in God, serving him until the last hour. His faith in God destroyed but his piety still strong, he searched for the saint in the forest only to discover that the saint too had died. With his death, piety, in the form of worship of God, vanished from the face of the earth. Yet piety itself persists, no longer as the worship of God, but as the effort to achieve redemption in God's absence. Perhaps having heard of Zarathustra's superhuman efforts to achieve redemption by mastering or loving eternity, the last pope proclaims Zarathustra "the most pious of all those who do not believe in God" (Z IV "Retired"). Zarathustra does not object to this title. Indeed, the two men become friends as the last pope recognizes in Zarathustra his legitimate heir and as Zarathustra, a lover of piety as the last pope correctly grasped, admires the last pope's errant but strong yearning for holiness or redemption.

Contrary to the last pope, who explains the death of God in terms of a natural process of aging and deterioration, Zarathustra takes personal credit for God's death. Echoing his remarkable inference that God must be a fiction because he wounded Zarathustra's vanity (Z II "Upon the Blessed Isles"), Zarathustra now reveals that it was not his envy but his piety that dealt the death blow to God. For God, according to Zarathustra, bungled his creation and then wreaked revenge on man for being bungled. This according to Zarathustra, "was a sin against *good taste.* There is good taste in piety too; and it was this that said in the end, 'Away with *such* a god! Rather no god, rather make destiny on one's own, rather be a fool, rather be a god oneself.'"

The last pope, exhibiting the alloy in his piety that attracts him to that before which he can kneel, lauds Zarathustra's speech as god-like. In fact, so enthralled is he with the fragrance of the old God wafting through Zarathustra's words that he fails to grasp that Zarathustra's piety makes the sacred and the profane one. The moral imperative stemming from Zarathustra's piety—"better a fool or deity than a believer"—undercuts the rank among souls Zarathustra himself had sought to preserve. For little is left of nobility or mastery when an expression of self-contempt—"Become a fool"—is seen as indistinguishable from the ultimate expression of human pride—"Become a god."

Although he corrects the last pope's account of the death of God, Zarathustra lets stand the old man's observation that it is piety that compels Zarathustra to reject God, and honesty that leads him beyond good and evil. Indeed, the last pope comes to regard Zarathustra as the model of piety and hence not perfectly godless: "Near you, although you want to be the most godless, I scent a secret, sacred, pleasant scent of long blessings: it gives me gladness and grief" (Z IV "Retired"). To this characterization Zarathustra gives his approval by proclaiming "Amen"; and confirming his blood bond to the priests, he declares that he "love[s] all who are pious" and warmly gives "the last pope" directions to his cave.

Charmed and reinvigorated by the strange interlocutors he has encountered, and no longer hostage to his repugnance to imperfection, Zarathustra proceeds cheerfully on his way. In this lighter mood he suddenly enters a "realm of death" (Z IV "The Ugliest Man") whose stark cliffs and creepy desolation evoke the gloomy mountain path "not cheered by herb or shrub" where, in the presence of the lame and lame-making dwarf, he elaborated his understanding of the moment and eternity (Z III "On the Vision and the Riddle" 1). Symbols linking the two underworld realms proliferate. Shepherds have named the valley that Zarathustra has just entered Snake's Death after the loathsome, fat, green snakes that come to die there—a potent reminder of the vision of the gagging shepherd that immediately followed Zarathustra's encounter with the dwarf. Struck with a distressing sense of *déjà vu*, Zarathustra sinks "into a black reminiscence" (Z IV "The Ugliest Man"). The grave weight that oppresses him and brings him to a standstill suggests the return of the spirit of gravity. Moreover, the "inexpressible" creature Zarathustra meets, the ugliest man, like the lame dwarf, challenges him with riddles, asking "What is *the revenge against the witness?*" and "who am I?"

Fighting off an onslaught of pity, Zarathustra cracks the ugliest man's riddle by recognizing him as the slayer of God. And Zarathustra's recognition induces the ugliest man to divulge how the motive of revenge impelled him to his murderous attack:

But he *had* to die: he saw with eyes that saw everything; he saw man's depths and ultimate grounds, all his concealed disgrace and ugliness. His pity knew no shame: he crawled into my dirtiest nooks. This most curious, overobtrusive, overpitying one had to die. He always saw me: on such a witness I wanted to have revenge or not live myself. The god who saw everything, *even man*—this god had to die! Man cannot bear it that such a witness should live. (ibid.)

Although Zarathustra distinguishes the ugliest man's way from his own, he too traces his repudiation of God to pride, his inability to suffer the indignity of the limitation on his will posed by God and gods (Z II "On the Blessed Isles"). The thinking of both prideful men testifies that beyond its role in spawning belief in the divine, the spirit of revenge is furiously at work in the destruction of such belief.[6] In other words, the impulse to eradicate the impulse to transcendence is also a potent form of the spirit of revenge.

Noting that the ugliest man is both a great despiser and a great lover,[7] Zarathustra returns to a theme he introduced in the prologue, and wonders whether the ability to despise oneself is a kind of height, and whether the ugliest man is not the higher man for whom he is searching. But the other strange individuals he has met also displayed a great and frustrated capacity for love that compelled them to despise not only their contemporaries but also themselves. If great love based on great contempt is the mark of the higher man, then Zarathustra has been dealing with higher men for some time now.

Whereas his encounter with the ugliest man was marked by gloom, his next encounter, with the voluntary beggar, a thinly veiled Jesus, arouses his tender affection and gentle derision (Z IV "The Voluntary Beggar"). The scene shifts from the cold, dark underworld to a sunny pasture. Sensing "unknown companions and brothers roam[ing] about," Zarathustra feels refreshed. But as he looks around he discovers, without expressing surprise or displeasure, that the source of his comfort and fellow feeling is a herd of cows gathered in a circle listening eagerly to a preacher. The herd's shepherd, the voluntary beggar, turns out to be a fellow victim of the great nausea, and like Zarathustra, a seeker of happiness on earth.[8] The "sermonizer on the mount" recounts how disillusionment with the rich drove him to the poor and meek, and then how disgust with the poor and meek drove him to become a teacher of cows. For the voluntary beggar, as for Zarathustra, the consequence of being a great despiser is to lose sight of the distinction between the greatest and smallest man and finally between cud-chewing beasts and human beings. Still not satisfied that he has found the origin of the cry of distress that had been resounding through his realm, Zarathustra bids the voluntary beggar join him at his cave and continues on his search.

Lost for a brief moment in the quiet of his solitude, Zarathustra is hailed by a shadow, a shadow that turns out to be his own. But having suddenly become annoyed with all the strange intruders roaming about on his mountain, and complaining that his "kingdom is no longer of *this* world" (Z IV "The Shadow"), he dashes away with his shadow in hot pursuit. In fact, Zarathustra's kingdom has for some time been open to the human world; having lost its air of exotic remoteness, it has become human, all too human.

When Zarathustra finally halts the chase and confronts the shadow he sees a dissipated creature, thin, swarthy, hollow—and a zealous seeker after eternity. The shadow reveals that he willingly braved the forbidden and repugnant, overthrowing all from which men had previously derived security and elevation, "all boundary stones and images," yet came up worse than empty-handed. The cry of distress of Zarathustra's shadow echoes the soothsayer's catechism of despair: "Nothing is true, all is permitted." Although motivated by love of truth, the shadow's quest ends in humiliation: "Too often, verily, did I follow close on the heels of truth: so she kicked me in the face." Echoing Zarathustra's songs of lament, his shadow reveals that his capacity for faith and love, including self-love, perished as a result of the knowledge he acquired. Homeless and heartbroken, afraid that he has exposed all horizons as illusory, Zarathustra's "best shadow" bitterly declares that he has repudiated the very idea of eternity.

With this display of candor from the shadow, Zarathustra can no longer withhold his recognition. His melancholy acknowledgment that the shadow is his own is linked to his exposition of the shadow's chief danger. He praises his shadow as a free spirit, but also warns him—and by extension he who casts the shadow—that he is placed in jeopardy by the powerful temptation to break faith with his grueling faithlessness and to exchange the brutal freedom won and preserved by honesty or the intellectual conscience for the soothing imprisonment offered by illusion: "To those who are as restless as you, even a jail will at last seem bliss. Have you ever seen how imprisoned criminals sleep? They sleep calmly, enjoying their new security. Beware lest a narrow faith imprison you in the end—some harsh and severe illusion. For whatever is narrow and solid seduces and tempts you now" (ibid.). And perhaps what is most narrow, solid, and severe, what offers the most extreme form of imprisonment, eternal imprisonment, is what tempts and seduces most of all.[9]

Zarathustra's shadow rounds out the band of higher men who, in a variety of spheres including politics, science and scholarship, art, philosophy, and religion, seek excellence. With the aid of the summary speech "On the Higher Man," one can sketch a composite portrait of Zarathustra's new companions. First, like Zarathustra, the higher man is a great despiser: he is repelled by the collective lie people call morality. Second, he is a great lover, longing to discover an object worthy of reverence. Third, he suffers a twofold estrangement called nausea that stems both from intense disgust with his fellow man and from mounting self-contempt as he flounders in his efforts to achieve elevation by finding or making himself a worthy object of reverence. Fourth, his contempt drives him from society but he lacks the strength to flourish in solitude. Zarathustra's preoccupation with the higher man represents a return to humanity after his consuming efforts to teach and bring into existence the highest type. Whereas prior to part IV he had focused on two extreme types, the superman and the last man, his new acquaintances attest to the existence of an intermediate type who partakes of the aspirations of the superman and the feebleness of the last man.

Although proclaiming the higher men heavy-footed failures, Zarathustra offers an alternative to their despair. He urges them to lift their hearts and to become good dancers, for revenge is overcome, he teaches, by lightness and gaiety of spirit: "Laughter I have pronounced holy; you higher men, *learn* to laugh!" (Z IV "On the Higher Man" 20, also 15). But as Zarathustra failed with the people in the marketplace and his disciples on his wanderings, so too he fails to impart his wisdom to the higher men: he is not capable of teaching them to laugh rightly (Z IV "The Awakening" 1); nor are they able to teach themselves. Indeed, Zarathustra becomes a party to their degradation. As the ass worship at Zarathustra's banquet illustrates, the higher man is distinguished by a pathetic betrayal of his innermost beliefs, a sinking back into the modes of behavior he has publicly condemned and continues to despise.

The Retreat from Eternity and the Return of the Lion

The ass festival occurs during the banquet Zarathustra throws in honor of the higher men. Zarathustra's momentary and premature optimism notwithstanding, the higher men retreat back to a nauseating kind of conduct. For no sooner does Zarathustra express his delighted conviction that "Nausea is retreating from these higher men" and that they are convalescing, than he finds his guests at once "kneeling like children, and devout little old women and adoring the ass" (ibid. 2). Just as Zarathustra was amazed when the people in the marketplace listened to him with deaf ears and cold hearts, he is now amazed to find the higher men having become pious again.

But the higher men are not alone. Zarathustra too, it seems, loses his capacity, in the face of nauseating behavior, to experience nausea. Smashing his own tablets, he leaps into the midst of the pious idolaters and "himself shouted Yeah-Yuh, even louder than the ass" (Z IV "The Ass Festival"; cf. BGE 269). From his position in the middle, ringed by worshippers, he accusingly queries each of the higher men how he could have reverted to belief in god, particularly such a laughable god. The various self-mocking and resigned replies reflect a drastic easing of the tension that spurred the higher men to pursue excellence. The higher men, Zarathustra serenely proclaims, have become like pious little children and hence fit for the Christian heaven. Perhaps one of the reasons he views this sad spectacle with equanimity—"such things are invented only by convalescents" (Z IV "The Ass Festival" 3)—is that he recalls his own convalescence and the embarrassing comfort he invented for himself. And perhaps he sees a connection between his own failure to achieve the sacred play of the child, his symbol of the totally unconditioned creator (Z I "On the Three Metamorphoses"), and the infantilization of the spirit manifested by the ass worship in which he takes a leading role.

Declaring that new festivals are necessary and that the higher men now appear to him to have become light in spirit, Zarathustra seems to approve of the degrading worship service in which he has permitted himself to indulge:

Do not forget this night and this ass festival, you higher men. *This* you invented when you were with me and I take that for a good sign: such things are invented only by convalescents.

And when you celebrate it again, this ass festival, do it for your own sakes, and also do it for my sake. And in remembrance of *me*. (Z IV "The Ass Festival" 3)

By characterizing the ass festival as the invention of convalescents, Zarathustra calls into question his love for and reconciliation with eternity, which he himself achieved or invented as a convalescent. And by linking his name to the celebration of the ass, Zarathustra evokes, in a mocking key, the festivals of atonement and sacred games Nietzsche's madman had proclaimed as the fitting response to the death of God. The aspiration to the supreme heights embodied in Zarathustra's quest to sanctify his world by making his will a law unto itself appears to lead to a descent to the humiliating depths of ass worship.

"The Drunken Song," alone among speeches in part IV, is devoted to the eternal return, and it points to the essential loosening of rational standards that makes possible Zarathustra's brief celebration of his interpretation of eternity. The higher men become inebriated by his drunken song and its renewed celebration of the joy of self-love, eternity, recurrence, and the prospect of "everything eternally the same." That their freedom from the constraints of reason is ill-gotten, acquired through inebriation rather than insight, is illustrated by the fact that the higher men persist in maintaining that Zarathustra has taught them how to love the earth while they unabashedly embrace a vision of eternity that drains the concrete moment of its significance.

Contentment, peace of mind, and a feeling of being at home in the world characterize the higher men after their worship of the ass (Z IV "The Drunken Song" 1). Their contagious self-satisfaction even envelops Zarathustra as he admits his fondness for them. The higher men's happiness springs from the presumption, voiced by the ugliest man, that they have fathomed the significance of Zarathustra's teaching and have learned, as Zarathustra teaches, to love the earth. But the ugliest man, who feels comforted and at ease but remains as ugly as before, only proves how easy it is to reduce Zarathustra's ethics to a snappy slogan, to turn his teaching into a hurdy-gurdy song. Moreover, the ugliest man's presumption notwithstanding, Zarathustra has contrasted the voice that speaks honestly of "the meaning of the earth" to the futile flight after "ultimate walls" and "eternal walls" (Z I "On the After-worldly" and "On the Gift-Giving Virtue" 2). The ugliest man and his companions seem altogether oblivious of the fundamental tensions that constitute Zarathustra's teaching. They are unaware that the injunctions to love the earth and to embrace eternity reflect extremes that Zarathus-tra does not succeed in harmonizing or reconciles only at tremendous cost to his intellectual conscience.

But with the sweet wine flowing none of the higher men seems much in the mood for seeing things as they are. Flushed with the warmth of convalescence, the higher men "jumped toward Zarathustra to thank, revere, caress him, and kiss his hands, each according to his own man-ner" (Z IV "The Drunken Song" 1). In their fawning and childish treat-ment of Zarathustra as a kind of savior, the higher men sink to the level of obsequiousness characteristic of the disciples Zarathustra had apparently abandoned. This spectacle, capped by the suggestion that the deified ass join the festivities, fortifies the conclusion that the feeling of convalescence to which Zarathustra had given his approval represents a form of weariness, a relaxing of stern ideals that have neither been refuted nor revalued.

Zarathustra is momentarily staggered by the spectacle unfolding be-fore him. After he "gradually recover[s] his senses to some extent" (ibid. 2), he is stricken by insight. His midnight wisdom conjures up old nightmares—"The dog howls, the moon shines" (ibid. 4)—evoking the very scene that marked the transition from his encounter with the lame dwarf to his vision of the gagging shepherd. And the eternal re-turn, representing both redemption and damnation, also reasserts itself in his thoughts. Yet he rejects the idea of sharing his crippling knowl-edge with his present companions: "Sooner would I die, die rather than tell you what my midnight heart thinks now" (ibid. 4).

Although Zarathustra conceals the content of his memory, its impact on him is immediate, inducing sharp criticism of and deep estrange-ment from his guests. Only moments before he had "fond thoughts" of the higher men. Now his dissatisfaction seems irremediable: "Alas! Alas! Have you flown high enough yet? You have danced: but a leg is no wing. You good dancers, now all pleasure is gone: wine has become lees, every cup has become brittle, the tombs stammer. You did not fly high enough" (ibid. 5). Applying harsh standards to the higher men, Zara-thustra passes a severe judgment: in coming to love the earth, the higher men have become earthbound. They lack the crucial capacity or sense that elevates and recognizes elevation: "You higher men, you do not smell it? A smell is secretly welling up, a fragrance and smell of eternity" (ibid. 6).[10] Rejecting the daytime, the period in which the higher men thrive, as "stupid, boorish, dumb" (ibid. 7), Zarathustra instead teaches that lordship of the earth belongs to the pure souls, "the most unknown, the strongest, the midnight souls who are brighter and deeper than any day" (ibid. 7). Such mastery entails usurping all previous claims to the title "lord of the earth." Such mastery means making oneself a god.

But the higher men do not perceive this demand. His words ringing with bitterness, Zarathustra accuses the higher men—his most public, vocal, and devoted admirers—of being deaf to his innermost needs and aspirations. He makes one last effort to explain himself:

> Woe entreats: Go! Away, woe! But all that suffers wants to live, that it may become ripe and joyous and longing—longing for what is farther, higher, brighter. "I want heirs"—thus speaks all that suffers; "I want children, I do not want *myself*."
>
> Joy, however, does not want heirs, or children—joy wants itself, wants eternity, wants recurrence, wants everything eternally the same. (ibid. 9)

But Zarathustra's distinction between an ethics of suffering and an ethics of joy constitutes a decisive self-criticism. For in his apparent reconciliation with eternity at the end of part III, he had indeed hoped to produce children in union with eternity (Z III "The Seven Seals"). But the love of eternity is now revealed to be inconsistent with the desire for anything but eternity. In view of the fact that Zarathustra characterizes the desire for children as an unworthy alternative to the desire for eternity, his hopeful concluding utterance in his final speech proclaiming that his "children are near" is a sign of his revaluation of the desire for eternity at the heart of his ethics of creativity (Z IV "The Sign").

Reaching the same conclusion as his animals did in part III, Zarathustra directly links the joy of the eternal return to the obliteration of differences, moral and natural:

> Do you not smell it? Just now my world became perfect; midnight too is noon; pain too is joy; curses too are a blessing; night too is a sun—go away or you will learn: a sage too is a fool.
>
> Have you ever said Yes to a single joy? O my friends, then you said

Yes too to *all* woe. All things are entangled, ensnared, enamored, if ever you wanted one thing twice, if ever you said, "You please me happiness! Abide moment!" then you wanted all back . . .

You higher men, do learn this, joy wants eternity. Joy wants the eternity of all things, wants deep, wants deep eternity. (Z IV "The Drunken Song" 10, 11)

In this topsy-turvy, radically egalitarian world where the extremes are entangled—the world seen from the perspective of the eternal return— it seems that the greatest is indeed indistinguishable from the smallest, and consequently that the highest type is no better than any other type.

Zarathustra does not dwell on this sobering consequence. This does not mean that he does not take it to heart. Responsible for inebriating his admirers and encouraging them in their abject ass worship by participating in it himself, he bothers neither to calm their inflamed yearnings nor to prepare them for reintegration into political life. Possessed of a new sobriety and dignity, he abandons his hung-over guests in the morning. He, as it were, awakens in his final speech from the dream or thought-experiment that embraces his announcement that God is dead, his revelation of the superman, his articulation of the ethics of creativity, and his attempt to make himself a god.

Zarathustra's final speech points directly back to the first speech of the prologue, and suggests a new beginning informed by modified hopes. Whereas in that very first speech Zarathustra addressed the sun in envy and painful neediness, on this occasion, as the morning sun spills over him, he speaks with dignified ease, rejecting the higher men as unsuitable companions. The appearance of the lion, the second of the three incarnations of the "spirit" (Z I "On the Three Metamorphoses")—and a form in which the spirit lacks the right to create new values—is taken by Zarathustra as a sign that his "children are near," that his heirs await him as the day blossoms (Z IV "The Sign"). Yet by his own reckoning, preoccupation with his children, even his true and proper children, signals the voice of a sufferer, one who himself has not attained joy and excellence (Z IV "The Drunken Song" 9; cf. BGE 296).

Moreover, Zarathustra's embrace of the perspective of the lion, the noblest but not the highest of his images of transcendence, reflects a turning away from the "dark wisdom" of his "midnight heart," an abandonment of the quest to speak the child's sacred yes, an abdication of the responsibility to invent sacred games and festivals of atonement, a renunciation of the ambition to command eternity, and a retreat from the duty to make himself a god by eternalizing necessity through the force of his own will.[11] He forgoes these imperatives of his wisdom because he has learned that he lacks the strength required for the impossible task his wisdom imposes upon him. Perhaps he has also learned that this lack is no disgrace. Either way, Nietzsche does not give his Zarathustra the opportunity to test this new knowledge in life.

Nietzsche survives Zarathustra's perilous attempt to command great things and master eternity. Henceforth, however, quietly assimilating Zarathustra's lessons, he will maintain a respectful distance. Never again will the will to power, the eternal return, the death of God, the superman, the last man, or the way of the creator undergo sustained scrutiny in his books. He will prudently refrain from the attempt to invent sacred games, notwithstanding the fact that his unswerving belief in the absence of cosmic support for morality, combined with his equally steadfast belief in an order of rank among desires, souls, and forms of life, requires such an effort. It is this retreat, suppression, compromise, or noble lie, the expression of a soul that prefers to will nobility rather than to will nothingness, that makes possible the bold, prankish, graceful, and golden lion's voice of *Beyond Good and Evil*, the acute psychological analyses of *On the Genealogy of Morals*, and the flawed gems of 1888.

9

The Ethics of Knowing:
Beyond Good and Evil

Beyond Good and Evil, perhaps Nietzsche's most beautiful book, has fallen into ill-deserved neglect. This neglect is not incompatible with the book's manifest appeal and popularity. Who would deny the sparkling gracefulness of language in *Beyond Good and Evil,* the staggering audacity of its attempt to comprehend and criticize the West in terms of a single error called Platonism, the arresting cheerfulness marking its vivisection of "modern ideas," the exhilarating brazenness of its summons to cultivate a new and nobler humanity in anticipation of a philosopher of the future? Yet if the importance scholars attach to a work is measured less by its ability to stimulate gushing encomiums and enthusiastic citations than by its capacity to provoke sustained critical reflection, one must conclude that *Beyond Good and Evil* does not command respect as a fundamental statement of Nietzsche's teaching.

Although scholars have eagerly availed themselves of favorite passages, few have undertaken to study *Beyond Good and Evil* as an ordered whole.[1] This avoidance seems to be based on the unstated assumption that Nietzsche's book, subtitled "Prelude to a Philosophy of the Future," lacks a plan, a unifying argument, or a comprehensive intention. The result is that *Beyond Good and Evil* has come to be treated as an introduction and overview to Nietzsche's thought, a showcase of styles, a handy compendium of catch-phrases, slogans, sensational insights, and conversation-stopping observations.

This prejudice is at odds with Nietzsche's own judgment. In a letter written shortly after publication of *Beyond Good and Evil* to a former colleague, the eminent historian Jacob Burckhardt, Nietzsche remarks that his new book, "says the same thing as my *Zarathustra*—only in a way that is different—very different."[2] This would imply that *Beyond Good and Evil* deals with the highest type and has the eternal return as its fundamental conception. Yet the extreme doctrines that mark Zarathustra's teaching—the death of God, the superman and the last man, the love of eternity—are not explicitly discussed in *Beyond Good and Evil.*

In his only remarks prepared for publication on the relation between *Zarathustra* and *Beyond Good and Evil*—in his brief review of *Beyond Good and Evil* in *Ecce Homo*—Nietzsche emphasizes how the two works differ in focus and aim. Whereas *Zarathustra* was affirmative, *Beyond Good and Evil* was critical. Whereas *Zarathustra* was primarily devoted to erecting a counter ideal, *Beyond Good and Evil* was "in all essentials a critique of modernity," particularly "modern science, modern art, and modern politics". Whereas *Zarathustra* was Nietzsche's most farsighted book, *Beyond Good and Evil* focused on what lies nearest and on the surface (EH III, on BGE, 1–2).

And, although Nietzsche does not call attention to the contrast, whereas Zarathustra suffers debilitating fits of nausea brought on by the sight of his fellow man, Nietzsche in *Beyond Good and Evil* describes and analyzes the symptoms of nausea but does not exhibit them.[3] In general, these contrasts comport with Nietzsche's insistence that the refinement and reticence that mark *Beyond in Good and Evil* reflect a "recuperation" from the agonizing ordeal he underwent in writing *Zarathustra* (ibid. 2), and an abandonment, he implies, of the godlike perspective he had adopted to explore Zarathustra's teaching.

These differences in orientation and aim imply that the different perspectives informing the two books are those of one and the same eye, and suggest that each perspective is in need of correction by the other to achieve an adequate view of Nietzsche's explorations of the highest type.[4] If *Thus Spoke Zarathustra* is Nietzsche's most farsighted work, and if *Beyond Good and Evil* focuses on what lies nearest, then perhaps one may achieve clear-sightedness, the mean between the extremes of far-sightedness and nearsightedness, by reflecting upon the manner in which the distinctive perspective of each work brings into focus that which is exaggerated or occluded by the other.

Indeed, *Beyond Good and Evil* and *Thus Spoke Zarathustra* provide distinctive perspectives of one and the same eye on the nature of human perfection. They are in agreement that knowledge about the cosmos and understanding of true or real human needs are the foundations of human excellence. They are bound together in opposition to the powerful inhibitions and stern strictures of modern political philosophy that proclaim questions about the good to be illegitimate, philosophically barren, or politically unwise. They appear to diverge by furnishing alternative accounts of the supreme type and the rank order of needs, kinds of souls, and forms of life. For whereas Zarathustra links his highest hope to the advent of the superman, in *Beyond Good and Evil* Nietzsche envisages, just beyond the horizon, philosophers of the future. Whereas Zarathustra is the herald and precursor of the superman, Nietzsche writes *Beyond Good and Evil* as "a free spirit." And although the "higher man" appears in both works, the higher men with whom Zarathustra consorts are pathetic buffoons, whereas the higher men of *Beyond Good and Evil* are depicted as worthy precursors to the new philosophers. Are then the superman and the philosopher of the future two or one? Can Nietzsche really say the same thing in *Beyond Good and Evil* as he said in *Zarathustra* if he says it in so very different a way?

In fact, from the perspective of both works the highest type excels in both philosophy and art by engaging in right making based on right knowing. Both the superman and the philosopher of the future are supposed to secure freedom by making the most comprehensive forms of necessity subject to their will. But despite basic agreement about the peak of human excellence, the two books view the possibility and desirability of reaching the peak of human excellence from different perspectives. Whereas *Thus Spoke Zarathustra* trumpets the necessity and reveals the impossibility of attaining godlike mastery, *Beyond Good and Evil* gradually raises the possibility of self-deification and then discreetly abandons the hope without quite explaining why.

Nietzsche gives the appearance in *Beyond Good and Evil* of overcoming or reconciling the context of extremes in his thought; but in fact his book deftly evades the problem. This evasion sustains an unfortunate illusion that distracts from the book's achievement, an achievement that consists in placing in perspective the good of freedom by clarifying the ways in which freedom depends on knowledge. By forcing the extremes into the background, by emphasizing the distinguished position of the free spirits in the rank order, and, in the last chapter of *Beyond Good and Evil*, by equating nobility with the self-knowledge of a noble soul,

Nietzsche carries forward the suggestion from the end of part IV of *Zarathustra* that the higher type who understands the reach but also the limits of the creative will is superior to the very highest type who engages in the vain quest to make his will a law unto itself.

The spirit of Nietzsche's philosophical explorations in *Beyond Good and Evil* is captured in Kant's motto for enlightenment: *Sapere Aude!*, Dare to be wise.[5] But Nietzsche breaks with Kant over what the philosopher knows. For Nietzsche, philosophy depends on courage because the truths that the philosopher brings to light and that set him free are ugly and deadly. Courage is the pinnacle of the moral virtues in *Beyond Good and Evil,* and loving the truth is the exemplary act of courage. One way to understand the overall argument of *Beyond Good and Evil* is that Nietzsche marries the Romantic celebration of the heroic individual with the Platonic exaltation of the philosopher by making philosophy the highest form of heroic individualism.

The Ethics of Knowing

In harmony with his famous conviction that the mark of a great philosophy is that it is brought into being and nourished by the moral and immoral intentions of its author (BGE 6), Nietzsche's attack on the prejudices of the philosophers of the past in part I throws into sharp relief the moral intentions or prejudices that govern his philosophical explorations and, on his view, will underlie the philosophy of the future. Although his arguments against past philosophers are often poor, frequently miss the mark, rely on gross caricature, and seldom compel assent, they are nonetheless fascinating and important for what they reveal about his prejudices or convictions about human excellence. What distinguishes Nietzsche's perspective in *Beyond Good and Evil* is not the idea that philosophical teachings are based upon will and represent a rationalization of interests—a common view with a long pedigree—nor the fact that his philosophy is governed by convictions that are not subject to demonstration—hardly a novel circumstance—but rather the distinctive character and content of his convictions: that there is an order of rank determining the dignity of prejudices, that the philosophy of the past has been mired in prejudices that reflect weakness, and that the prejudices that will govern the philosophy of the future will spring from daring, courage, and the love of truth.

Part 1 of *Beyond Good and Evil* presents Nietzsche's most sustained discussions of the history of philosophy. In spite of their weaknesses, his criticisms of ancient philosophers, modern scientists, Spinoza, Descartes, Kant, and others pose formidable challenges and reveal unexamined vulnerabilities. Nietzsche, however, is not primarily interested in refuting philosophical doctrines (BGE 18, 21), but rather in discovering the moral and immoral intentions that support them.

In fact, Nietzsche is no conventional scholar of the history of philosophy. He does not explore texts, he rarely cites authors, he seldom examines an idea from multiple angles, and he almost never considers alternative explanations. The point is not to fault Nietzsche for caricaturing the philosophical positions he criticizes nor to harp on the defects of his supposed refutations, but rather to understand that he approaches the history of philosophy as a "genuine historian."[6] Just as in his histories, where he reconstructed or poeticized the past to clarify the moral significance of art, morality, and religion, so too as a genuine historian in *Beyond Good and Evil* he sacrifices precise understanding of the history of philosophy so as to understand precisely philosophy's moral significance, its value for life.

I shall not discuss Nietzsche's specific criticisms. Rather, I shall focus on the one big prejudice that, according to him, has crippled philosophy, namely the prejudice about what philosophy itself is. Philosophy is not, as commonly supposed, what scholars and professors of philosophy do. The tantalizing hypothesis with which Nietzsche opens the preface to *Beyond Good and Evil* ("Supposing truth is a woman—what then?") establishes a common ground with the philosophy of Plato and Aristotle by viewing the desire for truth as a kind of love. Although classical philosophy leaves unresolved whether the philosopher's love of truth is more akin to the enduring marriage of true minds or the romantic lover's blazing passion,[7] Nietzsche speculates, in agreement with Plato and Aristotle, that philosophy rightly understood is the love of truth, a mark of distinction, a real and perhaps the most resplendent human longing.

By supposing that truth is a woman, the elusive object of passionate desire, Nietzsche implies that the love of truth is not easily or commonly satisfied. Philosophers have been bumbling suitors and enfeebled lovers because they have been deficient in *eros*. Deficiency in eros results in clumsy, dogmatic philosophizing. Yet Nietzsche's own suggestion that dogmatism is a symptom of deficiency in eros swiftly undergoes transformation into a dogmatic statement of fact: truth is a woman and

"What is certain is that she has not allowed herself to be won" (BGE Preface).

Dogmatism, however, is not in Nietzsche's book an unmitigated evil. Although philosophical dogmatizing has throughout the past drawn sustenance from superstition and prejudice, it has kept alive the love of truth, bearing a promise through the millennia. It has inscribed in the human heart "eternal demands [*ewigen Forderungen*]."[8] But, weighted down by errors mistaken for truths, philosophy has so far failed to fulfill its great promise. Much like Hegel, who aspired to transform philosophy or the love of wisdom into science or actual wisdom, Nietzsche proclaims his aspiration to fulfill philosophy's promise by achieving "wakefulness itself."[9] This requires correcting "the worst, most durable, and most dangerous of all errors so far . . . Plato's invention of the pure spirit and the good as such" (BGE Preface). This catastrophic error involved "standing truth on her head and denying *perspective*, the basic condition of all life" (ibid.).[10] But if truth is to be stood on her head, she must have a head to stand on. The fight against the Platonic error, as it requires that truth be set upright, implies that truth has a characteristic look and posture. Thus Nietzsche asserts that perspective is the condition of all life from a vantage point that allows for a correct perspective on the relation between perspective and life.

Embracing as his own the struggle to return truth to her feet and restore her dignity, Nietzsche defends truth's honor by challenging not only Plato but Christianity, the form in which Platonism has conquered Europe. The struggle against Christianity has opened up tremendous new possibilities; it "has created in Europe a magnificent tension of the spirit, the like of which has never yet existed on earth." Note that Nietzsche not only makes philosophy, and its political reflection in Christianity, responsible for the worst, most durable, and most dangerous of all errors, but, in proclaiming that "with so tense a bow we can now shoot for the most distant goals," he also finds in philosophy the source of his highest hope.[11] That most distant goal, which he speculates is only now coming into view for "good Europeans, and free, very free spirits," among whom he classes himself, is a philosophy of the future.

Impelled by the grand ambition to shoot for the most distant goals, Nietzsche cheerfully announces that the will to truth "will still tempt us to many a venture" (BGE 1). This reckless will to truth is the very same "famous truthfulness of which all philosophers so far have spoken with respect" (BGE 1). By proclaiming the truth that the will to truth is a prejudice, Nietzsche does not turn his back on truth but exhibits his fidelity to it, and proclaims his superiority to the philosophers in precisely the sphere where they seek to reign supreme. The risky ventures to which the will to truth tempts consist primarily in asking daring questions. The most daring questions concern the origin of the will to truth and the value of the desire for truth.[12] While cheerfully hinting that the problem of the value of truth "does involve a risk, and perhaps there is none that is greater" (BGE 1; cf. Z Prologue 2), Nietzsche plunges ahead prepared to risk all for truth's sake.

To determine the value of truth, he questions the fundamental faith of the metaphysicians, *"the faith in opposite values"* (BGE 2). But questioning the faith in opposite values must not be confused with attacking the very idea of a hierarchy of values. More daring and careful thought may yield the insight that a higher and more fundamental value for life must be ascribed to deception, selfishness, and lust than to truth, selflessness, and moderation. Indeed, Nietzsche encourages the hope that questioning the faith in opposite values will result in overcoming prejudice and determining rightly which values are high and fundamental. The possibility that the passions and values that have been traditionally vilified are of higher value than those which have been conventionally esteemed is a "dangerous 'maybe'"; and the new species of philosophers he envisages will be "philosophers of the dangerous 'maybe' in every sense" (BGE 2).

New philosophers must grasp philosophical thinking as it really is. Accordingly, Nietzsche boasts of delving beneath surface appearance to discover that philosophical thinking, contrary to its claim to be governed by the sovereign dictates of logic, is in fact guided by instinct (BGE 3). Moreover, logic rests upon concealed valuations, for example, that "mere appearance" should be "worth less than 'truth'" (BGE 3). By calling the traditional estimate a "foreground estimate," he implies that the traditional view of the relation of surface to depths is superficial and that the hitherto reigning estimation of the comparative worth of appearance and truth is false. Nevertheless, by reversing the traditional estimate of appearance and reality, he vindicates the traditional distinction between them. The dangerous insight that informs the opinion that old metaphysical truths, though useful, may nevertheless be "mere foreground estimates" is that truth is not determined by will, utility, or human need: "not just man is the 'measure of things'" (BGE 3). The traditional assumption underlying Nietzsche's critical argument that philosophers of the past have merely rationalized as moral imperatives conventional beliefs about what is useful, is that useful belief differs fundamentally from true belief or knowledge of what is.

Similarly, Nietzsche's opinion that "the falseness of a judgment is for us not necessarily an objection to a judgment" (BGE 4) presupposes a tenable distinction between truth and appearance. To determine the worth of a belief in accordance with the degree to which it is "life-promoting, life-preserving, species-preserving, perhaps even species-cultivating," as Nietzsche recommends, requires making exacting judgments about the desire and longings of the human soul or self, precise evaluations of the advantages and disadvantages of competing forms of social and political life, accurate classifications of species, and fine discriminations between beliefs that promote and beliefs that stultify life. To conclude, as Nietzsche invites the reader to do, that logic and mathematics are fictions, that it is precisely the falsest judgments that are indispensable, and that untruth is an indispensable condition of life, is to see through the pretensions of mathematics and logic, to affirm the capacity to distinguish true from false judgments, and to identify the indispensable conditions of life.

So far from teaching that the truth about things is inaccessible to reason, permanently shrouded in the mystifications and ambiguities of language, Nietzsche expounds an ethics of knowing grounded in the nonskeptical opinion that the truth is intelligible, life-impairing, and species-destroying. Although false judgments serve life, true judgments about the role of false judgments in life serve the philosophic life. While false judgments are useful and perhaps indispensable to the life of the species, the knowledge that such indispensable judgments are false is the precious, though dangerous, acquisition of the most outstanding members of the species. Nietzsche opposes life and assumes the ultimate risks for the sake of exposing the dangerous truth about the role of untruth in human affairs.

In contrast, at least as Nietzsche sees it, his philosophical precursors and contemporary rivals betray truth by failing to see, much less pursue, dangerous questions about truth's value. He reproaches the philosophers for their innocent and childish dishonesty "when the problem of truthfulness is touched even remotely" (BGE 5). Despite virtuous words and pious poses on behalf of disinterested reason, the truth of the matter, according to Nietzsche, is that philosophical opinions are typically just dressed-up prejudices. Philosophers have been "advocates who resent that name, and for the most part even wily spokesmen for their prejudices which they baptize 'truths'"(BGE 5).

The discovery that the history of philosophy is the story of the rationalization of prejudice is not prejudice but knowledge. This knowledge is made possible by a moral virtue, "the courage of conscience" (BGE 5). Accordingly, for Nietzsche, as for some forms of Christianity, intellectual error is rooted in moral vice. By singling out courage as a practical necessity for the attainment of knowledge, Nietzsche implies the fearful character of knowledge. By invoking the courage of *conscience,* he emphasizes that he persists in his dangerous investigations not because knowledge is pleasant or useful but because its attainment is a kind of moral imperative.

Not only is philosophy grounded in morality but also a philosopher's morality reveals accurately "in what order of rank [*Rangordnung*] the innermost drives of his nature [*Natur*] stand in relation to each other" (BGE 6). Through philosophy the "basic drives of man" make their claim to supremacy: "every single one of them would like only too well to represent *just itself* as the ultimate purpose of existence and the legitimate master of all the other drives. For every drive wants to be master— and it attempts to philosophize in *that spirit*" (BGE 6). In this war within the soul of all against all, one drive, philosophy, surpasses the rest, for philosophy is the "most spiritual will to power" (BGE 9). Philosophy designates both the natural inclination or pretension of every drive to rule and the name of the rightful ruler among the soul's many drives. As the supreme form of mastery, philosophy also designates a kind of soul and a way of life. The philosopher's "morality bears decided and decisive witness to *who he is*—that is, in what order of rank the innermost drives of his nature stand in relation to each other" (BGE 6). Thus, on the assumption that the structure of the soul and the moral intention of a philosophy are intelligible, Nietzsche presents the philosopher as an animate morality of the highest order.

The tight connection between philosophy and character helps explain why Nietzsche regards psychology, correctly conceived, as "again the path to the fundamental problems [*Grundproblemen*]" (BGE 23). The fundamental problems primarily concern the foundations of morality and the character of the soul (BGE 23; cf. 45).[13] Courage is a chief prerequisite for the new psychologist because of the deadly nature of the knowledge he seeks.[14] Even he who possesses a "hale and hearty conscience" will altogether lose his bearings as he gains a correct understanding of the value of morality.

Indicating that he has already encountered the new and dangerous knowledge whose acquisition he urges, Nietzsche reveals that traveling the path to the fundamental problems means not only abandoning but destroying what has hitherto been regarded as morality. Though morality suffers a violent death, all is not lost: the intellect or intellectual integrity, Nietzsche stresses, survives the frightful voyage intact. Indeed, he implies that morality, or conventional morality, must be sacrificed in order to preserve the intellectual conscience. Then the intellect will have been set free to pursue its higher calling, the exploration of the "fundamental problems." In short, the overcoming of conventional morality is justified by imperatives arising from the ethics of knowing.

Who Is Nietzsche's Free Spirit?

Psychology, or an unprejudiced and fearless exploration of "the depths," is according to Nietzsche's final remark in part 1 of *Beyond Good and Evil* the way once again to "the fundamental problems" (BGE 23; cf. 45). Part 2, "The Free Spirit," reveals that freedom is one of the fundamental problems. But not freedom understood in conventional or political terms. Freedom for Nietzsche depends upon both moral virtue and intellectual virtue, yet it is neither exercised in or nor achieved through political life. That does not mean that Nietzsche's account of freedom is devoid of political implications. To the contrary, his peculiar identification of freedom with philosophy and mastery reflects a rank order of values in which political liberty and legal slavery are essentially indistinguishable—both, from the perspective afforded by the commanding heights above political life where the free spirit dwells, are equally forms of unfreedom.

Who is Nietzsche's free spirit? What are his virtues, and what keeps him from being a philosopher of the future? These are not arbitrary or incidental questions. Rather they are posed by Nietzsche himself in *Beyond Good and Evil*, for the free spirit is not just any admirable character, outstanding figure, or "higher man," but rather a type of which

Nietzsche regards himself as one.[15] Writing as a free spirit, one amply endowed with the "piety of the search for knowledge" (BGE 105), Nietzsche's account of the free spirit in part 2 takes on heightened significance because of the light it promises to throw on the perspective from which *Beyond Good and Evil* was written and the moral and immoral intentions out of which this "Prelude to a Philosophy of the Future" grew.[16]

Part 2 opens with the genial observation that freedom is in abundant supply (BGE 24). But this "almost inconceivable freedom" is purchased at the cost of a strange simplification and falsification. It is dependent upon a form of knowledge, scientific knowledge, that itself is erected upon a "solid, granite foundation of ignorance" (BGE 24). Disapproving of the will to knowledge that drives science because it produces pleasing lies, Nietzsche indicates that however pleasurable the freedom enjoyed as a result of science, however well-suited to serving life, it is disreputable because it rests on a "thoroughly artificial" and "suitably falsified" world. Freedom thus differs from its appearance, and the free spirit is in need of a more precise understanding of freedom's foundations.

Addressing a "serious word" to "the most serious," Nietzsche connects freedom to devotion to the truth (BGE 25). While he warns "philosophers and friends of knowledge" about the temptation to martyrdom involved in "suffering 'for the truth's sake'!" (BGE 25), he nevertheless indicates that the truth is worth seeking for those fit for freedom and solitude. Whereas scientific knowledge serves life by fostering ignorance, philosophical knowledge seems to undermine life by estranging the knower from society. Whereas the scientist, a lover of ignorance from Nietzsche's perspective, is destined to a pleasant unfreedom, the philosopher, in Nietzsche's sense of the term a lover of truth, achieves an excruciating freedom through fidelity to his vocation. This fidelity consists in a measured skepticism directed toward all doctrines, accompanied by a prudent withdrawal from political life.

Nevertheless, the tension between human excellence and political life is practically universal: "Every choice human being" is imperiled by "the crowd, the many, the great majority" (BGE 26). Yet the "choice human being," the free spirit, does not flee from society but rather "strives instinctively for a citadel and a secrecy" amid other human beings. To make his home within society the free spirit must become an expert in the art of wearing masks. As a "knower in the great and exceptional sense," he is likely to be driven out of his citadel and forced to endure an almost nauseating intercourse with others in order to satisfy his restless curiosity. And yet Nietzsche maintains that, though disagreeable, "the long and serious study of the *average* man" is a necessary part of the philosopher's education (BGE 26).

The free spirit is aided in his obligatory study of the average man by the cynic (BGE 26). The cynic is a base soul who honestly proclaims his baseness, but basely infers from his experience that hunger, sexual desire, and vanity are the sole motives of human action. The cynic wrongly and maliciously reduces all human beings to clever beasts or complicated machines. In spite of his faulty generalizations and noisy fulminations based on a narrow range of experience, the cynic provides instruction to the "lover of knowledge" *(Liebhaber der Erkenntnis)* about what is low and common in human beings. While indignation-racked moralists may be ranked higher than cynics from the perspective of conventional morality, Nietzsche ranks them very low because they contribute little to the free spirit's quest for knowledge; one can learn little from them because "no one *lies* as much as the indignant do" (BGE 26).

The independence that is the reward for daring and free-spirited thought can be neither granted nor withdrawn by the political order, but such freedom is nevertheless a matter of right. It is suited "for the very few; it is a privilege [*Vorrecht*] of the strong," but a strong spirit who freely chooses to seek independence, even with "the best right [*Rechte*]" is "daring to the point of recklessness." The road to real freedom brings about a loss of orientation and control over one's destiny, throws one into an unwelcome solitude, unleashes a fearful attack of conscience, and results in permanent estrangement from other human beings (BGE 29).

Yet the terrible burden of freedom does not cause Nietzsche to doubt its worth, or to question the possibility of discriminating between higher and lower types of men on the basis of their capacity to achieve knowledge and freedom. Men's different capacities for knowledge are at the root of the distinction he draws between the exoteric and esoteric (BGE 30), a distinction that for him is not primarily political but moral. The exoteric and the esoteric in *Beyond Good and Evil* do not essentially refer to a kind of layered writing with an external or political meaning and an inner or philosophical meaning, but rather reflect two basic perspectives for seeing, estimating, measuring, and judging.[17] Indeed, for Nietzsche the distinction between the exoteric and the esoteric is rooted in two basic human types. And the distinction between the two basic types is a function of the height of the insight to which each can attain, the loftiness of the perspective from which each sees, estimates, measures, and judges. That the insights of the higher man would poison the lower type, and that the virtues of the common man "might perhaps signify vices and weakness in a philosopher," does not mean that Nietzsche believes universal standards are lacking. To the contrary. The different perspectives that according to Nietzsche characterize the higher and lower types reflect universal standards about what counts as high and what counts as low.

Higher souls have higher tasks. Overcoming morality is a task "for the finest and most honest, also the most malicious, consciences of today, as living touchstones of the soul" (BGE 32). The overcoming of morality does not include the silencing of conscience. To the contrary, it is under the dictates of conscience that Nietzsche asks the reader, as he had in the opening of the preface, to entertain a provocative hypothesis (BGE 36). This hypothesis, a curious mixture of skepticism and dogmatism, involves the denial of the reality of almost everything, but the affirmation of the reality of our desires, passions, and drives. The promised reward is nothing less than a comprehensive explanation of the world, something physics as "only an interpretation and exegesis of the world" could not give (BGE 14).

Yet even were there no reward involved, the attempt to explain the world in terms of real human drives is, Nietzsche declares, demanded by the "conscience of method." Ascending from the reality of human drives to a comprehensive explanation of the world is also an obligation arising from a "morality of method." This morality of philosophical inquiry, or ethics of knowing, turns out to be more basic than the drives that it commands one to posit as real, and thus it is the real foundation for Nietzsche's thought experiment, a thought experiment that results in the inference that the will to power is the fundamental faculty at work in the world. Since it is the conscience or morality of method, on Nietzsche's account, that compels one to assume the reality of basic human drives and to undertake the reductivist inquiry that transforms the world into the work of the will, the will to power, at least as presented here in *Beyond Good and Evil,* is not an expression of the free spirit's own will, but rather a necessary conjecture stemming from an authoritative ethical vision. Nietzsche does not account for the will to power as an expression of his will but rather as an inference of his reason, a conclusion stemming from the "conscience of method" that limits the free spirit's will (BGE 36).

The ethics of knowing positively forbids establishing human pleasure or improvement as the measure of truth. But it is not equally hostile to all such measures. Accordingly, Nietzsche entertains sympathetically the hypothesis that "Something might be true while being harmful and dangerous in the highest degree" (BGE 39). What follows, morally speaking, from the assumption that truth is debilitating or deadly? Nietzsche envisages a decisive test of character:

> Indeed, it might belong to the fundamental character of existence [*Grundbeschaffenheit des Daseins*] that those who would know it completely would perish, in which case the strength of a spirit should be measured according to how much of the "truth" one could still barely endure—or to put it more clearly, to what degree one would *require* it to be thinned down, shrouded, sweetened, blunted, falsified. (BGE 39)[18]

Although Nietzsche presents as a hypothesis the view that knowledge of the fundamental character of existence is fatal, it only follows from this hypothesis that strength of spirit may be measured by how much "truth" one could endure on the assumption that knowledge of the fundamental character of existence, or philosophy, is good.[19] Though subsequently in *Beyond Good and Evil* he will associate philosophy with creativity, commanding, and legislating (BGE 211), while he discusses the free spirit Nietzsche has little to say about imposing one's will on the world as a defining achievement of the higher type of man. Rather, he drives home throughout the part entitled "The Free Spirit" that the touchstone of human greatness and the ground of freedom is not making or creating but the capacity to discover and endure spirit-crushing truths.[20]

Although the free spirit sees clearly into what is, he is not easily seen into. As a profound spirit, the free spirit is a kind of "concealed man" who assiduously fashions masks so as to remain hidden even from his friends (BGE 40). Masks also grow spontaneously around him "owing to the constantly false, namely *shallow*, interpretation of every word, every step, every sign of life he gives" (BGE 40). Solitude is thus a basic feature of freedom or independence. This is entirely consistent with the identifying marks, predominantly negative, of fitness for freedom that Nietzsche mentions: not to stick to or rely upon one's country, lover, or friend; and not to become enslaved to one's sense of compassion, desire for science, or own virtue (BGE 41).[21] Apparently, the only reward a free spirit may expect for the drastic renunciations imposed by freedom is knowledge of the fundamental character of existence.

The free spirit's knowledge and freedom are not the highest of which human beings are capable. The highest awaits the advent of a "new species of philosophers" (BGE 42–44). These future philosophers are especially characterized by the risky experiments they undertake. They probably will be "friends of 'truth'" and very likely will love "their truths," but, Nietzsche insists, they "will certainly not be dogmatists" (BGE 43; note Nietzsche's quotation marks around *truth* in the first case and omission of them in the second). By this he does not mean that the new philosophers will lack beliefs they hold to be true, but rather that they will refrain from insisting that what is true for them must be "a truth for everyman." Yet so far from reflecting a leveling doctrine that celebrates the equality or dignity of all opinions, Nietzsche's understanding of dogmatism is rooted in the deeply aristocratic view that only the "higher type of man" is fit to hear, and to live in accordance with, the highest insights (BGE 30).

Nietzsche conjectures that philosophers of the future will say to themselves, "'My judgment is *my* judgment': no one else easily has a right [*Recht*] to it" (BGE 43). It is not that all truths are equal, but that human beings are radically unequal in their capacity for, and right to, the highest truths. Although there may be many perspectives, there is for Nietzsche only one rank order determining the importance of the various truths and the worth of those who seek them. Nietzsche is not denying, as Alexander Nehamas implies in remarking on this passage, that truth is one and universal,[22] but rather is asserting that there is no reason for the superior individual to insist that everyone recognize the shape and requirements of the highest and most comprehensive truths. Common, popular opinions—the beliefs of the multitude of men and women about what is good—are not serious rivals to what free spirits and philosophers of the future view as good, because "whatever can be common always has little value" (BGE 43). And the superiority of the philosopher's truth is in Nietzsche's opinion not mere opinion but necessary and universal: "In the end it *must* be as it is and always has been: great things remain for the great, abysses for the profound, nuances and shudders for the refined, and, in brief, all that is rare for the rare" (BGE 43; cf. TI "What the Germans Lack" 5). The moral and intellectual superiority of the judgments of the philosophers of the future stems from the knowledge, beyond the grasp of the common view, that there is an order of rank with philosophers at the peak.

While the free spirit remains the new philosopher's herald and precursor (BGE 44), there is a chasm on the opposite side between the freedom of the free spirit *(der Freie Geist)* and the freedom of the "falsely so-called 'free spirits,'" that is, the freethinkers *(Freidenker)*, the democrats, all the "goodly advocates of 'modern ideas'" (BGE 44). Free thinkers reveal their unfreedom in their "basic inclination" to see aristocratic political life as the root of all suffering and misfortune. Nietzsche discovers in the democratic interpretation of political life the same offense against truth that he claims Plato perpetrated, for it is "a way of standing truth happily up on her head" (BGE 44; see also Preface, 48, 62, 220). Democratic freethinkers, wishing to spread material prosperity, guarantee comfort and security, establish universal equality, and most characteristically abolish suffering, are blind to the rank order of human types and hence enslaved to ignorance.

What is so terrible from Nietzsche's point of view in the promotion of democratic, bourgeois notions of the good is not simply that the democratic interpretation of man is false but rather that, like Socrates' theoretical interpretation of reality and Christianity's religious interpretation of the world, the democratic interpretation cripples those of high rank by poisoning the air that free spirits breathe. The free spirit is educated and elevated not by material prosperity but by deprivation, not by comfort and security but by fear and isolation, not by equality but by slavery, not by the abolition of suffering but by the release of "everything evil, terrible, tyrannical in man," and not by happiness but by "malice against the lures of dependence that lie hidden in honors, or money, or offices, or enthusiasms of the senses" (BGE 44). Nietzsche knows of no interest that supersedes, recognizes no right that limits, and sees no good beside that of the higher type. This is not a matter of calculation but of principle. The promotion of what is highest in humanity is in *Beyond Good and Evil*, as it is for Nietzsche in his histories, in *Zarathustra,* and throughout his thought, the sole criterion for judging what is good and bad in politics. Another way of capturing the spirit of his considered moral intention is that the natural right of the best is the exclusive determinant of political right.

In sum, the free spirit is one who, thanks to hardness, cunning, clarity of sight, freedom from illusion, independence from political attachments, and emancipation from the bonds of love and friendship, attains true but deadly knowledge of the fundamental character of existence. The free spirit is more philosophical than almost all previous philosophers.[23] Practical dependence of all forms is poison to the free spirits who are "born, sworn, jealous friends of *solitude*" (BGE 44). The connection between freedom of spirit and solitude is not a result of contingent circumstance, but arises from the ethics of knowing. And although Nietzsche does not trumpet them, his portrait of the solitary free spirit has harsh political implications: if bone-chilling knowledge is not only freedom pure and simple but the only freedom worth talking about, political liberty and conventional slavery lack a relevant moral difference. Nietzsche sets the requirements of freedom so high that political life in all its variety is consigned to the realm of unfreedom.

Who Is Nietzsche's Philosopher of the Future?

A major puzzle that arises from the first two parts of *Beyond Good and Evil* concerns the relation between the free spirit and the philosopher of the future. If freedom is based on knowledge, and if the free spirit is a knower, what must be added to his freedom and his knowledge to make him a philosopher of the future? Perhaps the most striking qualities, conspicuous by their absence from Nietzsche's account of the free spirit, are creativity and will. Whereas the free spirit is obliged to undertake the philosophical experiment of understanding the world in terms of the will to power (BGE 36), his freedom does not depend on imposing his will on the world or creating new values. In contrast, Nietzsche proclaims that philosophers of the future will not only be knowers but also creators, commanders, and legislators (BGE 211). But whom or what will these "genuine philosophers" (*eigentlichen Philosophen*) command (BGE 211)? What will they create? And for whom? As in *Zarathustra,* so too in *Beyond Good and Evil:* the highest type is obliged to create the conditions of its own freedom, to command the greatest things, to legislate necessity.

The connection between freedom and creativity begins to emerge in Nietzsche's account of the essence of religion in part 3, "The Religious Being." The free spirit, a kind of religious being, may be seen as the exemplar of noble religiosity in Nietzsche's age, for the demand, characteristic of the ethics of knowing, for the renunciation of belief in every form of transcendental comfort can bespeak the same passionate devotion that once renounced everything before God. But the free spirit's piety imposes a more than saintly renunciation, calling ultimately for the sacrifice of God (BGE 53–55).

Beyond the free spirit and his predominantly negative deeds, his renunciations and repudiations, is an even higher type. Under the rubric of "the religious being," Nietzsche introduces the type of "the most high-spirited, alive, and world-affirming human being," who not only affirms but ardently wants *"what was and is* to be repeated into all eternity" (BGE 56).[24] This highest type who makes his own need to eternalize necessity necessary, Nietzsche suggests, is tantamount to *"circulus vitiosus deus,"* a vicious circle as God, or God as a vicious circle. He thereby indicates the religious character of the ambition that compels the highest type to affirm the world exactly as it is without reference to good and bad, the awesome presumption underlying the deification of necessity. Like the ethics of creativity in *Thus Spoke Zarathustra*, the ethics of knowing in *Beyond Good and Evil* gives rise to the demand to become a god.

The religious man, in the best sense, is a higher kind of artist, falsifying the world and making life more beautiful than it really is on the basis of having once seen accurately the world's true but deadly character (BGE 59). This comprehensive recasting of existence, this thoroughgoing remaking of the world, this revaluation of all values, prompts Nietzsche to suggest that the religious man "might be included among artists, as their highest rank" (BGE 59). This union of knowledge, creativity, and piety indicates that the supreme type is at once philosopher, artist, and saint.[25]

Nietzsche reserves the title "philosopher of the future" for the type that unites knowing and making by engaging in right making based on right knowing. The philosopher—or as Nietzsche variously refers to the type throughout part 6, "the true philosopher" (*der rechte Philosoph;* BGE 205), "a real philosopher" (*wirklichen Philosophen;* BGE 211), "the genuine philosophers" (*die eigentlichen Philosophen;* BGE 211)—is the supreme master (BGE 9). But what does the philosopher rule? Nietzsche invokes Heraclitus, Plato, and Empedocles, ancient Greeks whom he describes as "royal and magnificent hermits of the spirit," as exemplars of philosophy (BGE 204). In contrast to these philosophers who exercised their royal prerogative in splendid isolation from human affairs, the modern world offers miserable charlatans, scholars who lack the right to the "masterly task and masterfulness of philosophy" (BGE 204). With presumption masquerading as humility, these modern impostors reduce philosophy to a theory of knowledge, a self-lacerating form of epistemology "that never gets beyond the threshold and takes pains to *deny* itself the right [*Recht*] to enter" (BGE 204). This righteous self-abnegation on the part of modern philosophy obscures philosophy's right to dominate.

But the question returns: what does the philosopher rule? Just as Nietzsche distinguishes between the highest forms of political rule and the "superroyal tasks" that are made possible for the few in a well-ordered society (BGE 61), he distinguishes kinds of commanding. Although he admires Cesare Borgia, Alcibiades, Caesar, the German Emperor Frederick II, and Napoleon (BGE 197, 200), regarding these "beasts of prey or men of prey" as healthy human types, head and shoulders above free thinkers and democrats, he deems them lower than free spirits and philosophers of the future. Political rulers stand decidedly higher in the order of rank than the ruled, but those who are free of the need to be commanded as well as of the need to command others occupy the highest ranks because they are free to command the greatest things. Politics may be necessary to ensure the well-being of the higher type, and "great politics," Nietzsche believes, has become necessary to overcome the sickness of will spread by modern democracy (BGE 208), but the peak of human excellence is not achieved through the practice of such politics.

It should be observed that Nietzsche's enthusiastic anticipation of "great politics" (BGE 208) occurs in the midst of his reflections on types of skepticism—a sickly democratic skepticism of the weak (BGE 208) and a "manly skepticism" of the strong (BGE 209)—and that he hopes for the advent of a bloody and momentous "great politics" precisely because it "may also favor the development of another and stronger type of skepticism" (BGE 209). In other words, his enthusiasm for "great politics" is rooted not in the conviction that politics is the forum in which greatness is exhibited, but rather in the conclusion that massive wars will have to be waged to restore an aristocracy of spirit.

The philosopher, or a philosopher of the future, is the peak of the aristocracy that Nietzsche envisages. The philosopher in the finest sense is a "complementary man," who, in contrast to the objective scholar, is a goal, a conclusion, and a sunrise. Indeed, inasmuch as he justifies existence, is a first cause and thereby a self-cause, and a self-reliant and supreme master, the complementary man or new philosopher is a kind of self-made god (BGE 207). Although Nietzsche hesitates before this extravagant conclusion, he insists on the comprehensive character of the philosopher's mastery:

> Genuine philosophers [*Die eigentlichen Philosophen*], however, are commanders and legislators; they say, "*thus* it *shall* be!" They first determine the Whither and For What of man, and in so doing have at their disposal the preliminary labor of all philosophical laborers, all who have overcome the past. With a creative hand they reach for the future, and all that is and has been becomes a means for them, an instrument, a hammer. Their "knowing" is *creating*, their creating is a legislation, their will to truth is—*will to power*. (BGE 211)

Nietzsche thus lays out the form but not the content of the union of knowing and making that typifies a philosopher of the future. Having identified the formal criteria that qualify one as a genuine philosopher, he himself wonders whether there are, or have been, or must be such philosophers.

Although he refrains from acknowledging any defects in his conception of the philosopher of the future, Nietzsche promptly initiates a visible though unheralded retreat from the idea that the philosopher is a commander and legislator. While noting in section 210 that philosophers are critics, but more than critics, and then in section 211 explaining that philosophers are more than critics in the sense that they are commanders and legislators, Nietzsche, in section 212, makes criticism the heart of the philosophical task. At least those in the past who deserved the title of philosopher "found their task, their hard, unwanted, inescapable task, but eventually also the greatness of their task, in being the bad conscience of their time" (BGE 212). Immediately after his most explicit statement about the merging of creativity, commanding, and knowing in the person of the philosopher of the future (BGE 211), Nietzsche returns to the very vision of the philosopher as critic he had only just described as an excellence of a lower order.

To be sure, Nietzsche continues to insist that philosophers have a task beyond criticism. Because of the hypocrisy, ignorance, and weakness that they discovered sustained conventional virtue, philosophers always sought a "new greatness of man . . . a new untrodden way to his enhancement" (BGE 212). In the modern era in which virtue is equated with specialization, opposition to convention means striving for wholeness. A philosopher in the modern era "would even determine value and rank in accordance with how much and how many things one could bear and take upon himself, how *far* one could extend his responsibility" (BGE 212).

But are there practical, moral, or natural limits to how far a single individual can extend his responsibility? Nietzsche's failure to say does not shake his conviction that there are objective and intelligible moral distinctions: "Ultimately there is an order of rank among states of the soul and the order of rank of problems accords with this" (BGE 213). The order of rank is supported by "the primeval law of things" (*Urgesetz der Dinge;* BGE 213), which, like premodern notions of a natural hierarchy and natural law, is seemingly independent of the human will and binding upon human action. The "primeval law of things" guarantees that only those who belong to the higher ranks may understand and grapple with the higher problems. To grapple with the highest problems one needs "a right [*Recht*] to philosophy" and virtue. The beautiful and intoxicating vision of the philosopher's virtues with which he brings part 6 to a close should not be allowed to disguise Nietzsche's failure to dramatize or provide an account of the form of life in which those virtues are to be exercised.

What Is Noble?

Parts 7–9 of *Beyond Good and Evil* continue the process of decoupling philosophy from commanding, legislating, and creating that began in the concluding sections of part 6. In accordance with this retreat from the maximum demands of knowledge and freedom as he understands them, Nietzsche, after part 6, does not refer again in *Beyond Good and Evil* to a philosopher of the future. Although he continues to praise philosophy as the highest activity and to regard the philosopher as the highest type of man, the philosopher he describes in parts 7–9 resembles more the free spirit, the courageous knower, than a new breed of philosopher who, thanks to and bound by his knowledge, legislates necessity and creates values. In the last three parts of *Beyond Good and Evil* Nietzsche blurs the distinction he himself forged in parts 1–6 between the higher type, the free spirit who comes to understand the reasons why the legislation of necessity becomes a moral imperative, and the very highest type, the philosopher of the future, who fulfills the moral imperative grasped by the free spirit by making himself a godlike master and creator. But Nietzsche neither explains nor shows why the equation between knowledge, freedom and mastery must be altered, what factors impel the retreat from the highest type, or why the will is unworthy to rule in the soul.

In part 7, "Our Virtues," Nietzsche turns away from philosophers of the future, or rather shows that the future of philosophy is profoundly continuous with its past. By his repeated use of the first person plural, he emphasizes that the virtues he discusses are his virtues, the virtues of a free spirit (BGE 214, 227, 230). The free spirit's virtues include a dangerous curiosity, a good conscience, the historical sense, a higher pity, a spiritualized cruelty, and honesty. These are either primarily intellectual virtues or honored by Nietzsche for their function in the acquisition of knowledge. They are also accompanied by obligations. Ridiculing the thoughtless inference that his critique of conventional morality issues in libertinism or hedonism, Nietzsche insists, contrary to "the dolts and the appearances," that as an immoralist he opposes conventional or herd morality in the name of sterner duties and higher tasks (BGE 226).

But is Nietzsche entitled to claim virtues for himself? After all, talk about virtue evokes traditional morality, the old-fashioned notion of a good conscience that safeguards virtue by constricting the understanding and placing dangerous questions off-limits. Virtue and conscience, as is well known, are bound up with traditional notions and metaphysical principles that Nietzsche has criticized as enfeebling prejudices. Although Nietzsche does oppose traditional morality in most respects, he is proudly aware of the debt his repudiation of tradition owes to tradition. Free spirits are radicals, but their need for self-knowledge places that radicalism in perspective and reveals its limits. At least "in one respect" free spirits are "worthy grandsons," the "last Europeans with a good conscience [*gutem Gewissen*]" (BGE 214). Like those from his grandfather's generation who acted under the sway of traditional morality, Nietzsche recognizes the authority of conscience and attempts to conform to its strictures. But the "good conscience" as he understands it and the virtues that serve it compel him to repudiate the traditional interpretation of morality. Although he fears the imminent disappearance of the good conscience (BGE 214), his break from traditional morality is by his own account, and is in fact, grounded in and a partial continuation of traditional morality.

The traditionally esteemed virtue "honesty" is at the center of the free spirit's virtues. Nietzsche places himself among the "last Stoics" because the perfection of honesty, the virtue most his own, requires, as well as courage, curiosity, and a "most spiritual will to power," hardness and severity (BGE 227). Honesty is in danger of becoming a vice in those who, having grown soft and lazy, cease to be honest about honesty itself, concealing from themselves the imperfect evidence attesting to honesty's status as a virtue. Put otherwise, honesty compels free spirits to acknowledge that judging honesty a virtue is a matter of opinion or prejudice, not knowledge. It is a mark of his honesty that Nietzsche both acknowledges that thinking honesty a virtue is a prejudice and affirms this prejudice as his own distinguishing mark.

The knower or free spirit is "an artist and transfigurer of cruelty" in the specific sense that his honesty compels him to discipline his spirit to recognize harsh, repellent truths that he would prefer to be other than they are (BGE 229).[26] Thus, just as creating must be based on knowing, so too knowing or philosophy must be based on creating, in that the philosopher must ruthlessly shape or discipline his spirit to enable it to attain and endure knowledge. Although the spiritualization of cruelty in the person of the free spirit depends upon a kind of extravagant honesty, speaking of cruelty is preferable to speaking of honesty. Not because honesty is not a virtue but because the term and others like it have been debased by common use:

> These are beautiful, glittering, jingling, festive words: honesty, love of truth, love of wisdom, sacrifice for knowledge, heroism of the truthful—they have something that swells one's pride. But we hermits and marmots have long persuaded ourselves in the full secrecy of a hermit's conscience that this worthy verbal pomp, too, belongs to the old mendacious pomp, junk, and gold dust of unconscious human vanity, and that under such flattering colors and make-up as well, the basic text of *homo natura* must again be recognized. (BGE 230)

In making it a matter of conscience to reject the common words routinely used to designate the virtues of knowers and philosophers, Nietzsche both exercises and reaffirms the virtues those words name.

Nietzsche's abstinence is in fact limited. In spite of his reluctance to use noble words debased by common tongues, he draws abundantly on terms hallowed by tradition—honesty, love of truth, sacrifice for knowledge, right, duty, nobility, virtue, and so forth—to designate the principles of thought and action most his own. Although he is inhibited from using the common words for describing the virtues by a deep respect for moral and intellectual virtue, both the inner structure of his argument and the outer form of his rhetoric testify to his dependence on traditional terms and notions without which he could neither think nor create.

Still, scorning pretty, high-sounding phrases, free spirits are freer to concentrate on the task given them by their cruel and extravagant honesty. Central to their task is "translat[ing] man back into nature" (BGE 230). This translation depends upon first stripping away the "overly enthusiastic interpretations that have so far been scrawled and painted over that eternal basic text [*ewigen Grundtext*] of *homo natura*" (BGE 230) so as to be able to gaze upon man's nature directly and see him as he really is. His investigations of man's nature thus far, Nietzsche concedes, leave him unable to satisfactorily answer the question "Why have knowledge at all?" (BGE 230). Thus knowledge or devotion to the examined life remains a prejudice for the free spirit. Nietzsche's knowledge that he lacks knowledge about the grounds of the goodness of knowledge lends pathos to the facts: knowledge is what Nietzsche yearns for most, is the goal of his philosophical explorations, and to the best of his knowledge is the thing most needed.

Indeed, for Nietzsche philosophy is what is noble. It should be noted that in raising the question of "What is noble," the title of part 9, the concluding part of *Beyond Good and Evil*, he cuts sharply against the grain of modern philosophy. Since around the time of Thomas Hobbes, the question of what is noble has been both formally and informally marginalized, though in practice never entirely expelled, from the domain of political philosophy. One important strand of modern political philosophy denies that there is a human good, another more modestly contends that human reason is incompetent to determine what the good is, and another concludes that for the purposes of politics it is best to bracket questions about the good life. The overall tendency has been for intensive exploration of the rights that citizens may exercise against and the entitlements a citizen may demand from government to preempt and often preclude an inquiry into the wisest exercise of the liberty provided by those rights and entitlements. By raising the question of what is noble, Nietzsche takes the side of tradition and premodern philosophy, which held that human excellence or perfection was a fit, if not a central, subject for philosophical exploration. Moreover, Nietzsche defies conventional usage by proclaiming that what is noble is not a function of "actions" or "works" or the desire for what is noble, or even of social status or aristocratic descent, but rather the self-knowledge of the noble soul.

Nietzsche's account of nobility begins with the restatement of a decisive equivocation on which the argument of *Beyond Good and Evil* rests. His hypothesis of the will to power (BGE 9, 13) commits him to the view that what is noble is invented by the will; yet he teaches throughout that, irrespective of what one wills, grasping that the will produces morality is the basis of freedom and what is noble. *Beyond Good and Evil* does not overcome the fundamental conflict between the views that the noble is made and that it is discovered. But it is a mark of Nietzsche's own nobility as a thinker that in section 260, the longest in *Beyond Good and Evil*, in a discussion of the origins of morality (expounded at much greater length in the *Genealogy*), he places this contest of extremes on prominent display.

There are, according to Nietzsche, two basic types of morality: master morality and slave morality. Although in higher cultures and sometimes "even in the same human being, within a *single* soul" these two moralities coexist (BGE 260), it is possible to identify the basic features of each. As in the *Genealogy*, Nietzsche finds that the difference between the two fundamental types is grounded in the health and the corruption of the human soul. And as in his earlier discussion of philosophers in *Beyond Good and Evil*, he contends that morality is the outward sign of the basic drives that govern specific types of natures. Thus, introducing master morality, he declares: "when the ruling group determines what is 'good,' the exalted, proud states of the soul are experienced as conferring distinction and determining the order of rank. The noble human being [*Der vornehme Mensch*] separates from himself those in whom the opposite of such exalted, proud states finds expression: he despises them" (BGE 260).

What makes master morality masterful is not that it comes from those who rule but that it expresses, honors, and institutionalizes in political life the exalted, proud states of the soul. That means that the exalted, proud states of the soul preexist the making of master morality. Consequently, the "good" and "bad" sanctioned by master morality— the rank order of values humanly or socially constructed by the noble man—reflect and receive their sanction from the pre-political rank order determining the health and nobility of the human soul. It is therefore of crucial significance that Nietzsche insists that the nobility of ancient Greece thought of themselves as truthful (BGE 260; cf. GM I 5). Whatever their subjective experience or perception, they were truthful, on Nietzsche's account, in the sense that the rank order which found expression in their moral values reflected the high rank order of their souls, itself a reflection of a rank order that preexisted the making of both master and slave morality.

The truthfulness of the noble man is consistent with the form of creativity that Nietzsche attributes to him. The "value-creating" of the noble man by which he "first accords honor to things" is more nearly imitation of what is noble than self-expression of what is unique (BGE 260). True, noble morality is a form of self-expression: "Everything it knows as part of itself it honors; such a morality is self-glorification" (BGE 260). But what is the self that is honored and what are the attributes that are glorified? The self of the noble man fits a definite mold. It is endowed with the "virtues of the powerful": courage, excess of power, severity, egoism, suspicion of pity, reverence toward age and tradition, the conviction that human beings are fundamentally unequal and that one has duty only toward one's peers, and the need for sophisticated friendship and worthy enemies (BGE 260). Master or noble morality is noble because, as the self-expression of noble souls, it imitates or mirrors, and glorifies, nobility. The art by which the noble man fashions a master morality is based on his understanding of how to honor (BGE 260). The noble type of man is value-creating not in the sense that he determines what is noble but rather in the sense that he makes human conventions—languages, beliefs, and institutions—that translate nobility of soul into practice.

As with master morality, the decisive factor in determining the char-

acter of slave morality is not political class but the rank of the dominating states or drives in the slave's soul. Accordingly, while slave morality is originally created by the ruled group, its specific valuations reflect
the creativity of the low and petty states of the soul, glorify what is
undeserving, and slander what is noble (BGE 260). Slave morality is a
form of utilitarianism because it attaches value to qualities that compensate for the slave's weaknesses and alleviate his suffering. Like noble
morality, slave morality involves a creative act. But not all creativity is
equal. In contrast to the creativity of the noble man which is good because it expresses and honors strength, the slave's creativity is bad
because it reflects sickly states of the soul and serves to empower the
weak. Whereas the powerful and healthy moralize nobility, the suffering
and weak moralize slavishness.

Where do the noble man and the slavish man stand in comparison
to Nietzsche's free spirit? Examination reveals that the noble man is not
altogether free, that the slavish man is not altogether ignorant, and that
the free spirit is kin to both. "The noble type of man experiences *itself*
as determining values" (BGE 260). But this experience is based on a
partial misinterpretation because the noble man fails to perceive the
myriad ways in which his will remains in fetters to ignorance and natural necessity. And the slavish man is partly right, or more truthful than
the noble man, for his quest for a morality that enables him to actualize
freedom springs from a recognition of his actual unfreedom.

Thus there is "one last fundamental difference" that separates noble
morality from slave morality. Slave morality is characterized by "the
longing for *freedom*" (BGE 260). Since freedom, albeit freedom rightly
understood, is the distinctive achievement of the free spirit, Nietzsche
indicates, by equating the longing for freedom with slave morality, the
respect in which slave morality is superior to noble morality and indeed
connected to the ethics of knowing. The noble man, though truthful, is
ignorant of the features of the human condition that render him unfree.
The slavish man, though knowledgeable about unfreedom, lies about
his capacity to actualize freedom. A higher nobility would combine the
truthfulness and reverence that mark the noble man with the knowledge
and longing for freedom characteristic of the slave.

Indeed, Nietzsche's understanding of the concealed weakness in
noble morality and the hidden strength in slave morality exemplifies the
newer, higher nobility that he celebrates in the concluding passages of

Beyond Good and Evil. Although usually thought of as a political designation, nobility for Nietzsche essentially refers to a definite kind of soul.
"Egoism belongs to the nature of a noble soul" (BGE 265).[27] The noble
soul views its egoism or self-love as rooted in "the primordial law of
things" *(Urgesetz der Dinge),* and is inclined to name this primordial
law "justice itself" *(Gerechtigkeit selbst;* BGE 265). While the noble soul
subordinates the interests of inferiors to its own aspirations, it respects
in those of its own rank "rights equal to its own" (BGE 265). The egoism
of the noble soul reflects not what is unique and inimitable but rather
what generally constitutes souls of high rank. Recognizing and respecting its equals is a mark of the egoism of the noble soul, because in hon-
oring its equals the noble soul honors what is of high rank in itself. The
noble soul believes that this form of respect "is of the nature of all social
relations and thus also belongs to the natural condition of things" *(na-
turgemassen Zustand der Dinge;* BGE 265). Within the natural condition
of things the noble soul attains an exalted perspective: *"it knows itself to
be at a height"* (BGE 265).

Although the noble soul is prepared to respect its equals, nobility
remains rare and difficult to recognize. There are signs, for the "values
of a human being betray something of the *structure* of his soul and
where it finds its conditions of life, its true need" (BGE 268; see also
BGE 6). But values must be interpreted. Common human beings whose
values reflect common experiences easily recognize one another,
whereas the higher men whose values reflect rare experiences are more
liable to misunderstand one another or pass one another by (BGE 268).

Indeed, the corruption of the higher type is the rule (BGE 269).
Where the common crowd sees in the statesman, conqueror, or discoverer a great man, the psychologist or student of souls sees the ruination
of a higher type of man. Where others succumb to the temptation to
project onto artists and philosophers the greatness manifest in their
great works, Nietzsche, as a student of the soul, has guessed the bitter
truth that great works too often reflect the broken spirits, unrealized
dreams, vengefulness, and vanity of their creators (BGE 270). Thus,
contrary to the aesthetic interpretation of his thought, Nietzsche himself argues that the production of a great literary work is neither a replacement for nor the expression of a noble soul, but all too often a
telltale sign of a noble soul's degradation.

Actions cannot prove nobility because they are unfathomable. Nor can literary or scholarly works, since they so often spring from a desire or need for what is noble. In contrast, the noble soul, being noble, does not seek nobility. To be sure, Nietzsche betrays an uncertainty about the theoretical status of this belief by first referring to it as "faith," and then recasting this religious formulation, speaking of "some fundamental certainty that a noble soul has about itself, something that cannot be sought, nor found, nor perhaps lost" (BGE 287). Whatever the cognitive status of the noble soul's belief, the root meaning of what is noble for Nietzsche is the conviction that the noble soul has of its height and dignity.

He expresses this fundamental thought in terms borrowed from Christianity: "*The noble soul [Die vornehme Seele] has reverence [Ehrfurcht] for itself*" (BGE 287). *Ehrfurcht* is a word with strong religious overtones signifying a combination of respect and awe or fear. In effect, Nietzsche transfers the passion that knowledge of God arouses in the soul of a pious Christian to the passion that knowledge of his own nature arouses in the noble soul. The mark of a noble soul is his self-recognition as divine, not his making himself a god. Thus, just as much earlier in his career Nietzsche reconceived justice, the basic political virtue, as a disposition primarily manifest in the search for and service to the truth (UD 6; cf. GM II 11), now he reconceives nobility, the highest of political virtues, as constituting the self-knowledge of one whose soul is worthy of reverence.

In accordance with this new definition of nobility as the self-knowledge of the highest-ranking soul, Nietzsche turns in sections 289 through 296, the final sections of part 9 and of *Beyond Good and Evil* as a whole, to the questions with which the book explicitly began and with which it was preoccupied throughout: Who is the philosopher and what sets him apart? The philosopher is a kind of hermit who writes books to mask his more fundamental thoughts and opinions (BGE 289; cf. 204). The philosopher prefers to be misunderstood both out of fear of doing an injustice to his opinions and out of compassion for others whom he wishes to protect from his painful thoughts (BGE 290). The suffering of the philosopher, which springs from his knowledge, is greater than the suffering of the common run of men, but whereas the common run preaches pity for the suffering, the philosopher embraces a gay science (BGE 293). Philosophers unite the profoundest suffering with golden laughter, and resemble gods of the future who, while they philosophize, will laugh in a "superhuman and new way" (BGE 294).

Nietzsche identifies this superhuman or godlike philosopher as Dionysus (BGE 295). This "genius of the heart" is capable of taking the measure of men's souls and elevating the spirit of whomever he meets. Nietzsche claims to be the "last disciple and initiate" of this "temptor god." Although he expresses reservations about showing his admiration for Dionysus by using "many solemn pomp-and-virtue names," he nevertheless is sorely tempted to praise Dionysus for his "explorer and discoverer courage," "daring honesty," "truthfulness," and "love of wisdom" (BGE 295). Indeed, Nietzsche has used such "solemn pomp-and-virtue names" throughout *Beyond Good and Evil* to praise free spirits and philosophers of the future. Although they are ultimately inadequate to the task of praising philosophy because of their corruption by common usage (BGE 295, 230), these terms of excellence remain among the most adequate means available for giving philosophy its due. While perhaps superhuman or godlike philosophers have no use for such words, those who anticipate such truly exalted figures, free spirits like Nietzsche, cannot do without them.

Nietzsche brings *Beyond Good and Evil* to a close by reminding his reader that philosophy differs from the praise of philosophy as thinking differs from writing a book. In a tone at once cheerful and melancholy he indicates that writing—the fixing and setting down of the results of thought—is inferior to thinking.[28] Free spirits who write books do not command, or create, or eternalize the greatest things. They are not therefore without dignity, for they are "eternalizers of things that *can* be written." Such free spirits eternalize "what cannot live and fly much longer—only weary and mellow things!" (BGE 296; cf. 39). The most characteristic practical activity of the free spirit, preserving the results of his quest for knowledge, is inferior in rank to, yet dependent upon, what he knows. Free spirits like Nietzsche who write books engage in a form, though not the highest form, of right making based on right knowing. It is a form of making that transpires high above politics, but beneath the task that Nietzsche repeatedly assigns the highest type: making oneself a god by eternalizing necessity.

Conclusion

Nietzsche writes in *Beyond Good and Evil* from the perspective of a free spirit. The free spirit's freedom stems from what he knows, not what he makes, invents, or wills. The free spirit, however, knows his freedom to be incomplete and understands the obligation to complete it by moving beyond understanding to creating, commanding, and legislating. The demand that the philosopher of the future create values and legislate necessity is paradoxically based upon the supposed knowledge that the will, not reason, is preeminent in the soul or self, and that comprehending this truth and its significance for life is the one thing needful. Such knowledge, on Nietzsche's view, makes it necessary for those who can do so to achieve absolute mastery by commanding necessity. Commanding or legislating necessity is the highest form of right making based on right knowing.

Mastery of necessity is Nietzsche's formal solution to the contest of extremes in his thought. But in *Beyond Good and Evil* he does not go beyond this verbal formula to provide an account of how "one can live in accordance with it," or an explanation of why such a formula defies realization in life. It is as if a political philosopher were to assert that in a society based on "the true principles of political right" obedience to general laws preserves and indeed purifies individual freedom, but failed to identify the conditions, practices, institution, and beliefs that make such a scarcely to-be-believed union between obedience and freedom possible. Or as if a poet were to give his character the beautiful lines, "My bounty is as boundless as the sea, / My love as deep; the more I give to thee, / The more I have, for both are infinite," without dramatizing the love begetting love of young lovers. Nietzsche's image of the philosopher of the future is a hypothetical and utopian extension of his ideas about knowledge, freedom, and mastery, a verbal formula that identifies the requirements and defines the task of the highest type but does little to show that the requirements can be met or the task accomplished.

Although he uses inspiring words to evoke the formal character of such a life, Nietzsche does not show what the life of a legislating philosopher would be like. He does not subject the philosopher of the future, as Zarathustra had subjected his superman, to "the only critique of a philosophy that is possible and that proves something, namely trying to see whether one can live in accordance with it" (SE 8, p. 187). Yet *Beyond Good and Evil* does make its distinctive contribution in the service of the intellectual conscience. For it brilliantly exemplifies Nietzsche's free-spirited skepticism, the very philosophical skepticism that can reveal Nietzsche's own dogmatic excesses and place them in perspective.

Although he fails in part 6, at the peak of his meditation on the philosopher of the future, to bring to light the character of the new philosopher's life, Nietzsche's account in *Beyond Good and Evil* of knowing and making, whether from the perspective of the free spirit or from that of the philosopher of the future, shows that freedom for him is a form of intellectual and moral excellence that has, in principle, nothing whatsoever to do with flourishing or failing in political life. The political consequence is that from the lofty heights where human excellence begins to emerge—the only perspective that Nietzsche regards as worthy of defending—political liberty and legal slavery, in the distant valleys below, cannot be spotted, much less distinguished.

Conclusion

Some cannot loosen their own chains and can nevertheless redeem
their friends.

Zarathustra

In keeping with his celebrated dislike of system, Nietzsche nowhere
elaborates or acknowledges the need for a systematic science of politics.
His thought may seem to defy classification in any recognizable tradition or genre in the canon of political philosophy. He provides no analysis comparable to Aristotle's detailed investigations of the causes that
preserve and destroy regimes; we lack evidence that he thought himself,
like Machiavelli, a shrewd student of the art of ruling; and his ferocious
scorn for modern man, modern ideas, and modern politics is antithetical to Hegel's understanding of the science of state as the endeavor to
articulate the rational structure inherent in the new political forms
brought forth in the modern age.

Nonetheless, the leading thinkers in the history of political philosophy, however various their interests and diverse their styles, found it
necessary to delve into ethics to clarify the great issues of politics. And
Nietzsche grapples with ethics or the character of right conduct with
scarcely rivaled tenacity, urgency, and singleness of purpose. In full
agreement with the tradition of political philosophy, he rests his judgments about politics on an understanding of what is essential to human
beings and sets them apart, that is, to use a term Nietzsche himself employs, a human being's nature. Yet opposing much of the tradition, he
teaches that the highest form of life culminates in a life above and beyond politics. The clarification of Nietzsche's ethics, and the denigration

of politics that it entails, is a task that falls squarely within the province of political philosophy.[1]

Despite both his dislike of and lack of system, Nietzsche's attempts to clarify the character of the highest type are marked by an exceptional unity of intention and execution. This unity is rooted in a conflict or contest of extremes in the very foundations of his thought. His thought is in part constituted by a pervasive and unresolved tension between his fundamental assumption that morality is made or willed by human beings and his unyielding conviction that there is a knowable and binding rank order of desires, souls, and forms of life. Of course Nietzsche cannot be adequately depicted as an old-fashioned Platonist for whom knowledge is virtue and contemplation the highest human activity. Nor, however, can he be correctly characterized as an up-to-date champion of the modernist and postmodernist ideal of self-making. As a matter of fact, both knowing and making count as virtues for Nietzsche and figure decisively in his philosophical explorations.

His view, reduced to a formula, is that the highest type must engage in right making based on right knowing. This formula or demand, rooted in definite convictions about the metaphysical structure of the cosmos and the rank order of true or real human needs, culminates in the moral imperative to command great things, to master eternity, to legislate necessity, in short, to become a god. But as the thought experiment that Nietzsche undertakes in *Thus Spoke Zarathustra* reveals, becoming a god is impossible for human beings. One of Nietzsche's great achievements is to show how and why the ambition to become a god arises from the ethics of creativity, and how and why this ambition is doomed.

Nietzsche's histories are themselves a form of right making based on right knowing. And this reflects the unity of his thought, for the uses to which he puts history are in harmony with his prescriptions for the right use of history. The "genuine historian," according to Nietzsche's account in *Uses and Disadvantages of History for Life*, fashions artworks, in the light of true metaphysical knowledge and accurate understanding of true or real human needs, out of raw materials drawn from history to provide an education in human excellence. This is what Nietzsche himself does in *The Birth of Tragedy, On the Genealogy of Morals,* and *The Antichrist*. But creativity is less praised than exemplified in Nietzsche's histories. While his histories are themselves examples of right making based on right knowing, instances of edifying poetry composed in accordance with metaphysical knowledge and an understanding of the rank order of true or real human needs, they are not the highest form of making because they do not make their maker free. The genuine historian displays but does not fulfill the demands of human excellence. Nietzsche himself explores most adequately the requirements of the highest life, that is, the most comprehensive manner of right making based on the most fundamental form of right knowing, in *Thus Spoke Zarathustra* and *Beyond Good and Evil*.

Thus Spoke Zarathustra is, I believe, as Nietzsche himself judged, the most profound and farsighted of his writings.[2] In *Zarathustra* Nietzsche explores more intransigently than in any of his other works the moral, political, and philosophical implications of his understanding of the highest type.[3] The new ethics Zarathustra proclaims rests on the knowledge that God is dead. From this foundation Nietzsche infers the obligation to radically emancipate and empower the creative will. The platitude that Nietzsche repudiates systems and systematic thought notwithstanding, Zarathustra carries out a methodical revaluation of virtue, the state, romantic love, and friendship that seeks to emancipate human beings from all forms of practical or human dependence. Nietzsche's new ethics demands the thoroughgoing stripping away of human attachments so as to purge the creative will of every trace of necessity. Gradually, Zarathustra's fantastic dream of transforming the will's affirmation into a divine pronouncement reveals itself as the aspiration to untrammeled and absolute freedom or autonomy. But this is not to be. Zarathustra comes to see that the creative will is thwarted in its striving for an unconditioned freedom by the implacable tyranny exercised by the past over the present and future.

The creative will, however, lashes out against its chains, seeking to liberate itself from time by becoming time's master. The doctrine of the eternal return emerges as a metaphysical interpretation of the cosmos, devised by Zarathustra to empower the will to command past and future by mastering the moment. But the solution it provides to the problem of mastering necessity is incoherent and unworkable. If the doctrine of the eternal return accurately described the cosmos, then willing the moment would entail mastery over both past and future; yet precisely under the conditions defined by the eternal return, willing the moment, indeed willing at all, becomes altogether impossible.

The theoretical defects that mark the eternal return are only part of the story. The moral intentions that compel Zarathustra to embrace the defective doctrine are made vivid by the tense drama that surrounds it, for Zarathustra adopts the eternal return under circumstances that expose it not merely as a stratagem for redemption but as a poisonous myth implanted in his heart and mind by the spirit of revenge. There is nothing of the wild and primeval exuberance of the spirit of Dionysus, nor of the severe and noble philosopher, in the florid, grossly overwrought love song Zarathustra sings to eternity. The corrupt doctrine of the eternal return impels him to betray his wisdom in exchange for a moment of debasing ecstasy and a fleeting feeling of redemption in a spurious reconciliation with his beloved.

On my reading, Zarathustra's redemption not only is false and fraudulent but is eventually experienced as such by Zarathustra. The unsilenceable and indomitable voice of Zarathustra's intellectual conscience inflicts severe punishment on his body and spirit, not only throughout his struggle to determine the significance of the eternal return but also in the aftermath of his capitulation to his self-proclaimed lust for eternity. His prodigious struggles to articulate and face up to the eternal return wreak physical and emotional havoc upon him, not because the doctrine is intrinsically life-denying and horrifying—as Nietzsche noted (WP 55) and Zarathustra's nausea and cowering suggest—but for almost the opposite reason. He is tormented by his attraction to a debilitating doctrine that he willfully misconceives as offering mastery over time, metaphysical comfort, and redemption from suffering. It is Zarathustra's abhorrence for the lie in the soul that impels him to comply with the imperative to command eternity that arises from the way of the creator. And it is his bad conscience, or the pangs of his intellectual conscience, stemming from his sham reconciliation with eternity that brings on his physical deterioration in part IV and triggers his descent into farce.

Part IV marks the end of Zarathustra's efforts to teach and to achieve godlike mastery. His dealings with the higher men reveal a profound change in orientation. He puts aside his solitary investigations of things aloft and under the earth, his attempt to storm the heavens and confront the abyss, and returns to the human world to confront the higher men—wounded spirits unable to overcome or renounce a world they despise. In the end, he abandons the higher men without having taught them to reconsider their notions of overcoming or to reevaluate the grounds of their contempt for conventional political life. It is a measure both of their wound and of Zarathustra's severe limitations as a teacher that he leaves the higher men in a more degraded condition than before he met them. At the same time, it is a mark of Nietzsche's achievement to have exposed Zarathustra's pedagogical failures as well as the incoherence and unworkability of his ethics of self-deification.

Nietzsche characterizes *Beyond Good and Evil* as an extreme inasmuch as he insists that it sets forth a criticism of modernity that at the same time points to a kind of excellence "that is as little modern as possible" (EH III, on BGE, 2). But what kind of extreme is it? *Beyond Good and Evil* is more beautiful than *Thus Spoke Zarathustra* in part because in *Beyond Good and Evil* Nietzsche does not allow the inner logic of the contest of extremes in his thought to play itself out. But the very source of its beauty also makes *Beyond Good and Evil* a less profound and less farsighted work than *Zarathustra.*

By exposing the prejudices that have led philosophy astray in the past, Nietzsche aims in *Beyond Good and Evil* to set philosophy on the proper course for the future. Just as in *Zarathustra* freedom emerged as a crucial precondition for, and the fruit of, creativity, so too in *Beyond Good and Evil* freedom, especially freedom from false and comforting belief, emerges as the foundation for, and the prize attained by, philosophy. Philosophy and the freedom of spirit that is its prerequisite depend upon the courage to confront ugly truths. But the big truth not confronted in *Beyond Good and Evil* is that the highest type, the philosopher of the future, cannot legislate necessity although he is obliged to do so. In the end Nietzsche discreetly retreats from the supreme demand he imposes on the philosopher of the future to a notion of human excellence more in harmony with the orientation of a free spirit, that is, the self-knowledge of a noble soul.

From the perspective of Nietzsche's free-spirited skepticism that honors "every little question mark" over "special words and favorite doctrines" (BGE 25), one must conclude that *Thus Spoke Zarathustra* is a more profound and farsighted book than *Beyond Good and Evil,* because while both show how knowledge of metaphysics and human nature gives rise to the moral imperative to achieve supreme mastery, it is Zarathustra's speeches and deeds that vividly expose the slavish lie that underwrites the unconditional freedom needed by a human being who wishes to make himself a god. Yet from the same perspective but in a different respect it is *Beyond Good and Evil* that is superior, for *Beyond Good and Evil*, which oscillates between the conviction that truth is elusive and mysterious (truth is a woman) and the belief that truth is ugly and poisonous (God is dead) more richly exemplifies the questioning characteristic of the free-spirited skeptic in whom honesty is a special virtue (BGE 227, 230), the desire for truth is a ruling passion (BGE 1), and conscience and courage combine in the perilous and exhilarating exploration of the fundamental character of existence (BGE 1, 5, 23, 39, 224). Although they differ in form and spirit, Nietzsche's most far-sighted book and his most free-spirited book provide, along with his histories, critical perspectives on the contest of extremes that forms his thought.

Virtue and Freedom

It is a commonplace that, while virtue was the central concern of ancient political philosophy, freedom came to be a dominant issue for modern political philosophy. But that valuable preliminary observation creates obstacles to understanding the highest ambition of Nietzsche's thought. At least for Zarathustra, who assumes the obligation to command the past, and for the philosopher of the future presented in *Beyond Good and Evil*, who seeks to legislate necessity, freedom is a virtue, the precondition for the attainment of the highest virtue, and virtue's reward. For Nietzsche as for Plato and Aristotle, virtue or human excellence is the central concern; and for Nietzsche as for much of modern philosophy, freedom is a dominant issue.

Nietzsche's ethics of creativity reflects the distinctive clash between ancient and modern in his thought. He thinks through radically a typically modern notion of freedom, but he does so on the basis of, and constrained by, moral and intellectual virtue. He affirms a version of what Isaiah Berlin famously called positive liberty, that is, a form of freedom "which consists in being one's own master."[4] For Nietzsche, at the peak of his reflections, the life dedicated to liberating the will from the myriad ways in which it is enslaved and imprisoned is the good life. Human excellence, so understood, consists in knowing and mastering the forms of necessity that condition the will.

Nietzsche's dream of total freedom and absolute mastery should be seen in light of the powerful tendency within modern philosophy to understand freedom in terms of obedience to self-given law. Self-given law is a characteristically modern solution to the problem of the conflict between freedom and necessity. Three key moments stand out in the modern effort to achieve freedom by willing or legislating necessity: freedom understood as political liberty; freedom understood as autonomy; and freedom understood as creativity.

The first moment occurs in social contract theory. Speaking very generally, freedom in the social contract theories of Hobbes, Locke, and Rousseau is equated with political liberty, or living under civil laws you have authorized,[5] consented to,[6] or formed.[7] Hobbes, Locke, and Rousseau reconcile freedom with necessity by moralizing political necessity.

The second moment receives its most powerful expression in Kant's practical philosophy. From Kant's perspective, so long as the will remains externally conditioned by the laws of natural necessity, political liberty, or the countless actions that take place within the framework of civil law, counts as little more than slavery. Shifting the focus of freedom from politics to morality, Kant defined freedom as autonomy, or acting out of respect for the moral law that one both legislates oneself and recognizes as universal.[8]

Nietzsche presses further in understanding freedom as obedience to self-given law.[9] He interprets freedom, at least at the peak of his reflections, as the most comprehensive form of creation, that is, making the world in which you live by mastering the most exalted and intractable forms of necessity—time and eternity. The common form of freedom—obedience to self-given law—linking Nietzsche's legislation of necessity to both Kantian autonomy and social contract political liberty should not obscure a basic difference: from the perspective of Nietzsche's account of freedom, both Kantian autonomy and social contract political liberty appear as forms of slavery, since both leave the self at the mercy of forces it has neither made nor mastered.

What accounts for the tendency in modern political philosophy to dwell upon freedom and to understand it in terms of obedience to self-given law? From the beginning, there was a tendency in modern philosophy to push aside the idea of authoritative normative standards external to the human will. At first, reason was enlisted to undermine the claims of nature and religion to guide life, so as to place the guidance of life on a solid and reasonable foundation. Eventually, reason became skeptical of its own authority, in the end leaving the various forms of necessity as the only legitimate restraints on freedom.

This process was disguised or mitigated by successive efforts to moralize necessity. Differences arose as to how necessity was to be defined and to what extent it could be overcome. The success of modern thought in subverting authoritative moral standards meant that if it were possible to master necessity there would be no reason to refrain from doing so. Indeed, there would even be a kind of compulsion or obligation to achieve and indeed expand mastery, for the choice in the end comes down to commanding or being commanded. What you do not master masters you, thereby arbitrarily diminishing your freedom and power.

While submitting to the necessity of self-preservation, social contract theory shows the way to a limited kind of freedom through the mastering of political necessity. While submitting to natural necessity, Kant shows the way to freedom through the legislating of the rational and universal moral law. Unlike his predecessors, Nietzsche, at the peak of his meditation on the ethics of creativity, will suffer no constraints whatever on freedom. The characteristically modern ambition to secure freedom by bringing necessity under the governance of the will culminates in his effort to identify the conditions for the possibility of commanding the greatest things, mastering eternity, and legislating the most comprehensive and intractable forms of necessity. This effort, thought through magnificently in Nietzsche's books, fails. The question therefore arises whether his effort to win freedom by making or legislating necessity is necessary. Must we vindicate our humanity by becoming gods?

A New Orientation

Nietzsche's philosophy fails to achieve its highest goal, but it fails in such a way as to show that human beings cannot become gods and that even the best are not obliged to make themselves gods. *Thus Spoke Zarathustra* represents an original and audacious thought experiment tracing the endeavor of a "devotee of the truth" to arrive at "the eternal goal of the true, the beautiful, and the good" (letter to his sister, 11 June 1865, in L, p. 7) on the basis of the conviction that morality is made, not discovered. On my view, *Thus Spoke Zarathustra* stands apart as a relentless and farsighted attempt to think through the characteristically modern aspiration to actualize freedom by mastering necessity. It is also, wittingly or not, an unparalleled criticism of that aspiration.

Zarathustra's failure to redeem himself from the bonds, both practical and theoretical, that, as he understands it, hold the will fast is not the result of an insufficiently powerful philosophical imagination. Indeed, the true measure of Nietzsche's accomplishment is to have pushed the antagonism between knowing and making to the breaking point. There is no final overcoming. Instead, Nietzsche's teaching, at the climactic moment, shatters. In Nietzsche's case, in contrast to a superb operatic voice that breaks on an unadorned, pure high note, it is not the voice but the music itself that breaks. Thanks to Zarathustra's severe ordeal we learn that distinctions of first importance to Nietzsche—between high and the low, noble and base, good and bad—cannot survive the alleged discovery that the source of order in the world resides exclusively in the brazen assertions, emotional expressions, arbitrary desires, private preferences, or even inspired creations of the human will.

Zarathustra's invaluable legacy teaches that the best life, conceived in terms of the ethics of creativity, is unobtainable. Nor is that all. As I have stressed, Zarathustra's ambition to make himself a god by mastering eternity compels him to betray his own doctrine, which, according to Nietzsche, stands alone because it "posits truthfulness as the highest virtue" (EH IV 3). Yet by displaying the truth about Zarathustra's lies Nietzsche attests to his own love of truth and abiding respect for the dictates of the intellectual conscience.

Zarathustra's speeches and deeds vividly portray three major consequences of the attempt to elevate the creative will to the position of undisputed ruler of the self or soul. First, enthroning the will withers the humane sensibilities, and not merely because it teaches that obligation, compassion, and love spring from envy and hatred. The will's insatiable appetite for total freedom becomes indistinguishable from the achievement of total domination, reducing every kind of friendship to an exclusively instrumental relationship and ultimately requiring the renunciation of all pleasures experienced through the company of others. Second, exaltation of the creative will instills an indiscriminate contempt for authority, limitation, and form: whatever constrains the will represents an intolerable "Thou shalt not." Finally, belief in the necessity of absolute freedom generated by the creative will promotes the practice of evaluating individuals and social and political arrangements on the basis of impossibly high standards.

The result is not to preserve an order of rank but to destroy it: Zarathustra's ludicrously inflated promises and inebriating visions represent utopian fantasies in the light of which the greatest and the smallest must of necessity seem beneath contempt. The pathos of Zarathustra's ethics is that it is forced to renounce and subvert the things Nietzsche most cherishes. But discovering the inhumane and ignoble consequences of the ethics of creativity should not be confused with refuting Nietzsche's views, much less with overcoming the formidable challenge posed by his philosophical explorations.

Grasping the significance of and forming a worthy response to the death of God—the general rejection of a natural, rational, or revealed order independent of the human will—is the basic task of Nietzsche's thought. But how does Nietzsche know that what is signified by God's death—that nature, reason, and revelation have once and for all been exposed as hollow idols—is true? In considering the status of this opinion in his thought one does well to examine the characters to whom he entrusts the various declarations of his true but deadly doctrine, as well as the argumentative context in which the opinion is set forth.

In *The Birth*, the half-deity Silenus is violently forced to reveal his secret knowledge, while tragic art is presented as revealing and transfiguring the metaphysics that Silenus's wisdom presupposes. In the *Genealogy*, compelling psychological conjectures about the origins of morality are misleadingly presented as documented happenings. In *The Antichrist*, Nietzsche furiously denounces Christianity for its falsification of reality and, from the exalted perspective of physician of the soul, condemns it for corrupting humanity. When Zarathustra proclaims that God is dead, he omits the reasoning that led him to this momentous conclusion. But in a candid moment he explicitly confesses that his rejection of belief in God and gods stems from envy of divine power (Z II "Upon the Blessed Isles"). And although Nietzsche speculates in the preface to *Beyond Good and Evil* that truth is a woman, hence elusive and mysterious, his analysis of knowledge, freedom, and mastery presupposes that God is dead or that the fundamental character of existence is knowable and deadly.

In sum, the primary evidence Nietzsche adduces for the death of God comprises coerced revelation from the gods, mythical histories, shrill tirades, prophetic visions, sickening nightmares, dubious conjectures about the history of philosophy and morality, and absolute statements about the fundamental structure of the cosmos. A depreciation of reason accompanied by a presumptuous claim to metaphysical knowledge is embodied in the figures and forms through which the death of God is presented. Consequently, a disquieting suspicion and liberating possibility emerges: is the alleged fact that necessitates the radical exaltation of the creative will—the death of God—essentially hypothetical? Did Nietzsche supplant one form of dogmatism with another? And has Nietzsche, through his brilliant evocation of the degradation that results from accepting the revelation of Silenus, the madman's pronouncements, the prophet's visions, the dwarf's temptations, and his own polemics, given us excellent reasons to probe whether to embrace the death of God is to acquiesce rashly to a debilitating myth?

Although the death of God broadly construed—the rejection of an external moral order that is independent of the human will—is fundamental to Nietzsche's thought, Nietzsche, as I have argued, has constant and critical recourse to those things—truth, wisdom, the soul, will, right, virtue, justice, nature, the rank order, nobility, philosophy— which were bound up with the God that supposedly died and the host of traditional convictions about human nature that allegedly perished with him. There are those who hope that this dependence can be understood as a misplaced nostalgia from which Nietzsche never managed to break free. In the end, this apology fails because it misidentifies the moral intention that gives birth to and governs Nietzsche's thinking. More basic than the speculations about perspectivism, thoughts about agency, and celebrations of the creative will, more primary than the convictions about the rank order and the prerogatives of the few, more fundamental even than the death of God to Nietzsche's thought is the intellectual conscience that compels Nietzsche to face up to God's death and to examine its moral and political significance for the good life.

To question Nietzsche's conjecture that the will is supreme is to challenge that form of dogmatism to which his philosophy is most prone. Yet such questioning does not depend on an appeal to standards from beyond the borders of his thought. For it is not contrary to but rather from the perspective of Nietzsche's free-spirited skepticism that the fundamental and broadly conceived conjecture that God is dead, along with all its awful and awesome implications, becomes deeply questionable. We not only may, in the face of Nietzsche's extraordinary challenge, study with a good conscience thinking that affirms that nature, reason, or revelation supplies moral and political standards; we must study such thinking in accordance with the demands of the intellectual conscience.

Nietzsche compares the free spirit to a solitary voyager obliged to set sail upon vast, uncharted seas. We are faithful to Nietzsche's legacy if, in full awareness of the gravity of the situation that requires it, we undertake that hazardous, uncertain voyage. Disciplined by Nietzsche's skepticism and consequently skeptical of his dogmatism, we shall navigate with less certainty than he that we are condemned to sail in solitude toward strange and undreamt-of horizons. Emboldened by the encounter with Nietzsche's tempting questions and chastened by the reach of his questionable convictions, we shall see ourselves and the world around us with brighter and sterner eyes. Open to wonder thanks to Nietzsche's bold explorations, we should be prepared for anything— even, who knows, for the rediscovery of venerable and forgotten lands.

Notes

Acknowledgments

Index

Notes

Introduction

1. A blindness Nietzsche cannot be said to have shared: "I have cast my book [*Human, All Too Human*] for the 'few,' and even then without impatience; the indescribable strangeness and dangerousness of my thoughts are such that a long time must pass before there are ears to hear them—and certainly *not* before 1901" (letter to M. von Meysenbug, 12 May 1887, in L, p. 266).
2. Alexander Nehamas, *Nietzsche: Life as Literature* (Cambridge: Harvard University Press, 1985), p. 91.
3. Ibid., p. 1.
4. Heidegger argues that the metaphysical position that the world is chaos remained "absolutely determinative" for Nietzsche. Martin Heidegger, *Nietzsche,* vol 2, trans. David Farrell Krell (San Francisco: Harper and Row, 1982), p. 93. I would qualify Heidegger's remark by omitting the "absolutely" because of the constant battle in Nietzsche's thought between the view that the world is chaos and the view that the world exhibits a rank order of desires, human types, and forms of life.
5. Nehamas denies that perspectivism entails a substantive and partisan moral doctrine. Yet if no view of the world is binding on everyone, then views such as the Platonic, Christian, and Kantian, which make universal claims are wrong views. Hence, perspectivism takes definite sides on questions of morality. Perspectivism is not, as Nehamas characterizes it, opposed to dogmatism, but rather is a contemporary form of dogmatism. Nehamas, p. 72.
6. Eric Blondel criticizes the tendency to reduce Nietzsche's philosophy to strategies for evacuating texts of meaning, in part because this reductivism obscures Nietzsche's basic ambition to evaluate reality and redeem life. Blondel, *Nietzsche: The Body and Culture,* trans. Seán Hand (Stanford: Stanford University Press, 1991), pp. 9–11, 53, 75. Blondel rightly argues that Nietzsche is a moralist from beginning to end, but overemphasizes the importance of culture to Nietzsche's morality. Ibid., pp. 64–65.

7. William Connolly does view the death of God in moral terms. For Connolly, the death of God serves Nietzsche "as an interpretation of the modern condition." Connolly, *Political Theory and Modernity* (Ithaca: Cornell University Press, 1993), p. 7. Connolly holds that the death of God gives rise to the imperative to abandon the effort to see the world in terms of definitive standards and authoritative convictions, and points toward an ethic or sensibility that aims at questioning, contesting, and problematizing beliefs and practices, particularly one's own. Yet precisely where Nietzsche's ethics needs most to be questioned vigorously, Connolly affirms unequivocally. That is, Connolly treats the death of God as true, the unproblematic basis for a philosophy of the future. He presents as a charitable interpretation of Nietzsche's teaching what looks on closer inspection like an uncritical embrace of an interpretation that he himself finds congenial or useful. This is unfortunate, for it encourages the conclusion that what Connolly favors is not exactly respect for difference and appreciation of ambiguity but rather *agreement* that dwelling upon difference and celebrating ambiguity are good for human beings. Connolly, pp. 7–15, 137–197.

8. In his remarkable study of nineteenth-century German thought, Karl Löwith emphasized that while one can find in Nietzsche's thought whatever one wishes, the contradictions in which Nietzsche's thought abounds reflect a fundamental unity: "Nietzsche's actual thought is a thought system, at the beginning of which stands the death of God, in its midst the ensuing nihilism, and at its end the self-surmounting of nihilism in eternal recurrence." Löwith, *From Hegel to Nietzsche*, trans. David E. Green (New York: Columbia University Press, 1991), pp. 192, 193.

    Similarly, Leo Strauss's most energetic discussions of Nietzsche emphasize the fundamental and unresolved tensions that form Nietzsche's thought. Strauss, "Note on the Plan of Nietzsche's *Beyond Good and Evil*," in *Studies in Platonic Political Philosophy* (Chicago: University of Chicago Press, 1983), esp. pp. 183, 185, 190; see also the Preface in *Spinoza's Critique of Religion*, trans. E. M. Sinclair (New York: Schocken, 1965), pp. 12–13, 30–31.

9. Mark Warren argues that "Nietzsche's refusal to use metaphysical categories of agency, such as 'will,' 'self,' 'soul,' or 'subject,' distinguishes his approach from his precursors in the German tradition from Kant through Schopenhauer." Warren, *Nietzsche and Political Thought* (Cambridge: MIT Press, 1988), pp. 9–10. But, as I will show, Nietzsche uses "metaphysical categories" freely and often. Of course he also severely criticizes metaphysical language and demands its repudiation. What call for explanation are the more fundamental considerations that drive Nietzsche both to repudiate and to embrace traditional metaphysical notions.

    Bernard Yack contributes to such an explanation by providing an enlightening analysis of Nietzsche's dependence on a dichotomy between human freedom and natural necessity that, Yack argues, he inherited from post-Kantian philosophy. Yack, *The Longing for Total Revolution* (Berkeley: University of California Press, 1992), pp. 310–365. But Nietzsche's thought is also dependent on opinions about moral and intellectual virtues more typical of ancient philosophy than of Kant. See, e.g., Karl Löwith, *From Hegel to Nietzsche*, pp. 188–200, 323.

10. See, e.g., BT ASC 1; BT 7; UD 6; GS 344; BGE Preface, 44, 48, 62; A 8, 51; EH IV 3.

11. See, e.g., BT 7, 18; GS 377; WS 86; Z Prologue 3, 4; Z II "The Child with the Mirror."

12. See, e.g., UD 4, p. 78; GS 382; Z Prologue 4, Z I "On the New Idol," Z II "The Dancing Song"; BGE 22, 30, 32, 45, 265, 287; GM III 14; 19, 20; A Preface, 37; EH I 8; letter to Carl Fuchs (18 July 1888) in BKSA VIII, pp. 358, 359.

13. See, e.g., Z I "On the Three Metamorphoses," "On the Way of the Creator," and Z II "Upon the Blessed Isles" and "On Redemption"; BGE 29, 44. See also Z Prologue 4, Z I "On the New Idol."

14. See, e.g., GS 382; BGE 11, 261, 265; GM III 14. Also Z I "On the Three Metamorphoses."

15. See, e.g., BGE 201, 214, 224, 227, 295.

16. See, e.g., UD 6; BGE 265; GM II 11; TI "Skirmishes of an Untimely Man" 48. Also Z I "On the Adder Bite"; Z II "On Scholars."

17. See, e.g., BT 7, 8; BGE 220, 265; A 57.

18. See, e.g., BGE 6, 30, 213, 219, 265, 287.

19. See, e.g., GS Preface 2; 344; BGE; GM Preface 1, 2; A 7.

20. Although Charles Taylor does not pursue the matter in connection with Nietzsche, this understanding of the contest of extremes in Nietzsche's thought is in harmony with his argument that many of the achievements that modernity most prizes have their roots in and are sustained by premodern categories of thought. Taylor, *Sources of the Self: The Making of the Modern Identity* (Cambridge, Mass.: Harvard University Press, 1987). For another account of modernity's fruitful entanglement with tradition see Robert Alter, *Necessary Angels: Tradition and Modernity in Kafka, Benjamin, and Scholem* (Cambridge, Mass.: Harvard University Press, 1991).

21. Heidegger, *Nietzsche,* vol. 1, trans. David Farrell Krell (San Francisco: Harper and Row, 1972), pp. 3–11; vol. 3, trans. Joan Stambaugh, David Farrell Krell, and Frank A. Capuzzi (San Francisco: Harper and Row, 1987), p. 8; also 187–192.

22. Ibid., vol. 1, p. 188.

23. Ibid., vol. 2, pp. 184–197.

24. See Heidegger, "The Word of Nietzsche: 'God Is Dead,'" in *The Question Concerning Technology and Other Essays,* trans. William Lovitt (New York: Harper and Row, 1977), p. 61; Heidegger, *Nietzsche,* vol. 2, p. 205; vol. 3, p. 166.

25. Jacques Derrida argues that deconstruction must work within the tradition of metaphysics to overturn and displace it. Derrida, "Signature Event Context," in *Margins of Philosophy,* trans. Alan Bass (Chicago: University of Chicago Press, 1982), p. 329. On the implausibility of the attempts by post-Nietzscheans to escape metaphysics see Alasdair MacIntyre, *Three Rival Versions of Moral Enquiry* (Notre Dame: University of Notre Dame Press, 1990), pp. 45–46.

26. Eric Blondel also stresses both the greatness of Heidegger's interpretation and its arbitrary truncating of Nietzsche's thought; see Blondel, *Nietzsche,* p. 5.

27. Heidegger, *Nietzsche,* vol. 1, pp. 3–6; vol. 2, pp. 5–8.

28. Ibid., vol. 3, pp. 1–9, 173–183, 230–231; vol. 4, trans. Frank A. Capuzzi (San Francisco: Harper and Row, 1982), pp. 8, 116–118. See also "Who Is Nietzsche's Zarathustra?" in ibid., vol. 2, pp. 232–233; and Heidegger, "The Question Con-

cerning Technology," in *Basic Writings*, ed. David Farrell Krell (New York: Harper and Row, 1977).

29. Almost twenty years ago Walter Kaufmann criticized the "methodological scandal" involved in Heidegger's interpretations of Nietzsche, which depend on "systematic preference for non-contextual readings—for taking bits out of context and using them willfully and arbitrarily." Kaufmann, *Existentialism, Religion, and Death* (New York: New American Library, 1976), pp. xiii, 29–30. Since Kaufmann wrote, Heidegger's methodology has become the norm.

30. Nehamas uses such a method while claiming to read carefully. But he does not use "carefully" in the ordinary sense of the word, that is, as denoting painstaking attention or precision: "We shall have to read a number of apparently unrelated passages and interpret them carefully (that is to say, creatively) in order to show that they are relevant to our concerns." See Nehamas, *Nietzsche: Life as Literature*, p. 47.

One example of such careful reading, crucial to Nehamas's overall argument, must suffice. According to Nehamas, Nietzsche employs a variety of styles as a rhetorical strategy to convey a basic theoretical truth, "that there is no single, neutral language in which his views, or any others, can ever be presented. His constant stylistic presence shows that theories are as various and idiosyncratic as the writing in which they are embodied" (p. 37). But it is very unlikely that Nietzsche understood his use of many styles as an effort to vindicate the theory of perspectivism, for he explicitly offers a quite different explanation. And, interestingly enough, he offers that quite different explanation in the very paragraph in *Ecce Homo* from which Nehamas quotes to provide the title for his chapter on Nietzsche's style, "The Most Multifarious Art of Style" (p. 19).

In the paragraph in question in *Ecce Homo*, Nietzsche makes clear that the problem for him is not, as Nehamas asserts (invoking for support a passage from *The Will to Power*), that there are no facts only interpretations (p. 20), but rather that of communicating accurately the facts about his inward states (EH III 4). For Nietzsche the question is not one of the perspectival character of all knowing, but rather how to make an accurate image of his inner experience available to others. For Nietzsche, at least according to the passage in *Ecce Homo* that Nehamas himself highlights, the aim in deploying a variety of styles is not grand and general, as if to contribute to the construction from his own experience and thoughts of a literary character in his works, but rather quite specific, to reveal the quality and variety of his actual inner life.

In sum, by transforming carefulness into creativity Nehamas can claim fidelity to Nietzsche's works while making Nietzsche teach nearly the opposite of what he says. One disadvantage of the creative redefinition of carefulness as creativity is that it obscures Nietzsche's account of the character of genuine creativity.

31. For example, Gilles Deleuze asserts, against those who understand the eternal return as the return of "a particular arrangement of things," that "on two occasions in *Zarathustra* Nietzsche explicitly denies that the eternal return is a circle which makes the same return." Deleuze, *Nietzsche and Philosophy*, trans. Hugh Tomlinson (New York: Columbia University Press, 1983), p. xi. But Nietzsche does not speak in *Zarathustra*. Rather, it is characters within *Zarathustra*, characters with their own complicated motives enmeshed in an elaborate narrative, who speak. Moreover, the denials are accompanied by affirmations. For ex-

ample, Zarathustra calls himself "the advocate of the circle" (Z III "The Convalescent" 1) and proclaims his "lust after eternity and after the nuptial ring of
rings, the ring of recurrence" (Z III "The Seven Seals"). If one may treat any
utterance by a character in *Zarathustra* as a teaching of Nietzsche's, then one
can make Nietzsche teach anything one wishes.

32. For an instructive discussion of this problem see Maudemarie Clark, *Nietzsche on Truth and Philosophy* (Cambridge: Cambridge University Press, 1990), pp. 17–21.

33. While one *could* advance any number of interpretations of Nietzsche's thought, Nehamas believes that a "single view," perspectivism, connects and accounts for the key paradoxes in his thought. Nehamas, pp. 1, 19, 105. Tracy Strong appears to have transcended the laws of perspectivism to discover that "Perspectivism . . . is at the center of Nietzsche's understanding of our presence in the world and of its availability to us." Strong, *Friedrich Nietzsche and the Politics of Transfiguration,* expanded ed. (Berkeley: University of California Press, 1988), p. 304. Mark Warren's observation that Nietzsche's "most pressing problems" lie in the historically, politically, culturally, and linguistically bound character of subjectivity appears to identify an objective feature of Nietzsche's thought. Warren, *Nietzsche and Political Thought,* p. 2. Jean Granier seems to have moved beyond interpretation to the knowledge that "one of the principal themes in Nietzschean thought" is the primacy of interpretation. Granier, "Nietzsche's Conception of Chaos," in *The New Nietzsche,* ed. David Allison (Cambridge, Mass.: MIT Press, 1985), p. 135. And so on.

34. Nietzsche himself affirms the continuity and unity of his thought in BT ASC and GM Preface 2, 8. Among the pioneering efforts to examine one of his books as a whole is Leo Strauss's "Notes on the Plan of Nietzsche's *Beyond Good and Evil,*" in *Studies in Platonic Political Philosophy* (Chicago: University of Chicago Press, 1983). In the last decade a number of studies have taken Nietzsche's books seriously. Foremost among these is Laurence Lampert's *Nietzsche's Teaching* (New Haven: Yale University Press, 1986). There is also a helpful collection of essay-length studies of individual books: *Reading Nietzsche,* ed. Robert C. Solomon and Kathleen M. Higgins (New York: Oxford University Press, 1988).

35. Derrida argues that "the hypothesis of a rigorous, sure, and subtle form is naturally more fertile." Jacques Derrida, "Plato's Pharmakon," in *Disseminations,* trans. Barbara Johnson (Chicago: University of Chicago Press, 1981), p. 67. And so it is. It remains an open question whether slow and careful reading, on "the hypothesis of a rigorous, sure and subtle form," results in the discovery of a secret, deeper organization than the one inscribed by the author, as Derrida contemplates, or rather of the organization and arguments the author inscribed.

36. There is no reason to forgo study of Nietzsche's unpublished writings. Although I shall refer to passages from his notebooks in the process of interpreting his books, I shall avoid invoking a statement from outside the book at hand as a basic premise or missing step in an argument. For a good discussion of the ambiguous status of the posthumously published collection of writings from Nietzsche's notebooks called *The Will to Power* see Bernd Magnus, "The Use and Abuse of *The Will to Power,*" in *Reading Nietzsche,* pp. 218–236.

37. "Immoralist" is a term Nietzsche uses in a variety of contexts to describe him-

self and to indicate the morality to which he believes himself subject. Speaking of "we immoralists," he holds, contrary to the "dolts and appearances," that immoralists are bound by exacting duties (BGE 226). In the preface to *Daybreak*, he emphasizes that he and his like are *"men of conscience"* who "still obey a stern law [*strengen Gesetze*] set over us—and this is the last morality [*die letzte Moral*] which can make itself audible even to us." This last morality requires the rejection of unworthy beliefs, of lies, and of compromise; and it says no to Christianity, romanticism, nationalism, and pleasure seeking. On account of this last morality, Nietzsche explains, "we still feel ourselves related to the German integrity [*Rechtschaffenheit*] and piety [*Frömmigkeit*] of millennia, even if as its most questionable and final descendants, we immoralists, we godless men of today, indeed in a certain sense as its heirs, as the executors of its innermost will . . . In us there is accomplished—supposing you want a formula—the *self-sublimation of morality*" (D Preface 4). Moreover, he declares himself "the first immoralist"; identifies Zarathustra with the achievement of immoralism—"the self-overcoming of morality, out of truthfulness"; and claims the word immoralist as "a symbol and badge of honor for myself" (EH IV 2, 3, 6; EH III, on UM, 2). Nietzsche's immoralism is the ethics of a type that deserves to be highest, and governs one who not only "conceives reality *as it is*" but also "is reality itself and exemplifies all that is terrible and questionable in it" and thereby achieves greatness (EH IV 4, 5). In a letter, Nietzsche recommended that he be characterized "as an *Immoralist*" and defined an immoralist as "the highest form, till now, of 'intellectual integrity' [*intellektuellen Rechtschaffenheit*]" (letter to Carl Fuchs, 29 July 1888, in L, p. 305).

38. In an early fragment, Nietzsche explains how art depends on philosophy: "The philosopher ought to *know what is needed;* and the artist ought to *make* it" (KSA 7, p. 423). Stanley Rosen comments on this fragment: "Nietzsche's relatively early statement (1872/73) on the relation between philosophy and art continues to hold true throughout his mature thought and writings . . . This [statement] is Nietzsche's Platonism." Rosen, *The Question of Being: A Reversal of Heidegger* (New Haven: Yale University Press, 1993), p. 174. I agree with Rosen's assessment and I would add that in his later writings Nietzsche envisages a supreme type who unites in his own person the work of the philosopher and that of the artist. In his sympathetic reconstruction of Nietzsche's thought, Leslie Paul Thiele asserts that "Nietzsche's aim was theoretically and practically to incorporate the philosopher, artist, and saint into one person." Thiele, *Friedrich Nietzsche and the Politics of the Soul: A Study of Heroic Individualism* (Princeton: Princeton University Press, 1990), p. 163. No contradiction arises from seeing the saint in the image of a supreme type who unites knowing and making, inasmuch as the saint, as Thiele himself observes (p. 155), is understood by Nietzsche as the highest-ranking kind of artist.

39. Rosen's examination of the tension between knowing and making is very helpful. See "The Quarrel Between Philosophy and Poetry" in his *The Quarrel Between Philosophy and Poetry* (New York: Routledge, Chapman and Hall, 1988) and "Theory and Interpretation" in his *Hermeneutics and Politics* (New York: Oxford University Press, 1987).

40. Charles Taylor develops the argument that even the most radical criticisms of morality, particularly the "neo-Nietzschean" criticisms that assume or seek to

show that morality is ultimately based on fiat or power, themselves of necessity issue from "moral orientations" that take a stand on what is right and good. Taylor, *Sources of the Self,* pp. 98–103. My account suggests that what Taylor claims is true of neo-Nietzschean theorizing is true as well for Nietzsche's philosophical explorations.

41. On the back of the original edition of *The Gay Science* Nietzsche wrote: "This book marks the conclusion of a series of writings by FRIEDRICH NIETZSCHE whose common goal it is to erect *a new image and ideal of the free spirit.* To this series belong: / *Human, All Too Human.* With Appendix: Mixed Opinions and Aphorisms. / *The Wanderer and his Shadow.* / *Daybreak: Thoughts about the Prejudices of Morality.* / *The Gay Science.*" (GS, p. 30). Although I do not give these books the attention they deserve, Nietzsche's remark about the common goal that unites them in conjunction with my own brief discussion of *The Gay Science* suggests that these books point to the constellation of problems inhering in Nietzsche's efforts to articulate the character of the supreme type. For a thoughtful discussion of the enduring philosophical significance of *The Gay Science* see Richard Schacht, "Nietzsche's *Gay Science,* Or, How to Naturalize Cheerfully," in *Reading Nietzsche,* pp. 68–86.

42. Nietzsche's account of the intellectual conscience also recalls the opening remark of Aristotle's metaphysics (*Metaphysics* 980a): "All men by nature desire to know."

43. In his final writings, Nietzsche describes the philosophical life he lived in characteristically ethical terms that evoke the intellectual conscience: "Philosophy, as I have so far understood and lived it, means living voluntarily among ice and high mountains—seeking out everything strange and questionable in existence, everything so far placed under a ban by morality . . . How much truth does a spirit *endure,* how much truth does it *dare?* More and more that became for me the real measure of value. Error (faith in the ideal) is not blindness, error is *cowardice* . . . Every attainment, every step forward in knowledge, *follows* from courage, from hardness against oneself, from cleanliness in relation to oneself . . . *Nitimur in vetitum* [We strive for the forbidden]: in this sign my philosophy will triumph one day, for what one has forbidden so far as a matter of principle has always been—truth alone" (EH Preface 3).

44. The aspiration to become a god is scarcely an isolated occurrence in German literature. For example, Goethe's Faust yearns to know the innermost secrets of the world (part I: 382, 383), wonders whether he is a god (part I: 439), is mockingly called a "superman" by the spirit he summons (part I: 490), and associates his passion for eternal truth and his sharing in God's creativity with the idea that he was created in God's image (part I: 614–622).

45. Because of his intense concern with the ultimate structure of the cosmos, Nietzsche's own term "antimetaphysician" is preferable to Richard Rorty's characterization of Nietzsche as one of modernity's "paradigm nonmetaphysicians." Rorty, *Contingency, Irony, Solidarity* (Cambridge: Cambridge University Press, 1989), p. 98. It is hardly, as Rorty argues, that Nietzsche has no opinion about the ultimate structure of the cosmos or that Nietzsche thinks his opinions about the cosmos lack moral and political significance. Rather, Nietzsche is opposed to metaphysicians of the past precisely because they misunderstood the true character of the cosmos.

46. Nietzsche himself suggests such an understanding in a notebook fragment, WP

617. I follow Heidegger in seeing great importance in this fragment. See, e.g., Heidegger, *Nietzsche*, vol. 1, pp. 19–20; vol. 2, pp. 201–204; vol. 3, pp. 156–158, 212–215, 245–246. For difficulties inhering in Heidegger's use of WP 617 see Krell's analysis in vol. 2, p. 257n2. I myself shall lay great stress on the act of falsification to which Nietzsche's note calls attention and which Heidegger sometimes overlooks. I shall suggest that WP 617—which links "the supreme will to power" and the idea that "everything recurs" in the attempt "to impose upon becoming the character of being" and which indicates that the success of this attempt depends upon a "twofold falsification"—articulates the character of Zarathustra's reconciliation with eternity and sheds light on the failure of Zarathustra's quest to make himself a god. But I must emphasize that I do not rely on this notebook fragment as a premise, but rather discuss it as a gloss on results gained by analysis of the text of *Zarathustra*. Here too I part ways with Heidegger, who insists that we could never understand the doctrine of eternal return but for Nietzsche's unpublished writings. Heidegger, *Nietzsche*, vol. 2, pp. 15, 141.

1. The Ethics of History: *On the Uses and Disadvantages of History for Life*

1. For example, whereas Nehamas finds in Nietzsche's writings the resources for fashioning a coherent, viable, and attractive model for self-creation, Heidegger decries the arrogant frame of mind that teaches that the will produces and imposes structure and value on the external world. Whereas Michel Foucault credits Nietzsche with introducing genealogy, a revolutionary and comprehensive form of social inquiry grounded in the assumption that morality and knowledge are, have been, and will always be nothing more than reflections of envy and desire for power, Alasdair MacIntyre, essentially embracing Foucault's characterization of genealogy, concludes that as a method of moral inquiry genealogy is hopelessly irrational. Finally, Mark Warren seeks to rescue what he regards as Nietzsche's central notion, human agency, from what he views as Nietzsche's repugnant and extraneous remarks about morality and politics. This stands in sharp contrast to Bruce Detwiler, who—proceeding from the premise, which he shares with Warren, that Nietzsche denies that morality has a rational, natural, or divine basis—argues that Nietzsche's sweeping denial is in fact intimately connected to his recurring accounts of a radically aristocratic political order. Alexander Nehamas, *Nietzsche: Life as Literature* (Cambridge, Mass.: Harvard University Press, 1985); Martin Heidegger, "The Word of Nietzsche: 'God Is Dead,'" in *The Question Concerning Technology and Other Essays,* trans. William Lovitt (New York: Harper and Row, 1977); Foucault, "Nietzsche, Genealogy, History," in *Foucault Reader,* ed. Paul Rabinow (New York: Pantheon, 1984); MacIntyre, *Three Rival Versions of Moral Inquiry* (Notre Dame: University of Notre Dame Press, 1990); Warren, *Nietzsche and Political Thought* (Cambridge, Mass.: MIT Press, 1987); and Detwiler, *Nietzsche and the Politics of Aristocratic Radicalism* (Chicago: University of Chicago Press, 1990).

2. See Nehamas, *Nietzsche*, pp. 13–20; and Eric Blondel, *Nietzsche: The Body and Culture,* trans. Seán Hand (Stanford: Stanford University Press, 1991), p. 18.

3. Perhaps Nehamas and Blondel overlook the importance of the genre of history in Nietzsche's writings because of the topical and thematic approach they adopt to interpret his thought. This approach, which passes by Nietzsche's books in favor of fragments drawn from them, has been called into question by a former practitioner. Tracy Strong has reached the conclusion that the topical and thematic approach is opposed to the manner in which Nietzsche wished to be read, and now looks forward to the day "when we will start reading Nietzsche as he wanted to be read, that is, to read his books as books and not as collections of sayings." Strong, *Friedrich Nietzsche and the Politics of Transfiguration,* expanded ed. (Berkeley: University of California Press, 1988), p. 317. A study of Nietzsche's histories can contribute to Strong's worthy hope.

4. Goethe's Faust is an example of one who suffers from the scholarly obsession with historical knowledge. Faust's colleague Wagner is an example of a man who does not know that he is afflicted (*Faust,* part I: 354–429, 522–602).

5. See also SSW in PT, p. 127, and PTG 1.

6. A preference he embraces in BT 7, GM III 24–27, and A Preface.

7. "The question of the degree to which life requires the service of history at all, however, is one of the supreme questions and concerns in regard to the health of a man, a people or a culture" (UD 1, p.67).

8. In the Preface to *Philosophy in the Tragic Age of the Greeks,* Nietzsche emphasizes that the reason for studying ancient philosophy is "to bring to light what we *must ever love and honor* and what no subsequent enlightenment can take away: great individual human beings" (PTG Preface, p. 24).

9. Plato's *Republic* 443c–445b, also 592b.

10. This is by no means an anomaly in Nietzsche's thought. For other discussions of justice as governing the service of truth see HH 636, 637; BGE 213; GM II 11. Of course, this is not the only understanding of justice in Nietzsche's thought. For example, Nietzsche also understood justice as an arrangement to secure self-preservation (HH 92) and as a prime manifestation of the drive to revenge (GM I 14; WP 255).

11. Nietzsche uses a related verb, *umzuprägen* (to mint), to describe the characteristic activity of the genuine historian (UD 6, p. 94).

12. See also UD 8, p. 103: "the thought of being epigones, which can often be a painful thought, is also capable of evoking great effects and grand hopes for the future in both an individual and in a nation, provided we regard ourselves as the heirs and successors of the astonishing powers of antiquity and see in this our honor and our spur."

13. Interestingly, Hobbes, for all his rhetoric about science and system, invokes the injunction "Read thy self" to indicate the foundation of moral and political knowledge, and asserts that the similitude or form of the passions, as opposed to the object of the passions, is the same in all men. One discovers the character or constitution of mankind by reading one's own character or constitution and finding what is universal in it. And according to Hobbes, moral and political knowledge admits of no other kind of demonstration. Hobbes, *Leviathan,* Introduction.

14. Nehamas infers that Nietzsche rejected the very idea of self-knowledge in the Socratic sense (see Nehamas, *Nietzsche,* p. 26). Sometimes Nietzsche does deny the possibility of self-knowledge. Yet no less frequently or importantly, he

affirms its reality and centrality to human excellence. Leslie Paul Thiele discusses the role self-knowledge plays in Nietzsche's understanding of the task of the educator and the philosopher. Thiele, *Friedrich Nietzsche and the Politics of the Soul* (Princeton: Princeton University Press, 1990), esp. pp. 207–214.

2. The Ethics of Art: *The Birth of Tragedy*

1. Nehamas, a leading proponent of the aesthetic interpretation, recognizes that the accent in *The Birth* is not on self-making through art but on the power of art to "intimate the final truth that the ultimate nature of the world is to have no orderly structure." Nehamas, *Nietzsche: Life as Literature* (Cambridge, Mass.: Harvard University Press, 1985), pp. 42–43. By contrast, Tracy Strong argues that Nietzsche held in *The Birth* that art did not imitate or represent a transcendental realm and did not intimate a "final truth" but rather was "an activity that built the very world to which it had reference." Strong, "Nietzsche's Political Aesthetics," in *Nietzsche's New Seas* ed. Michael Allen Gillespie and Tracy B. Strong (Chicago: University of Chicago Press, 1988), p. 160. Contrary to Strong but consistent with Nehamas, *The Birth* frequently repeats and, as I shall argue, critically depends upon the view that art reveals a realm that it does not make (see esp. BT 6–8). Indeed, in his major works Nietzsche affirms at critical junctures final truths about the ultimate nature of the world.

2. For a more skeptical view of art see ch. 4, "From the Souls of Artists and Writers," in *Human, All Too Human*.

3. In the summer of 1870, after the outbreak of the Franco-Prussian War, Nietzsche voluntarily enlisted as a nurse orderly in the Prussian Army. Within a month he collapsed from exhaustion and severe illness and by mid-autumn he was in Basel convalescing. Ronald Hayman, *Nietzsche* (New York: Penguin, 1982), pp. 126–130.

4. So, for example, Nietzsche speaks of "higher moralities" in contrast to herd morality (BGE 202). And in the draft of a letter to Paul Rée, he claims that his own is the most severe morality (PN, p. 102; BKSA 6, p. 309). Long ago, Karl Jaspers accurately characterized the matter: "*Nietzsche attacks morality in every contemporary form* in which he finds it, not in order to remove men's chains, but rather to force men, under a heavier burden, to attain to a higher rank." Jaspers, *Nietzsche: An Introduction to the Understanding of His Philosophical Activity*, trans. Charles F. Wallraff and Frederick J. Schmitz (Tucson: University of Arizona Press, 1965), p. 139.

5. Heidegger fairly asserts that "by 'morality,' Nietzsche usually understands a system of evaluations in which a transcendent world is posited as an idealized standard of measure." Martin Heidegger, *Nietzsche*, trans. Joan Stambaugh, David Farrell Krell, and Frank A. Capuzzi (San Francisco: Harper and Row, 1982) vol. 4, pp. 76, 77. I would add that Nietzsche's criticism of reality typically presupposes a transcendent world.

6. Cf. GM Preface 6, where morality is also characterized as the "danger of dangers" and for the same reason—because it thwarts human excellence.

7. See also AOM 220, where Nietzsche elaborates this opinion.

8. Cf. Aristotle, *Metaphysics*, 1072a18–1075a10; and *Nicomachean Ethics* 1177a11–1179a33.

9. There is a considerable measure of agreement among Nietzsche and Plato and Aristotle concerning the imitative and pedagogic powers of music. Plato, *Republic* 401d–e; Aristotle, *Politics* 1340a18–23, 1340b12–13. The crucial difference is that Nietzsche believes that music not only educates but reveals the character of human passions and through the passions the very essence of the world.

10. In contrast, Plato and Aristotle primarily analogize knowing to the sense of sight. The parable of the cave abounds in image metaphors. Plato, *Republic* 514–520. See also Aristotle, *De Anima* 432a1–10.

11. Music, for the mature Nietzsche, remains a vehicle for the presentation of wisdom and also one of the great corrupting influences on elevated souls. See e.g., BGE 255; CW 1, 2, 12; WP 810.

12. Cf. Plato's *Apology of Socrates* 22b; and *Ion* 534–536.

13. The twofold movement consisting of a shattering knowledge that is somehow transformed into redemptive insight resembles the experience Nietzsche describes in his first major presentation of the doctrine of the eternal return (GS 341) and the two episodes that compose Zarathustra's pivotal account of the eternal return (Z III "On the Vision and the Riddle").

14. In notes from the period in which he wrote *The Birth* Nietzsche characterizes the philosopher as a Promethean hero who finally is rescued from his suffering through *"reconciliation in the highest tragic art"* (P 85).

15. Whereas Nietzsche here equates the slave with the ordinary man who is sunk in silly pastimes and oblivious to what is noble, in his mature writings Nietzsche distinguishes between the passionate desire for vengeance that fuels the slavish man's elaborate construction of a transcendent sacred world (GM I 8–17) and the lusterless, withered spirit of the last man incapable and undesirous of undertaking formidable deeds (Z Prologue 5). Although demonstrating in *The Birth* a less subtle appreciation of the varying types of enemies of the noble than in subsequent works, Nietzsche nonetheless underscores his severely moralistic view that art must be judged not merely by its capacity to imitate and represent forms of life, nor simply by its power to provoke and to inspire, but primarily by its capacity to mirror the metaphysical character of the cosmos and real human needs.

16. Interestingly, the tendency to overreach, to mistake expertise in one area for wisdom as such, is precisely the error that Plato's Socrates claims to have discovered among the politicians, poets, and craftsmen, an error the understanding of which Socrates sees as the basis of his "human wisdom." See *Apology of Socrates* 20d–22d.

17. This assertion of the unity marking Nietzsche's thought accords with Thomas Mann's observation in his eloquent tribute: "the completely unified and compact character of Nietzsche's life work cannot be sufficiently stressed." See "Nietzsche's Philosophy in the Light of Contemporary Events," in *Nietzsche: A Collection of Critical Essays,* ed. Robert Solomon (Notre Dame: University of Notre Dame Press, 1973), p. 355.

18. Nietzsche calls *The Birth* "my first revaluation of all values" and explicitly describes the "tragic feeling" as an affirmation of "the eternal joy of becoming." He emphasizes that as "the teacher of the eternal return" he is "the last disciple of the philosopher Dionysus" (TI "What I Owe to the Ancients" 5). Moreover,

reviewing his career in *Ecce Homo,* he declares that *The Birth* brings to light "a formula for the highest affirmation . . . a Yes saying without reservation, even to suffering, even to guilt, even to everything that is questionable and strange in existence" (EH III, on BT, 2). That formula is "'the doctrine of the eternal return,' that is, of the unconditional and infinitely repeated circular course of all things" (EH III, on BT, 3). And Nietzsche declares the eternal return "the fundamental conception" of *Zarathustra* (EH III, on Z, 1). In Zarathustra's hands, the eternal return becomes a peculiar interpretation—neither necessary nor arbitrary—of the view that understanding "the primordial contradiction and primordial pain in the heart of the primal unity" redeems (BT 6).

3. The Ethics of Morality: *On the Genealogy of Morals*

1. The subtitle is on the back of the original title page. See the explanatory note in KSA 14, p. 377. Nietzsche also refers to the *Genealogy* as a polemic in *Ecce Homo* (EH III, on GM), and in a letter to Peter Gast of 18 July 1887 (L, p. 269).

2. Foucault, "Nietzsche, Genealogy, History" in *Foucault Reader,* ed. Paul Rabinow (New York: Pantheon, 1984), p. 76.

3. Foucault of course sometimes admitted that he was unconcerned with fidelity to the text: "The only valid tribute to thought such as Nietzsche's is precisely to use it, to deform it, to make it groan and protest. And if commentators then say that I am being faithful or unfaithful to Nietzsche, that is of absolutely no interest." Foucault, *Power/Knowledge: Selected Interviews and Other Writings, 1972–1977* (New York: Pantheon, 1980), pp. 53–54. The trouble with Foucault's apparently forthright statement is that it is incoherent and obscures his actual practice. The statement presupposes the importance of what it appears to deny, namely understanding Nietzsche's thought, for before manipulating Nietzsche's thought to bend it to his own use, Foucault implicitly claims to have understood it well enough to know that painful deformation constitutes a valid tribute to it. In fact, Foucault, as he says, does painfully deform Nietzsche's thought; but by also cultivating the appearance of carefully interpreting it he has persuaded many readers that his painful deformations are in fact faithful interpretations.

4. Nehamas argues that Nietzsche's criticism of Christianity is that it "conceal[s] and den[ies] its own interpretive status," pretending to be for everyone when it actually reflects and serves "the particular needs and desires" of some. Nehamas, *Nietzsche: Life as Literature* (Cambridge, Mass.: Harvard University Press, 1985), p. 105. But Nietzsche's criticism of Christianity goes much further. He attacks Christianity because he believes its beliefs are false and its dominion has been a catastrophe for the human spirit.

5. Here I disagree with Strong, who argues that the logic of genealogy requires the abandonment of God and that genealogy shows that "moral valuations are the result of illusions." Tracy B. Strong, *Friedrich Nietzsche and the Politics of Transfiguration,* expanded ed. (Berkeley: University of California Press, 1988), pp. 15–16, 29–49, 189, 272–273. In my reading, it is the logic of the death of God that requires genealogy. And genealogy does not show but rather presupposes that moral valuations are illusions. The death of God is in its primary sense a theoretical speculation that can neither be refuted (or established) by

history nor falsified (or proven) by logic. History can show that people have ceased to believe in God, and logic can show that conventional beliefs are incoherent, but neither historical studies nor logical analysis can establish the nonexistence of a supersensible world or the absence of objective ethical standards. Furthermore, genealogy follows the death of God not only logically but also chronologically in Nietzsche's thought. Nietzsche introduces the death of God and variations on that theme long before he presents genealogy, and in the preface to the *Genealogy* Nietzsche indicates that his major hypothesis about the origins of morality precedes the discovery of genealogy (GM Preface 4). In sum, the death of God is a conjecture that transforms all morality into a prejudice and thereby makes genealogy, the search for the human origins of practices and beliefs, look like the only appropriate method for studying morality. To borrow Charles Taylor's terms, the death of God belongs to the "background picture" or "moral ontology" that frames Nietzsche's orientation toward questions of what is good. Charles Taylor, *Sources of the Self: The Making of the Modern Identity* (Cambridge, Mass.: Harvard University Press, 1989), p. 41, and more generally pp. 3–111. See also Bernard Williams, *Ethics and the Limits of Philosophy* (Cambridge, Mass.: Harvard University Press, 1985), p. 33.

6. In stressing that genealogy is "an effort to take history itself very seriously and to find it where it has least been expected to be" (p. 112), Nehamas, I believe, overlooks a prominent form of Nietzsche's aesthetic tendency—the poeticization of history. Similarly, Deleuze understands genealogy as a new form of historical science, one that "shows how the word 'good' was originally created by the masters." Gilles Deleuze, *Nietzsche and Philosophy,* trans. Hugh Tomlinson (New York: Columbia University Press, 1983), p. 75. But rather than showing this in a scientific or scholarly sense, Nietzsche reconstructs history on the basis of speculations about the cosmos and human excellence. What Deleuze calls Nietzsche's "new philology" is actually a part of Nietzsche's practice of monumental history.

7. See Aristotle, *Politics,* 1254a, "But then we must look for the intentions of nature in things which retain their nature, and not in things which are corrupted." Rousseau uses this remark as the epigraph to his *Discourse on Inequality.*

8. Much earlier Nietzsche had directed a similar criticism, but with greater rhetorical fireworks, against David Strauss, a well-known German writer (DS).

9. The "historical sense" resembles Weber's celebrated concept of *Verstehen,* the empathetic understanding of the framework of beliefs and values that organizes a people's religious practices, economic institutions, and social order. Max Weber, *Economy and Society,* ed. Gunther Roth and Claus Wittich (Berkeley: University of California Press, 1968), pp. 3–24. Yet by comparison to Weber's social science, Nietzsche's exercise of the "historical sense" appears narrow and idiosyncratic. But then again rigorous comparative analysis and disinterested knowledge are not Nietzsche's goals. His declaration that the historical sense is one of his specific intellectual virtues camouflages his lack of interest in precise historical knowledge and the suprahistorical character of the knowledge he claims to achieve.

10. Nietzsche, in effect, revives the old charge that Rousseau leveled against Hobbes. Hobbes had sought to examine man in the state of nature to shed light on

the political significance of the right of nature and the laws of nature, but according to Rousseau he inadvertently transplanted civilized man into a prepolitical setting. On Rousseau's account, Hobbes failed to disentangle man's natural passions from the bad habits and artificial wants foisted upon him in civil society. Rousseau, *Discourse on Inequality,* trans. V. Gourevitch (New York: Harper and Row, 1986), p. 139. Similarly, on Nietzsche's account, the English utilitarians mistakenly took the contingent traits exhibited by Englishmen and the characteristics valued by English morality as the universal features of human nature. He does not criticize the English psychologists by denying the existence of a universal human nature, but by insisting that the English have failed to grasp it. Interestingly, marshaling the charge against Nietzsche that Nietzsche marshaled against the English, Alasdair MacIntyre maintains that Nietzsche in fact read his own peculiar conception of individualism into the ancient world. MacIntyre, *After Virtue,* 2nd ed. (Notre Dame: Notre Dame University Press, 1984), p. 129.

11. According to one such declaration, "There is *only* a perspective seeing, *only* a perspective 'knowing'" (GM III 12). Yet the continuation of this remark shows that Nietzsche both seeks and presupposes a kind of objectivity. He advises his fellow philosophers to view "one thing" from as many angles as possible. But the collection of multiple perspectives of "one thing" presupposes that the "one thing" under examination stays the same and that its look or nature can be pieced together by synthesizing views attained from many angles. Far from endorsing radical perspectivism, this key passage advances a method for overcoming or neutralizing the inevitable distortion that results from viewing a multifaceted object from a single vantage point. Maudemarie Clark, on the basis of a close examination of the passage in GM III 12, reaches a somewhat different conclusion but agrees that Nietzsche's account "does invite us to think of a thing that is independent of the perspectives on it." Maudemarie Clark, *Nietzsche on Truth and Philosophy* (Cambridge: Cambridge University Press, 1990), p. 136, and generally pp. 127–158.

12. Contrary to Strong, who argues that "*genealogy, as Nietzsche uses it, brackets the things themselves so as to be left with only the constituting human elements,*" Nietzsche emphatically evaluates the creations of the nobles and slaves with reference to an external rank order, finding the products of the former good because they conform better to the rank order and the creations of the latter bad because they distort or promulgate lies about the rank order. Strong, *Nietzsche and the Politics of Transfiguration,* p. 47.

13. It is worth recalling that the opinion that the weak invent morality to control the strong, closely associated with Nietzsche and his genealogy, long precedes Nietzsche and the invention of genealogy. See, e.g., Aristotle, *Politics* 1318b4–5: "The inferior always seek equality and justice; those who dominate them take no thought for it." It can be found in Thrasymachus's defense of the opinion that justice is the advantage of the stronger in Plato's *Republic* 338c; in the Unjust speech in Aristophanes' *Clouds* 890–1104; and in the words of Shakespeare's deformed and outcast king: "Conscience is but a word that cowards use / Devised at first to keep the strong in awe." *Richard III* V.iii.309–310.

14. The original forms of right or higher law *(Recht)* and positive law *(Gesetz)*

differ from the perverted forms instituted by slave morality. According to the second essay the true aristocrats of spirit, in accordance with the demands of justice *(Gerechtigkeit),* establish right or higher law through the positive law to check the subversive demands of the majority (GM II 11).

15. Similarly, Nietzsche cautions against prematurely introducing "the concept of 'revenge'" in the effort to understand how inflicting pain served as compensation for injury (GM II 6).

16. This account of justice recalls that offered in UD 6, which I discussed in Chapter 2.

17. Nietzsche makes a related point in regard to self-creation in BGE 225.

4. The Ethics of Religion: *The Antichrist*

1. Werner Dannhauser is one of the rare commentators to offer a reason for passing by *The Antichrist,* but his reason is unpersuasive. He makes the sweeping charge that in *The Antichrist* "everything he [Nietzsche] says is colored by his unbridled polemical passion and shaped by his desire to attack Christianity by any and all means." Dannhauser, *Nietzsche's View of Socrates* (Ithaca: Cornell University Press, 1974), pp. 233–234. Yet Nietzsche viciously attacks Christianity in many works. What distinguishes *The Antichrist* is not primarily its polemical fury but rather its rationalism, the frequency of its invocation of intellectual virtue as a standard for condemning Christianity and praising Christianity's rivals.

   In his analysis of the Christian dimension of Nietzsche's thought, Karl Löwith emphasizes that the critique of Christianity in *The Antichrist* is not only of a piece with Nietzsche's earlier writings but "is the culmination of a line of criticism which began with the *Unzeitgemässe Betrachtungen.*" Löwith, *From Hegel to Nietzsche,* trans. David E. Green (New York: Columbia University Press, 1991), p. 369.

   Gary Shapiro provides a thoughtful reading of *The Antichrist* which seeks to restore interest in it particularly among those concerned with Nietzsche's views on interpretation. Shapiro, "The Writing on the Wall: *The Antichrist* and the Semiotics of History," in *Reading Nietzsche,* ed. Robert C. Solomon and Kathleen M. Higgins (New York: Oxford University Press, 1988).

2. The evidence in *The Antichrist* refutes Nehamas's contention that in Nietzsche's later writings the idea that the aim of art is to intimate the world as it actually is drops out in favor of the view that there are no facts, only interpretations. Nehamas, *Nietzsche: Life as Literature* (Cambridge, Mass.: Harvard University Press, 1985), pp. 42–44. This is not to deny that in later writings—especially *The Will to Power* but also in early works—one can find Nietzsche "deny[ing] the very contrast between things-in-themselves and appearances" (p. 43). But one also finds—in abundance—Nietzsche affirming such a contrast. As Maudemarie Clark observes, *The Antichrist* and also *Twilight of the Idols* "exhibit a uniform and unambiguous respect for facts, the senses, and science." Clark, *Nietzsche on Truth and Philosophy* (Cambridge: Cambridge University Press, 1990), p. 105.

3. Stanley Rosen provides an extended analysis of the significance of Nietzsche's

self-identification with the Hyperboreans in *The Question of Being* (New Haven: Yale University Press, 1993), pp. 140–148.

4. On this understanding, Socrates would seem to be a model of the free spirit.

5. Similarly, in the *Genealogy* he praises the noble mode of valuation because it falsifies the world less seriously than does the slavish mode of valuation (GM I 10).

6. Karl Löwith suggests a very strong connection between the overall argument of *The Antichrist* and the doctrine of the eternal return: "How little Nietzsche had outgrown Christianity is shown not only by his *Antichrist*, but also by its counterpart: the theory of eternal recurrence. It is an avowed substitute for religion; no less that Kierkegaard's Christian paradox, it is an escape from despair: an attempt to leave 'nothing' and arrive at 'something.'" Löwith, *From Hegel to Nietzsche*, p. 373. In this connection, Löwith cites Nietzsche's letter to Erwin Rhode of 23 May 1887. See BKSA 8, pp. 80–81.

7. Nietzsche views this betrayal as the expression of a general rule holding that veneration "blots out the original, often painfully strange features and idiosyncrasies of the venerated being—*it does not even see them*" (A 31). So too, I shall argue, with Zarathustra's disciples.

8. Nietzsche views Jesus' doctrine of redemption as aptly symbolized by the child, the very image that Zarathustra—who also embraces a doctrine of redemption which secures the experience of eternity in this world—invokes to represent the highest form of perfection (Z I "On the Three Metamorphoses").

9. The slavishness of Jesus' love for eternity comes into sharper focus in the light of Nietzsche's unconditional judgments in *Beyond Good and Evil* that the taste for the unconditional is the worst of tastes (BGE 31), that "the slave wants the unconditional" (BGE 46), and that "everything unconditional belongs in pathology" (BGE 154). The underlying decadence or pathology of will that Nietzsche associates with the demand for the unconditional should be kept in mind when it comes to Zarathustra, who seeks, to the exclusion of all else, eternity within or mastery over time.

10. For closely related statements about the need to sacrifice for the sake of truth see BT 7, 9; GS 125; Z Prologue 3, 4 and I "On the Three Metamorphoses"; BGE 39; GM I 1; WP 1041.

11. His account of the healthy political order as exemplified by the law of Manu closely resembles his accounts of political health stretching back to his earliest writings. See *"Der Griechische Staat"* in KSA 1, pp. 764–777; SE 5, 6; and BGE 61.

12. See Alfarabi, "The Political Regime," in *Medieval Political Philosophy,* ed. Ralph Lerner and Muhsin Mahdi (Ithaca: Cornell University Press, 1963).

13. This opinion is repeated in similar language several times in Nietzsche's writings: e.g., Z II "On the Tarantulas"; BGE 221; TI "Skirmishes of an Untimely Man" 48.

14. See Mark Warren, *Nietzsche and Political Thought* (Cambridge, Mass.: MIT Press, 1987), pp. 207–248.

15. In a letter to Peter Gast, Nietzsche records his pleasure at having "found *Manu's* book of laws in a French translation in India under strict supervision from the most eminent priests and scholars there." Characterizing the laws of Manu as "absolutely Aryan" and the supreme example of "moral lawgiving," he asserts

that "even Plato seems to me in all the main points simply to have been well instructed by a Brahmin" (31 May 1888 in L, pp. 297, 298).

5. The Beginning of Zarathustra's Political Education: *Thus Spoke Zarathustra* (Prologue)

1. See also PTG 2, p. 37, letter to Mathilde Maier, 15 July 1878, in L, p. 168, and letter to Georg Brandes, 10 April 1888, in L, p. 292.

2. Leslie Paul Thiele expounds sympathetically what he calls Nietzsche's ideal of heroic individualism. Although Thiele himself emphasizes that for Nietzsche the test of this ideal, as of any philosophy, is the attempt to live in accordance with it, Thiele refrains from undertaking the investigation that his reconstruction of Nietzsche's ideal suggests is most necessary: to judge Nietzsche's ideal in terms of Zarathustra's attempt to live in accordance with it. See Thiele, *Friedrich Nietzsche and the Politics of the Soul* (Princeton: Princeton University Press, 1990), p. 221.

3. The leading study of *Zarathustra* is Laurence Lampert's *Nietzsche's Teaching* (New Haven: Yale University Press, 1986). Like Lampert, I believe that of Nietzsche's books, *Zarathustra* "yields the greatest reward" (p. 9). And I share with Lampert "the currently unfashionable view that Nietzsche's writings present a specifiable teaching about beings and human being" (p. 9). But I differ sharply with him over the moral and political significance of Nietzsche's teaching about beings and human being: whereas Lampert argues that Nietzsche's Zarathustra is the teacher of a new and desirable ethics, I argue that Zarathustra's new ethics is undesirable and self-defeating. This fundamental disagreement encompasses many others.

   According to Lampert, *Zarathustra* reveals that Nietzsche's teaching is "the most comprehensive wisdom that can guide the most spiritual beings" (p. 10). Moreover, Lampert believes that "Nietzsche's art of writing" avoids what is shameful and corrupting and is accurately attuned to its intended audience (pp. 45, 46); that Nietzsche overcomes nihilism "through the teachings of will to power and eternal return" (pp. 103–104); that Nietzsche achieves a total revaluation of all values (p. 190); that Zarathustra overcomes the spirit of revenge and attains redemption by willing the eternal return (pp. 213, 246); and that Nietzsche is the "genius of the heart worthy of being followed" who has demolished the old tradition and established a new one (p. 273).

   Contrary to Lampert, I argue that Nietzsche's insight into the human condition is severely limited; that Nietzsche's art of writing and Zarathustra's speaking descend into the shameful and fail to discriminate finely among interlocutors; that the doctrines of will to power and eternal return do not escape the nihilism they are meant to overcome; that Zarathustra's so-called redemption reflects the supreme manifestation of the spirit of revenge; and that Nietzsche, far from demolishing the old tradition and accomplishing a revaluation of old values, remains fundamentally dependent on the tradition he sought to transcend.

4. Letter to Franz Overbeck, 11 February 1883; letter to Karl Knortz, 21 June 1888; in L, pp. 207, 299. See also the letter to Carl Fuchs, July 18, 1888, in BKSA VIII, 358, 359; EH Preface 4; and EH III 1, 4. Nietzsche even goes so far

as to declare *Thus Spoke Zarathustra* mankind's "most profound book" (TI "Skirmishes of an Untimely Man" 51), and a work that "stands altogether apart" (EH III, on Z, 6).

5. Derrida makes just such an inference. From the real ambiguity surrounding the context and intention of the fragment "I have forgotten my umbrella," he wishes to infer the radical ambiguity of all of Nietzsche's writings. Jacques Derrida, *Spurs*, trans. Barbara Harlow (Chicago: University of Chicago Press, 1978), pp. 133–134. Such an approach obscures the difference between kinds and degrees of ambiguity.

6. In part IV the "last pope" characterizes Zarathustra, with Zarathustra's approval, as "the most pious of all those who do not believe in God" (Z IV "Retired"). Moreover, Nietzsche characterizes the spirit that animates his philosophical explorations as a form of piety (GS 344).

7. Zarathustra's rare autobiographical revelations, which tend to revolve around his weakness, need, and envy, are all the more striking for the heavy silence that they shatter. See e.g., Z I "On the Afterworldly"; Z II "The Night Song," "The Dancing Song," and "The Tomb Song."

8. The worry is that, lacking a past, Zarathustra is shielded or rendered immune to an analysis of his beliefs in terms of his needs, receiving an arbitrary exemption from a universal explanatory framework. Nevertheless, the secrecy regarding his past may forestall the misuse of the historical approach outside its appropriate domain: "Against the doctrine of the influence of the milieu and external causes: the force within is infinitely superior; much that looks like external influence is merely its adaptation from within. . . . A genius is not explained in terms of such conditions of his origin" (WP 70).

9. Nietzsche, himself forced to give up reading for long stretches of time as a result of chronic eye troubles, calls his deliverance from books "the greatest benefit I ever conferred on myself" (EH III, on HH, 4).

10. We can obtain perspective on Zarathustra by looking at another figure who seeks solitude and perfection in the distant mountain heights. In a poem about divine aspirations, solitude, and friendship that followed the original text of *Beyond Good and Evil*, Nietzsche depicts the austere mountain peak as a remote and dangerous waiting place for friends, inhospitable to all but the strongest and rarest: "Higher than mine no table has been set: / Who lives so near / The stars or dread abysses half as sheer? / My realm, like none, is almost infinite, / And my sweet honey—who has tasted it?—"(BGE "From High Mountains. Aftersong").

The poem's narrator longs for friends despite his avowal that few men are capable of dwelling alongside him on the edge of the abyss and in the presence of the infinite. His ardent longing for friendship is condemned to disappointment by his greater need to explore the extremes of nature. When his old friends at last draw near, they no longer recognize him. As a result of his ascent to the summit of unexplored, bleak regions, he sees sights, feels fears, and undergoes changes that estrange him from his friends without satisfying or alleviating his need for others. Participation in the realm of the infinite and enjoyment of the realm of the intimate are in tragic tension. Having achieved fundamental knowledge, the poet, like Nietzsche's Oedipus (BT 9), is "wounded and stopped by his own victory." Knowledge separates and fundamental knowledge separates fundamentally. Knowledge brings emancipation from traditional religious piety but also results in exile from political life. The poet reluctantly discourages his friends—for their sake, for fear of the pain they might suffer due to their unfitness to endure the heights—from completing their climb and so guarantees his own tortured solitude: "You leave?—My heart: no heart has borne worse hunger."

In the end, in place of friendship with another human being, the poet welcomes the imagined Zarathustra as his friend and "guest of guests." Both mountain-dwellers—the poet of Nietzsche's "From High Mountains" and Zarathustra—probe the secrets of metaphysics and thereby discover the true but deadly doctrine that God is dead. However, whereas the poet chooses knowledge, solitude, and invented spirits for friends, Zarathustra, when we first see him, having grown impatient with his solitude, weary of his wisdom, and anxious to promulgate his new doctrine and win recognition as a teacher and redeemer, chooses to seek his fortune among mankind.

11. See Z I "On the Three Metamorphoses" and below in Chapter 5, "A Parable on the Spirit." Cf. Matthew 18:3; Mark 10:13–15.

12. Although I agree with Bernard Yack that a notion of human dignity animates Nietzsche's scathing indictment of modern cultural and political institutions, I believe Yack is mistaken to take Zarathustra's statement that he loves man as evidence of Nietzsche's general love of humanity. Bernard Yack, *The Longing for Total Revolution* (Berkeley: University of California Press, 1992), p. 312. Zarathustra immediately corrects his statement, and it is contradicted by the overall thrust of the vast majority of his speeches. Zarathustra's love of man is love of the superman or the highest type, and this love requires contempt for, and the recognition of the utter superfluousness of, the multitude of mankind (Z I "On the New Idol" and "On the Flies of the Marketplace"). As additional evidence of Nietzsche's general love of man, Yack (pp. 321–322) cites Nietzsche's remark in "The Greek State," "The human being only has dignity in so far as he is, consciously or unconsciously, a tool of genius." But this does not reflect, as Yack contends, a kind of Kantian universal human dignity, because the dignity of the multitude is a byproduct of the benefits the genius derives from the use of the inferior human being. It is the dignity of a slave who is treated always as a means and never as an end. It is not that Nietzsche cannot leave the multitude of humanity "condemned to a less than human life" (Yack, p. 320), but rather, and to the limited extent that Nietzsche entertains political hopes, that Nietzsche wishes to harness the less than human lives led by the multitude to support the higher lives of the few. The same love of man that informs Nietzsche's consignment of the mass of humanity to slavery in "The Greek State," that animates Zarathustra's critique of the state and the marketplace, and that engenders Nietzsche's savage disgust with "the sick" in the *Genealogy* (GM III 14–15) is made absolutely explicit in *The Antichrist:* "The weak and the failures shall perish: first principle of *our* love of man. And they shall even be given every possible assistance" (A 2).

Nietzsche's radically aristocratic political intention is instructively discussed by Karl Löwith in *From Hegel to Nietzsche*, trans. David E. Green (New York: Columbia University Press, 1991), pp. 260–262, and carefully connected to the major themes in his thought by Bruce Detwiler in *Nietzsche and the Politics of Aristocratic Radicalism* (Chicago: University of Chicago Press, 1990).

13. Zarathustra's stiff-necked desire to impose his ideal on others is at odds with

his view that justice declares that men are unequal (Z II "On the Tarantulas" and "On Poets").

14. Cf. BGE 63. In a letter to his sister written shortly after the completion of part IV of *Zarathustra*, Nietzsche reflected: "It seems to me that a human being with the very best of intentions can do immeasurable harm, if he is immodest enough to wish to profit those whose spirit and will are concealed from him" (March 1885, in PN, p. 441).

15. Instead of keeping Walter Kaufmann's "overman," I have followed Bruce Detwiler in translating *Übermensch* as "superman." As Detwiler argues, the disadvantage of evoking false associations with the popular comic book character is outweighed by the advantage of preserving the possible connection to a number of important Nietzschean *über* words—such as supramoral, suprahistorical, and superhuman—that require the English prefixes of "super" and "supra." See Detwiler, *Nietzsche and the Politics of Aristocratic Radicalism,* pp. 48–49.

16. While it is a commonplace that *Zarathustra* parodies the New Testament, it is less remarked that Zarathustra pays Jesus a high honor by recognizing him as his rival, by imitating him in crucial respects, and by seeking to outdo him as a teacher to mankind. Like Jesus, Zarathustra brings a dramatic new message to mankind about the connection between God and human well-being. Like Jesus' disciples, Zarathustra must become a fisher of men (Z Prologue 7 and IV "The Honey Sacrifice"). Like Jesus, he condemns as corrupt the prevailing morality and religion. Like Jesus, he summons mankind to break sharply with its past for the sake of a new form of life. Like Jesus, he exhorts the people to reorient their lives in terms of their ultimate happiness and ultimate degradation. And just as Jesus promises as a reward eternal life *(das ewige Leben),* so too Zarathustra promises a reconciliation with eternity in the doctrine of the eternal return *(die ewige Wiederkunft).* The Christian counterparts to Zarathustra's quest and ideas are discussed by R. J. Hollingdale in the introduction to his translation of *Thus Spoke Zarathustra* (New York: Penguin, 1969), pp. 27–29. By drawing attention to these similarities I do not mean to obscure the profound difference between one who comes to reveal a new message from God and one who proclaims that human beings must, as a worthy response to God's death, make themselves gods.

17. Nietzsche's own contradictory attitudes toward recognition and fame are reflected in the tension between the seclusion he sought out and contended was characteristic of the thinker's life, and his excitement in 1888 upon learning that the Danish professor Georg Brandes would be lecturing on his thought in Copenhagen. Cf. Nietzsche's account of "The Type of my Disciple" in WP 910 with the letter to Overbeck, 3 February 1888, in L, pp. 282–283, the letter to Knortz, 21 June 1888, in L, pp. 298–299, and the letter to Fuchs, 29 July 1888, in L, pp. 304–305.

18. Heidegger's opinion that "Anxiety reveals the nothing" is closely related, and also reflects the opinion that internal disorder is an accurate reflection of the chaos without. Heidegger, "What Is Metaphysics," in *Basic Writings,* ed. David Farrell Krell (San Francisco: Harper and Row, 1977), p. 103.

19. "Man would rather will *nothingness* than *not* will" (GM III 28).

20. Similar misgivings about Zarathustra's concern for the independence of those

who follow him arise in connection with his subsequent statement that he anticipates "a companion and fellow creator . . . one who writes my will on my tablets to contribute to the greater perfection of all things" (Z III "On Involuntary Bliss"). Furthermore, the old man Zarathustra meets in the woods on his way to bury the tightrope walker seems to be a caricature of Zarathustra's propensity to equate the needs of others with his own needs: like Zarathustra, who orients his teaching in terms not of his students' needs but of his own, the old man, while professing to wish to feed the hungry, insists that whoever knocks at his door must take what he offers (Z Prologue 8).

21. See Soren Kierkegaard, *Fear and Trembling*, in *Fear and Trembling/Sickness unto Death*, trans. Walter Lowrie (1941; rpt. Princeton: Princeton University Press, 1974), pp. 49–52; Plato, *Republic* 496a–e, 592a; BGE 26; GM III 8.

22. Heidegger discusses the relation between Zarathustra's eagle and serpent and the doctrine of the eternal return in "Who Is Nietzsche's Zarathustra?" in Martin Heidegger, *Nietzsche*, trans. David Farrell Krell (San Francisco: Harper and Row, 1984), vol. 2, pp. 209–233.

6. The Ethics of Creativity: *Thus Spoke Zarathustra* (Part I)

1. See, e.g., Rousseau, *Social Contract*, ed. Roger D. Masters, trans. Judith R. Masters (New York: St. Martins, 1978), I viii, p. 56; and Kant, *Groundwork of the Metaphysic of Morals* (New York: Harper and Row, 1964), trans. H. J. Paton, ch. II, pp. 98–102. Robert Pippin explores the relation between autonomy and Nietzsche's philosophy in *Modernism as a Philosophical Problem* (Cambridge, Mass.: Basil Blackwell, 1991), pp. 80–116.

2. Although Zarathustra's disciples are exclusively men and Zarathustra caustically disparages women, it was a woman, Lou Salomé, who engendered Nietzsche's highest hope as a disciple. See Walter Kaufmann, *Nietzsche: Philosopher, Psychologist, Antichrist* (Princeton: Princeton University Press, 1974), pp. 47–62. See also letter to Peter Gast, 13 July 1882, in L, p. 1860; letter to Lou Salomé, end of August, 1882, in L, p. 191; letter to Franz Overbeck, October 1882, in L, p. 195; letter to Overbeck, 22 February 1883, in L, p. 209.

3. Thomas Pangle provides a valuable overview of Nietzsche's critique of democracy, but in my view does not give sufficient attention to the fact that Zarathustra expounds an ethics that results in a denigration not just of democracy or bourgeois modernity but of all forms of political life. Pangle, "Nihilism and Modern Democracy in the Thought of Nietzsche" in *The Crisis of Liberal Democracy*, ed. Kenneth L. Deutsch and Walter Soffer, corrected ed. (Albany: State University of New York Press, 1987). Leslie Paul Thiele discusses the severely antipolitical character of Nietzsche's philosopher in *Friedrich Nietzsche and the Politics of the Soul* (Princeton: Princeton University Press, 1990), pp. 22–224. On Nietzsche's recurring visions of an aristocratic political order, see Bruce Detwiler, *Nietzsche and the Politics of Aristocratic Radicalism* (Chicago: University of Chicago Press, 1990).

4. Contrary to Bernard Yack, who assimilates Nietzsche's longing for total freedom to a "left Kantian" longing for a total transformation of the social and political world, for Nietzsche total freedom is achieved in total solitude and is ultimately independent of political reform or revolution. Yack, *The Longing for*

Total Revolution (Berkeley: University of California Press, 1992), pp. 310–364. Nietzsche's Zarathustra does not preach, as Yack would have it, a total transformation of political life, but rather practically its opposite, a total transformation of a few solitary individuals which leaves the social and political world exactly as it was.

5. Karl Löwith, in his masterly study of nineteenth-century German thought, views this speech as encapsulating Nietzsche's thinking. Löwith, *From Hegel to Nietzsche*, trans. David E. Green (New York: Columbia University Press, 1991), p. 193. According to Löwith (p. xv), "Hegel and Nietzsche are the two end points between which the historical course of the German spirit in the nineteenth century moves." There is a unity that underlies the differences between Hegel and Nietzsche. For example, Zarathustra's parable is itself a kind of phenomenology of spirit inasmuch as it depicts the necessary stages through which the spirit must pass on its ascent to a final and absolute end. Like Hegel, Zarathustra deserves to be considered a philosopher of the absolute. The crucial difference of course concerns the nature of the end. Whereas Hegel argued that self-consciousness completes itself in absolute knowledge, Zarathustra contends that the satisfaction of spirit consists in the exercise of unfettered, absolute creativity. Yet absolute creativity is, for Zarathustra, based on absolute or fully adequate knowledge about humanity's place in the cosmos.

6. Zarathustra's account comports with Nietzsche's discussion of "a long compulsion" that signifies the vital role played by submission to the tyrannical laws of morality in the education of free spirits and philosophers of the future (BGE 188, 189; also WP 910).

7. Cf. BT ASC 1; GS 268; BGE 225; WP 852, 910.

8. The mistake of believing everything monsters tell you is brought out in the speech "On the New Idol," in which Zarathustra exposes a monster who whispers "dark lies," falsely claiming for itself greatness and even divinity (Z I "On the New Idol").

9. Consider Nietzsche's provocative observation: "Our vanity desires that what we do best should be considered what is hardest for us. Concerning the origin of many a morality" (BGE 143). The question arises whether the ethics of creativity is born of excessive pride and vanity. And similarly, whether the lion is like the "many people" who "exaggerate the worth of their foes so as to be able to show with pride that they are worthy of such foes" (AOM 263).

10. See BT ASC 1; and Z I "On War and Warriors."

11. This question becomes especially acute when viewed in light of Nietzsche's criticism of the desire for the unconditional (BGE 31, 46, 154) and his speculation that there may be more truthfulness in questions than in "special words and favorite doctrines" (BGE 25).

12. Zarathustra himself alludes to some such vested interest: "For in order that the superman [*Übermenschen*] should not lack his dragon [*Drache*], the overdragon [*Überdrache*] that is worthy of him, much hot sunshine must yet glow upon damp jungles" (Z II "On Human Prudence").

13. The madman and Zarathustra use strikingly similar religious language to describe the moral imperative that arises from mankind's new situation. The madman speaks of inventing "festivals of atonement" and "sacred games" *(heiligen Spiele)*. Zarathustra envisages a child who plays a new "game of creation"

(Spiele des Schaffens) and embodies a "sacred Yes" *(heiligen Ja-sagens;* GS 125 and Z I "On the Three Metamorphoses").

14. On other occasions Nietzsche himself recognizes the fundamental ambiguity in establishing the child as the image of the supreme type. See HH 147, 159. Cf. Z IV "The Ass Festival," in which the wish to become like a little child reflects, according to Zarathustra, a degrading Christian longing for heaven. Hannah Arendt has occasion to notice the child's natural and pre-political helplessness in "What Is Authority," in *Between Past and Future* (New York: Penguin, 1954, 1977), p. 92. Hans-Georg Gadamer, in suggesting the superiority of the child to free spirits, overlooks the dark side of Nietzsche's metaphor. See "The Dance of Zarathustra," in *Nietzsche's New Seas* ed. Gillespie and Strong (Chicago: University of Chicago Press, 1988), p. 231.

15. See Karl Marx, "For a Ruthless Criticism of Everything," in *The Marx-Engels Reader,* ed. Robert C. Tucker (New York: Norton, 1978), p. 13.

16. "And may everything be broken that cannot brook our truths!" (Z II "On Self-Overcoming"). See also GM III 14; WP 246, 247, 964.

17. This effusive praise of the ego echoes Nietzsche's much earlier identification of the satyr as a pure embodiment of human nature (BT 8). In both instances the body, the earth, and the physical are exalted at the expense of the soul, heaven, and the intelligible; and in both instances the exaltation of the nonrational is carried out in the name of the real needs and essential nature of human beings. Just as Nietzsche regarded the satyr of Greek tragedy as superior because it accurately reflected the natural order, so too Zarathustra presents the voice of the ego as superior to the sage's reasoned defense of sleep and virtue on the grounds that the ego declares correctly that heaven is a human creation. There are differences: while Nietzsche's satyr and Dionysian artist are mouthpieces of wisdom but not themselves wise, Zarathustra's ego seems to both know its own worth and create new meaning.

18. Similarly, Nietzsche argues that exploitation rooted in the will to power is "the primordial fact [*Ur-Faktum*] of all history" (BGE 259).

19. See, e.g., *"Der Griechische Staat"* in KSA 1, pp. 764–777; SE 5–6; BGE 61; A 57.

20. Nietzsche reaffirms elsewhere the imperative to behave decently toward one's acts: "Not to perpetrate cowardice against one's own acts! Not to leave them in the lurch afterward! The bite of conscience is indecent" (TI "Maxims and Arrows" 10). This imperative, along with his criticism of the pale criminal for the incapacity to bear the image of his deed, presupposes the very distinction between doer and deed that Nietzsche flatly denies in the *Genealogy* (GM I 13).

21. Nietzsche gives a similar account of the relation between chastity and sensuality in GM III 2.

22. Cf. Machiavelli, *The Prince,* ch. 21. Notice the dramatic discrepancy between Zarathustra's fanatical view and Nietzsche's exquisite praise in *The Daybreak* of the Jewish practice of securing spouses for all adult members of the community (D 205). This illustrates the serious difficulties in simply identifying Zarathustra as Nietzsche's spokesman.

23. Reminiscent of Socrates' account of Diotima's teaching in the *Symposium,* Zarathustra views love for another human being as a prelude and training for a more perfect form of love. Diotima identifies the highest form of love with an erotic yearning to contemplate the eternal Form of Beauty, while Zarathustra,

it would seem, has forfeited the right and renounced the intention to seek beyond the human world a higher world.

24. Nietzsche frequently characterizes the superior type of man as a solitary or hermit. See, e.g., BT 9; BGE 204 and "From High Mountains. Aftersong"; GM III 7–9; A Preface.

25. See also BGE 41 and letter to Malwida von Meysenbug, 12 May 1887, in L, p. 266; letter to Georg Brandes, 2 December 1887, in L, p. 280; and letter to Overbeck, 3 February 1888, in L, p. 282.

7. The Lust for Eternity and the Pathos of Self-Deification: *Thus Spoke Zarathustra* (Parts II and III)

1. It should not be a surprise that Nietzsche offers differing accounts of or perspectives on the eternal return. Perhaps the most discussed alternative to the account in *Zarathustra* is associated with the formula *amor fati*, the grateful acceptance of and love for "what is necessary" (e.g., EH II 10). Interestingly, one finds in *Human, All Too Human*, a work that precedes *Zarathustra*, several extended explorations of the tension between necessity and the freedom to take responsibility for one's deeds that anticipate the constellation of problems Zarathustra aims to solve by means of the doctrine of the eternal return (HH 39, 91, 105, 106, 107, 133, 588; AOM 33). Nietzsche's own testimony from *Ecce Homo* provides good reason to pay special attention to the eternal return as Zarathustra teaches and experiences it. What one should avoid is lumping together Nietzsche's many statements from different books and notebooks about the eternal return as if he were always referring to exactly the same notion.

2. See Alexander Nehamas, *Nietzsche: Life as Literature* (Cambridge, Mass.: Harvard University Press, 1985), pp. 167–169.

3. See Tracy B. Strong, *Friedrich Nietzsche and the Politics of Transfiguration*, expanded ed. (Berkeley: University of California Press, 1988), pp. 260–293.

4. See Maudemarie Clark, *Nietzsche on Truth and Philosophy* (Cambridge: Cambridge University Press, 1990), pp. 266–270.

5. See Laurence Lampert, *Nietzsche's Teaching* (New Haven: Yale University Press, 1986), pp. 176, 256.

6. Martin Heidegger, *Nietzsche*, vol. 1, trans. David Farrell Krell (San Francisco: Harper and Row, 1979), pp. 18–24; vol. 2, trans. David Farrell Krell (San Francisco: Harper and Row, 1984), pp. 5, 133, 98–105, 228.

7. Robert Pippin also finds that Zarathustra is motivated by a kind of revenge that he cannot overcome. Pippin, "Irony and Affirmation in Nietzsche's *Thus Spoke Zarathustra*," in *Nietzsche's New Seas*, ed. Michael Allen Gillespie and Tracy B. Strong (Chicago: University of Chicago Press, 1988), p. 55.

8. In 1947, in the attempt to refute the charge that his way of thinking undermined human dignity, Heidegger wrote, "the highest determinations of the essence of man in humanism still do not realize the proper dignity of man. To that extent the thinking in *Being and Time* is against humanism. But this opposition does not mean that such thinking aligns itself against the humane and advocates the inhuman, that it promotes the inhumane and deprecates the dignity of man. Humanism is opposed because it does not set the *humanitas* of man high enough." Heidegger, "Letter on Humanism," in *Basic Writings*, ed.

David Farrell Krell, rev. and expanded edition (San Francisco: Harper and Row, 1993), pp. 233–234. Heidegger's apology overlooks that human dignity can be diminished not only by setting the *"humanitas* of man" too low but also by setting it too high.

9. Pippin provides an illuminating analysis of the dramatic structure in *Zarathustra* and Zarathustra's evolving attitudes toward the superman and the eternal return. Pippin, "Irony and Affirmation."

10. Zarathustra's degradation both confirms Nietzsche's judgment that "extreme positions are not succeeded by moderate ones but by extreme positions of the opposite kind" (WP 55) and corroborates Socrates' closely related thought that "anything that is done in excess is likely to provoke a correspondingly great change in the opposite direction . . . the greatest and most savage slavery out of the extreme of freedom." Plato, *Republic* 563e–564a.

11. Elsewhere Nietzsche describes a similar "tortured tension" and asserts that it signals *"the advent of nihilism"* (WP Preface 2).

12. See also Z II "The Dancing Song"; Z III "On the Vision and the Riddle"; and Z III "On the Spirit of Gravity." The spirit of gravity and the spirit of revenge are closely related. The difference, perhaps, is that the spirit of gravity is more the malevolent force that keeps things down (Z III "On the Spirit of Gravity") while the spirit of revenge is more the malevolent human reaction to being kept down (Z II "On Redemption").

13. Later, Zarathustra traces disbelief to conscience (Z III "On Apostates" 2). Elsewhere Nietzsche argues that rejection of God is rooted in the quest to redeem the world (TI "The Four Great Errors" 8).

14. See also EH II 1.

15. Moreover, in Nietzsche's view, the priest's blood courses through the philosopher's veins (WP 140).

16. See also Z II "On Scholars."

17. Elsewhere Nietzsche observes that preoccupation with past sorrows and old wounds is a sign of decadence (WP 233).

18. Shakespeare, *Antony and Cleopatra* I.i.48–51. Just as Antony's stormy love for Cleopatra impairs his judgment and leads to his humiliating military defeat, so too Zarathustra's love for life eventually compels him to shamelessly sacrifice his wisdom so that he can embrace eternity (Z III "The Other Dancing Song"; "The Seven Seals").

19. "And once more Zarathustra shook his head and wondered. 'What shall I think of that?' he said once more. Why did the ghost cry, 'It is time! It is high time!' High time for *what?*" (Z II "On Great Events").

20. My account of this speech and its connection to the eternal return is indebted to Karl Löwith's incisive observations in *From Hegel to Nietzsche*, trans. David E. Green (New York: Columbia University Press, 1991), pp. 193–197.

21. Nietzsche himself seems to be of two minds. He both asserts that the task of redeeming the world compels him to reject Christianity (TI "The Four Great Errors" 8) and condemns the need for redemption as "the most honest expression of decadence" (CW Epilogue).

22. Heidegger's view that Zarathustra should be primarily understood as a teacher or advocate encourages such apologetics. Heidegger, "Who Is Nietzsche's Zarathustra?" in *Nietzsche*, vol. 2, pp. 211–233.

23. For a valuable discussion that takes this speech as a point of departure see Karsten Harries, "The Philosopher at Sea," in *Nietzsche's New Seas,* ed. Gillespie and Strong, pp. 29–36.

24. Heidegger observes that in describing the moment, "the two of them, the dwarf and Zarathustra, say the same thing. Between them lies only 'the smallest gap': in each case it is an other who speaks the same words." Heidegger, *Nietzsche,* vol. 2, p. 53.

25. In *The Antichrist* Nietzsche describes the manner in which Jesus' disciples mis-understood and betrayed him in terms that could easily be applied to Zarathus-tra's disciples (A 31).

26. *Ein Toller.* In Nietzsche's parable it is a madman *(Der tolle Mensch)* who reveals that God is dead (GS 125).

27. For similar formulations, see Z II "On Scholars"; TI "Skirmishes of an Un-timely Man" 48.

28. Nietzsche entertained the idea that the doctrine of the eternal return obliterates all moral distinctions: "If becoming is a great ring, then everything is equally valuable, eternal and necessary" (WP 293). And in the same vein: "Becoming is of equivalent value every moment . . ." (WP 708).

29. Similarly, Nietzsche presented "metaphysical comfort" *(metaphysische Trost)* as a reward of tragic wisdom (BT 7). In linking the achievement of comfort to having seen the world as it really is and overcoming what is terrible in it, Nietzsche and his Zarathustra have an important precursor: In Luther's trans-lation of the Bible, Jesus proclaims: "In der Welt habt ihr Angst; aber seid ge-trost, ich habe die Welt überwunden" (Johannes 16:33: "The world holds dis-tress for you: but be comforted, I have conquered the world.")

30. Nietzsche equated such a condition with decadence (WP 44).

31. In a photo from 1882, the pose for which Nietzsche is said to have arranged, Lou Salomé stands in a small wagon wielding a whip; Paul Rée and Nietzsche, like beasts of burden, pull the wagon. Ronald Hayman, *Nietzsche: A Critical Life* (New York: Penguin, 1980), p. 246.

32. For the philosopher's temptation to resort to myth see P 87; WP 428.

33. See Nietzsche's discussion WP 54, 55.

34. Like Nietzsche's Wagner, Zarathustra, it seems, has cowardly succumbed to the "Eternal Feminine," the great danger for artists and geniuses (CW 3). See also HH 431, 434.

35. Sometimes Nietzsche conceived of the eternal return not as a source for restor-ing meaning to a meaningless world but as the deepest expression of the world's meaninglessness: "Let us think this thought in its most terrible form: existence as it is, without meaning or aim, yet recurring inevitably without any finale of nothingness: *the eternal recurrence*" (WP 55).

8. Retreat from the Extremes: *Thus Spoke Zarathustra* (Part IV)

1. See letter to Franz Overbeck, 22 February 1884, in L, pp. 220–221; letter to Karl von Gersdorff, 12 February 1885, in L, p. 235; and letter to Carl Fuchs, 29 July 1888, in L, p. 304.

2. In *Beyond Good and Evil,* Nietzsche reveals a change in perspective by using "higher man" as a term of praise designating a type, intrinsically vulnerable,

that occupies a lofty rung in the rank order of types. See, e.g., BGE 62, 212, 228, 256, 269, 274.

3. Nietzsche stressed the connection between spiritual decay and physical deterioration. See TI "Skirmishes of an Untimely Man" 20; letter to Lou Salomé, 2 July 1882, in L, p. 185; letter to Rohde, 15 July 1882, in L, p. 187; EH I 6; EH III, on Z, 4; and WP 43, 47.

4. Nietzsche refers to Wagner as an "old magician" (CW 3). See also Karl Löwith, *From Hegel to Nietzsche*, trans. David E. Green (New York: Columbia University Press, 1991), pp. 180–181.

5. So too were those to whom Zarathustra revealed his "vision of the loneliest" (Z III "On the Vision and the Riddle") and Nietzsche's madman (GS 125). See also BGE 42, 210.

6. Similarly, Nietzsche argues in *The Will to Power* that Christianity ultimately perishes from the virtue of honesty to which it gave birth and which it cultivated (WP 1–3, 5). See also Löwith, *From Hegel to Nietzsche*, pp. 368–373.

7. The ugliest man's ugliness and ambiguous greatness call to mind Nietzsche's ambivalent account of Socrates (TI "The Problem of Socrates"; BT 13).

8. See A 27–37, where Nietzsche distinguishes Jesus as one who seeks eternity on earth and within time from the organized Christianity founded by Paul that construes redemption in otherworldly terms. See also above, Chapter 4.

9. On the ambiguous character of the will to eternalize see GS 370. Zarathustra's warning to his shadow also recalls his dire pronouncement that the will that discerns its captivity to the past is provoked to wrath, lashes out at others who lack its insight, and is doomed to redeem itself foolishly (Z II "On Redemption").

10. Nietzsche regarded the sense of smell as a philosophical sense. See EH I 1, 8; III, on BT, 2, and on D, 1; and IV 1.

11. Deleuze finds in the concluding speech of *Zarathustra* evidence that Zarathustra achieves his highest aim, but overlooks the significance of Zarathustra's abandonment of the child, the highest form of the spirit. Gilles Deleuze, *Nietzsche and Philosophy*, trans. Hugh Tomlinson (New York: Columbia University Press, 1983), p. 192.

9. The Ethics of Knowing: *Beyond Good and Evil*

1. Two notable exceptions are Leo Strauss, "Note on the Plan of Nietzsche's *Beyond Good and Evil*," in *Studies in Platonic Political Philosophy* (Chicago: University of Chicago Press, 1983), and Alexander Nehamas, "Who Are 'The Philosophers of the Future'?: A Reading of *Beyond Good and Evil*," in *Reading Nietzsche*, ed. Robert C. Solomon and Kathleen M. Higgins (New York: Oxford University Press, 1988). Both essays attach great importance to determining the character of the philosopher of the future. Strauss argues that *Beyond Good and Evil* embodies a fundamental tension between Nietzsche's ambition to repudiate nature and reason and his pervasive reliance upon them, a tension that Nietzsche does not overcome (pp. 177, 183). In contrast, Nehamas contends that Nietzsche overcame the perplexities involved in making nondogmatic statements about perspectivism by fashioning a narrative voice that constantly called attention to the personal and tentative character of its own judgments.

In stressing the unsettled conflict between opposing opinions, Strauss better respects the conflicting perspectives in Nietzsche's book than does Nehamas who views *Beyond Good and Evil* from only the angle of perspectivism.

2. Letter to Burckhardt, 22 September 1886, in L, p. 255.

3. See, e.g., BGE 203, 224, 263, 269, 270, 282.

4. The assertion that *Zarathustra* and *Beyond Good and Evil* deal with the same thing but in different ways recalls Nietzsche's suggestion that objectivity consists in assembling and synthesizing multiple perspectives on "one thing" (GM III 12).

5. Immanuel Kant, "What Is Enlightenment," in *Kant's Political Writings*, ed. Hans Reiss (Cambridge: Cambridge University Press, 1970), p. 54.

6. See UD 6 and above, Chapter 1.

7. While Nietzsche indicates that the truth should arouse passionate romantic love, the term "philosophy," composed of the Greek words love *(philia)* and wisdom *(sophia)*, equates the philosopher's love of wisdom with the fondness characteristic of a friend's love *(philia)* as opposed to sexual, erotic love *(eros)*. Nevertheless classical political philosophy knows both opinions. While philosophy emerges as the peak of Aristotle's classic account of friendship, according to Socrates' recollection of Diotima's speech, philosophy is the perfection of erotic love, a love which begins as love or *eros* of beautiful bodies and culminates in knowledge of the beautiful. See Aristotle, *Nicomachean Ethics* 1155a–1172a15; Plato, *Symposium* 201d–212a

8. Accordingly, like Jesus' teaching that promises "eternal life" *(ewige Leben)* and "eternal punishment" *(ewigen Strafe)*, philosophy, on Nietzsche's view, is essentially concerned with eternity. See *Lutherbibel* Matthäus 25:46.

9. See Hegel, *Phenomenology of Spirit*, trans. A. V. Miller, preface, pp. 3–4.

10. Nietzsche accuses Plato of inflicting the same indignity on truth that Marx accuses Hegel's philosophy of carrying out against the dialectic. See Marx, *Capital*, afterword to the 2nd German ed., in *The Marx-Engels Reader*, ed. Robert C. Tucker (New York: Norton, 1978), pp. 301–302.

11. Like his madman, who saw in the death of God an unparalleled catastrophe for the human spirit but also a grand new opportunity for human beings to make themselves gods, and like Zarathustra, who presents the superman as the only worthy response to the knowledge that God is dead, so too Nietzsche in *Beyond Good and Evil* sees a monumental breakthrough arising out of an epoch-making spiritual crisis.

12. Nietzsche compares he who dares to inquire into the value of truth to the tragic hero Oedipus. His Oedipus acquires wisdom by solving the Sphinx's riddle, and as a result suffers "the dissolution of nature in his own person" (BT 9). In *The Birth of Tragedy* Nietzsche emphasized that the consequence of the attainment of wisdom is the gruesome violation of the most basic prohibitions governing social and political life.

13. During the period in which he was working on *Beyond Good and Evil* Nietzsche indicated that the meaning of his life consisted in knowing. See letter to Overbeck, 17 October 1885, in L, p. 248; see also EH Preface 3.

14. Nietzsche repeatedly employs various forms of the German *"wagen,"* meaning to venture, dare, or risk, in section 23 as well as in section 1.

15. At the end of the preface, Nietzsche includes himself among the small, very

select group of "free, very free spirits" in Europe who confront unprecedented opportunities for spiritual greatness. Identifying himself as a free spirit at the end of part 2, he says that the free spirits are heralds and precursors of philosophers of the future who will themselves be free spirits but also something more (BGE 44). And again in part 3, counting himself among the free spirits, he presents the perspective of the free spirit as particularly advantageous for discerning the tasks and responsibilities of the philosopher (BGE 61).

16. Nietzsche also wrote *Human, All Too Human* from the perspective of a free spirit. As in *Beyond Good and Evil,* the free spirit of *Human, All Too Human* is defined not by a doctrine but by a problem, namely *"the problem of the order of rank"* (HH Preface 7). And in *The Antichrist* as well, Nietzsche identifies his outlook with that of the free spirit and defines the free spirit in terms of intellectual virtue (A 13).

17. Elsewhere Nietzsche expresses a somewhat different opinion. In the polished but unpublished piece "The Greek State," he praises what he regards as Plato's "secret teaching" on, and essentially correct understanding of, the aim of the perfect state. While he thinks Plato was correct that the aim of the perfect state is the cultivation of genius, he does gently reproach Plato for failing to include the artist alongside the "genius of wisdom and knowledge" in the general concept of genius (KSA 1, *Der Griechische Staat,* pp. 776, 777).

18. By enclosing the word *truth* in quotation marks Nietzsche reveals his misgivings about the term, but just as important, he reveals his incapacity at this crucial juncture in his explorations to do without it. Sometimes he encloses *truth* in quotation marks, but often he does not, as for example later in the section now under study (for a few additional examples see BGE Preface, 1, 43, 44, 48, 81, 202, 210, 220, 261). His sporadic resort to quotation marks appears to reflect an ambivalence, a wish to abandon the notion of *truth* coupled with an implicit acknowledgment of the unfeasibility, for free spirits, of doing so.

19. Though he presents it as a hypothesis in *Beyond Good and Evil,* in *The Will to Power* Nietzsche says that the question "How much truth can a spirit *endure,* how much truth does a spirit *dare?*" became for him "the real [*eigentliche*] standard of value" (WP 1041).

20. This exaltation of knowing in the life of the "free-spirited philosopher" is reinforced by a striking observation Nietzsche attributes to Stendhal, whom he admiringly calls the "last great psychologist," to the effect that the philosopher shares with the successful banker the ability to see clearly into what is (BGE 39).

21. The free spirit of *Human, All Too Human* is also a solitary who acquires his freedom outside of and aloof from political life (HH 638).

22. Nehamas, *Nietzsche: Life as Literature* (Cambridge, Mass.: Harvard University Press, 1985), p. 33. Eric Blondel brings out the aristocratic tendency inhering in Nietzsche's teaching about perception according to which "the philologist's fine hearing" results in a certain deafness to mediocre minds and superficial problems. Blondel, *Nietzsche: The Body and Culture,* trans. Seán Hand (Stanford: Stanford University Press, 1991), pp. 100–106.

23. See also WP 465.

24. Heidegger considers this passage to be Nietzsche's third major presentation of

the doctrine of the eternal return. According to Heidegger's scheme, the first presentation occurs in GS 341, and the second is found in *Zarathustra* taken as a whole. See Martin Heidegger, *Nietzsche,* vol. 2, trans. David Farrell Krell (San Francisco: Harper and Row, 1984), pp. 63–69; also 19–27, 32–36. Heidegger's scheme is useful but somewhat forced because of what it excludes: the account of Dionysian tragic wisdom in *The Birth* (BT 7), the description of the suprahistorical vantage point and the activity of the genuine historian in *Uses and Disadvantages* (UD 1, 6, 10), and the exploration of the relation between freedom, necessity, and responsibility in *Human, All Too Human* (HH 39, 91, 15–107, 133, 588; WS 33).

25. This corresponds to Nietzsche's earlier opinion that the "perfecting of nature" consists in the cultivation of the three forms of the genius: the philosopher, the artist, and the saint (SE 5, 6).

26. Such honesty is also a virtue of the genealogist (GM I 1).

27. Deleuze thus oversimplifies by arguing that Nietzsche wishes to reject egoism in general because it is based on a bad interpretation of the will and a false assumption about the reality of the ego. See Gilles Deleuze, *Nietzsche and Philosophy,* trans. Hugh Tomlinson (New York: Columbia University Press, 1983), pp. 7–8. Rather and characteristically, Nietzsche seeks to distinguish noble from base forms of egoism.

28. Cf. Plato's Socrates on the inferiority of writing to thinking: *Phaedrus* 274c–276.

Conclusion

1. Cf. Aristotle, *Nicomachean Ethics* 1094a20–28; *Politics* 1323a13–17.

2. See TI "Skirmishes of an Untimely Man" 51; EH Preface 4; EH III 1, 4, and, on Z, 6; letter to Overbeck, received 11 February 1883, and letter to Knortz, 21 June 1888, in L, pp. 207, 299.

3. Cf. Löwith, *From Hegel to Nietzsche,* trans. David E. Green (New York: Columbia University Press, 1991), p. 258.

4. Isaiah Berlin, "Two Concepts of Liberty," in *Four Essays on Liberty* (Oxford: Oxford University Press, 1969), pp. 131–134.

5. Thomas Hobbes, *Leviathan,* chs. 17, 21.

6. John Locke, *Second Treatise,* secs. 15, 112, 119, 121, 122.

7. Jean-Jacques Rousseau, *On the Social Contract,* ch. I, sec. 6.

8. Immanuel Kant, *Groundwork of the Metaphysic of Morals,* trans. H. J. Paton (New York: Harper and Row, 1964) pp. 98–113. While consigning that which partakes of the contingent and empirical and that which is relative to human inclination and need—that is, the greater part of practical life—to the realm of unfreedom, Kant compensates by recommending the hypothesis that history is governed by necessary laws that tend in the direction of decent republican constitutions. Kant, "Idea for a Universal History with Cosmopolitan Purpose" and "Perpetual Peace: A Philosophical Sketch," in *Kant's Political Writings,* ed. Hans Reiss (Cambridge: Cambridge University Press, 1970), esp. pp. 50–53, 108–114. Hegel and Marx follow Kant in viewing history in terms of progress guaranteed by objective laws. All three support freedom by moralizing and rationalizing historical necessity.

9.   Heidegger also understands Nietzsche's highest aim in terms of the purification of self-legislation. Martin Heidegger, *Nietzsche,* vol. 3, trans. Joan Stambaugh, David Farrell Krell, and Frank A. Capuzzi (San Francisco: Harper and Row, 1987), pp. 224, 240; vol. 4, trans. Frank A. Capuzzi (San Francisco: Harper and Row, 1982), pp. 90, 136–138. Heidegger, however, views Nietzsche's radicalization of self-legislation in light of the Cartesian ego which prescribes the standards of certitude and truth.

   Other scholars have seen a Kantian dimension to Nietzsche's fundamental aspiration, although of course they differ on the character and significance of Nietzsche's Kantianism. See, e.g., Bernard Yack, *The Longing for Total Revolution* (Berkeley: University of California Press, 1992), pp. 310–311, 317–318, 348–349, 355–356; Mark Warren, *Nietzsche and Political Thought* (Cambridge, Mass.: MIT Press, 1987), pp. 116–126; and Robert B. Pippin, *Modernism as a Philosophical Problem* (Cambridge, Mass.: Basil Blackwell, 1991), pp. 80–116.

Acknowledgments

James Kurth, professor of political science at Swarthmore College, was the first to ask me questions I thought important but could not answer. I am grateful that he has continued to ask me such questions.

I owe much to my teachers at Yale. Joseph Hamburger has graciously supported my work and looked out for my interests. At an early stage, Karsten Harries directed my attention to difficult riddles in Nietzsche's thought. Rogers Smith and Steven Smith have given much sober advice over the years. In their different ways they have both made vivid for me the truth in Zarathustra's remark that "one repays a teacher badly if one always remains only a pupil." As a graduate student I was fortunate to take the Research and Writing seminar taught by David Mayhew. Although I thought I knew better, Professor Mayhew managed to impress upon me that in most cases clear thought is achieved through the practice of clear writing. During my four and a half years in New Haven I was especially fortunate to study a wide range of subjects, including politics and philosophy, with Rabbi James Ponet: no teacher taught me more about the things really worth knowing.

At a crucial juncture in my studies, Harvey C. Mansfield, Jr., took an interest in my work. In his incisive but unobtrusive way. he has helped me to better understand Nietzsche's formidable challenge. The late Judith N. Shklar welcomed me to Harvard with open arms. Her extraordinary spirit contributed much to making the government department a fascinating place in which to practice political theory. In Jerusalem, where many parts of this book were first written and later revised, I met David Hartman, director of the Shalom Hartman Institute. His enthusiasm for my work and his persistent encouragement over the years have been a pleasant and steadying influence.

I am grateful to Michael Aronson of Harvard University Press for taking charge of the transformation of my study of Nietzsche into a book. It is a better book thanks to the sharp eye and keen sense of proportion of Camille Smith, also of Harvard Press.

Marilyn Paul long ago tactfully suggested to me that a writer ought to give some thought, and certainly more than I had, to his reader. And I wish to thank Barry Shain for his outrageous provocations.

During the 1992–93 academic year I was on leave, supported by a John M. Olin Faculty Fellowship. That year several friends from a variety of disciplines joined me in a study group on Nietzsche. Our lively discussions helped me to collect my thoughts and to clarify my opinions.

This book has benefited immensely from Evan Charney's intelligent and painstaking work. Linda Berkowitz corrected drafts of each chapter. Nathan Tarcov urged me to aim high and to confront Heidegger's challenge. I thank Mark Lilla for reminding me that the job of an introduction to a book is to introduce. Jay Wink prodded me to cultivate the virtue of brevity. Out of the blue, Robert Howse wrote to me to share his learning and his insight into the significance of Nietzsche's achievement. My account is more balanced and accurate owing to what I learned from him. The many acute observations and hard questions about Nietzsche and political philosophy put to me by the remarkable students it has been my pleasure to teach at Yale and Harvard have improved my understanding and placed me in their debt. And without Jessica Korn's unfailing confidence, good instincts, and shrewd judgment, this book would be far more imperfect than it is.

Index